The Manner of Men

9 PARA's Heroic D-Day Mission

STUART TOOTAL

JOHN MURRAY

First published in Great Britain in 2013 by John Murray (Publishers)
An Hachette UK Company

2

© Stuart Tootal 2013

The right of Stuart Tootal to be identified as the Author of the Work has been asserted by him in accordance with the Copyright, Designs and Patents Act 1988.

Maps drawn by Rodney Paull

A CIP catalogue record for this title is available from the British Library

Hardback ISBN 978-1-84854-677-6
Ebook ISBN 978-1-84854-678-3

Typeset in 11.5/14 Monotype Bembo by Servis Filmsetting Ltd, Stockport, Cheshire

Printed and bound by Clays Ltd, St Ives plc

John Murray policy is to use papers that are natural, renewable and recyclable products and made from wood grown in sustainable forests. The logging and manufacturing processes are expected to conform to the environmental regulations of the country of origin.

John Murray (Publishers)
338 Euston Road
London NW1 3BH

www.johnmurray.co.uk

For Flt Lt Jack Tootal, RAF – one who did not make it home

What manner of men are these who wear the maroon red beret? They are firstly all volunteers, toughened by hard physical training. They have jumped from the air and . . . have conquered fear. Their duty lies in the van of the battle. They have shown themselves to be as tenacious and determined in defence as they are courageous in attack. They are, in fact, men apart – every man an Emperor

Field Marshal Bernard Montgomery

Contents

Maps

Preface

A T FIFTY MINUTES past midnight on 6 June 1944, over 600 paratroopers from the 9th Battalion the Parachute Regiment began jumping from their aircraft into the moonlit skies of Normandy. With 20,000 other British and American airborne troops, 9 PARA formed the spearhead of the Allied invasion to liberate occupied Europe from the Nazis. The D-Day landings were the biggest combined armed operation the world had ever seen, involving hundreds of thousands of troops, over 5,000 ships and 11,000 aircraft. But its success was not a foregone conclusion. The Supreme Allied Commander, Eisenhower had already prepared a note, in which he stated that in the event of failure, responsibility would be his alone.

Despite the shifting fortunes of the Allies, their meticulous planning for the opening of the second front and the vast resources at their disposal, launching an amphibious operation against a defended enemy coastline was an extremely hazardous undertaking. Much would depend on the paratroopers' and glider troops' ability to secure the flanks at either end of the invasion area before the main Allied seaborne force hit the beaches. What they achieved in the first few hours and days would be crucial while the Allies raced to build up their forces and establish themselves firmly ashore before the Germans could bring the full weight of their own strength to bear and drive them back into the sea. 9 PARA were given the critical behind-the-lines task of destroying the heavily fortified German gun emplacement at the Merville Battery to prevent it slaughtering British troops as they came ashore at Sword Beach on the east flank of the Normandy landings. It was the toughest of all the D-Day missions given to Airborne Forces and the one considered most essential to the success of Operation Overlord.

But the mission went badly wrong from the start. It was beset by faulty intelligence, blighted by command intrigue and a disastrous drop. Only 20 per cent of Lieutenant Colonel Terence Otway's force made it to the rendezvous for the attack on the battery; many died when they were dropped wide into flooded marshland and half became casualties during the costly assault on the gun position. Many more were to die over the following six days of bitter fighting, as Otway's small band of paratroopers clung on desperately to a small patch of vital high ground on the Bréville Ridge. Undermanned and under-equipped, they fought to hold it against vastly superior German forces to prevent them from getting through to the beaches when the Allied foothold on the enemy coastline was at its most tenuous.

Numerous credible authors have written about the D-Day landings. But, however commendable their works, they have tended to cover the entirety of the Normandy campaign, focusing on the generals and their broad sweeps of grand strategy and operational plans. The experience of men in combat is essential to our understanding of war, yet the view of the ordinary soldier is largely confined to individual anecdotes from a range of different units, often covered in just a few sentences.

This book is about D-Day seen through the prism of one single unit, in one distinctive time and space. It concerns the individual soldier rather than the famous commanders, such as Eisenhower and Montgomery who fought from maps in rear headquarters, where shot and shell and the smell and fear of battle rarely penetrated. The following pages seek to unveil the human dimension of war at the sharp end, where the soldiers' focus was limited to the slit trench they lived in, the enemy position only a stone's throw away behind the next hedgerow and whether they would live to see the end of an artillery bombardment.

This is 9 PARA's story of what has been described as the Parachute Regiment's most incredible feat of arms during the Second World War, which took those who were part of it to the edge of human endurance. This book attempts to tell it from the perspective of those who took part in it. The ranks of surviving veterans have been depleted and wearied by age and many of their accounts have been taken on the periphery of living history. On occasion their recollections of events have varied, just as they would have done if they were captured the day after the battle, where total recall is neither complete nor precise; this is the natural order of things and the consequence of the passage of time. I have balanced accounts against archive recordings, orders, official operational reports and intelligence summaries, as well as questioning them with experts who have made 9 PARA's exploits in Normandy a significant part of their own lives. I have walked the battlefield with some of the veterans, where ranges, visibility and the sequence of events have been discussed in detail in order to gain a sense of the terrain and the circumstances where the fighting took place.

Their accounts confirm that war is a random, bloody business, where the weird geometry of chance has its play and its frictions abound around human fallibility and fragility. Battle is fast-moving, confusing and often bewildering. There is no perfect science, only perfect intent that is unlikely to withstand first contact with the enemy and the realities on the ground. All were at play in 9 PARA's attack on the Merville Battery and defence of the Bréville Ridge. Rightly their exploits are one of the key battle honours of the Parachute Regiment. But the realities of war underline the need for caution over sanitized official accounts. In the following pages I have tried to tell it as it was, my only concern being that I have done justice to the remarkable courage and fortitude of the men who fought there and particularly those whom I was so privileged to get to know. Seven decades on, their remarkable spirit remains undiminished.

Prologue

I T WAS RAINING when Leutnant Raimund Steiner cycled back to his small concrete observation post among the sand dunes at the mouth of the River Orne, where it opened into the Channel twelve kilometres north of the ancient French city of Caen. A squall blew across the estuary, making it unusually rough for the time of year. The wind had a chill edge to it, although it was nothing compared to the bitter temperatures of a winter on the Russian Front where Steiner had also served. In spite of the cold, the unseasonally bad weather had a silver lining, as it meant that no invasion would be expected to come that night. According to the German high command's meteorological predictions, the summer storm that blew into the Channel from the west would prevent the anticipated Allied landings for at least another two weeks, until the moon state and the tides would be favourable again in the middle of the month.

At twenty-five years old, Steiner was already a veteran of numerous German campaigns. He had joined the Wehrmacht's mountain artillery in 1939, and had been wounded in the bitter fighting for Murmansk in 1941, where he was awarded the Iron Cross. Wounded again at Stalingrad and during subsequent fighting in the Crimea, his gallantry had marked him out for a commission from the ranks. But, despite his fighting prowess, Steiner was no Nazi; an Austrian by birth, his father had been the leader of Innsbruck city council in 1938 when Germany annexed Austria. Arrested and sent to a series of concentration camps for his opposition to Hitler, Ludwig Steiner died as a result of his internment two months after being released from Dachau. His son fought hard as an officer in the Wehrmacht in an attempt to protect the rest of his family from further persecution.

Wounded once more fighting Yugoslav partisans in Trieste, Steiner had been sent to the French coast to convalesce in the spring of 1944. The gun battery he commanded was part of an under-strength division that formed part of the 7th Army stationed in Normandy to guard against the threat of Allied invasion. But the Calvados region was supposed to be a quiet sector, and many of his men were unfit to serve in more active theatres of operations, or like him were sent there to rest. Other fronts took priority as regards men and materiel; as did the 15th Army based around the Pas de Calais where the Germans expected the Anglo-American Allies to attempt their long anticipated landing.

Steiner was exhausted. He had spent the day overseeing the final repairs to his battery just over two kilometres away, on the other side of the small village of Merville. The bombing raids against the guns had started in May and the RAF had visited several times since, but none of the 4,000-pound bombs had penetrated the heavy casemate bunkers that sheltered the four field artillery pieces. The havoc they wreaked to the rest of the position not protected by two metres of reinforced concrete with compacted earth on top was another matter.

Since the beginning of May, the RAF had been bombing along the entire northern French coast in earnest. The last raid took place in the early hours of the preceding Friday morning and it had taken three days to recover the bodies of Steiner's men from collapsed trenches, re-dig the surrounding machine-gun pits and repair the gaps blown in the thick wire obstacle belt and minefield that surrounded the battery. Steiner was in need of a good night's rest and he ignored the orders to sleep in his uniform and climbed into bed in his pyjamas. Normandy wasn't the predicted sector for any landing and the weather was further reason to expect a quiet night.

It seemed he had only been asleep for a moment when the telephone woke him. The voice on the other end of the line was filled with alarm; it was his battery sergeant major, Hauptwachtmeister Johannes Buskotte, who was stationed at the gun position. Buskotte was another veteran from the Russian Front and someone whom Steiner trusted. '*Herr Leutnant!* A glider has landed on the battery and we are in close combat!' Steiner told him to secure the guns behind

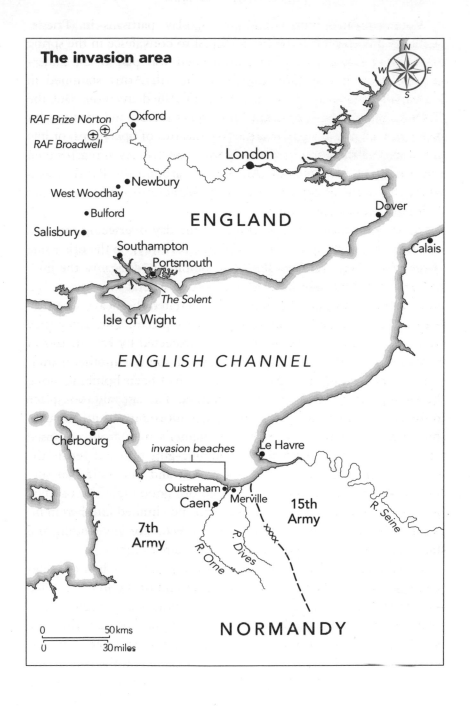

The invasion area

RAF Brize Norton
Oxford
RAF Broadwell

London

ENGLAND

Dover
Calais

Newbury
West Woodhay
Bulford
Salisbury

Southampton
Portsmouth
The Solent
Isle of Wight

ENGLISH CHANNEL

Cherbourg
invasion beaches
Le Havre

Ouistreham
Caen
Merville
R. Seine

7th
Army

15th
Army

R. Orne
R. Dives

NORMANDY

0   50 kms
0   30 miles

the steel doors of the thick concrete casemates, fight off any attack and wait for him to get there. After alerting the infantry soldiers stationed in a command bunker less than 100 metres behind his own bunker; Steiner then put a call through to his divisional headquarters.

The commander of 716th Infantry Division, Generalmajor Wilhelm Richter, was asleep at his headquarters on the northern side of the city of Caen when Steiner's call came in. Richter's division was responsible for defending forty kilometres of the Normandy coastline running westwards from the banks of the River Dives a few kilometres east from where the Orne flowed into the sea. He was irritated at being woken up, which was not helped by the fact that he had taken a dislike to the young Austrian lieutenant who now commanded one of his divisional artillery regiment's four gun batteries. '*Herr General*, an enemy glider has landed on the Merville Battery and my troops are under attack. I believe the invasion has begun.' Richter was incredulous at what he heard Steiner say.

'One crashed aircraft doesn't make an invasion. Don't get excited and don't bother me with trivialities,' he snapped back at Steiner, then slammed down the receiver.

Still in his pyjamas, Steiner shivered in the cold night air inside the small cramped observation bunker, as the wind blew in the narrow observation platform that faced the sea. He looked at his watch; it was just after 0130 hours DST* on Tuesday, 6 June 1944.

Four kilometres away on the other side of Merville, Lieutenant Colonel Terence Otway was also in a foul mood. D-Day was less than an hour old, but things had already begun to go badly wrong for him and the men of the 9 PARA who had jumped into Normandy forty minutes earlier. Otway had missed the planned dropping zone for his battalion and struck the side of a house, which was being used as a German company headquarters. Narrowly avoiding capture, he had struggled through thick hedgerows and deep irrigation ditches to get to the unit's rendezvous point. Before he reached the RV he had

---

* DST – Double Summer Time: two hours ahead of GMT used as a daylight saving measure by the Allies during the war.

had to watch one of his men drown in a flooded ditch. Otway and his batman had tried to pull the stricken man out, but they were too late and the poor unfortunate, carrying over 100 pounds of weapons and ammunition, was sucked beneath the murky water by the weight of his equipment.

Reaching the rendezvous Otway had expected to see a mass of activity, as the 640 men who jumped from his unit collected their equipment and made their way into the allotted rallying point. But there was hardly anyone there except for the few members of the RV marking party and only fifty other paratroopers. As the moonlight struggled to break through the stormy clouds that scudded above him, he made out a few more stragglers emerging from the darkness to join them; but it was hardly enough to form a credible assault group to take the gun battery at Merville.

Otway was a twenty-nine-year old Ulsterman and as a regular pre-war officer, commanding his own battalion in action was the moment he had been waiting for. He was beside himself with rage, cursing his luck and the RAF for the disastrous drop of his men and equipment. He kept glancing at his watch and wondered how long he could delay in the hope that more of his men would turn up to make up their depleted numbers. Otway knew that if he didn't get going soon, he wouldn't make it to the battery in time for the arrival of another part of his force that would assault directly on to the battery in three gliders. Already short of numbers, he desperately needed the fifty-eight additional men that they would bring and it was essential the attack was coordinated with their arrival.

Time was now Otway's biggest enemy: he was racing against the approach of first light. At dawn the seaborne invasion fleet would start landing on the beaches at Ouistreham, the full length of which were covered by the guns at Merville. If the guns remained intact when the first wave of infantry hit the shoreline, the Allied troops risked being blown to pieces by the German battery as they struggled out of the landing craft and assaulted across the open stretch of sand on Sword Beach.

Sergeant 'Paddy' Jenkins noted his CO's anger as Otway stomped about the field next to where he crouched in the wet grass. Paddy had concerns of his own. As a twenty-one-year-old platoon sergeant, he was the next senior man in his platoon of thirty-five Paras, but so far less than half of them had shown up at the rendezvous. Among the missing was his platoon commander, which meant that he was now in charge and he wondered how he would measure up. Their mission had been well drilled into them through painstaking and meticulous training in England. He knew the risks involved. But he also knew that they had just increased exponentially with the loss of so many men before they had even started.

I

Fortress Europe

O N 20 JANUARY 1944 a large black Horch drew through the gates of the Merville Battery on the east bank of the River Orne in the Calvados region of Normandy. Erwin Rommel stepped stiffly from the rear of the car. A thick leather belt buckled his field–grey overcoat against the cold winter air, which blew in off the sea from across the mouth of the river. Rommel's back hurt. But the field marshal was not going to allow an attack of lumbago to distract him from his programme of inspecting all the units in his new command.

Rommel's appointment as Commander-in-Chief of Army Group B had been confirmed five days previously by Oberkommando der Wehrmacht (OKW), the German military high command. It included the 7th and 15th armies of the Wehrmacht, which were responsible for defending approximately 900 kilometres of coastline stretching from the Belgian frontier to the Spanish border. 15th Army was centred on Pas de Calais with an area extending southwards to the east bank of the River Dives. Starting with the 716th Infantry Division, 7th Army's sector started on the other side of the river and ran west across the Cotentin Peninsula and south into Brittany. The gun position at Merville belonged to the 716th's divisional artillery regiment and sat just at the extremity of 7th Army's eastern sector.

At five feet eight inches tall, Rommel was smaller than his reputation and German propaganda newsreels suggested. But his air of natural self-confidence and energy inspired his subordinates. Although not a party man, his performance as a divisional panzer commander during the Blitzkrieg campaign in France in 1940, and the dazzling victories of the Afrika Korps against the British in North Africa a year later, had made him a personal favourite of Hitler. It was a reputation and position that rankled with his immediate superior, Commander-in-Chief West.

Aged sixty-nine, Field Marshal Gerd von Rundstedt was cold and aloof. He was an archetypical Prussian general of traditional Junker stock, the antithesis of the younger field marshal, whom he considered a flashy impetuous upstart. His opinion was not helped by the fact that Rommel was the son of a Swabian schoolmaster, he had not fought on the Russian Front and he was not a member of the General Staff. Eschewing the traditional route to senior rank in the Wehrmacht, Rommel had chosen continuous field command. It was a successful preference, which Reich propaganda minister Joseph Goebbels used to make Rommel a darling of the German people and media. In contrast, Hitler had sacked von Rundstedt for his ultimate failure to capture Moscow in 1941. Brought out of forced retirement the following year, he had been given responsibility for all German land forces in north-western Europe. Compared to the Eastern Front, military command of occupied France, Belgium and Holland was a strategic backwater appointment.

At the beginning of 1942 a large-scale Allied invasion of north-west Europe was but a remote possibility. The impact of America's entry into the war was still to be felt, while Hitler's armies stood at the gates of Egypt and continued to press deep into Russia. But after the German defeat at Stalingrad in 1943 the tide had begun to turn. By the end of the year, Wehrmacht forces had been driven out of North Africa and had withdrawn from Sicily. As the British and Americans advanced up the Italian peninsula, the last great German offensive in the east had already died out around Kursk. By December the Red Army had crossed the Dnieper and were on the Polish border. The U-boat battle of the Atlantic had been lost and the Reich struggled to provide its collapsing fronts with men and materiel. In the skies above Germany the Luftwaffe was being bled white as it failed to stop thousands of Allied bombers pounding its cities by both day and night.

By the beginning of 1944, an invasion of north-west Europe was only a matter of time. The Germans expected a landing to be attempted in the spring or summer, when the tides and weather in the Channel were best suited for amphibious and air operations. Forced back on the defensive, Hitler had ranted about Fortress Europe. In the wake of the disastrous Anglo-Canadian landing at Dieppe in August 1942 he had boasted about the ability of his Atlantic Wall defences to throw the Allies back into the sea. But although a costly failure, Dieppe had been only a raid. It had been readily defeated because it was launched against a heavily defended port. The harsh reality was that where the Atlantic Wall existed, it did so in just a few places and the coastal defences beyond the other major ports such as Calais, Boulogne, Le Havre and Cherbourg were thin.

While the ebb of military victory flowed in their favour, the German defences along the intervening coastline had been neglected; now they could no longer be ignored. By 1943 half a million forced labourers, locally contracted workers and soldiers under the administration of the Todt Organisation, which was responsible for coordinating all major civil and military engineering works in Germany and the occupied territories, were building concrete gun positions, pill-boxes and bunkers from Antwerp to the Pyrenees. However, the progress of work was slow and the defences left much to be desired.

In January 1944 von Rundstedt had fifty divisions, including the armies under Rommel's command, to defend the entire length of the Atlantic seaboard of Nazi-occupied Europe. But despite the growing threat of an Anglo-American invasion, 200 German divisions would remain committed to the Russian Front. Of those in the west, twenty-six were dedicated to manning the fixed defences of the Atlantic Wall and were low-grade static formations, which were substantially weaker than normal Wehrmacht line infantry divisions. They relied on horse-drawn transport and had limited offensive capability. Their units were forced to rely on a motley collection of captured enemy equipment, as obsolete British, French and Czech vehicles and weapons were pressed into service.

Many of their troops were too old or unfit to serve on the Eastern Front and combat experience tended to be limited to soldiers convalescing from wounds and the rigours of service in Russia. In an attempt to make up their shortfall in manpower, 'near-Germans', such as Czechs and Poles from the eastern occupied territories, were conscripted into their ranks. Units formed of Soviet prisoners of war known as Hiwis were also added to the order of battle in what were termed as 'East' or Ost battalions. Although wearing Wehrmacht uniform and serving under German officers, the loyalty of non-German troops in the coming battle would be suspect from the outset.

Under the command of Generalmajor Wilhelm Richter, the 716th Infantry was a typical static division. With its headquarters in the city of Caen, it defended ninety kilometres of the Normandy coast running from the Orne to the Carentan Estuary in the west. Since Richter had only two German battalions, each of 600 men, in his two infantry regiments, the 726th and 736th, he was forced to spread out his men in isolated company strength positions like a 'string of pearls' across his entire front. This meant that his positions lacked depth and were too far apart to provide mutual support to each other with their direct-fire weapons. Richter's men were also responsible for guarding the bridges over the River Orne and Caen Canal at Bénouville and Ranville with a platoon of soldiers from the 736th Regiment. In addition the division could call upon one Ost battalion of 1,000 Hiwis, which had its headquarters in the small village of Le Plein on the Bréville Ridge overlooking the Orne from its eastern side.

The division had very few vehicles and the guns at Merville were horse-drawn. The battery was one of four other howitzer batteries, each of four guns, which made up one of the three sections of the 1/716th Artillery Regiment. The regiment provided fire support for the division's infantry units, which were also supported by a pioneer battalion, signals and supply troops. The division also had a single Panzerjäger company equipped with 35 R Panzerkampfwagen self-propelled assault guns. The 35 Rs were old Czech 4.7cm calibre Pak guns mounted on captured French 35 R Renault tank chassis and were a classic example of the Wehrmacht's ability to recycle captured and outdated equipment.

The quality of von Rundstedt's other formations and units varied enormously. The line infantry divisions such as the 346th Infantry

Division near Le Havre were better manned and equipped than the static divisions and were organized for both attack and defence. But their offensive capability was reduced by a lack of integral transport and limited armoured fighting vehicles in comparison to the much more capable motorized panzergrenadier and panzer divisions. However, von Rundstedt had relatively few of these formations.

Von Rundstedt, the man who had outflanked the Maginot Line and encircled large Soviet armies on the Russian Front, had little faith in either the static divisions or the defences they manned. Unlike Hitler, he doubted that the Allies could be prevented from getting ashore by fixed positions and remained true to the doctrine of blitz-krieg: the mass use of concentrated armoured force to manoeuvre to a position where a decisive defeat could be inflicted on the enemy in a massive counterstroke. He believed that the invasion force could only be defeated once it had landed and exposed its flanks as it attempted to advance inland. In von Rundstedt's opinion this could only be achieved by a large-scale counter-attack by armoured divisions, held sufficiently far back from the coast to be able to crash into an advancing flank once it had been identified.

Von Rundstedt's preference for offensive manoeuvre meant that little of his energy had been directed towards overseeing the construction of the Atlantic Wall. His lack of conviction was not helped by the competing demands of repairing bomb damage in Germany on the one hand and building U-boat and launch installations for Hitler's new V-1 rockets on the other. Instead, von Rundstedt had invested his time trying to persuade OKW and Hitler of the need for more panzer units and to stop redeploying troops away from his command to meet the insatiable demands of the Russian Front.

Hitler knew that another massive Soviet onslaught in the east was only a matter of months away following the spring thaw, but he also knew that he could not continue to ignore the demands in the west. If he defeated the Allies in the west first, he hoped to then be able to transfer the bulk of his divisions in France to the Russian Front. It was a strategy enshrined within Führer Directive Number 51, issued on 3 November 1943. But while the Führer acknowledged that he could 'no longer justify further weakening of the west in favour of other theatres of war' and directed that forces in the west should be strengthened, Hitler didn't immediately give von Rundstedt the divisions he wanted; instead he got Rommel.

Before taking over Army Group B, Rommel had been Inspector General of the Atlantic Wall defences, where he had been shocked at the lack of progress in preparing the defences. His report to OKW at the end of 1943 led to his being given operational command of 7th and 15th armies. But while Rommel's return to field command gave him some operational authority to adjust the static defences within his area of responsibility, he could not move any of the divisions in his armies without the sanction of Commander-in-Chief West.

Initially, Rommel agreed with von Rundstedt's assessment that an Allied landing in the Pas de Calais area offered the Allies obvious advantages, which made it the most likely place for the coming invasion. It was the shortest distance across the Channel from England and provided the most direct route into Germany. Landing in the Calais area would also give the British and Americans a major port from which to sustain the logistical inflow of men and materiel necessary for a subsequent breakout from their beachhead. Von Rundstedt's view held sway with Hitler and OKW. But Rommel also considered a landing further south in the Bay of the Somme and along Normandy's Cotentin Peninsula a strong possibility. Consequently, he wanted a continuous system of defence along the whole shoreline, which would extend three to four miles inland and would include offshore anti-landing craft obstacles, beach obstacles, bunkers, gun emplacements, minefields and anti-glider and parachute troop defences in all possible landing areas within seven miles of the coast.

The conviction Rommel attached to improving the fixed defences was part of his fundamental belief that any invasion had to be defeated on, or close to the beaches, before the Allies could establish a consolidated beachhead. He maintained that the most vulnerable period for the enemy would be at the 'moment of their landing', where the static defences would slow them and fix them while the armoured units counter-attacked as they attempted to struggle ashore. For this he wanted the panzer divisions already allocated to his armies, but stationed fifty to sixty miles inland in the vicinity of Paris, to be brought closer to the coast. This would enable them to intervene at the point of landing in the first critical hours and days of the Allied invasion. If they were too far back, he was convinced that the advance of their long armoured columns would be halted by Allied airpower before they got anywhere near the beaches. Rommel believed that, if the Allies were able to get ashore in sufficient numbers, their subsequent breakout and drive into Germany would be unstoppable.

In contrast von Rundstedt was adamant that holding the panzer forces further back from the coast was the right strategy. He argued that it avoided the risk of committing them to the wrong place, should the Allies choose to land away from the German forward positions; while keeping them at a greater distance would give them time and space to identify the direction of the Allied thrust and then be able to challenge it. Von Rundstedt's strategy of keeping the panzer divisions further back in reserve was supported by OKW, but if necessary Rommel was prepared to use his personal influence with Hitler in an attempt to alter that decision.

While he debated the issue with von Rundstedt, OKW and anyone else of influence who would listen to him, Rommel threw himself into his mission to improve the defences along the Atlantic Wall. Having established his headquarters in Fontainebleau, his intensive tour of inspections had resumed the day after his appointment as Army Group B's commander. On 20 January Rommel started a nine-day tour of Generaloberst Friedrich Dollman's 7th Army positions in Brittany and Normandy. Given its rocky coastline and limited road network inland, Rommel assessed that a landing in Brittany was unlikely. However, he agreed with Dollman's commander of 84th Corps, General Erich Marcks, that Normandy offered a more likely prospect given that the coastline along the Bay of the Seine was flat and well suited for landings on its beaches. Marcks was a widely renowned strategist who had lost a leg fighting on the Russian Front and walked with the aid of an artificial limb. Respected by Rommel, he was also one of the few senior Germans who believed an attack would come along the 400 kilometres of the Cotentin Peninsula, which the five divisions under his command, including the 716th Division, were responsible for defending.

Marcks's assessment struck a chord with Rommel, who also noted his view that the bocage country around Caen offered ideal ground for Allied airborne operations. Marcks pointed out that while there were sufficient potential landing zones to the north-east of the city, the thick hedgerows that criss-crossed the land between them would make it difficult to organize rapid counter-attacks against any troops landing by glider or parachute. However, the prevailing conventional thinking of von Rundstedt and OKW remained wedded to Calais. As a result 15th Army continued to be the priority in terms of men and materiel at the expense of 7th Army, whose thirteen divisions had only 170 75mm and sixty-eight 88mm anti-tank guns across its entire frontage of 900 kilometres.

To help fill this shortage of firepower, Rommel directed that artillery field batteries needed to be sited closer to the coast. But he also recognized that they needed to be encased in concrete and earth if they were to be protected from heavy naval and air bombardment, which was bound to precede an amphibious assault. With Rommel's arrival, plans were put in place to increase the number of concrete gun emplacements, which included the Merville Battery. However, the allocation of concrete to protect field batteries along the coast also reflected the precedence given to Calais. In 15th Army ninety-three of its 123 heavier guns were to be placed in casemates, compared to twenty-three of the forty-seven guns in 7th Army's sector.

Like much of the equipment in Richter's division, the guns of the Merville Battery had not been made for the Wehrmacht. The four Type LFH 15/19 (t)s were of Czech manufacture and had been used by the Austrian Army in the First World War. Upgraded with longer barrels by the Krupp armaments company, they were 100mm calibre howitzers, which fired two-part ammunition, consisting of an M28 high-explosive shell and a brass case of propellant charge-bags. Using all six charge-bags they could fire a shell, weighing 31.21 pounds, a distance of 9.8 kilometres.

Work had begun on placing the four guns at Merville under concrete in June 1943. Until then they had been sited out in the open in three hectares of pastureland on the outskirts of the village of Merville and the tiny hamlet of Descanneville. The fields had been requisitioned from local farmers and lay at the end of a narrow lane that ran up from the crossroads in Descanneville past the mairie, a small schoolhouse and a number of shuttered Norman cottages. The school and the mairie had also been requisitioned by the battery for accommodation and messing. The Château de Merville, a short walk away, served as the unit's administrative headquarters and stores.

The unit had moved to Normandy from Germany with the rest of 716th Division in December 1942. Merville was considered to be a sleepy occupation duty in the back end of nowhere, where life was mundane and dull. But few of the soldiers complained. It was in marked preference to being sent to fight on the Eastern Front, which was a constant dread, especially among those who had been posted to France because they had been judged unfit for service in Russia. An upgrading in their medical status was deemed tantamount to a death sentence.

Relationships with the local Normans were cordial if not friendly. For the local schoolchildren the arrival of the Germans had been exciting and meant a source of extra food at a time when produce was scarce. While their parents suffered the strictures of rationing, schoolchildren such as twelve-year-old Lucien Yvonne and his friends enjoyed impromptu meals in the soldiers' soup kitchen. Lucien befriended a young crossed-eyed gunner who gave him a lift to school on a horse-drawn cart. Known as 'One Eye' by Lucien and his friends, impaired sight had spared him service on the Eastern Front. But others were not so lucky and Lucien often saw other German soldiers sobbing uncontrollably when they discovered that they were about to be transferred to Russia.

Some members of the battery enjoyed the benefits of the slow pace of life and relationships with the locals more than others. Hauptmann Karl Heinrich Wolter was sent to France from Russia after suffering from combat fatigue and was a renowned womanizer and drinker; he regularly cavorted with a local woman in his billet in the mairie and had a fondness for the region's famed calvados and cider. Wolter was also the commander of 1/1716th Battery and was strongly suspected of running a black market racket sending local agricultural produce back to his contacts in Germany.

Although Wolter looked the epitome of professional military efficiency in his steel helmet and polished jackboots as he snapped to
attention and saluted Rommel on the afternoon of 29 January, the
man who did the real work in the battery was Wolter's twenty-eight-
year-old sergeant major, Hauptwachtmeister Johannes Buskotte.
Buskotte came from a strict Catholic family in Osnabrück and had
joined the regiment in 1939 when it was raised in Detmold. He
enjoyed exercising the horses in the surrounding countryside, but he
was sober, responsible and oversaw the maintenance and administration of the battery, leaving Wolter to pursue his extra-curricular
activities undisturbed.

The task of building the concrete casements for the battery had
already begun in June 1943. The work had been subcontracted out
through the Todt Organisation to a local building firm in Cabourg.
By the time Rommel visited, work on the concrete casemates for the
battery was far from complete and only two of the four planned casemates had been cast. Priority had been given to the Number One
emplacement on the north-east corner of the site. This contained the
ranging gun, which would be used to adjust fire on to targets called
in by the observation position located a mile and a half away on the
coastline near the seaside town of Franceville. Once the gun's fire
was registered as being accurate, the adjusted data would then be sent
to the other guns to bring their fire down accurately on to the
designated target.

The casemate consisted of two-metre-thick concrete walls and
overhead cover, with another two metres of earth banked up at the
sides and on the top of the structure. Underground chambers for
ammunition and accommodation were sunk four metres into the
foundations; as it breached the water table, a pump system was
installed to keep the casemate dry. Once manhandled inside, the gun
and its crew could be secured from the outside world by heavy steel
doors to the rear and steel shutters over the gun ports and an air filtration system to guard against a gas attack. The bunker was built to
exact measurements mandated by the Todt Organisation and was
strong enough to withstand anything but a direct hit from the heaviest of Allied bombs. Work had also started on a cookhouse and a

command bunker. But while the precision of the Todt specifications suggested Teutónic efficiency, progress on the other three casemates and the surrounding defences did not.

Rommel inspected the position flanked by his staff and the senior officers of 7th Army. The battery was little more than a building site of mechanical diggers, large wooden mouldings for the concrete to be poured into and large mounds of piled earth. A defensive mine-field had been laid round the perimeter and the excavation of an anti-tank ditch in front of the casemates had been started. But there was no barbed-wire obstacle belt to keep out enemy infantry, save a single-strand wire fence, which prevented grazing cattle from wandering on to the position from the neighbouring fields.

Rommel was unimpressed. He noted that any sense of urgency was 'underrated' and made it clear that not enough was being done to complete the position. It was indicative of the general state of defences along the entire length of the Atlantic Wall. With the approach of spring and better weather, Rommel knew that he had only four to five months to make the necessary improvements if he was to stand a hope of defeating the coming invasion. His arrival heralded the end of the tranquil pace of life for the men of the bat-tery. But Rommel and his entourage were not the only ones who were interested in the progress being made to the gun battery at Merville.

The sound of the supercharged Merlin engines of the two Spitfires would have been unmistakable as they flew in at low level towards the battery. The group of staff officers and generals scattered as the aircraft approached at maximum speed. Rommel's naval adviser Admiral Friedrich Ruge stood beside Rommel and watched the air-craft come in. When the operations officer next to him dived for cover, he decided to follow the army man's lead and did likewise. There was a frantic fumbling of activity around the battery's one 20mm 38 Flak gun, as the crew rushed to bring the single-barrelled anti-aircraft weapon into action.

Rommel remained standing, impassive and alone, as he watched the Spitfires swoop in low over the battery; but they did not fire. As PR, or photographic reconnaissance, variants of the famous fighter, they were not armed. But the mission they were engaged in and the equipment they carried in their wings and fuselage, in lieu of machine guns and cannon, were to have profound implications for both the German gunners at Merville and the men of 9 PARA who would be tasked with their battery's destruction.

2

Operation Tonga

THE MARK XI PR Spitfire relied on speed and agility for protection. Travelling at 400 miles per hour, the aircraft, which flashed low over the Merville Battery at 1,000 feet, had been 'cottonized'. By stripping out their guns and radios, the weight of their airframes had been reduced to allow them to carry a configuration of photographic reconnaissance equipment. The sortie that flew over Rommel and his party were fitted with F.24 cameras with fourteen-inch focal lenses, which enabled them to take low-level oblique-angle photos. The aircraft could also carry F.52 cameras with larger lenses to take vertical pictures from altitudes of up to 30,000 feet, but the mission they flew over the Merville Battery required greater detail and that meant going in low.

Each Spitfire carried one sideways-looking F.24 mounted in a porthole behind the cockpit on the port side of the fuselage. Producing a five-by-five-inch negative, each exposure provided a coverage of 1,667 by 1,667 yards of ground. Once enlarged, the negatives produced a 1:12,000 scale image, with sufficient detail to pick out a single man, or a group of men running for cover. But it wasn't just the scale that was important. Two additional F.24s, with smaller five-inch lenses, were fitted under the wings and angled towards each other so they could take overlapping photos of the same target. When consecutive photos were viewed with a stereoscope, they gave a three-dimensional effect, akin to looking at a still from a modern film with 3-D glasses.

Achieving the 3-D effect depended on the interval of exposures between frames being matched against the speed of the aircraft. Consequently, flying a low-level 'dicing' mission to get the necessary detail was a tricky and intricate business that required skill and entailed risk, as, lacking height, the pilots were more vulnerable to enemy aircraft above them and flak below them.

To capture the right image, the pilots' navigation had to be spot-on; even a small deviation from the pre-planned flight path could lead to missing the target by several hundred yards. Flying close to the ground at high speed, the lead pilot had little time to line up his aircraft and aim the camera by aligning a tiny black cross etched on the blister of his bubble canopy with a small black strip painted on his aileron. At the same time he had to mentally calculate his speed and adjust the camera control box on his joystick to ensure it was set at the right exposure to start taking the pictures.

Trusting that his wingman was with him, the aviator glanced at his airspeed dial, checked his bearing and then focused on the crosshair and target alignment. He thumbed the camera control switch as the terrain of green fields and hedgerows flashed past beneath him; at the moment when all three points of reference lined up, he flicked the switch on his control column and the cameras started taking photographs at one-second intervals.

Surprise was also an important part of the aircraft's protection and the pilot put more faith in it than in the single sheet of armoured plating in the back of his seat. He knew he had to get the alignment right first time. There would be no second chance. He had to bounce the target and get in and out fast, before the anti-aircraft gunners had time to react and fill the air around him with flak. If he missed the target, or his photos were not of the right quality, he would not be allowed to revisit the target for several days.

The pilot in the lead Spitfire was concentrating too hard to realize that the gunners of the single 20mm 38 Flak gun at the battery had failed to get their cannon into action against him or his wingman. He hoped he had got what he wanted as he flicked off the camera control switch and pulled back aggressively on his joystick to begin climbing hard for altitude.

The danger was far from over. The pair of reconnaissance aircraft may have been too fast for the crew of the 20mm gun mounted on the cookhouse bunker of the battery, but they still had to run the gauntlet of the nearby anti-aircraft positions stationed along the coast if they were get home safely with the information they had captured. By now the Germans were alerted to the presence of enemy fighters in the area and thick black puffs of exploding flak and tracer marked the air as the Spitfires pulled up steeply to reach a height of 5,000 feet to give them a chance of evading enemy fire as they crossed the coast. This is where the two-stage supercharged Merlin 60 engine, with its excellent climb rate, did its business.

The engines screamed for power, calling on the maximum performance of their 1,560-brake horsepower to get their aircraft out of trouble. Both pilots fought against the crushing effects of the G-force, as the horizon dropped away below them and their airframes surged upwards. They were not out of it yet. As the blood began to drain to their lower extremities, they struggled to remain focused. The need to keep scanning the skies above them and the rear-view mirror for enemy aircraft was paramount, as was checking that the aircraft's fuel gauges, oil pressure and heading were all still good.

Within an hour of clearing the coast the two aircraft were back at their base at RAF Benson in Oxfordshire. As their props feathered and wound down at their stands on the apron of the airfield, the ground crews of the squadron's photographic section were already waiting to meet them. While the crews switched off their engines, unstrapped and climbed out of their cockpits to head for debriefing by the intelligence officer in the operations room, the magazines of the cameras were being unloaded. The film was taken to a requisitioned manor house in the neighbouring village of Ewelme, where it could be developed. Within forty-eight hours the negatives had arrived at RAF Medmenham in Buckinghamshire for detailed analysis.

Medmenham was a sister organization of Bletchley Park and specialized in photographic intelligence and interpretation. Much of the work they conducted was in 3-D using a stereoscope. The stereoscope was a bi-optical viewing device, akin to a pair of magnifying spectacles mounted on a small four-legged metal frame. When positioned over an overlapping air photograph, it gave the 3-D image. Being able to view captured images in three dimensions was crucial, because it brought the enemy landscape and installations they studied to life, and allowed the interpreters to examine features of an object, such as the angles of shadows, to make assessments about the height of a particular structure or weapon types. It was a monotonous and painstaking task, but the photographic intelligence work at Medmenham was instrumental to the planning of D-Day in assessing enemy dispositions, strengths and capabilities.

In the run-up to the invasion, the teams of interpreters at Medmenham would study and file reports on 16 million photographs of enemy-occupied territory. It was an immense undertaking and the interpreters worked round the clock to provide those charged with planning D-Day with vital information. The majority of effort was concentrated along the coastline between Calais and Cherbourg, but no one area received particular attention so as not to give away the intended location of the invasion.

The stereoscope was Medmenham's secret weapon; while the British and Americans worked in three rather than two dimensions, the Germans did not. Scouring the prints of the Merville Battery for every detail, the interpreters could give an appraisal of the progress of the casemates' erection, noting that two had been completed and that two remained under construction. They could also provide an estimate of the thickness of the concrete protection, pick out the detail of perimeter defences and compare the progress of the work against later photographs. This was all important information, but the study of the photographs could not confirm the calibre of the guns at Merville. It was a vital piece of missing detail, as the position of the battery and the frantic work being conducted to improve its defences were of profound concern to the man responsible for planning the Allied invasion of France.

By January 1944, Lieutenant General Sir Frederick Morgan had been working on the planning for D-Day for several months. At a meeting in Washington in May 1943 the Combined British and American Chiefs of Staff had taken the final decision to invade Nazi-occupied north-west Europe and had set a provisional date of May 1944. Morgan had been selected as the Chief of Staff Supreme Allied Command. As COSSAC, he and a small team of Anglo-American officers were responsible for the joint planning of the largest, most complex combined arms operation ever to be mounted. They had decided to codename it Operation Overlord and had also decided that it would take place in Normandy.

COSSAC's detailed planning had identified the advantages of landing in Calais, but their work also confirmed that it was heavily defended. The disaster of Dieppe highlighted the need to avoid landing in areas of main enemy troop concentrations and had been reinforced by the experience of Allied landings in Sicily and Italy. German troop dispositions in Normandy were more thinly spread and could be more readily isolated by bombing the bridges over the Seine, which the bulk of German reinforcing units would have to pass across. Intensive reconnaissance and intelligence analysis had also confirmed that the gently sloping beaches along the Cotentin Peninsula were suitable for a landing and were within the range of Allied fighter cover. Additionally, the terrain and inland road network were suitable for the logistic build-up of a beachhead and subsequent breakout towards Paris.

While Normandy offered clear advantages to Morgan and his planners, it also had its problems. One was a matter of logistics. Cherbourg was the nearest major port most suitable for the subsequent logistical build-up behind the main beach landing, but its heavy defences precluded a direct assault from the sea. This was overcome by the simple, but ingenious decision to take a port with them in the form of the Mulberry portable harbours and by laying fuel pipelines under the Channel. But the issue of neutralizing the gun battery at Merville was an altogether thornier problem, which could not be overcome by the application of physics and science alone.

On the other side of the River Orne from the Merville Battery lay the small seaside resort of Ouistreham, where the mouth of the river flows into the Bay of the Seine and the beaches of Normandy start their long curve west along the flat shelving shoreline of the Cotentin Peninsula towards Cherbourg. Codenamed Sword by the Allied planners, the beach at Ouistreham was at the eastern end of the Allies' chosen landing area. It was also where the left-hand British assault division would touch down on the morning of D-Day.

Given their position, the guns at Merville were capable of sweeping the entire length of the beach with artillery fire. Drawing on the lessons from Dieppe, where British and Canadian troops had been caught out in the open shingle as they disembarked from their landing craft, Morgan and his team were in no doubt of the devastation that a well-defended battery could wreak on troops struggling to get ashore on Sword. Additionally, the position of the guns meant that they would be capable of engaging ships out to sea as well as the slow-moving landing craft as they ran into the beach.

Although it had not been confirmed by photo reconnaissance, the COSSAC planners suspected that the guns were 150mm-calibre field howitzers. While none of the artillery pieces had been captured on camera, when viewed under a stereoscope the shape and shadow at the rear of the casemates indicated that large entrances were being constructed. If they were naval ordnance, the guns would have been bolted permanently inside the bunkers and would have no need of large rear entrances. Consequently, photographic interpretation suggested that the casemates were designed specifically to take field guns, which could be manhandled in and out of the concrete shelters.

Given the extraordinary lengths the Germans were going to in order to protect the guns, it was logical for the planners to deduce that they would be one of the heavier and more valuable Wehrmacht field types. The largest standard field gun the Wehrmacht possessed was *schwere* or 'heavy' Feldhaubitze 18. It had a calibre of 150mm and could hurl a shell weighing sixty pounds over ten miles, a distance that brought every inch of Sword Beach within range and meant that vessels could be engaged several miles out at sea.

While the Allies placed a heavy emphasis on PR aircraft to gain intelligence on the Atlantic Wall defences, they were not their only source of information on the preparations being made on the other side of the Channel. The build-up of German troops at the beginning of 1944 and the frenetic building activity had not gone unnoticed by the French Resistance. Eugène Meslin was the Vichy government's chief engineer in Caen and was responsible for handling relations with the Todt Organisation. Meslin was also the head of the Resistance's intelligence section at their western headquarters based in the city and his job meant that he was ideally placed to conduct the principal Resistance task of spying on the German coastal defences and reporting on their progress to the Allies. Through his network of fellow engineers and artisans working for the Germans on the defences, the details of every pill-box, wire entanglement and gun emplacement were being reported back to London by Meslin's outfit.

Louis Bourdet was a member of Meslin's network and had been subcontracted to work on the gun position at Merville. When completing electrical work at the battery he had managed to slip his hand into the mouth of one of the guns. Once his shift had finished, Bourdet raced home and measured the span of his hand with the aid of a piece of paper and a ruler. The ruler showed 120mm and the information was duly fed back to London. The Germans did not possess 120mm-calibre field guns, but the measurement of Bourdet's hand suggested that the guns in the casemates were definitely larger than the Wehrmacht's other standard-issue field howitzer, the smaller *leichte* or 'light' Feldhaubitze 18, which had a calibre of 105mm.

The lengths the Germans were going to in order to protect the battery, combined with the information provided by the Resistance, was enough to convince Morgan that the guns at the battery must be of 150mm calibre. When considering the significance of artillery, size matters. The circumference of the barrel dictates the weight and the explosive content of the shell, which in turn dictates its lethal effect. The weight of the projectile it fired meant that a shell bursting from a 150mm gun would have a lethal splinter distance radius of up to 200 metres. A salvo from four 150mm guns, firing in close proximity, could spread their jagged metal shrapnel over the area of a football pitch and would easily devastate a unit of infantry advancing over an open beach in a matter of minutes.

The existence of the battery, set back a mile from the coast, presented a significant threat to the landings and it was vital that it was eliminated before the troops touched down on the beaches. Bombing lacked precision and offered no guarantee when the casemates could withstand anything but a direct hit from the heaviest Allied bombs. Morgan therefore needed an insurance plan that the guns would be put out of action before the troops landed on the beaches. A pre-emptive attack launched from the sea entailed too much risk; getting a raiding party to the battery undetected would be no easy task and could alert the Germans in advance of the landing of the main invasion force.

Morgan's bosses shared his concern and had no illusions about the hazardous nature of mounting an amphibious landing on a defended shoreline against fifty enemy divisions who were expecting an inva-sion. General Dwight Eisenhower's appointment as Supreme Allied Commander of the invasion had been confirmed at the Tehran Conference in December 1943, where Churchill, Stalin and Roosevelt decided to open the second front. Ike had arrived in Britain in January 1944 to assume command of the Supreme Headquarters of the Allied Expeditionary Force (SHAEF) at the same time as General Bernard Montgomery returned from commanding the 8th Army in Italy to take over command of the British contribution to the landings. As well as commanding 21st Army Group, Montgomery had been selected to command all the Anglo-American land forces under Ike and was tasked with overseeing the planning for the entire operation.

The experience of Dieppe and near disaster of the invasion of Sicily and Italy a year earlier increased Ike and Monty's apprehension of what the Allies were about to undertake. If the invasion failed the implications for the conduct of the war would be significant: an Anglo-American landing could not be reattempted for some consid-erable time, and defeat in France would allow Hitler to transfer the bulk of his divisions to face the onslaught from the Red Army in the east. Consequently, like the Germans, the Allies saw the success or failure of the invasion as a strategic decision point and agreed with Morgan on the need to eliminate as many risks as possible to get the maximum number of troops safely ashore.

While one of the risks centred on neutralizing the Merville Battery, Ike and Monty agreed with Morgan's assessment that the risk of counter-attack by German mobile reinforcements into the flanks of the landing also needed to be reduced. But in reviewing Morgan's plan they felt that his intended invasion frontage of three assaulting divisions in the first wave was too narrow. With Eisenhower's agreement, Montgomery expanded the length of the invasion area to include the whole of the Cotentin Peninsula. He also increased the number of divisions in the first wave from three to five, landing on five separate beaches instead of three. Two US divisions would land in the western sector along two beaches codenamed Utah and Omaha. One Canadian and two British divisions would land to their east along Juno, Gold and Sword beaches.

The Allies had thirty-seven divisions stationed in England for the invasion, but it would take days and weeks to take them all across the Channel. To Montgomery, success depended on breaching the Atlantic Wall and getting enough troops ashore to consolidate the beachhead before the Germans could bring the combined weight of their panzer divisions against him. Like Rommel, he saw the first hours and days as critical. A successful breakout from Normandy could only come after the Allies had won the race to build up sufficient force ratios ashore to beat off the panzers as they moved to counter the landing.

In line with Morgan's initial estimate regarding the risk of German attacks into the flanks during the early phases of the operation, the one aspect of the COSSAC planning work that Montgomery did not change was the simultaneous dropping of US and British airborne troops on the eastern and western ends of the invasion beaches. The east flank of Sword Beach where the 3rd British Division would land was a particular concern, given its proximity to the concentration of the majority of German formations around the Seine. Focused on responding to a threat of invasion in the Pas de Calais area, the panzers would come from this direction once the enemy realized that the real threat was in Normandy.

The quickest and most direct approach for German reinforcements moving westwards towards Sword Beach lay across the Dives and Orne rivers, which ran into the sea astride the wooded high ground of the Bréville Ridge. If the German mobile divisions were able to cross these rivers they would have an opportunity to roll up the flank of the invasion from east to west before the Allies had time to land sufficient numbers of their own armoured forces to counter such an attack.

27

The western side of the ridge, closest to Sword Beach, had the added benefit of the Caen Canal. Fed from the mouth of the Orne, it flowed beside the river along the bottom of the ridge towards Caen. There were only two bridges across the double water feature at the villages of Bénouville on the Orne and over the canal as it passed through Ranville. The bridges were the vital ground and the ridge was the key terrain to defending the left flank of the invasion. Whoever held the bridges would control the most direct access to Sword Beach, and whoever held the Bréville Ridge would have a marked advantage in controlling the high ground that dominated them.

Trying to take the ground from the sea by landing on the beaches to the east of the River Orne would bring the invasion fleet into the effective range of the Germans' large-calibre naval guns at Le Havre. Consequently, Morgan's plan to protect the left flank advocated using the British 6th Airborne Division to seize and hold the vital ground and terrain by dropping them behind the Atlantic Wall during the night immediately preceding the arrival of the main seaborne forces on the morning of D-Day. It was a daring and ambitious plan and not without its detractors, particularly among the British Air Staff.

Its leading opponent was Air Marshal Sir Trafford Leigh-Mallory. Following the catalogue of errors that had occurred during the Sicily landings, the chief air planner in COSSAC had profound misgivings. Leigh-Mallory pointed to the heavy losses of gliders in the Mediterranean and the inaccuracy of the parachute drops where many of the paratroopers had been dropped wide of their drop zones, or DZs. Leigh-Mallory doubted that the fate of airborne forces in Normandy would be any different. In fact he expected it to be worse. The troops landing by parachute and glider would be lightly armed and dispersed, whereas their opponents would be able to concentrate and bring their heavier weapons systems, in terms of tanks and artillery, against them. Given the circumstances, he forecast that the airborne troops would expect to incur 75 per cent casualties.

The more powerful voices of Eisenhower and Montgomery were convinced of the utility of airborne forces and the critical role they had to play in D-Day. Sicily had been the first mass use of Allied glider and parachute troops. While it revealed the need for many improvements, landing airborne troops in advance of the main sea-borne force had made a significant contribution to the success of the landing and also convinced Churchill of its possibilities in Normandy. Endorsed at the highest levels, and as a subset of Overlord, the British airborne phase of the invasion would be called Operation Tonga.

Although backing the use of airborne forces, SHAEF's final adjust-ment of the plan was one of timing. The shortage of assault landing craft for the invasion meant that the date was put back to 5 June. Delaying by another month allowed more time for the pre-invasion bombings to continue to soften up German defences, and would also align the date of the Allied assault on the beaches with the launch of the Red Army offensive in the east. Additionally, it would provide more time to build up the capability of the airborne forces and improve on the lessons from Sicily. Monty had wanted to increase the number of British airborne troops taking part in the operation, but had been frustrated by the lack of available aircraft to lift them. While the US 82nd and 101st airborne divisions could be lifted in their entirety and dropped on the right flank at the western end of the Cotentin Peninsula, the RAF had insufficient aircraft to fly in all of 6th Airborne Division. With a month's delay Monty hoped that he might just get the additional aircraft he needed in time.

Two weeks after the photographs of the Merville Battery had been taken, the nominal head of British Airborne Forces was in less opti-mistic mood as he drove to the headquarters of 6th Airborne Division to give its commander his orders for D-Day. Lieutenant General Frederick 'Boy' Browning was a bright young Guards general with a dapper dress sense who had spotted the potential of parachute forces as a brigade commander at the start of the war. His early interest in the development of the airborne arm had led to his rapid promotion, command of the first British Airborne Division and his further pro-motion as it expanded into a corps-sized capability. But he didn't feel particularly bright about the message he would have to give to its commander, General Richard Gale.

In terms of appearance, Richard Gale, or 'Windy' as he was nick-named, was everything Browning was not. With his regulation

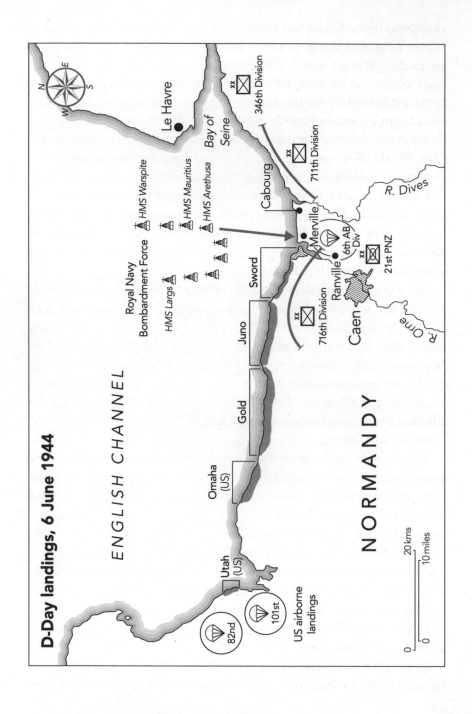

D-Day landings, 6 June 1944

ENGLISH CHANNEL

Le Havre

Bay of Seine

R. Dives

xx
346th Division

xx
711th Division

Cabourg

HMS Warspite

HMS Mauritius

HMS Arethusa

Royal Navy
Bombardment Force

HMS Largs

Merville

6th AB
Div

Ranville

xx
21st PNZ

xx
716th Division

Caen

R. Orme

Sword

Juno

Gold

Omaha
(US)

Utah
(US)

82nd

101st

US airborne
landings

NORMANDY

20 kms

10 miles

0

0

military moustache, he had the look of a typical Indian Army 'Poona' officer or affable uncle, who would not have seemed out of place in an Evelyn Waugh novel. Although aged forty-three and without a trace of grey in his hair, he looked older and had a portly air about him, not helped by his incongruous style of wearing an open-zipped parachutist's Denison smock and riding jodhpurs over standard-issue Army boots. He was awarded the MC as an infantry subaltern in the First World War, and might have ended his career as a passed-over lieutenant colonel had it not been for the outbreak of war in 1939. But by 1944, Gale had already worked on airborne staff matters in the plans directorate of the War Office and commanded a parachute brigade. Gale awaited Browning's arrival with anticipation, eager to discover the role his division would play in the invasion. He was about to be disappointed.

Browning informed Gale that his division would be dropped at the British end of the beaches, around the Bréville Ridge and would then secure the left flank of 3rd Division prior to its landing on Sword Beach. But due to the shortage of lift for his two Para brigades and brigade of glider troops, he was told that he would have to accomplish it by providing only one of his parachute brigades under command to 3rd Division. For a commander who had built up his division from scratch since its formation in April of the previous year it was a bitter blow.

Gale's single parachute brigade was given three principal tasks. The primary mission was to capture and secure the bridges across the Orne and Caen Canal and destroy the heavily fortified gun battery at Merville. These tasks were to be completed no later than half an hour before daylight on D-Day, prior to the start of the landing of the seaborne forces. The secondary task was to delay the movement of enemy reinforcements westwards by blowing the bridges over the River Dives not more than two hours after the landings, and then by holding key access points across the Bréville Ridge.

It was an ambitious undertaking for one brigade. Composed of 2,200 men formed into three battalion groups, each of approximately 750 soldiers, including supporting arms, such as engineers, signallers and medics, the units would be without the support of heavier conventional forces until the leading elements of 3rd Division landing across the beaches could link up with them. Until that happened, they would have to rely on naval gunfire support to bridge the gap in their limited firepower.

Gale was convinced that what he had been asked to do was beyond the means of one brigade. As he lobbied to be allowed to take his whole division, his staff began to make their plans for the mission with what they had been given. The majority of their planning took place in a heavily guarded farmhouse that had been requisitioned as the intelligence cell of 6th Division's headquarters. The Old Farm at Brigmerston House was in the village of Milston two miles north of Bulford on the southern edge of Salisbury Plain in Wiltshire. It was ringed with a thick concertina barbed-wire perimeter and a detachment of military policemen; no one got in or out of the building without a specially issued pass.

The precautions taken at the farmhouse reflected the tight ring of security and secrecy regarding all the planning for D-Day. Operation Tonga was no exception. The circle of knowledge beyond COSSAC was kept to an absolute minimum of a few key officers on Gale's staff and the commander of the 3rd Parachute Brigade, Brigadier James Hill, whose brigade Gale had selected for the mission. The rest of the division were kept deliberately in the dark about what was afoot. But as the war tipped irrevocably against the Germans and the inflow of Anglo-American manpower and materiel began to build up in England from January 1944, most people knew that the second front was coming. But like the Germans on the other side of the Channel, they knew neither when nor where. As the planning continued in the Old Farm at Milston the lives of thousands of men of the 6th Airborne Division were being irrevocably drawn into the events that would unfold on 6 June 1944.

The 6th Airborne Division was one of two battle-ready airborne divisions stationed in England at the beginning of 1944 and had been raised specifically to take part in the invasion. Since its formation, Gale had worked the division hard to declare it ready for operations by the end of the year. It was a major accomplishment and although the division was still to be tested in battle, and regardless of the paucity of aircraft to lift it, the fact that the British could lay claim to having two airborne divisions in their order of battle was an impressive achievement in itself. Four years previously, the very existence of airborne forces was little more than a pipe dream in the minds of a few men and the vision of one man in particular was of seminal significance.

3

Hard Landings

D AWN ON 26 April 1941 was cold and bleak for the time of year, hardly the ideal weather conditions for a demonstration of Britain's fledgling military parachute capability. The windsock at the end of the runway strained at its mast in a gusting wind that swept down from the Pennines, as six ageing Whitley aircraft lumbered into a menacing grey sky over Ringway Aerodrome on the outskirts of Manchester. The twin-engine bombers that had been converted to drop paratroopers were slow and obsolete, but they were all that could be spared by the RAF.

They climbed to a height of 1,000 feet before turning back to begin their run in over the airfield at 100 miles per hour. One by one, small dark figures emerged from the bellies of each of the aircraft. Winston Churchill watched them, as each man was swept away by the slipstream and static lines yanked out parachutes to deploy into thirty-two billowing white canopies. They came in to land in a gusting wind, pulling hard on their rigging lines to reduce their airspeed across the ground. After they struggled out of their harnesses, they ran to collect their weapons and equipment from cylindrical metal containers that had been dropped with them, then formed up in sections at their rally point ready to attack some imaginary target.

The parachute demonstration was over in little more than a minute and was the culmination of the tireless work of a small group of pioneers at Ringway. Lacking any previous experience and with completely inadequate resources, they had been asked to do the near impossible, namely create a completely new branch of the armed forces, at short notice and when the priority of the nation's war effort was focused elsewhere. Despite the obstacles they faced, they had managed to train a total of 400 parachutists and create the genesis of a brand-new military capability.

Given the circumstances, what the small band of pioneers had managed to achieve might have been remarkable, but Winston Churchill was less than impressed. The demonstration fell well below his expectations of the force of 5,000 parachutists for which he had agitated less than a year previously. The paltry numbers of men paraded and dropped from the sky reflected the fact that the military chiefs and the policy makers in the War Office and Air Ministry did not share his vision of parachute forces and the vital contribution he believed they could make to winning the war.

In Britain during the inter-war period, parachuting was a means of escaping from a stricken aircraft, not a method for delivering soldiers into battle. Although the American and Italian armies had carried out small-scale experiments with military parachuting in the late 1920s, it was the Russians who were the first to recognize the potential of conducting large-scale airborne operations. In 1935 the Red Army invited foreign military attachés to watch a force of 1,200 military parachutists jump from large Tupolev aircraft, as part of manoeuvres in the Kiev military district. The visitors were suitably struck by the spectacle of masses of parachutists tumbling off the wings of the large six-engine transports and landing in the fields around them. Among them was Major General Archibald Wavell, who later wrote that if he had not witnessed it he 'would not have believed such an operation was possible'.

But while impressed by the novelty of what he had seen, Wavell, like the majority of his fellow military observers, doubted that the demonstration proved parachuting had much practical utility as a new method of warfare, believing such lightly armed troops would be quickly overwhelmed by heavier conventional forces. It was a view that conformed to the official War Office opinion that there was 'little scope for airborne forces being used on a scale that could have any meaningful bearing on the outcome of a military campaign'. The demonstration also came at a time when the conventional military mindset was focused on preparing to confront an old enemy on more traditional terms. Their scepticism was not shared by their German counterparts.

Through secret military cooperation agreements signed with the Soviets in the 1920s, the Germans had been following Russian military research into new forms of warfare with great interest and the coming to power of the Nazis provoked more innovative military thinking. The use of airborne forces meshed with Hitler's policy of rearmament. The Russians' achievement over the skies of Kiev captured the imagination of the German observers, the use of parachute troops fitting neatly into their emerging philosophy of blitzkrieg. As a new form of warfare based on manoeuvre, the avoidance of costly battles of attrition and the use of speed and surprise to defeat an enemy by attacking him in a manner and location least expected, airborne operations offered great potential.

By the outbreak of war in 1939, the German order of battle consisted of a complete parachute division of 9,000 *Fallschirmjäger* and a separate division of troops who could land by glider or transport aircraft. Although they did not take part in the Polish campaign in the autumn of 1939, Hitler personally instructed German parachute forces to be used in the invasion of western Europe. Small numbers of parachute troops were dropped with mixed success to capture strategic objectives during the German invasion of Norway and Denmark the following April. But it was the use of airborne troops in operations in the Low Countries a month later that was to provide a far more convincing demonstration of their utility.

On the night of 10 May 1940, seventy-eight *Fallschirmjäger* landed silently by glider on the flat grass-topped roof of the heavily defended Belgian fortress of Eben-Emael. The massive structure of reinforced concrete was considered impregnable. Occupying a strategic point on the Dutch–Belgian border, its 120mm and 75mm guns dominated three bridges over the Albert Canal, bridges that were deemed critical to the success of the German invasion. The small force used shaped charges to cripple the guns and began to blast their way into the fortress, supported by troops landing by parachute, who captured two of the three bridges intact. Surprise was complete. Trapped inside and unable to dislodge the paratroopers above them, the garrison of 650 were forced to surrender after thirty hours of fighting, having suffered over 100 casualties. Losses to the much smaller German force amounted to six men killed and nineteen wounded. To their north, the Germans used the rest of their airborne forces to capture strategically important bridges over the Maas, which led to the rapid capitulation of Rotterdam and the defeat of Holland. Combined with the spectacular feat of arms at Eben-Emael, the success of the daring use of parachute and glider troops in the Low Countries confirmed Hitler's faith in their utility; it also stirred the imagination of Britain's new Prime Minster.

Within a month of the fall of Eben-Emael, France had been defeated and the British Expeditionary Force had quit Europe from the beaches at Dunkirk. While Britain stood alone in the face of the seemingly unstoppable Nazi war machine, Winston Churchill was already thinking about the means of striking back across the Channel and laying the foundations for the eventual return to the Continent. On 22 June, struck by what had been achieved by the Germans in Belgium and Holland, Churchill wrote a memorandum to the Chiefs of Staff.

The note directed them to raise a corps of at least 5,000 parachutists and he was anxious that they should take advantage of the remaining summer months to do so. Along with the creation of commando units to raid the enemy coast and the training of Special Operations Executive (SOE) agents to encourage the resistance movements to set occupied Europe ablaze, the aspiration to develop airborne forces chimed with the new leader's offensive spirit. It also showed a remarkable foresight.

A school, under the Directorate of Combined Operations, had already been set up at Ringway Aerodrome to conduct experiments into parachuting. Under the command of Squadron Leader L.A. Strange, its initial purpose was to develop training that would allow SOE agents to be dropped into Europe. In response to Churchill's note, the Chiefs of Staff ordered Major John Rock to move to Ringway to begin the training of airborne forces. But despite endorsement at the highest level, Rock was given little guidance by the War Office and found it impossible to get any information regarding the policy or task he had been set. Rock was a Royal Engineer officer and although Strange was a pilot who had been highly decorated in the First World War, neither of the two men had the faintest idea about parachuting.

It was quite clear to them that they would have to make it up as they went along. With great energy and determination they set about trying to achieve in less than twelve months what the Germans had taken over four years to accomplish. Their enthusiasm was not shared by the War Office or Air Ministry. In 1940 conventional thinking in the senior echelons of both services saw preparing the Army to meet the imminent threat of invasion, building up the strength of RAF fighters to defend the country's skies and bombers to take the war back to Germany as the priorities for manpower and resources. They also viewed the success of German airborne operations in Europe as a one-off; the War Office noted that it doubted that parachute troops would be used again 'on a serious scale in major operations'. The conventional minds in the ministries considered fulfilling Churchill's aspiration to be an unwarranted distraction. It was a view that was reflected in the lack of urgency accorded to the establishment of the Parachute Landing School.

Ringway's selection was not due to its suitability as a parachute training centre, but because it was out of the way of the RAF's main operating areas for its fighters and bombers. Situated in the peaceful Cheshire country, it was subject to the notoriously bad weather of the upper Midlands. The vagaries of the north-east wind, which swept down from the Pennines, and rain-laden weather fronts pushing in across the Irish Sea regularly hampered training. In addition, the area was prone to fog and industrial smog from Manchester during the winter months. However, the principal problem was the lack of suitable aircraft for dropping parachutists and an almost complete lack of practical experience to draw on.

The school's instructors were drawn from the physical training branches of the RAF and Army and were equipped with 1,000 modified Irvin aircrew parachutes and parachute packers from the RAF. With no prior knowledge of parachuting, they would have to learn on the job. The instructors were augmented by a number of parachute stunt jumpers from Cobham's Air Circus, who had thrilled the crowds before the war. No doubt their expertise added value, but their skill was individual and very different to the requirements for training 5,000 soldiers to jump into action under battle conditions. Strange and Rock began experimenting with dummies and on 13 July the first live jump was made over the nearby drop zone of Tatton Park.

The slow and obsolete twin-engined Mark II Whitley bombers were initially converted to carry eight paratroopers; however, the crew doors in its fuselage were too small to allow paratroopers wearing parachutes and equipment to jump through them in quick succession. In order to modify the bomber for parachuting, the rear turret was removed to create a pulpit-type platform from which the parachutist could jump from the aircraft using the 'pull off method'. One of the first men to make a parachute jump using this technique was Captain Martin Lindsay of the Royal Scots Fusiliers. Lindsay was posted to Rock's small staff of four other officers in July 1940 after he had taken part in the disastrous British operation to central Norway, which had failed to stall the German invasion of the country two months earlier.

Born into a traditional Scottish military family, Lindsay was a driven high achiever and adventurer. His father had died when he was a young boy and Lindsay was brought up by his mother; money had always been in short supply and the young Lindsay knew that he would have to fashion his own path in life. He won a scholarship to attend Wellington School, where he proved to be an accomplished scholar with a flair for writing, then went on to Sandhurst and was commissioned into the Army in 1925.

By the time he was twenty-three he had led his first transcontinental expedition, crossing Africa from west to east, funding himself by shooting game as he went and collecting pygmy artefacts for the British Museum. He was also an accomplished steeplechase jockey and when in Ajuba won the Nigerian Grand National. In 1930–31 he took part in the British Arctic Air-Route Expedition and was awarded the Polar Medal. Three years later he defied the experts and crossed Greenland again, completely unsupported. His epic journey made the *Guinness Book of Records* and his acclaimed account of the adventure, entitled *Sledge*, sold over 100,000 copies and established his name as an explorer of renown.

Despite his thirst for adventure, Lindsay was undeniably frightened when he made one of the first pull off jumps from the back of a Whitley. His apprehension was not helped by the fact that the planned parachute descent had been delayed by a searing wind that had blown across the aerodrome for four days without respite. On the fifth day the wind abated and Lindsay drew and fitted his chute for the jump. As he waited to board the Whitley he felt the nervous dread that reminded him of sitting in the jockeys' dressing room waiting for his race to be called. However, what he was about to do was no steeplechase but a feat that few others had ever attempted.

At six foot one, Lindsay was not the ideal size for a paratrooper; having crawled to the back of the aircraft along the gloomy and cramped fuselage, he sat uncomfortably as the Whitley took off and climbed to a jump altitude of 800 feet above Tatton Park. The drop zone was only ten minutes' flying time from Ringway, but to Lindsay it seemed an interminable age as he sat uncomfortably giddy from airsickness, his palms sweating.

Lindsay tried not to look at the green patchwork of countryside as he took up position on the small square-foot jump platform at the rear of the bomber. His mental struggle became a physical one as he attempted to stand up into a 100-mile-per-hour slipstream and had to hold on grimly to a bar across the open platform to prevent being blown off. Turning to face his flight sergeant instructor, Lindsay watched the little light on the side of the platform flash from yellow to red. 'Not long now!' shouted the instructor above the roar of the engines and blast of the rushing slipstream. 'Oh God!' Lindsay said to himself. 'Oh God!' As the light flashed green, the instructor chopped his hand down hard, Lindsay gripped his D ring on his left shoulder and pulled sharply.

An instant later he felt a terrific jerk as his chute opened, caught the slipstream and yanked him violently from the aircraft into the void behind him. Seconds later Lindsay was astonished to find himself floating under a taut white canopy. He drifted across the trees of the parkland, the lake below him shimmering in the sun. The bucolic calm of his surroundings was soon rudely interrupted by the approach of the ground rushing up to meet him. He landed with a bump and sprawled in an ungainly heap, but he was down, safe and unhurt. Exhilaration and a sense of confidence surged through him; the bogey of fear had gone and another dragon was slain.

The pull off technique was not only a horrendous method of making a parachute jump, it was also slow and cumbersome. Only one student could be dispatched at a time, meaning men were widely dispersed across the drop zone, when tactical considerations dictated that they needed to land close together. The solution was arrived at within a few days by removing the aircraft's dorsal gun turret and cutting a hole in the bottom of the aircraft, which would allow the parachutists to jump in quick succession with the use of an American-designed 'statichute'.

Equipped with a static-line ripcord attached to a strongpoint inside the aircraft, the parachute would be automatically pulled out of its pack once the jumper dropped through the hole and fell away from the aircraft. The 'Whitley Hole' allowed ten parachutists to be dispatched from the aircraft in ten seconds and jumping one after the other considerably reduced their dispersal from each other when they landed on the ground. However, it was not without its problems.

The aperture cut in the underside of the Whitley produced a three-foot-deep shaft between the floor of the fuselage and the outer skin of the aircraft's belly. The jumper had to remain absolutely rigid and upright as he dropped through the hole. If he caught his parachute pack on the edges it would pitch him forward, making him strike his face on the side of the shaft as he exited through it. The resultant bloody noses and facial bruises were known as 'ringing the bell'. This awkward method of jumping could also lead to twists in the rigging lines, as a less than clean exit made the jumper tumble uncontrollably in the slipstream and serious twists could cause a canopy to malfunction. On 25 July Ringway suffered its first fatality, when twists prevented a soldier's canopy from deploying properly. More deaths were to follow.

It was hardly surprising that death and injury were common, since the method of British military parachuting developed by trial and error against pressing deadlines. Fatalities often halted jumping until the reason for the death had been investigated and improvements to equipment and technique made. However, an early training technique of jumping backwards from three-tonne Army trucks moving at fifteen to twenty miles per hour was quickly discontinued when the instructors realized that they were in danger of injuring more men than they were qualifying. But slowly the men at Ringway began to master their art.

Technical improvements led to the design of the British X-Type statichute. The new parachute suspended the jumper from twenty-eight rigging lines and attached him to four harness lift webs, which allowed the rigging lines to be pulled from the parachute pack to their full extension before the canopy deployed. The more progressive deployment of the chute reduced some of the shock of the canopy opening and the risk of twists. Becoming caught on the tail wheel of the Whitley was another risk. The problem was solved by the pilot applying enough flap to alter the trim of the aircraft and lift the wheel when dropping personnel, but the technique was only developed after a tail wheel hang-up had claimed the lives of several men.

Despite its design improvements, the round-shaped X-Chute was prone to oscillation, with even the slightest breeze causing the chute to swing the parachutists violently from side to side like a leg-snapping pendulum, as they came in to land. The parachute also tended to make men land backwards, taking the shock of impact on the base of the spine. Consequently, broken backs and concussion were common, as were shattered and twisted limbs. Training men to keep their feet and knees pressed tightly together and to roll when they landed reduced the risk of injury. If the correct position was maintained the force of impact was absorbed by the combined strength of both legs and the softer parts of the thighs.

The continual advances notwithstanding, parachuting was not for the faint-hearted. It required a special type of soldier with the right kind of physical and mental qualities to risk life and limb even before battle had been joined. Every jump was fraught with risk and entailed a certain amount of luck. The experience was not helped by having to jump from a Whitley, which was uncomfortable and the means of exit nerve-racking. The dark gloomy interior gave rise to the Whitley's nickname: the 'flying coffin'.

The first body formed to undergo parachute training at Ringway was Number 2 Commando. The commandos were all volunteer units; initially drawn from the ranks of the Army, they had undergone demanding physical selection and training. While some men jumped because they felt compelled to fulfil the obligations of what they had signed up for, others actually enjoyed the thrill of parachuting, but most jumped because of their fear of failure and the ignominy of being RTU'd, or returned to unit. Some, however, even among the hardest of men, found the act of throwing themselves out of a completely serviceable aircraft beyond the limits of their undoubted courage and toughness.

Of the 342 commandos who volunteered to undergo parachute training, thirty refused to jump, two were killed and twenty were injured or declared medically unfit to continue training. But, despite the tribulations and hazards, by the end of 1940 the parachute school had conducted over 2,000 jumps and trained over 500 parachutists. Some were SOE agents who were trained to drop into occupied Europe, but most were from Number 2 Commando, which was renamed the 11th Special Air Service Battalion in November. It was little more than a nascent force, but it was impatient for action and was about to be tested on operations for the first time.

On the night of 10 February 1941 thirty-eight members of the battalion's X Troop, took off in six Whitleys from Gibraltar under a full moon and cloudless sky for their target in Italy. Their mission was to blow up the Tragino aqueduct near Calitri to disrupt the supply of water to military forces stationed in the south of the country, thereby hampering Axis efforts to conduct operations in North Africa. Five of the aircraft managed to drop their paratroopers within one mile of the aqueduct, although a lack of explosives meant that the structure was only badly damaged rather than destroyed. All the raiding party were subsequently captured, but the mission demonstrated the potential to strike deep into enemy territory against a key target.

The operation against the Tragino aqueduct had convinced Churchill that he had been right to demand the creation of an airborne capability, but the paucity of the demonstration he later witnessed at Ringway dismayed him. Churchill felt that a whole year had been wasted and the programme he had set down the previous summer was hopelessly off-track. When informed that only 500 men had been trained as parachutists he noted tersely: 'I said 5,000.' Five weeks after his visit to Ringway, events in the Mediterranean were to give the Prime Minister an added spur to battle through the inertia of his ministries and commanders in developing the airborne force that he demanded.

On the morning of 20 May the first wave of 530 German transport aircraft began dropping 10,000 *Fallschirmjäger* of the 7th Flieger Division over the olive groves of Crete. Their mission was to seize the island and deny the Royal Navy the use of its harbours, thus circumventing British naval supremacy, which would have defeated a seaborne landing. It was a daring attack against a numerically superior enemy, who through Ultra intelligence intercepts knew that the force was on its way. After two days of bitter combat, and suffering heavy casualties, the Germans had captured all their primary objectives and the ebb and flow of battle shifted irrevocably against the defenders.

By 30 May the Chiefs of Staff in London conceded that the position was hopeless. At 0842 hours that morning General Sir Archibald Wavell, as the commander of the Middle East theatre, informed Churchill that the fight was lost and recommended that an evacuation of the island be ordered. It was an ironic twist of fate for the man who delivered the message. The devastating success of the *Fallschirmjäger* was the epitome of the very capability he had doubted when he witnessed the Russians' use of parachutists in 1936 and the loss of Crete would cost Wavell his command.

Crete was the high-water mark of German parachute operations: 10,000 paratroopers and 5,000 air-landed mountain troops had defeated a British, Commonwealth and Greek force of 40,000. It was the first time the *Fallschirmjäger* had been used on such a large scale; Operation Mercury dwarfed anything that had been seen at

Eben-Emael or Rotterdam. But the costs had been prohibitively high and shook the Führer's faith in large-scale airborne operations. Over 4,000 men had been killed; 400 of 600 men of the third battalion of the 1st Assault Regiment, who jumped in the morning, were dead by the end of the first day and the Luftwaffe had lost 284 aircraft, losses Hitler could ill afford as he prepared to embark on the invasion of Russia. Although the airborne arm of the Luftwaffe continued to expand in size, it would never make a mass drop again. Instead it would bleed itself to death fighting as normal infantry in the snows of the east and the fields of Normandy.

As the Germans broke faith with the capability they had pioneered, the British military establishment began to find theirs. With the Prime Minister's direct intervention and the shock of Crete still fresh in their minds, senior officers came to recognize the incontrovertible effectiveness of large-scale parachute operations and began to implement the lessons that were already apparent to Churchill and the small band of pioneers at Ringway.

On 31 May the military Chiefs of Staff issued a joint paper outlining plans to raise two parachute brigades, an air landing brigade and to start production of troop-carrying gliders. Orders were issued to form the 1st Parachute Brigade under Brigadier Richard Gale in July. Gale folded 11th SAS into the new formation as the 1st Parachute Battalion and set about finding volunteers from the rest of the Army to form his other three battalions. The Chiefs also agreed that while one brigade should be held in England, the second should be raised for deployment in the Middle East. Each brigade needed an established strength of nearly 2,500 troops and the throughput at Ringway was expanded to meet the increased demand to train 5,000 of them by January 1942.

In October Brigadier Frederick 'Boy' Browning was promoted to the rank of major general and appointed as the commander of Airborne Forces. He was tasked to set up a divisional headquarters to oversee the development of all glider and parachute troops. In December the War Office announced the formation of the Army Air Corps as the parent regiment, which would include the newly formed Glider Pilot Regiment of Army pilots trained by the RAF to fly the gliders that were beginning to come off the production lines. The first forty candidates would begin training at the RAF Elementary Flying Training School at Haddenham in Oxford the following month. Within two years the strength of trained glider pilots in the new regiment was to grow to over 2,500.

Regardless of whether they would be delivered into battle by parachute or glider, all Airborne troops wore a distinctive maroon beret that immediately marked them out against the drab khaki serge forage caps and berets worn by conventional units. On their right upper arm they wore the Airborne flash of Homer's hero Bellerophon astride the winged horse Pegasus etched in sky-blue against a maroon background. While the choice of blue was obvious, maroon happened to be the favourite colour of Browning's wife, the novelist and socialite Daphne du Maurier.

In August 1942 the War Office announced the formation of the Parachute Regiment as part of the Army Air Corps and by placing the administration and organization of all parachute battalions under a single regimental identity helped encourage an *esprit de corps*. However, generating the right ethos was more than just about corps colours, unit identity and insignia. The German experience demonstrated that the greatest value of airborne forces was in taking critical objectives that would be difficult to achieve by other means. But air assault operations entailed risk and required the ability to fight under exceptional circumstances. Paratroopers were expected to land behind enemy lines, surrounded by an enemy with greater numbers and heavier weapons. They would be isolated until a ground forces link-up or withdrawal could be achieved. Jumping from an aircraft and then to fight in such circumstances would require a special type of soldier, where courage, physical fitness and personal initiative would be key. But they would also need to have the right attitude of mind, self-confidence and determination to succeed when the odds were stacked against them. Consequently, the ethos of the force would have to encompass more than just skill at arms and physical training. In order to standardize the selection criteria and assessment for service with Airborne Forces, the Airborne Forces Depot was opened at Hardwick Hall in Derbyshire in April 1942, where all volunteers had to pass a rigorous period of two weeks' physical and tactical field training before being allowed to move to Ringway to train as a parachutist. The course was deliberately designed to weed out the unsuitable and only the most determined of men got through.

By early 1942 Ringway was capable of producing 100 qualified parachutists a week, but the problem now was less one of capacity but of finding enough volunteers of the right calibre to pass the stringent medical, survive the rigours of Hardwick and then make it through parachute training. The training of the first parachute units had proved that only one man in three who volunteered possessed the necessary qualities. But the number of volunteers dwindled and attrition of their ranks through injury, sickness and refusals made it impossible to produce a second parachute brigade of another three battalions. The lack of volunteers was accounted for in some measure by the fact that in 1942 the paratrooper was still a novel kind of soldier.

In order to make good the shortfall, a publicity and recruiting campaign was launched, which called for volunteers from across the Army and recruiting teams were sent out to find them from regular units. However, commanding officers were understandably reluctant to lose their best officers and men, and only the most determined soldiers were capable of overcoming the obstacles of a system that espoused loyalty to their own regiment. The recruitment drive therefore proved unable to attract enough trained volunteers to meet the expanding requirements of the newly formed Parachute Regiment. The remedy was found by converting existing line infantry battalions into parachute troops.

In October 1942 the 5th and 6th Battalions were generated from the 7th Battalion of the Cameron Highlanders and the 10th Battalion of the Royal Welch Fusiliers. Converting complete units had the advantage of adding a new capability on to the basis of an existing unit, which already had its own established ethos and administration structure. Every individual in the chosen units still had to be willing to volunteer, although they could now do so with the additional motivation of volunteering out of loyalty to their parent unit. Volunteers nonetheless had to meet the demanding standards of becoming a paratrooper. On average, out of over 600 men in a converting unit, only 150 men would make the grade, but even so it was a faster way of raising new Para battalions using an existing cadre of individuals.

By February 1942, the newly forming Parachute Regiment had already demonstrated its operational worth when C Company of the 2nd Parachute Battalion had captured components from a Würzburg radar station on the coast of France that month. By November the 1st Parachute Brigade deployed to North Africa where it captured a number of enemy airfields by direct parachute attacks. The same month 1st Airborne Division achieved its status as an operational formation of three brigades and a decision was taken to raise a third parachute brigade.

The 3rd Parachute Brigade was formed using existing units: the 10th Somerset Light Infantry, 13th Royal Warwickshire Regiment and the 10th battalion of the Essex Regiment were converted to become the 7th, 8th and 9th battalions of the Parachute Regiment respectively. Due to shortages of equipment, the need to complete retraining and find additional volunteers, the process of raising the new brigade would be slow. The 9th Battalion the Parachute Regiment would be no exception. Its original Essex Regiment commanding officer was too old to transfer to the new airborne role and over the period of the next eighteen months the new battalion would have a succession of no fewer than three different COs. Each was a formidable character in his own right and the intricate dynamics of the relationship that existed between them and the men under their command would have a significant part to play in 9 PARA's journey to D-Day and the fighting in Normandy.

4

Emperors

O N A BRIGHT sunny day in late autumn 1942 twenty-one-year-
old Sergeant Paddy Jenkins formed up on the barrack square in
St Albans with the other 644 officers and men who made up the 10th
Battalion of the Essex Regiment. He didn't know what to expect,
but to Jenkins the senior officer who stood in front of them looked
every inch the Para general. Dressed in his camouflage Denison
smock and wearing the distinctive maroon beret, Boy Browning
waited for the regimental sergeant major to stand the assembled ranks
at ease. Then he told them about the formation of the new airborne
division and that the 10th Essex was to be part of it.

Browning explained that the unit had been chosen by the War
Office to convert to the parachute role and would be renamed the
9th (Eastern and Home Counties) Battalion the Parachute Regiment,
which would also be known as 9 PARA. After that he told them that
they had a choice: they could either volunteer to stay with the battalion and undergo selection for parachute duties, or they could elect
to be posted elsewhere.

There was a pause, a murmur of hesitant discussion in the ranks
and then the first man stepped forward; virtually every man followed
suit. As far as Jenkins was concerned it took real courage not to volunteer in front of the general and their commanding officer. The
menacing presence of the company sergeant majors undoubtedly
helped persuade any who hesitated. Some, like twenty-year-old
James Baty, stepped forward because they wanted to stick with their
mates, but Jenkins had a particular reason for wanting to volunteer.

The 10th Battalion had spent most of its time wiring obstacles on
beaches for an invasion that never came. As the threat receded the

men had been sent into the countryside to help the farmers pick sugar beet, as Britain struggled to feed its population at the height of the German U-boat campaign. Their efforts might have made a small contribution to staving off the threat of starvation, but it wasn't what Jenkins had joined up for. The unit had little ammunition and rifles had to be shared, which did little to convince Jenkins that he was at the heart of the war effort. Volunteering to convert to a parachute battalion was an opportunity to change all that. Although military parachutists were a new type of soldier, there was a certain cachet about them that seemed to offer something more exciting than the dull monotony of his current circumstances. Like the rest of the men in the battalion, Paddy didn't really know what to expect, although he anticipated that it was going to be tough.

Over the next few days the battalion's gymnasium echoed to the shouts of Army physical training instructors (PTIs) and the grunts of their charges. The PTIs were assigned to the battalion from the 1st Airborne Division and their job was to weed out the unsuitable by putting the volunteers through a series of selection tests. If a man could not run a mile and a half in under nine minutes or complete a set number of pull-ups, they were posted from the unit. The medicals were equally stringent. Poor dentures, eyesight or a perforated eardrum were enough to disqualify a man and by the time the newly designated 9th Battalion moved to its new barracks on Salisbury Plain, its ranks had thinned to little more than 200 men, less than a third of the 650 soldiers required to form a properly manned parachute unit.

The number of survivors from the initial selection process at St Albans would reduce further when their training started in earnest in the New Year. Paddy made it to Kiwi Barracks near Bulford in Wiltshire, but the high spirits he had first felt on making the selection grade for the Paras were soon replaced by a depressing gloom when the remnants of the battalion took up residence in 9 PARA's new base just before Christmas 1942.

Kiwi Barracks is located near the Wiltshire village of Bulford. Built into the lea of Beacon Hill ridge, the barracks sit on the southern edge of Salisbury Plain, where the rolling fringe of open grassland and wooded plantations meets the more cultivated and settled part of the county. The barracks form part of the larger Bulford garrison, which in 1942 was a mix of old redbrick Victorian buildings and Nissan huts thrown up hastily to accommodate an expanding wartime army. 9 PARA had the good fortune to be accommodated in a modern Hore-Belisha barracks, named after the War Minister who ordered their construction in 1939 following the Munich Crisis the year before. As a champion of soldiers' welfare, Hore-Belisha had ensured that the new two-tiered spider-blocks barracks were built with hot showers, central heating and recreation facilities. They were good for their day, especially for a generation of young working-class men who had lived through the privations of the Great Depression of the 1930s.

Despite the quality of the accommodation, Jenkins remained in high dudgeon. To him Bulford was a dreary windswept place in the 'arse-end of nowhere'. The cold east wind swept over the chalk badge of a large New Zealand Army kiwi carved into the slopes of Beacon Hill and cut down across the raised parade ground beneath it. Like the Anzac troops that had garrisoned Bulford during the First World War, Paddy felt a long way from home. He had been looking forward to spending the festive season in St Albans where he had friends, since the 10th Essex's barracks had been located in the town and the battalion had integrated well with the local community. Now he knew no one, many of his mates had not made it to 9 PARA and the nearest town of Amesbury was four miles away and uninviting.

After a miserable Christmas in Bulford, the depleted ranks of the battalion headed north to Derbyshire, where the serious part of the selection process would begin at the Airborne Forces Depot at Hardwick Hall near Chesterfield. For the next three weeks they would be at the total mercy of the Airborne physical training instructors. All were qualified parachutists and many had recent operational experience. The sergeant major who greeted the men on their arrival was still recovering from wounds he had received the previous February during the Bruneval raid, when three bullets had passed through his guts. He left the volunteers in no doubt about the regime at the depot. He told them, 'You will move at the double at all times except when you leave the dining hall after a meal, but at any other time, even after dark, if you are found walking you will have me to deal with.'

The sergeant major also made it quite clear that there would be no exception for rank, so majors, captains and subalterns found themselves running up and down the slopes of the camp at double time just like the NCOs and privates. Regardless of rank, most men wondered what they had let themselves in for as they were 'beasted' between accommodation and equipment stores, where they drew bedding and the extra kit they would need for the course, before being allowed to settle down for an uncertain night between rough Army blankets in poorly heated wooden barrack huts.

The real agony started the next day. At 0600 hours all ranks paraded in full battledress with rifle and pack, then set off at a shin-burning pace along the hilly roads connecting the surrounding Derbyshire mining villages. They forced-marched hard up the steep inclines and then doubled down the other side and on the flats. Distances became progressively longer and the weights heavier. If someone started to flag or drop behind the rest of the squad of running men, officers were expected to take the lead in motivating them and dragging them back into formation. If a man could not keep up the punishing pace, he had his kit stripped off him and passed round the rest of the members in his ten-man section or 'stick'. Should anyone drop out altogether, his card was marked and he was destined for failure.

Arriving back in camp bathed in sweat with heaving chests and aching lungs, those who had kept up the pace would have a few minutes to double back to their bunks, change out of their heavy serge battledress into PT kit and then be hammered through circuit training until lunchtime. The afternoons were taken up with tactical field training and assault courses until seven o'clock in the evening. Sticks would be expected to hump a five-gallon metal drum filled with earth across obstacles, or conduct squad runs carrying logs the size of telegraph poles over demanding cross-country routes and obstacle courses.

They learned to fire the Sten gun, a cheap mass-produced British weapon prone to stoppages and accidental discharges. But at £5 a piece it was substantially cheaper than the US Thompson sub-machine gun, which cost ten times as much to manufacture. Weighing only seven pounds, the Sten was light, ideal for parachute forces if properly handled and could be fired on single shot or on fully automatic from a thirty-two-round side-fed box magazine. Effective out to 100 metres, it was good for close-quarter work too. Its 9mm round was interchangeable with German ammunition of the same calibre, another advantage for lightly equipped parachute troops where resupply would be limited and pillaging enemy stocks would form a key part of their ability to sustain themselves.

They were trained in the use of the Gammon bomb, another weapon favoured by Airborne Forces, which would lack heavy anti-tank weapons. Containing two pounds of plastic explosive in a sticky coated stockinette bag, the bomb was designed to squash and attach itself on to armoured plate when thrown against the side of a tank. When it exploded it caused lethal scabs of metal to flake off from the other side of the armour, which would be blown around the crew compartment like shrapnel. As well as using standard-issue British infantry weapons, such as the two-inch hand-held mortar and Mark 36 fragmentation grenade, the volunteers were introduced to more specialist weapons such as the US .45 Colt automatic pistol. This weapon, was reliable and at close range was a good man-stopper, with the added benefit of being easier to reach than a rifle or Sten gun, for a man encumbered with parachute gear could still strap a pistol to his leg when he jumped.

Physical fitness and weapons handling were only one part of the activities at Hardwick. As well as assessing a man's fitness and endurance, the selection course at the depot also tested a student's potential aptitude for parachuting when they moved to Ringway for the next phase of their training. High-wire confidence courses and cliff-climbing exercises were designed to establish whether candidates had a head for heights and the nerve to make a parachute jump. There were no safety nets. A fall from the ropes and narrow plank walkways set up high in trees, or from a standing jump across a gap that gave the illusion of being an impossible task, all invited serious injury. Any hesitation or refusal to react instantly to an instructor's word of command to leap for a rope or throw oneself across a void would result in failing the selection process and being 'returned to unit'. Repeated failure to keep up the punishing pace, or dropping out of a battle march would also result in being returned to unit. The ignominy of being RTU'd was dreaded by all those who entered the depot and many men left Hardwick with tears in their eyes after having been informed that they had not made the grade.

The test phase of the course followed after two weeks of building up a candidate's fitness and was designed to gauge the individual's determination, team spirit, aggressiveness and behaviour under stress. It would determine whether a man had the self-discipline and motivation required to serve with Airborne Forces and therefore earn a place on the parachute training course at Ringway. The test events involved timed speed marches over varying distances and terrain. Squad races with heavy logs and stretchers and assault courses, were each designed to simulate a particular battle activity and the hardships associated with airborne operations where men would have little in the way of vehicle support and would have to march hard to an objective carrying all their equipment with them. One part of the tests involved completing a ten-mile battle-march in full kit in less than one hour and fifty minutes to simulate force marching to an objective after having landed on a drop zone by parachute. Another test event was called 'milling', a form of boxing where each candidate, wearing sixteen-ounce boxing gloves, was expected to land as many blows on his opponent as possible in three rounds of controlled violence. The objective was to demonstrate relentless attack and candidates would be marked down and could risk failure if they displayed defensive behaviour, such as attempting to block or avoid an opponent's punch.

To graduate from the course a potential parachutist needed to pass each of the tests, but injuries were also common and added to the attrition rate of those who failed. Men broke bones as a result of falling from high platforms and scramble nets or suffered lower leg injuries from the constant pounding of forced marches while carrying heavy loads. A candidate could also elect to withdraw from the course at any time and the combination of voluntary withdrawal, RTU and injuries meant that the pass rate for those who entered Hardwick was rarely more than 30 per cent. Success earned the candidate the right to wear the maroon beret and set the benchmark entry standard for Airborne Forces. It also provided a thread of shared experience that tied all members of the new Parachute Regiment together. Regardless of rank or seniority, each paratrooper knew that the comrades he served alongside had been through the same rigorous course.

The lack of any differential between ranks made a marked impression on Paddy Jenkins and was at odds with what he had been used to in a traditional line infantry regiment. The fact that the officers were expected to do everything that was asked of the rank and file as a matter of course was a key strength of Airborne Forces and brought about a degree of instant respect between its officer corps and its soldiers. The fact that they had to do everything the men did also had a marked impact on the officers who would serve with 9 PARA.

Captain Bill Mills had been due to attend the Army Staff College. Selection was competitive and attendance at the year-long course at Camberley in Surrey was essential for career advancement as a regular officer. However, Mills had been the adjutant of a training regiment where he was the senior captain responsible for administering discipline to young conscript soldiers. He was tired of sitting behind a desk and wanted to get into the war, so he turned down his place at Camberley to volunteer for Airborne Forces. Grunting and sweating with the rank and file at Hardwick was a new and levelling experience and particularly tough after having enjoyed near god-like status in another training establishment.

The egalitarian nature of the Airborne fraternity continued when they moved to start their parachute training at Ringway, where the officers also went through exactly the same training as the men and where the inherent fear associated with parachuting was no respecter of rank and could affect all students equally, whatever their status. Passing parachute training further strengthened the bond between officers and men and confirmed their full club membership of Airborne Forces and their sense of being an elite. However, after the rigours of Hardwick, the physical regime at Ringway was mercifully easier. The emphasis was on learning skills and parachute techniques, rather than muscle-busting exercises and arduous physical endurance.

By the time Jenkins arrived at Ringway, the training had been consolidated into a three-week course of eight qualifying jumps, two from a balloon and six from a Whitley. But first he would have to undergo several days of synthetic ground training in the great hangar gymnasium where the men practised techniques for exiting an aircraft and parachute landing falls that would allow the body to absorb the impact of hitting the ground while minimizing the risk of injury. In 1943 the numbers passing through Ringway had increased substantially and the hangars on the edge of the airfield rang to the sound of tumbling bodies thumping on to crash mats and the RAF instructors repeatedly shouting, 'Keep your feet and knees together, elbows close to the side of the body and your head tucked in. Now fall on your side and roll!'

Initially they practised rolling on to crash mats on the floor; then they progressed to jumping and landing from benches and ramps from increasing heights. They made simulated exits from mock-ups of aircraft fuselages and landings in harnesses attached to swings and slides designed to induce motion into their parachute rolls. Before graduating from the hangar to make their first jump for real, each candidate would also have to make several simulated descents from the 'Fan'. This involved jumping from a thirty-foot-high platform set high up in the rafters of the hangar while wearing a harness connected to the drum of a large industrial paddle fan by a steel cable. As the student stepped off the platform on the command 'Go!' the wire pulled through the drum of the fan and turned the blades, which arrested the speed of the man's fall towards the floor to a speed similar to that of being under a parachute canopy.

While the approach of the RAF instructors differed from that of the Army PTIs at Hardwick, the threat of RTU remained. Heavy emphasis was still placed on a student's instant reaction to orders.

Hesitation to climb a ladder or jump from the platform would preclude a student from further training, as it was better to weed out someone showing reluctance on the ground before he got into the air where the fear factor would be far greater. A slowness to learn ran the risk of being RTU'd too. Failure to perform exit drills from aircraft mock-ups or execute regulation parachute landings to the satisfaction of the instructors could also lead to being declared unsuitable. To most students jumping from the Fan for the first time was a heart-thumping experience. For some it was too much and provoked refusals and the inevitable RTU. But it was nothing compared to the first real jump from a balloon and the biggest test would come over the drop zone at Tatton Park.

Jumping from balloons was not new. During the First World War artillery observers had used parachutes to escape from balloons suspended behind the trench lines when enemy fighters attacked them. But it was a last-chance life-saving expedient, not a means of entering battle. However, to the instructors at Ringway the balloon was an ideal way of training parachutists at a time when aircraft were in short supply. Converted barrage balloons used to protect British cities from low-flying German bombers were not only plentiful, but three times as many men could jump from them in an hour as could be dropped from a Whitley. Additionally, the balloon could be used at night and when mist descended on the area and precluded flying. In theory jumping from a balloon made for an easier first jump, as the absence of an aircraft's slipstream reduced the oscillation in the canopy, making it easier to control and land. But while an ideal training platform, the balloon was not a popular innovation among the men who had to jump from it.

In reality, jumping from the balloon was a far more terrifying experience than making a parachute exit from an aircraft. The confines of the fuselage and noise of the engines in a plane gave a sense of detachment from the ground and the blast of the slipstream forced the parachute to open before the jumper was aware that he was falling. In the balloon the absence of the slipstream meant that the student would experience the full effect of plummeting a gut-wrenching 200 feet before the parachute deployed fully. The slow methodical clank of the winch cranking the balloon to the right jump height, while the students clung to the sides of a rickety cage to avoid falling through the hole in its floor, watching the ground get smaller and smaller below them, all added to the psychological edge of what a man was about to be asked to do: namely to commit his life to the thirty-pound bag of silk that he had strapped to his back.

When Paddy Jenkins made his first jump, he eyed the hole in the bottom of the cage nervously, and as the balloon rose higher his sense of exposure increased as Tatton's parkland was spread below him. He was scared to hell. The sudden stop of the winch was followed by a foreboding silence, broken only by the wind sighing through the wire cables that attached the metal-framed hessian cage to the silver globe of the barrage balloon. The RAF jump instructor reminded him that everyone on the ground was looking up at him and he expected to see a good clean exit. He motioned Jenkins forward from the side of the cage and clipped the static line of his chute into the 'D' bar above the hole. Then he ordered him to swing his legs into the aperture and sit on the edge of the hole. Paddy was ordered to look up and told to get ready. He tensed himself and then the instructor shouted, 'Go!' and slapped him on the back.

To Paddy it was another test of demonstrating that he deserved to be wearing the three stripes of a SNCO on his arms. He certainly didn't want to be a 'jibber'. Thinking of the example he needed to set, Paddy arched his back, pushed himself bolt upright, at the same time gripping tightly to the seams of his trousers to ensure that he dropped smartly through the bottom of the cage. Paddy felt the dead drop as he left his stomach behind and plunged towards the ground. It was like jumping out of nothing into nothing. While his body's instincts told his brain that he was falling to his death, for an instant the fact that he was wearing a parachute didn't register. Then he heard the sharp crack of the chute as it deployed, the raisers tugged sharply at his shoulders, and the billowing canopy of silk caught the air and arrested his fall earthwards. He was floating and he experienced the surreal feeling that his life had been saved. Jenkins was brought back to reality by an instructor on the ground shouting through a megaphone to tell him to begin steering the parachute and adopt the right position for landing. Suddenly the ground rushed up towards him, his feet touched, his bent legs buckled, absorbing the impact and he rolled his body on to its side with a bump.

Although most parachutists considered jumping from the balloon to be their most frightening experience, nobody ever forgot their first jump from a Whitley. Jenkins felt even more apprehensive, because as the senior man in the stick of ten students he would have to help the dispatcher open the cover of the hole in the bottom of the fuselage and then watch the others go out before jumping last. In the 1940s the majority of students who went through Ringway had never flown in an aircraft before, let alone made a parachute jump from one. They also had no reserve parachute to call on should their main canopy fail. An additional parachute strapped to their front was too bulky and prevented the jumper from making a clean exit through the floor of the bomber; it was also deemed too expensive. Wearing leather rubber-rimmed training helmets, shapeless jump smock jackets and single parachutes, the students clambered into the narrow fuselage through the small crew hatch in the forward underside of the aircraft and crawled to their allotted space on the cold metal floor of the Whitley's bomb compartment.

As the converted bomber approached the dropping zone, Paddy helped open the cover of the jump aperture. He felt the icy blast of the slipstream and could see hedges and trees whipping past below at 100 miles per hour. The instructor barked the command of 'Action stations!' above the roar of the engines and the first man swung his legs into the well of the exit hole. Poised rigidly on the lip of the aperture, back arched and head up looking at the face of the dispatcher stationed on the other side of the hole, the first student waited for the red warning light to flash green, his face white and tense as he anticipated the next command.

As the light turned green, the jump instructor would yell, 'Go!' An instant later the first student pushed himself ramrod straight and dropped like a stone through the belly of the Whitley from a height of 1,000 feet. If he got it right he would exit cleanly into the rush of slipstream and be whipped downwards and away from the aircraft. A clean exit was important as it would reduce the likelihood of twists in the rigging lines which at their worst could make the chute malfunction.

Paddy watched the grimacing features of fear-etched faces of each member of his stick slip through the hole, disappearing into oblivion one after the other from either side of the hole. He did not relish the prospect of following them. When his turn came he sat on the edge of the hole and repeated the drill. The red light flashed, then turned green and with the shout of the dispatcher he dropped neatly through the aperture in the belly of the Whitley. For a moment he fell earthwards, until the reassuring tug at his shoulders and sight of the canopy snapping taut confirmed that his parachute had deployed. The relief was short-lived, as he kicked out violently against the twists in his rigging lines, tried to assess his drift and then prepared for the landing. Paddy was under his canopy for little more than thirty seconds before he felt the sickening crunch of his collision with the ground. Paddy didn't care whether he managed to execute a proper parachute roll or landed in an ungainly heap, the key thing was that he was uninjured and had made his first parachute jump from an aircraft.

At the end of his third week at Ringway, six jumps later, including one more jump made from a balloon at night, Paddy paraded with the rest of the course to be awarded his wings. The senior course officer personally presented each of those who had successfully completed all eight parachute descents with his white and blue parachutist's badge. The ceremony of the occasion was limited and had a serious edge to it. They were informed that it had cost the War Office £800 to train each man and that once they accepted their wings, refusal to jump in future would result in an automatic court martial, imprisonment and being ejected from Airborne Forces. Paddy and the rest of the course were invited to take one pace forward if they wished to be freed from the obligation; nobody did. The right to wear the maroon beret and parachute wings sewn under the distinctive shoulder flash of Airborne Forces transformed the way the men felt about themselves. Regardless of whether they were pre-war regulars, like Company Sergeant Major Jack Harries, or younger soldiers like Paddy Jenkins, they now felt part of an elite club of volunteers. But if gaining full club membership of Airborne Forces had been tough, life as a fully fledged paratrooper was to get even tougher under their new commanding officer when they returned to Bulford.

The original CO of 10th Essex Battalion, Lieutenant Colonel Tom Hearn, had been deemed too old to undertake parachute training and had been replaced by Lieutenant Colonel James Hill in February 1943. Hearn had earned the affection of his men for his kindly disposition and the interest he showed in their welfare. He was remembered fondly for his regular visits to the soldiers' cookhouse in St Albans, where he would enquire whether the men were getting enough to eat and urge them to eat more. Hill also cared about the welfare of the soldiers under his command, but he was an altogether different proposition from his predecessor and arrived in Bulford with an already established reputation as a combat-proven Parachute Regiment officer.

Aged thirty-two when he was selected to command 9 PARA, Hill had previously commanded a parachute battalion in action during the Tunisian campaign in North Africa. Before volunteering for Airborne Forces he had won a Military Cross serving with the British Expeditionary Force during the retreat through France in 1940.

James Hill had been commissioned from Sandhurst where he won the Sword of Honour in 1931 and joined his family regiment the Royal Fusiliers. His decision to marry before he had reached the regimentally acceptable age of twenty-eight gave him little option but to resign his commission and pursue a career in the family business in 1936. The outbreak of war led to Hill being called back to join the second battalion of his old regiment. Serving as a junior staff captain in France in 1940, Hill was on the last destroyer to leave Dunkirk. He served in a number of other staff positions, was promoted and passed Airborne selection and parachute training in the spring of 1942. He joined the 1st Battalion of the Parachute Regiment as the battalion's senior major, and had assumed command of the unit by the time that 1 PARA deployed to North Africa in November 1942 with the 1st Parachute Brigade. As one of the combat elements of the 1st British Army, the brigade formed part of the Allied effort to hasten the destruction of Rommel's Afrika Korps after its defeat by Montgomery's 8th Army at El Alamein. On 16 November Hill led the first Allied unit level drop near the Tunisian town of Beja. His task was to attack German forces in the area and encourage French forces garrisoning Beja to come over to the Allied cause.

Five days after the drop, Hill was severely wounded when attempting to bring about the surrender of three enemy tanks during an operation to destroy enemy armour located on a ridgeline near Beja. He climbed aboard the first two tanks and persuaded their Italian crews to come out at the point of his revolver. The third tank was crewed by Germans and the panzer commander's response to Hill banging on his turret hatch was to emerge and shoot him through his neck, chest and shoulder at point-blank range with his Luger. Hill received lifesaving field surgery at Beja before eventually being evacuated to an Allied hospital in Algiers and later flown back to England for further treatment. On 11 February 1943, while still convalescing at Tidworth, Hill was awarded the Distinguished Service Order (DSO) for his inspirational leadership and the gallantry he had shown leading 1 PARA. He was also selected to command the newly formed 9 PARA.

James Hill was not a man to sit still, recovering from wounds or not; he discharged himself from hospital without recourse to the medical hierarchy and travelled the short distance to Bulford to take up his new command at Kiwi Barracks. He overcame the 9 PARA Regimental Medical Officer's reluctance to declare him fit by challenging him to a race to the top of the steep slopes of Beacon Hill behind the barracks. Hill won the race convincingly and the MO had little option but to sign off his new CO as being medically fit enough to command the battalion. Hill's impact was immediate. Like the rest of those who had made it back to Bulford, Paddy Jenkins had survived everything that the Parachute Regiment selection had thrown at him and considered himself in peak physical condition. Hill, however, was soon to disabuse him of that assumption.

Hill quickly proved that he could march the legs off any man. Having demonstrated his fitness to the unit doctor, he turned his attention to the rest of the men under his command. Parading the 156 ranks who had made it through their training to join 9 PARA, Hill informed them, 'Gentlemen, you don't look very fit. We will alter that, your miserable bodies are coming with me.' He then proceeded to lead them on a route-march at a blistering pace that many struggled to keep up with. His men knew that he was still recovering from his wounds and it earned him instant respect, while for Hill it also confirmed his initial assessment. At the end of it he declared, 'Gentlemen, you are not fit. But don't let this worry you because from now on we are going to work a six-and-a-half-day week. You can have Saturday afternoons off.' This was the start of a demanding training regime, with physical fitness at its core. Drawing on his experiences in North Africa, Hill knew that his men would have to rely on their physical resilience to prevail on the battlefield. Hill wanted his men to be able to move fast across country while carrying all their equipment. Fitness would also give them a toughness to endure when the odds were stacked against them. After the first route-march they moved at the double everywhere round Kiwi Barracks. On Sundays after attending the unit's church parade at the garrison church of St George, 9 PARA would collect their weapons and equipment they had left stacked on the neat lawns outside the neo-Gothic building and proceed on a twenty-mile battle march with Hill at their head.

This was typical of Hill, who led from the front in all he did. He also moved everywhere at speed using a long thumb-stick to lengthen his stride, which quickly became his trademark. His pace earned him the nickname of 'Speedy', which was a term of respect; his men were impressed by the tall, gaunt and handsome officer who came into their midst while still recovering from wounds sustained in combat. Hill was undoubtedly tough, he led by impressive example and, while calm and quietly spoken, his energy and professionalism were infectious. Compassion for his soldiers was also a stated core tenet of his command style, but by setting and maintaining exacting standards many of his troops felt a degree of trepidation in his company and that they would fail to measure up to the example he set. While Hill's impact on 9 PARA was immediate his tenure in command of the unit was to be brief. His influence, however, would be enduring.

In mid April 1943 Hill was promoted to the rank of brigadier and took over command of the 3rd Parachute Brigade. His new command included 9 PARA, the 8th Battalion of the Parachute Regiment and the 1st Canadian Parachute Battalion, which would arrive in England later that summer. The brigade also included 244 (Parachute) Field Ambulance, 3rd Parachute Squadron Royal Engineers and a headquarters staff. The following month, the brigade was selected to form the nucleus of 6th Airborne Division, which was raised by the War Office specifically for D-Day.

At thirty-three, Hill was not particularly young to be commanding a brigade in an expanding wartime army, where death, wounds and incompetence in action created opportunities for rapid advancement for the ablest of relatively junior officers. However, he was still significantly younger than and comparatively junior, in terms of traditional Army List seniority, to the man who replaced him as the commanding officer of 9 PARA.

Lieutenant Colonel Martin Lindsay was thirty-eight years old when he assumed command of 9 PARA on 14 April 1943. In 1936 he had resigned from the Army before the outbreak of war to contest the Labour-held parliamentary seat of Lincolnshire for the Conservative Party and like Hill had been recalled to the Colours in 1939. As well as standing senior to Hill in the Army List, Lindsay had arguably more parachuting experience: he was not only one of the pioneers of parachuting at Ringway in 1940, but he also formed and commanded 151st Parachute Battalion in the Indian Army Parachute Brigade before his return to England to take over command of 9 PARA from Hill. Lindsay had also proven himself on active service, winning a Mention in Dispatches as a brigade reconnaissance officer in Norway, where he played a key role in enabling the British expeditionary force to extract itself under fire after retreating across the frozen snowfields and mountain valleys to the Norwegian port of Namsos. But while Lindsay was noted for his particular energy and courage, he lacked Hill's combat command experience at unit level, which made the younger man the more obvious choice to lead 3rd Para Brigade.

Lindsay was an extrovert and didn't mind courting controversy if there was a point of principle in the balance. As an unconventional and uncompromising leader, he was prepared to ask awkward questions, challenge orthodoxy and adopt imaginative practical solutions, which not only often defied regulations but also irked his seniors. Although only a captain, his concern regarding the conduct of the disastrous British campaign in Norway prompted him to contact Clement Attlee, the leader of the opposition, on his return to England. At a clandestine meeting at the Oxford and Cambridge Club in Pall Mall, Lindsay told Attlee that if further operations were conducted in such a manner, Britain was in serious danger of losing the war. Armed with a memo provided by Lindsay charting the ineptitude of British performance in the Norway campaign, Attlee and Herbert Morrison used the information as ammunition to move a cross-party vote of no confidence against Neville Chamberlain during the two-day 'Norway Debate'. The debate opened against the government on 7 May. Three days later, Chamberlain resigned as Prime Minister.

Given the military disaster that was also unfolding in France, Lindsay's contribution to Chamberlain's downfall should not be overstated, but it demonstrated an independence of thought and action, with a willingness to risk upsetting the chain of command if he believed there was an important issue at stake. This disposition often brought him into conflict with his seniors on more routine matters. Hill was no exception. Early in his command of 9 PARA, Lindsay defied the stricture of Army dress and parachuting regulations by promising his men that they would be allowed to wear parachute wings on both shoulders of their uniforms if they completed fifteen further training jumps from a balloon tethered over the Bulford training fields. It worked as an incentive and the rank and file were queuing up to complete extra parachute descents, until Hill heard about the unorthodox practice and brought it to an abrupt stop.

While there may have been something of a professional difference between the two men, there were also similarities. Wearing the all-white King's Polar Medal on his chest, awarded for the remarkable feat of endurance he had shown in participating in the British Arctic Air-Route Expedition in 1931, Lindsay quickly became known as 'Polar Joe' by the rank and file in the battalion. To Paddy Jenkins he was the archetypical 'gentleman explorer'. The nickname was a mark not only of his renown for previous exploits, but also the fact that he could march anyone in the battalion off their feet. Like Hill, he led the battalion battle marches from the front, with an unrelenting endurance and a marching technique that gave the impression that he was forging through deep snow. The superbly fit Lindsay pushed his men to the limit, but he would not ask them to do anything that he was not prepared to do himself.

The premium both men placed on leading by example and physical fitness provided 9 PARA with a certain continuity of command. But what Hill handed over to Lindsay was hardly the makings of a fully manned parachute unit of five companies made up of over 700 officers and men. By the time Lindsay took over command, 9 PARA numbered a little over 200 men. A third of those who made it from the Essex Regiment had been pre-war regulars, the majority of whom were the more senior officers and senior NCOs such as Harries and Jenkins. Although the predominance of senior ranks provided a foundation to build on, as a fighting entity the battalion was far from being ready for war.

To reach its war establishment and be ready for operations, the battalion would need to man three rifle companies; designated A, B and C Company, the rifle companies would be the principal assault elements of 9 PARA, which would be expected to take and hold ground by closing with the enemy and killing them. Each rifle company would need 120 men and five officers to form three platoons of thirty-six paratroopers and a company headquarters. The platoons were divided again into three sections of ten men commanded by a sergeant; the platoons themselves were commanded by a lieutenant and a senior platoon sergeant.

The forth company was a reserve training sub-unit, while the fifth company in a parachute battalion formed the headquarters and support element. The headquarters company not only contained the signallers, medics, logistics and administrative staff for the battalion, but also provided the unit with its heavier support weapons made up of four Vickers medium machine guns and six three-inch mortars organized into individual platoons with their own officers. The crew-served weapons provided the fire support to the fighting troops, but, like the rifle companies, they would also need trained personnel to man them. To make good the shortfall in numbers the Parachute Regiment looked to individual volunteers from the rest of the Army to reinforce the battalion.

At the outbreak of the war the Army could muster 224,000 men, and by the end of 1942 conscription had swelled its ranks 2.5 million. But while British soldiers fought in the Mediterranean and Burma, the majority of the Army was stationed in England. With the threat of a German invasion over, most men under arms had been engaged in a monotonous routine of training, guard duties and providing additional labour for the war effort. Those stationed at home who had willingly joined up to fight for their country suffered from boredom as they waited for the coming of the second front. Undoubtedly, some were content to be inactive, but countless young men were impatient to see action. The call for volunteers to join the Parachute Regiment provided the opportunity that many had been waiting for. From the beginning of 1943, individual reinforcements began to fill the depleted ranks of 9 PARA. They came from a diversity of backgrounds, from across the class divide and from different parts of the country. Together they formed an eclectic mix of pre-war regulars, butchers, factory apprentices, school leavers and schoolboys, who found themselves serving alongside lords, actors and professional dancers.

Their origins and routes to the battalion may have varied and few had any real understanding of the risks they would face, but they had other things in common: they knew that they wanted to be different, they were young, had a sense of adventure and many were attracted by the prospect of earning the extra two shillings a day paid to qualified parachutists.

The extra money tripled Sid Capon's pay as a private soldier conscripted into the line infantry. He was the youngest of seven children and came from a working-class family living in Mortlake. As a teenager he had lived through the London Blitz and had watched Spitfires chase German bombers across the burning skies of London and fantasized about becoming a fighter pilot and shooting down 'Hun' aircraft. When Capon was called up in 1942, colour blindness ended his dream of joining the RAF and he was sent to the Army and the

East Surrey Regiment. The additional pay was not the only attraction for joining the Paras. Capon's character and fitness made him stand out, but they also attracted the unwarranted attention of the less imaginative NCOs. He saw volunteering for the Parachute Regiment as a means of escaping the petty bullshit and tyranny of a regime where a basic infantry soldier was not expected to think for himself.

Although the line infantry provided the bulk of volunteers, they came from every conceivable cap badge in the Army. Geoff Pattinson, like Capon, was called up in 1942 and applied to join the RAF. He too was rejected for aircrew training on the basis of a medical imperfection. However, impaired hearing in his right ear did not prevent him from being conscripted into the Army and he found himself in the Royal Armoured Corps being trained to drive and maintain antiquated tanks and Bren-gun carriers. Dissatisfied with his lot, he put his name down for parachute training after a Parachute Regiment recruiting team visited his unit. Once at Hardwick Hall, he almost failed the medical, although not on account of his hearing.

At only eight stone seven pounds, he was not considered a prime candidate for Airborne training. He asked to be given a chance. A bristling muscle-bound physical training instructor admired his pluck and agreed to let him have a crack. Each night Geoff marvelled that he had survived another day and had just enough strength left to roll into his rough Army blankets and pray that he would survive the next. Although it took everything he had, he passed. Hugh Pond was another non-infantryman volunteer who found Airborne selection particularly tough, even more so as he was an officer. Newly commissioned into the Royal Tank Regiment, Pond was impatient to command troops and get into action, but a motorcycle injury meant he missed being deployed to the Middle East as a tank troop commander. Volunteering for the Parachute Regiment was preferable to hanging around the RAC depot in Dorset where he was bored and had little to do.

Not all those who volunteered were legally eligible to do so. At sixteen years old, Fred Glover was too young to be called up. Had he been old enough, his engineering apprenticeship was classed as a reserve occupation and would have exempted him. But Fred wanted to serve his country. He had watched his father die from the effects of being gassed in the trenches in the First World War and in 1942 his brother had been posted missing in action in North Africa. One day he walked out of the factory where he worked in Brighton and went to the local recruiting office. There he lied about his age and the recruiting sergeant didn't ask to see his birth certificate. He was sent to an infantry training unit in Canterbury, and was duly posted to the Middlesex Regiment. But instead of being sent overseas, his unit was dispatched into the fields of Sussex to pick potatoes. While the close proximity to the Land Girls held obvious attractions, thoughts of his dead father and missing brother made him feel that he should be doing more for the war effort. When a Parachute Regiment recruiting team visited his unit it was an easy choice to volunteer. Fred had little trouble passing the initial selection and went on to complete his parachute training.

Nineteen-year-old Gordon Newton volunteered to join the Paras because he wanted 'those wings' and 'some of their glory'. Before being conscripted into the infantry, he had been a factory worker in High Wycombe producing aircraft dials that calculated the tow angle between a glider and a tug aircraft. He had no idea what he had been making at the time, but when he next saw the strange luminous gauge it would be under very different circumstances. After passing through Hardwick and Ringway, Newton reported to Bulford with the other new recruits; together, they added another thirty-one men to the ranks of the battalion that had grown to 231 since the start of the year.

The new unit continued to draw heavily on the officers and SNCOs of the 10th Essex who had made it through the selection process. But despite the advantages of a harsh selection process and having a nucleus of the original members of the 10th Essex, the unit's real ethos, cohesion and fighting spirit would come through the tough training that 9 PARA would endure as it prepared for war.

Under Martin Lindsay, there would be little respite in pace or the focus on physical training. He not only shared Hill's passion for route-marching, but also had to train the unit in accordance with the direction of his brigade commander. Hill had four cardinal principles regarding the way the units under his command would train to fight: speed, physical fitness, simplicity and control.

It was an emphasis that drew on Hill's experience of fighting in North Africa and reflected the fact that airborne troops were likely to be used to take objectives that could not be seized or destroyed by other methods. It would mean that they would need to be prepared to be dropped behind enemy lines, where they would expect to be surrounded by an enemy superior in numbers and more heavily armed. The men would be isolated from the main Allied forces until a link-up could be achieved and would have to be self-reliant, with little access to vehicles, tanks and artillery. Resupply of ammunition and food would also be extremely limited. In essence they would need to fight and survive with what they could jump with and carry on their backs.

The training at Hardwick and Ringway was an initial schooling of character, courage and self-confidence, providing the basic tactical and parachute skills that the men would need as paratroopers. However, it was a long way from the collective and specialist skills 9 PARA would need to fight as a cohesive unit. In addition, the majority had spent relatively little time in the army and had undergone only basic training aimed at the mass ranks of a growing conscript army, whereas as a parachute unit, 9 PARA's training would have to be more specialized. But first the men would need to become expert in the standard infantry work of marksmanship, bayonet drill, map reading and fieldcraft.

Every man had to become accomplished in handling general-purpose infantry weapons, such as the Lee Enfield bolt-action rifle, Bren and Sten guns. The Mark 4 version of the Lee Enfield single-shot, magazine-fed rifle was the main firearm used by British forces. Although old in terms of original design it was reliable, accurate and capable of firing fifteen rounds a minute out to a range of 600 metres in the hands of a practised rifleman. It was complemented by the short-range automatic firepower of the new Mark V Sten gun. Issued to parachute troops in 1944, the improved version of the simple mass-produced weapon was fitted with a wooden pistol grip, fore grip and stock; it could also hold a short 'pig-sticker' bayonet, which was interchangeable with the rifle. The sten would provide a lightly equipped force with a ready weight of firepower when the automatic fire from heavier machine guns would be in short supply.

The Mark V was easier to fire and more reliable than earlier versions of the Sten gun, but it was still prone to stoppages and accidental firing if not carefully handled. In comparison, the Bren gun was reliable, accurate and had an effective range of 600 metres. Providing the section with a light automatic support weapon, the 'Bren' was equipped with a bipod, weighed twenty-five pounds and fired the same .303 ammunition as the Lee Enfield. It was capable of delivering a rate of fire of 500 rounds a minute but only if the Bren operator and his number two's drills were slick in changing the distinctively curved thirty-round magazine and swapping the barrel between sustained bursts of firing to prevent it from overheating. Issued on a scale of one per section, the gun could be fired from the shoulder or hip, but it was most effective when fired from its bipod and when two or more Brens were grouped together to produce a heavier and more dispersed rate of fire.

Regardless of the personal sidearm they were issued with, everybody was expected to be proficient in handling all the weapons available to a platoon. The men practised marksmanship on the steep sandbanked gallery ranges at Bulford and during tactical live-firing manoeuvre exercises on the rolling chalk lands of the Cranborne Chase and West Wiltshire Downs. They also learned to fire captured German weapons and equipment in the highly probable event that they would have to be used to supplement their own firepower.

What they became expert in by day had also to be applied by night. On occasion the battalion's training programme was altered so that they would sleep during the day and then get up at 6 p.m. to work through the night until the next morning. They trained until they became adept at firing, loading and stripping weapons in complete darkness. Night training was not popular, but it was indicative of Lindsay's unconventional and imaginative approach to training. Lindsay was also a stickler for field discipline and the proper execution of basic tactical drills had to be faultless. His rationale was simple: if his men couldn't get it right in training, poor fieldcraft would cost lives in battle. If he felt that his troops had made too much noise during a night march, he would form them up in the morning and make the whole battalion practise lifting their feet and marching silently around him until he was satisfied that they could move without making a sound.

The type and level of training may have varied, but the one constant was the endless physical training and route-marching. 9 PARA paraded early each morning in all weathers on the battalion square before breakfast in PT shorts and vest for a cross-country run. If they weren't running they were marching. Ten miles in full battle kit was the basic distance and had to be completed in less than two hours. The distances and loads carried were gradually increased to twenty miles and then fifty miles, which had to be completed in twenty-four hours. The men in 9 PARA soon came to know every bend in the roads and the gradient of every hill round Kiwi Barracks. They also completed battle marches from further afield and marching back from training conducted in the next county became a standard practice; each march was a test of endurance and the men would arrive back in Bulford exhausted, with blistered and bloody feet. Gradually they became fitter, tougher and harder.

The training was meant to be hard. Perhaps suspicious of his origins as a tank officer, when Lindsay first interviewed Hugh Pond he told him, 'This is not a glamour unit, it is for the toughest infantrymen only.' Pond found out just how tough shortly after joining the battalion. During a fifty-mile battle march carrying full kit, he collapsed from dehydration and mineral loss five miles from the finish point; he had forgotten to take his salt tablets. Lindsay was furious, especially as Pond was a platoon commander. He made him do the whole route again on his own the following week, much to the amusement of the soldiers in Pond's platoon. It illustrated the fact that officers completed exactly the same training as the men and under the same conditions.

Rank would also be no protection against bullets and shells in combat, and the nature of parachute operations meant that the attrition rate of a Para unit's officers and SNCOs in battle was liable to be high. Consequently, over-reliance on a relatively small core of appointed leaders entailed risking the success of a mission, especially when up to a third of any airborne force was highly likely to be widely dispersed during a drop. Additionally, to succeed and maximize the surprise of landing by parachute, an inserting unit would need to concentrate quickly after a jump and attack with what troops it had immediately available. If some of the officers and SNCOs did not make it, the attack would have to go in without them. As a consequence each section of ten men also had their own sergeant in addition to the normal complement of corporals found in standard infantry platoons.

Emphasis was placed on fostering initiative, self-reliance and training each man, regardless of rank, to do the job of the man above him. A culture of resilience and self-confidence had therefore to be inculcated in the most junior of private soldiers when the odds were likely to be stacked against them. The ability to step up and fill a void in leadership, which might result from dispersal or casualties, was regularly practised during exercises. Officers and senior NCOs were often 'killed off' by umpires who awarded them casualty cards, which precluded participation until they were 'brought to life' again. This forced subordinates to take over and continue the mission without them. Platoon commanders practised taking over command of their companies, sergeants their platoons and private soldiers stepped into the shoes of corporals.

As the cold winter months of 1943 began to recede with the coming of spring, the numbers of 9 PARA steadily increased and they began to bond together as a unit. The better weather also brought the opportunity to practise parachute training as formed groups. By the summer, although still far from being a fully manned parachute battalion, 9 PARA began jumping as a single unit with full equipment. On 9 August two squadrons of converted Whitley bombers from the RAF's 38 Wing took off from Thruxton airfield in Hampshire to make a daylight drop along the banks of the River Spey near Grantown in Scotland. The 500-mile flight took nearly six hours and the men of the battalion had to endure the mind-numbing cramp of being wedged tightly together on the cold metal floor in the dark confines of the aircraft's fuselage, their full equipment loads and weapons competing for every inch of space.

Used to making short flights to Tatton Park, or dropping zones over Salisbury Plain, part of the objective was to accustom 9 PARA to long-distance flying. The men's misery was compounded by air-sickness, as the antiquated aeroplanes bucked and bounced in the turbulence and crosswinds as they droned steadily northwards. If paratroopers needed to vomit, they would have to jump with sick bags full of puke stuffed down the front of their smocks. The sleeve-less denim jump jackets they wore over their smocks and equipment to reduce snagging provided little insulation when flying at altitude in an unheated, bitterly cold fuselage. So most found it a blessed release finally to jump from the aircraft and be free of the wretched conditions.

Despite the discomfort of flying such long distances, the drop was made with a remarkable degree of accuracy. James Hill jumped with them and landed on top of the DZ smoke marker in the middle of the drop zone. However, the relief of escaping from the cramped Whitley bomber and making an accurate jump was short-lived. The objective of the nine-day exercise was to operate in the Spey Valley and then capture a strongpoint on the top of Ben Macdui, Scotland's second highest mountain in the middle of the Cairngorms. During the first few days they patrolled in the lower lying ground of the valley and were billeted in farm buildings and outhouses, but the real test would come with the weather when they carried out a final attack against troops defending the top of the 1,309-metre peak.

By 1943, the extraordinary attire of specialist parachute clothing of spring-loaded rubber jump boots and padded leather helmets spawned by the early pioneers at Ringway had been discarded in favour of more practical military apparel. Standard Army boots were issued and reflected the fact that parachutists were expected to fight once they had jumped. A flat-edged steel helmet, distinct from the normal soup bowl design of the standard British military helmet, had no protrud-ing rim that might interfere with rigging lines, or cause injury on landing. A pale fawn camouflage Denison smock with knitted cuffs was also made, with press-studs and a full-length zip in preference to buttons, which also reduced the line-snagging hazard. Together with the Para helmet, the smock was to become a distinguishing mark of the British paratrooper. It was worn over standard battledress with extra pockets sewn in the trousers to hold additional shell dressings, which also provided some padding for backward landings. Made of a wind- and showerproof material, the smock was especially developed as a component of a layered insulated clothing system. It was worn as part of a combination of loosely woven string vests and undergarments of shirt, jumper and battledress jacket, and provided a lighter weight alternative to standard British infantry field kit. Depending almost entirely on what they could carry into battle when they jumped, greatcoats and blankets were considered luxuries and unnecessary weight that could be dispensed with in favour of carrying extra water, rations and, above all, ammunition. Without the support vehicles available to general line infantry, tents were completely out of the question and gas capes that could be joined together provided the only means of protection against the elements.

For those who climbed through the mist up the steep grey granite scree slopes of Ben Macdui, the lack of standard field baggage seemed to make hardly any difference, as they struggled and sweated under sixty-pound loads of belt-kit, weapons and small packs stuffed with ammunition, water and rations. But as they climbed higher the weather closed in. At 500 metres, the lashing rain and wind chill were biting. At 1,000 metres it started to snow. Attacking in such extreme conditions, the battalion took the peak's defenders by surprise. But as night fell conditions worsened and the lightly dressed troops of 9 PARA suffered. Where their clothing failed them, discipline, ethos and the junior NCOs stepped in. Geoff Pattinson's section commander slapped him repeatedly as the temperature dropped well below freezing. Lacking surplus body fat, it was the shock his slight body needed to stop him succumbing to exposure. Other men huddled together for collective warmth among the rocks and wished the night away.

With the coming of dawn, they descended the southern slopes of the mountain into the relative shelter of the Dee Valley. They force-marched the twenty miles to Aviemore, where they boarded trucks that would take them to parade in Aberdeen and Edinburgh and then a train that would carry them southwards to London. The vim of physical exercise thawed out frozen limbs and eased cold-induced stiffness, while empty stomachs hankered for more than a hard tack biscuit for breakfast from a stripped-down twenty-four-hour ration pack. Most men slept the sleep of the dead as the train pulled out of Edinburgh's central railway station. Unbeknown to most, the plan had been to march the men from Aviemore to Aberdeen, but Lindsay recognized that his men were done in and decided to truck them north before boarding the train.

Marching through London was Martin Lindsay's idea. It was a chance to show off the battalion and the War Office felt it would be good for public morale to see one of the new Para units parading through the streets of the capital. The men had handed in their sodden smocks in Scotland where they changed into clean battledress. They were also issued with .38 revolvers, which they wore holstered to their hips specifically to add a certain cachet to their appearance. Unencumbered by their normal field kit of smocks, webbing and packs, they stepped off in marching formation from Euston to Liverpool Street station, with Lindsay at their head. The march was also an opportunity to show the public what the battalion had achieved in little over nine months. Although still undermanned, 9 PARA were now a formed unit; they could insert by parachute as a group, form up and take a demanding objective regardless of the weather.

9 PARA were pleased with themselves. They had always been told that they were part of an elite regiment and now they felt it as they marched with pride through their capital. Proud families were invited to watch their menfolk and see what had become of their boys. The more discerning among them might have noticed that the men of 9 PARA still wore the 10th Essex badge in their maroon berets. But official Parachute Regiment cap badges were not the only things in short supply. Although still well below its full establishment, it took the combined efforts of two squadrons of Whitleys to drop 9 PARA in Scotland. The fifteen aircraft were the total number of converted bombers available to the RAF's 38 Wing, which had been charged with training the new and growing 6th Airborne Division. It reflected the woeful lack of RAF air transport capacity in the middle of 1943.

A month before 9 PARA made its training jump in Scotland, the first British Airborne Division had taken part in the Allied invasion of Sicily, but their participation had only been made possible by using DC-47 transport aircraft and crews belonging to the United States. The development of a British-built transport aircraft was beyond national production capabilities, at a time when the priority of the war effort was with building bomber and fighter planes. Despite the lack of a suitable troop carrier, Churchill was determined that the RAF should keep pace with the Army's expanding airborne capability. He pushed the Chief of the Air Staff, Air Marshal Sir Charles Portal, to provide more converted bombers for parachute training. But his call to allocate 100 more aircraft to 38 Wing had met with stubborn resistance ever since the wing had been formed in January 1942.

Churchill's intervention had caused an explosive outburst from Air Chief Marshal Arthur Harris. As head of Bomber Command, and like most other senior RAF officers, Harris doubted the operational utility of parachute operations. He also considered providing Airborne Forces with converted bombers as a distraction from his main effort of expanding Bomber Command as a strategic war-winning weapon. The matter was still not settled by the summer of 1943. Harris was backed by Portal who argued that attacking German industry would make an incomparably greater contribution to winning the war.

The prevailing strategic priorities meant that Churchill and the Army were forced to accept that no more RAF personnel or aircraft would be supplied to support Airborne Forces. But as senior men in the corridors of power wrangled, shortages of aircraft or no, 9 PARA continued to train. While opportunities to conduct jump training from aircraft would be limited, there was plenty of scope to practise street fighting using live ammunition. The German Blitz of 1940 and 1941 had left large swathes of British cities and towns as bombed-out wasteland. Rebuilding would have to wait until after the war and a number of severely damaged suburbs were turned over to the War Office. Once clear of local residents, the shattered streets provided a training ground for soldiers to practise fighting in built-up areas in preparation for fighting in European towns and cities when the time came. During 1943 and 1944 the battalion trained in bombed-out areas around Battersea Park in London and in Southampton. As a major port on the south coast and main production centre for Spitfires, Southampton had been a prime target for the Luftwaffe who dropped 2,300 bombs on the city during the Blitz. They had missed the Spitfire engine factory near the River Itchin, but much of the city centre and residential areas had been destroyed.

The house-clearing range set up on Blackball Street across from the Itchin provided an ideal environment to practise fighting in built-up areas. Wearing stripped-down webbing equipment to ease movement, each of the companies rotated through a three-day street-fighting package. Sections and platoons were taught how to clear a house by posting a grenade through the front door and then raking the interior with Sten guns on full automatic, and afterwards entering to repeat the process room by room. They were taught how to 'mouse-hole' by using wads of explosive gun cotton on a rudimentary timber frame to blow a gap through partitioning walls. It was dirty work and they would emerge covered in brick dust and grime. Training in Southampton had the advantage of being within marching distance of Kiwi Barracks, so after three days of street-fighting drills in the once neat rows of terrace dwellings, each company would march the thirty blistering miles to Bulford in full fighting order, arriving back at the barracks footsore, filthy and exhausted.

Marching long distances to and from training became standard, but on occasion it pushed the men to the edge of their endurance. Major Allen Parry was the officer commanding A Company, a pre-war regular from the 10th Essex who took things in his stride in an easy-going, relaxed manner and was highly regarded by officers and men alike. But on one occasion, as the summer sun beat down on him and his men as they exerted themselves to keep up with the relentless pace set by Lindsay during a forced march back from the Wiltshire Downs, he pleaded with his CO that the men should be allowed to take a break and drink from their water bottles. The men had marched the best part of twenty miles, forbidden to touch their water, they were drenched with sweat and their mouths stuck thick with swollen tongues. Despite the appeals of his senior company commander, Lindsay only relented when the medical officer insisted that the men should be allowed to drink.

Like other parachute units, being an all-volunteer force meant they were somewhat set apart, but they were also human and they lived for the prospect of a thirty-six-hour leave pass. Leave passes were precious commodities and vital to morale. Granted on an average of two per month, passes were issued at midday on a Saturday and usually followed the return from an exercise and several days' hard living in the field. Before passes were issued, the barracks were a hive of activity and anticipation as men relished the prospect of women-folk, alcohol and, above all, a brief respite from the relentless tempo of training and exercises. They cleaned equipment and weapons, handed them into stores and armouries, then showered, shaved and changed into their best battledress with renewed gusto. Once their company officers and sergeant majors were satisfied all was in order, they joined the throng of paratroopers heading out of the camp gates, setting off to see wives, girlfriends or family.

Most single men headed for London. The bright lights might have been diminished by the blackout, but the draw of women and beer retained its usual appeal to young men preparing for war. The Paras lodged in cheap accommodation such as Salvation Army canteens and the Union Jack Club across the road from Waterloo station. Their pay went on booze, trying to attract girls and finding enough to eat. Although they were well fed by the Army and considered themselves fortunate compared to civilians suffering the strictures of wartime rationing, they were always hungry and any spare money was spent on extra food. Dance halls where live bands played swing and jazz were the main attractions for off-duty soldiers. For a few short hours, the lights, music and dancing allowed men who knew that one day soon they would be going into action to forget their relentless training and the danger of what lay ahead.

The Bodega was the only dance hall in Salisbury and the best one in striking distance of Bulford, which made it a favourite haunt for 9 PARA soldiers when they had a rare evening off duty. It was also a magnet for the large numbers of other soldiers in the area. Charged with testosterone, the combination of booze and competition for girls led to inevitable fistfights between men of competing units. As 1943 began to draw to a close, better paid American soldiers became their main challengers for the attentions of the fairer sex and the rivalry between British paratroopers and their US airborne counterparts was particularly marked.

The American 82nd and 101st airborne divisions had been formed in 1942 and sailed for England in September 1943. The headquarters of 101st Airborne Division was in Newbury with units based across Berkshire and into Wiltshire, which brought the Americans into close proximity in the pubs and dance halls of places such as Salisbury and Marlborough. The appeal of their more affluent and exotic cousins from across the Atlantic to local British women led to numerous Anglo-American punch-ups. Fuelled by alcohol, it was a rivalry exacerbated by their comparative status as elite forces in their own armies. The frequency of fighting was enough to cause Eisenhower to express his concern about it when visiting British Airborne units.

Off-duty fighting was an unsurprising disciplinary issue in a large expanding conscript Army encamped in close proximity to an increasing number of Allied soldiers. Returning late from leave, petty theft and absenteeism were also common disciplinary offences, although the incidence of soldiers 'absent without leave' or AWOL was comparatively low among 9 PARA given their all-volunteer status. However, the cardinal sin a paratrooper could commit was to refuse to jump, regardless of the circumstances. After making a successful exit from the belly of a converted bomber, a junior NCO witnessed the man jumping behind him plummet past him and fall to his death when his chute failed to open. Seeing the lifeless body of the dead man on the DZ was enough to make him lose his nerve and he refused to jump again. The corporal was placed in the battalion jail, awaiting sentence. He was subsequently court-martialled, demoted and sentenced to eighty-four days' detention in a military glasshouse. Although not common, there were other refusals.

Most men who engage in military parachuting would admit that if they ever thought of refusing, it was the fear of personal shame that motivated them to get through the door. But in some isolated cases,

men simply refused to jump; often because they had something on their mind that interfered with their confidence or dimmed their focus, or simply because they suddenly ran out of the right stuff to make a parachute descent. In some cases a man might be offered the chance to redeem himself by being ordered to jump from a balloon in the presence of spectators that included WAAFs from the local RAF camp at Netheravon. It was thought that the presence of women might prick his male ego and compel a man to jump. In some cases it worked, but if a man had really made up his mind that he was not going to jump then he would be charged and the inevitable route that Fred Walker took to prison and being RTU'd from the regiment would follow. Like Walker, if the man had rank, he would also expect to lose it.

Jumping from the gloomy confines of a converted bomber through a hole cut in its belly was not conducive to parachuting. But as 1943 drew to a close 9 PARA would have a new and more encouraging aircraft to jump from. While the Americans brought an added dimension to the discipline of off-duty Airborne soldiers, they also brought with them the Dakota aircraft. The twin-engine Douglas DC-47 Dakota was specifically adapted from the civilian DC-3 airliner to drop paratroopers. Powered by Pratt and Whitney Twin-Wasp fourteen-cylinder radial engines, it was capable of carrying 26,000 pounds of freight or twenty-eight fully equipped parachutists. The Americans had brought over the DC-47s in troop carrier commands to support the 82nd and 101st divisions and although they were made available to help train 6th Airborne Division, British parachuting capability improved dramatically with the direct provision of 150 Dakotas to the RAF under the Lend-Lease scheme in January 1944. Equipping five squadrons stationed at airfields in Oxfordshire and Wiltshire, the new aircraft were used to form 46 Group.

By the end of 1943, 38 Wing had also been upgraded and was re-designated as 38 Group. The Americans had been early converts to parachute operations and their faith extended to Eisenhower and their Joint Chiefs of Staff. The invasion of Sicily had also done much to convince those in the British military establishment of the value of

using mass airborne troops. So by the autumn of 1943 a combination of Sicily, Churchill's own personal enthusiasm and the influence from Washington convinced the Air Ministry in London to agree reluctantly to replace the limited numbers of the obsolete Whitleys with Halifax, Albemarle and Stirling bombers converted to drop parachute troops. But it was the arrival of the Dakota that would make the biggest improvement to the expansion of the British fleet of aircraft capable of deploying airborne troops. The DC-47s were much better suited for dropping paratroopers than the newer bombers made available to 38 Group. Like the Whitley, the bombers had jump apertures cut in their belly floors, which, although wider than those in the Whitley, still required the jumper to assume an awkward crouched position to make a clean exit through the hole.

Designed to carry people, the Dakota was easily converted to drop them. The fuselage was roomy enough to stand up in and had benches running either side of its length, which allowed troops to sit facing each other. When they stood up to prepare to jump, the static lines of twenty-eight jumpers could be clipped to one of two wire cables that ran along the central length of the fuselage roof, which would deploy the chutes as they exited the Dakota through the side door between the port wing and tailplane. The size of the fuselage and the side door meant that each paratrooper could make a standing jump wearing full equipment. After the first man jumped, the men behind could rapidly follow him out of the door without breaking step. Capable of travelling at 120 miles per hour, the aircraft would throttle back to just above its stalling speed of ninety miles per hour to reduce the shock of the parachutes opening when the men jumped. At that speed, a fully loaded DC-47 could clear a complete complement of parachutists within thirty seconds with a dispersal of only fifty metres between each man when they landed.

The size and position of the jump door also brought the benefit of being able to jump with a heavy kitbag strapped to the leg of each parachutist. British paratroopers in North Africa using US aircraft conceived the idea of the leg bag, but until the arrival of the DC-47 in England weapons and equipment that could not be carried on the body were dropped in separate six-foot cylindrical metal containers.

Broken Horsa gliders litter the open fields around the landing zones at Ranville. The anti-glider poles that Rommel ordered to be erected as a precaution against Allied airborne operations are clearly visible

A member of the A Company glider force with a Wehrmacht prisoner. A luminous skull and crossbones badge is painted on his Dennison smock as a recognition symbol

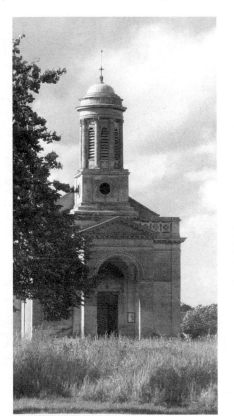

The church at Le Plein where Russian 'Hiwis' fighting for the Germans engaged 9 PARA from its slatted tower

The Château St Côme on the Bréville Ridge, showing the stables and the stirrup-shaped drive that ran towards the Bois du Mont where 9 PARA established their main defensive position

The rear of the Bois du Mont with the graves of 9 PARA's fallen, who were hastily buried during temporary lulls in the near-relentless German attacks on the position

Sergeant Major 'Dusty' Miller, who took part in the reconnaissance of the battery just before 9 PARA's attack. He became the unit's RSM after his predecessor was killed on the Bréville Ridge

Sergeant Sammy McGeever who commanded the unit's Vickers machine-gun platoon

Corporal Jim 'Mara' McGuinness, the tough Geordie who, with McGeever, used the Vickers medium machine guns to devastating effect to break up German attacks at the Bois du Mont

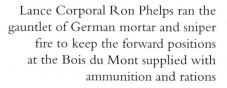

Lance Corporal Ron Phelps ran the gauntlet of German mortar and sniper fire to keep the forward positions at the Bois du Mont supplied with ammunition and rations

The sunken lane, which formed the left flank of the position around the Bois du Mont and from where the Black Watch made their forlorn attack on Bréville

Smashed German vehicles of 346th Grenadier Division in the side streets of Bréville. The cannon in the foreground is a 20mm 38 Pak Flank gun similar to the anti-aircraft weapon at the Merville Battery, which wounded Fred Glover as his glider circled overhead

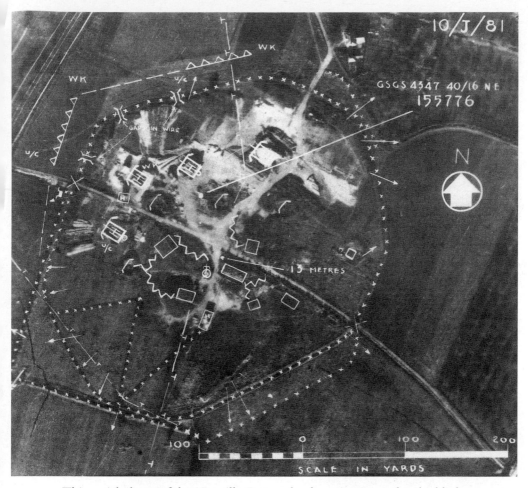

This aerial photo of the Merville Battery has been interpreted to highlight the defences around the casemates. Otway planned his attack in minute detail, but did not account for the disastrous drop by the RAF

The rear of Casemate One of the Merville Battery taken in the 1980s, when British Army engineers began to restore the bunkers. The two-metre thick concrete meant that it could withstand the heaviest RAF bombing raid

Lieutenant Alan Jefferson had a bad premonition due to the successful dress rehearsal attack on the mock-up practice battery in England. He dislocated his shoulder during the jump and stepped on a mine during the real attack on the Merville Battery

Captain Hal Hudson, the adjutant who was shot through the guts during the attack on the battery

The shattered crucifix at Calvary cross where 9 PARA rallied after the bloody attack on the battery in which half the attacking force was either killed or wounded

The Château St Côme after the fighting

The temporary graves of thirty-eight members of 9 PARA buried in a bomb crater by the Germans after they were killed by American bombers in a friendly fire incident on D-Day

(*From left to right*) Fred Glover, Gordon Newton and Geoff Pattinson
standing in front of the drive to the Château St Côme, June 2012

The Ranville Cemetery where the dead of the 6th Airborne were eventually buried. Most of
9 PARA killed in action lie in the top left-hand corner. The trees in the distance follow the
line of the Caen Canal running adjacent to the Orne River as it flows out towards the sea.
Had the Paras' positions on the Bréville Ridge and bridges fallen, the entire British left flank
would have been open to a direct attack on the beaches by Rommel's panzers

Equipped with their own parachute, the containers would be loaded into bomb bays, or under the wings of an aircraft and were dropped in between sticks of paratroopers to be retrieved on the ground. The sole use of the container meant that a parachutist would be without his weapon when he landed and would have to find the container and open it before he was ready to fight. The dispersal risk during a drop, especially at night, meant that it could take time to find the containers. If a drop was widely scattered, they might not be located at all.

The idea of the leg bag was trialled and developed at Ringway in January 1944 in Dakotas attached to the school. It consisted of a robust canvas kitbag, which could be stuffed with radios, small packs and extra ammunition and rations, and was attached to the parachute harness by a twenty-foot nylon rope. The bag was then fastened to the parachutist by a long thin metal pin, which ran through three D-rings of a leather scabbard strapped to the man's right leg as he made his exit from the aircraft. Once under canopy, the pin would be pulled from the quick-release mechanism and the bag would fall away under the control of a hand-held friction device, which would allow it to dangle from the jumper on the end of the rope. Striking the ground first, the sound of the bag's impact provided the jumper with a crude form of early warning that his own landing was imminent, which was an added advantage especially at night. The Dakota's side door also meant that bulkier weapons, such as the Lee Enfield rifle and Bren gun, could be fastened to the man, sewn into a felt valise cover which would prevent snagging in the parachute rigging and the risk of causing a malfunction. The weapons sleeve was attached to the body when jumping, but could then be lowered with the leg bag. However, it was crucial that the valise and leg bag were lowered as soon as the parachutist was under canopy, as landing with either the bag or long-barrelled weapon cover attached to the body would invite serious injury.

To paratroopers used to jumping from the belly holes of converted bombers, the Dakota was the Rolls-Royce of jump aircraft. It was not only more comfortable to fly in, but the more conducive nature of jumping from it reduced the incidence of refusals. Having to perch precariously on the edge of an exit hole before dropping through it, with the risk of 'ringing the bell', was a thing of the past. The sense of vertigo was also reduced, as men jumping further back in the stick only had a moment to experience the exposure of their position when they turned in to the door. If a man hesitated and thought about refusing, it was usually too late as the momentum of those pushing up close behind him was enough to carry him out of the aircraft. But while the arrival of the American aircraft may have been the answer to a maiden's prayer as far as the British Airborne were concerned, it was not without its hazards.

A member of Sid Capon's stick was killed when converting to jumping from Dakotas at Ringway. The soldier's chute became entangled on the Dakota's tail wheel when the aircraft was caught in turbulence as the man jumped. Without a reserve, there was no option of trying to cut the poor unfortunate away and he was killed when the aircraft landed. Further incidents of becoming 'hooked up' led to the adoption of a drill of flying out to sea; the entangled para-trooper would then be cut away as the Dakota made a low pass over a harbour area, with a rescue launch standing by to pick him up. But while a soldier was likely to be alive when he was cut loose, he was often dead when he was fished out of the water. At least two Airborne soldiers were to lose their lives in this manner, before it was discovered that the risk could be reduced by altering the trim of the aircraft, which would lift the Dakota's tail wheel as it made its run into the drop zone. As D-Day approached, it was a costly reminder to the men of 9 PARA of the dangerous business they were in.

5

Battle Preparation

THE OPENING OF the second front was on everyone's lips as the winter primroses poked through the frost-covered ground of Bulford to herald the start of another year. 9 PARA had also begun to blossom, and by January 1944 it was approaching full strength. After twelve months of intensive training, the battalion had bonded as a cohesive unit with its own sense of identity and ethos, which came from being part of an elite outfit. They were confident in their abilities as trained paratroopers and they were hungry for action. As the New Year dawned, every man had one predominating thought on his mind. When would the invasion come?

They knew that 6th Airborne Division had been raised to take part in the Allied entry into the western Europe, but none of them knew when or where it would take place. Widely held rumours that it would be France were speculative and the secrecy-obsessed Allied planners at COSSAC intended to keep it that way. Only the unit commanders knew for sure that it would be France, although even they did not know the precise timing and location of the landing. Scant and imprecise as the information was, simply the knowledge that it would be France would be sufficient to cost Martin Lindsay dearly as D–Day approached.

Before departing on Christmas leave in 1943, Major General Richard Gale had been directed by the War Office to mobilize his division for the second front and to be ready to commence operations by 1 February 1944. With the subsequent confirmation that only one brigade would be used, Gale and Browning lobbied hard to have their orders for D–Day changed to include the whole of 6th Airborne Division. The decision to use only the 3rd Parachute Brigade had been made on the basis of a lack of available RAF aircraft, but Gale and Browning argued that both the division's parachute brigades and its air landing brigade would be required to protect the left flank of the British invasion beaches. Their petition fell on fertile ground and it took them little more than a week to convince General Bernard Montgomery, and so Bomber Command was ordered to make more aircraft available to lift the complete division in two waves on D-Day.

As the senior Allied officer responsible for planning D-Day, Montgomery wanted the American and British airborne divisions to shield the flanks of the seaborne invasion and protect the assault divisions landing on the beaches from counter-attack by German armoured forces. If they could hold the panzers off for long enough, the Allies could buy themselves enough time to establish a sufficiently large beachhead with adequate forces ashore to break out from Normandy towards Paris and ultimately into Germany itself. Montgomery agreed with the COSSAC assessment that the left flank would be the most critical and most vulnerable part of Overlord. Given the concentration of panzer divisions and more mobile units around Calais, this was the direction from which the German armoured counter-attack would come.

Montgomery knew that if Rommel moved his panzers across the Seine, then got them across the River Orne and Caen Canal, which ran in parallel to each other south to the city of Caen, it could spell disaster. The wide water features of the Orne and the canal lay less than a mile from Sword Beach, where the British 3rd Division, the Allies' easternmost formation, would land. The far side of the river and canal from the beaches was dominated by the Bréville Ridge and beyond that lay the marshy Dives valley and river. The topological combination of three water lines and the thickly wooded ridge presented a significant obstacle to armour. But if the panzers moved fast enough, they might be able to cross the Dives, breach the ridge and then cross the bridges on the Caen Canal and River Orne and attack the British flank. If they did this while the ground was undefended, there was a real risk that the Germans could roll up the entire seaborne assault divisions from the east before the Allies could get enough of their own armour ashore to stop them.

The Allied planners were particularly concerned about the 21st Panzer Division and 12th SS (*Hitlerjugend*) Panzer Division. 21st Panzer was already close to the Caen area and would be in striking distance of the eastern beaches, while 12th SS was not much more than a day or two's march away. Consequently, the first few hours and days of the invasion would be crucial. If 6th Airborne Division could seize and defend the two bridges across the Orne and the Caen Canal, hold the high ground and blow the bridges over the River Dives on its east side to delay the advance of the panzers, possession of this vital ground could provide Montgomery with the protected flank he was seeking. Once dominated and held, he could bring in enough of his own combat power across the beaches to meet any further threat as more German armour headed towards the coast. Additionally, he could build up sufficient forces to start his breakout from Normandy.

The existence of the Merville Battery across the Orne from the seaside town of Ouistreham posed another problem. Its guns enfiladed the entire length of Sword Beach, where 3rd Division would touch down on D-Day. The battery threatened to cause carnage among the densely packed landing craft running into the shoreline and those troops who survived as they came off the ramps and attempted to advance across the exposed openness of the beach. The task of silencing the guns at Merville before the start of the seaborne landings would therefore have to be given to 6th Airborne Division.

While the scale and significance of the operational requirement made for easy argument with Montgomery, even with the division's full complement of 3rd and 5th parachute brigades and the 6th Air Landing Brigade of glider troops, Gale would have to hold twenty square miles of country against the onslaught of one or more German divisions. He would be reinforced by the 1st Special Services Brigade, which was commanded by Lord Lovat. But even after Lovat's four commando units had landed on the beaches and linked up with Gale's men, it would be an ambitious undertaking. If 6th Airborne Division failed, the very opening of the second front might also fail.

On 24 February 6th Airborne Division was placed under the command of 1st British Corps, which would form the left flank of the

Allied landing. With sanction secured to use his whole division, Gale and his staff officers began detailed planning in earnest at their D-Day headquarters at the Old Farm at Brigmerston House. Gale's planning team included airmen from the RAF's 38 and 46 Group, who would carry his troops to Normandy, as well as a commando planning team from Lovat's brigade. The Old Farm was codenamed Broadmoor. Given the extensive security measures and the frenetic pace of planning activity there, the headquarters staff thought that it was aptly named.

On 18 March the divisional commander gave his orders to his subordinate brigade commanders. Initially, Gale intended to use Brigadier Hugh Kindersley's 6th Air Landing Brigade to capture the bridges on the Orne and Caen Canal, which lay between the small Norman towns of Bénouville and Ranville. Landing at night in 250 troop- and equipment-carrying gliders, Kindersley's men could insert with a greater degree of accuracy around the bridges than parachute troops, which might be widely dispersed during a drop. Additionally, the gliders could bring in six- and seventeen-pounder anti-tank guns to protect the approaches to the bridges from the panzers. However, having pioneered the very concept of airborne warfare, the Germans were alive to the threat posed by Allied parachute and glider forces, which had been used against them in North Africa and Sicily.

Not long after Gale had issued his first set of orders, air reconnaissance revealed small holes being dug across the proposed landing sites. The analysts at RAF Medmenham deduced that the Germans were erecting anti-glider poles. Initial concerns that the Allied plan might have been discovered abated when further air recce sorties confirmed that similar anti-airborne obstacles were being erected along the entire length of the enemy coastline. Hewn from pine plantations, the poles were eight to ten feet high, and some were enhanced by trip wires and topped by explosives. Whether enhanced or not, they represented a significant hazard and spelled potential doom to any wooden-framed glider unfortunate enough to strike one when coming in to land at speeds approaching 100 miles an hour. As a result, Gale reallocated the task of capturing the bridges to

Brigadier Nigel Poett's 5th Parachute Brigade. Poett's three parachute battalions would jump in, seize the area around the bridges and
clear the glider landing zones of obstacles so that the 6th Air Landing
Brigade could fly in before last light on D-Day on the second lift of
aircraft.

The one part of the original plan that Gale did not change was the
use of six gliders to land a reinforced company directly at the bridges
in a *coup de main* operation. Intelligence reports indicated that the
structures had been prepared for demolition, and Gale wanted to
capture them intact before the Germans could destroy them.
Although the surrounding fields were strewn with anti-glider poles,
aerial photographs suggested that there was just enough clear space to
land two or three gliders close to each of the two structures. Success
would depend on surprise, speed and dash. But if the gliders could
get close enough to the bridges, the troops they carried could overwhelm the defenders before they could set off the demolition charges.
The operation was audacious in its conception and drew its inspir-
ation from the German use of gliders to capture the Belgian fort at
Eben-Emael.

While two-thirds of the division focused on seizing and securing
the area around the bridges, Hill's 3rd Parachute Brigade was given a
more diverse and geographically spread range of tasks for its three
battalions. The 1st Canadian Parachute Battalion would drop on the
flat ground to the north of the Bréville Ridge, secure the drop zone,
codenamed DZ 'V' for Victor, and destroy the bridges over the
River Dives at Varaville and Robehomme. 8 PARA, under Lieutenant
Colonel Alistair Pearson, would jump in on DZ 'K' to the south and
would blow up the other two bridges at the southern end of the ridge
at Troarn and Bures. Pearson's battalion would then hold the wooded
feature of the Bois de Bavent along the centre of the high ground.
Having denied the crossing points on the Dives to German armour,
the Canadians and 8 PARA would fight a defensive battle on the
ridge to delay enemy reinforcements approaching from the eastern
side of the high ground. Hill planned to place his headquarters
between the two battalions at a farm complex across from an old
brickworks near the Le Mesnil crossroads that cut across the middle

of the feature. While the bulk of his brigade would be focused on seizing and holding the Bréville Ridge, Hill reserved his most difficult task for 9 PARA.

In order to eliminate the threat posed to the British landing craft and troops coming ashore on Sword Beach, the Merville Battery would have to be silenced in advance. Defended by a garrison estimated to be in the region of 160 to 180 men, with dug-in machine-gun pits and surrounded by extensive minefields and a coiled barbed-wire perimeter several metres thick, it would be a tough nut to crack. In 1944 the RAF lacked a precision-bombing capability and numerous heavy bombing raids had failed to score direct hits against any of the four concrete and earth casemates that protected the guns. Continued bombing had no guarantee of success and sustained RAF attacks ran the risk of drawing attention to Allied intentions in the area. Consequently, a parachute assault was considered the only means of ensuring the guns would not be able to fire on the morning of D-Day when the seaborne landing on the beaches began. Once 9 PARA's mission at the Merville Battery was completed, the battalion would destroy a German radar station located at Sallenelles, on the east bank of the Orne, and then move up to the ridge to capture and hold the village of Le Plein until relieved by Lovat's commandos.

The two waves of the divisional plan were given codenames. The initial fly-in of the parachute brigades, which would involve 9 PARA and a more limited number of gliders during the night prior to D-Day, remained codenamed Operation Tonga. The subsequent fly-in of the bulk of 6th Air Landing Brigade on the evening of D-Day was called Operation Mallard. The final detail of the brigade's plans would not be set until April, but Gale was in no doubt about the superior odds his units would face, or what he expected from his brigade commanders and their men when he told them, 'What you get by stealth and guts, you must hold by skill and determination.' But while their divisional commander's intent was clear and his concept of operations had been briefed to his immediate subordinate commanders, there was still much to be done.

Whether landing by parachute or glider, the infantry units of the division, which would be expected to hold the ground and close with and kill the enemy, could not be expected to fight in isolation. The parachute battalions and glider units would need the assistance of the division's support arms: its engineers to enhance mobility and remove obstacles, its artillery to provide indirect fire support and crew anti-tank guns and its medics to treat their casualties. 6th Airborne Division had four field squadrons of engineers, two batteries of anti-tank guns and a light artillery battery. Each brigade also had a medical field ambulance unit, which consisted of field surgical teams and a main dressing station. Every supporting unit had to be able to deploy by the same means as their troops so their equipment had to be light and compact enough to be carried in by glider or dropped by parachute, which meant that standard Army kit had to be adapted for airborne operations, or new items had to be identified, designed or procured.

By 1944, the six-pounder crew-served anti-tank guns had become the standard British infantry weapon for dealing with tanks. Modified with a shortened axle, the gun could be manhandled into a Horsa glider. In terms of punch it was still a relatively small-calibre weapon and could not defeat the frontal armour of the Panzer Mark IV, which was the Germans' main battle tank. The British seventeen-pounder gun was capable of knocking out the heaviest enemy armour, including the much better armoured Tiger and Panther tanks, but its larger size and weight meant it could only be flown in the huge cargo-carrying Hamilcar glider. 6th Airborne Division had one squadron of lightweight Tetrarch tanks, but they were designed for reconnaissance duties and since they too could only be flown in by Hamilcar gliders their numbers would be limited, besides which they had little capability to take on heavier enemy armoured vehicles.

Men of the 53rd Light Air Landing Artillery manned the division's anti-tank guns and the regiment's gunners also crewed the American 75mm pack howitzer. Designed for use in the mountains, this small field piece could be stripped down and carried by a mule; it also fitted into the back of a Horsa glider. However, while accurate, its size meant that it lacked range and lethality and its rate of fire would be limited by the relatively small amount of 75mm ammunition that could be flown in with the first lift of glider troops, or dropped in later by parachute resupply. Deficient in integral punch, 6th Airborne Division would have to rely on the guns of the Royal Navy light cruisers, which would be stationed in the Channel, to provide bombardment support to the Allied troops when they put ashore. Additional support would come from the main Army assault divisions, but only once their artillery regiments had landed and established their batteries ashore.

Besides lacking its own firepower, the division would be short of vehicles to tow its guns and carry other stores and equipment. Standard British military vehicles were too large and too heavy to fit into a glider. The answer came in the form of the ubiquitous quarter-ton Willys Jeep that had begun to arrive in England from America towards the end of 1941. Compact, lightweight, rugged and with excellent 4×4 cross-country mobility, the Jeep became the standard mover for all Allied airborne forces. Two Jeeps, or a combination of one six-pounder anti-tank gun or a trailer and a Jeep, could be squeezed into a Horsa glider. Although their numbers would be limited, the Jeeps' lift capacity would be increased by the use of trailers and they were allocated to headquarters units, engineers and medical teams to carry their equipment and provide a degree of mobility.

The medical treatment and evacuation of casualties would be a major challenge for airborne troops and 6th Airborne Division. Normal field evacuation from the point of wounding would be by stretcher to a unit's Regimental Aid Post, known as the RAP. Casualties would then be sent to advanced dressing stations at brigade level before onward evacuation and treatment at the Main Dressing Station (MDS) at division, followed by final evacuation to general hospitals in the rear areas or in the UK. In an airborne operation, the casualty evacuation chain would stop at the MDS until a link-up with conventional forces had been made. Consequently, life-saving surgery would have to be carried out further forward by the specially trained Field Surgical Teams, or FSTs. They would have to be trained to fly in by glider, or to jump in by parachute with specially adapted medical equipment that could be transported in a Jeep's trailer or carried in under canopy. In order to increase the chances of a casualty's survival, each unit's medical doctor was supported by a medical section of thirty men from the Royal Army Medical Corps field ambulance units, which were attached to the brigade. Many of the medics were conscientious objectors and although they refused to fight for their country, they were willing to parachute unarmed into occupied territory to save the lives of British soldiers. They also insisted that they would be allowed to provide equal treatment to enemy casualties.

Despite being declared ready for operations at the beginning of February, 6th Airborne Division was still in the process of making good its equipment and personnel shortfalls by the time Gale gave his orders to his brigades. At a time when every unit in England expected to cross the Channel was clamouring for its full complement of men, vehicles and weapons, meeting 6th Airborne Division's requirements was all the more complex given the specialist nature of the type of soldiers and kit it would need. A surgeon who could conduct open chest surgery to save a man's life, or a naval gunnery officer who could direct the fire of a light cruiser as well as parachute were not easy billets to fill. While Gale's staff pored over equipment tables and lobbied the War Office for more resources, the training of the division's units became more focused and the tempo of their own preparations increased.

Although the divisional concept of operations and brigade mission had been issued, in order to maintain absolute secrecy the location and dates of the specific tasks were kept secret from the battalions who would execute them. But even while COs were kept in the dark, the broad outline of their likely tasks had been briefed down to unit level. Martin Lindsay instructed his officers on the layout of a generic gun battery using a cloth model in the billiard room of the officers' mess. With four casemates facing west, a thick barbed-wire perimeter and a surrounding minefield, it was remarkably similar to the Merville Battery. But as his commanders listened to the briefing from the intelligence officer and then broke into syndicated groups to discuss how they might attack it, none of them had any idea of its name or location. Virtually all the subsequent exercises the battalion conducted incorporated attacking a battery whose configuration was always the same: four guns, defending machine-gun pits, wire and lots of mines.

During Exercise Thrust in late March, the battalion's orders were to attack a coastal battery at Fox Covert on Salisbury Plain. The battery was described as consisting of four 150mm enemy guns, inside a double belt of barbed wire with extensive minefields protecting it. Defended by 150 to 200 troops, it was also described as consisting of machine-gun pits and a 20mm flak gun. The road line running from Warminster and through the villages of Chitterne and Tilshead was used to represent a coastline and in the 'Ground' paragraph of the exercise instruction the topological relief of the area was described as follows: 'This part of France is marshy with a large number of wide drainage ditches.' It seemed to confirm what most men suspected, but while Lindsay alone knew for certain that 9 PARA would be jumping into France, he did not know where.

The unit may have had a specific focus for the continuation of their training, but while seizing strongpoints and breaching and assault drills became a key part of the programme, general themes remained the same. Field firing with live ammunition took place at Cranborne Chase where the men practised firing Sten and Bren guns from the hip and every rank had to throw a live 36 Mills grenade and Gammon bomb. They also practised jumping as more aircraft became available. Since the beginning of February the battalion had started to fly in the newly arrived Dakotas and they parachuted in sticks of twenty. By the end of the month they were jumping with leg bags full of 112 pounds of sand and long-barrelled weapons encased in felt valises. The new aircraft reduced the dispersal of a stick and required rehearsing new RV drills and working out minor details, such as the provision of sick bags, and more serious issues such as how to deal with refusals. All the men were searched at the airhead before boarding the aircraft to ensure that they were not carrying any documents that might compromise security; it was to become standard operating procedure from then on. The battalion and the brigade had also begun to practise dropping en masse. During Exercise Cooperation 1,370 parachutists, including 9 PARA and its attached arms of medics and engineers, jumped on to the DZ at Winterbourne Stoke on the southern edge of Salisbury Plain at night.

Through it all they continued to march. All ranks were expected to complete a twenty-mile battle march once a month and the emphasis Lindsay placed on physical fitness and honing the toughness of his men remained undiminished. His concern at the number of soldiers reporting sick with severe blisters after route-marches resulted in a terse directive being issued to his officers. It chastised them for not ensuring that the men looked after their feet and instructed platoon commanders to conduct 'constant foot inspections' to ensure that the troops' feet were kept in 'a healthy and hard condition'. Drawing on his own experience, Lindsay recognized that the small details of field discipline were important; if his soldiers did not look after their feet, they risked becoming ineffective in the coming battle. Lindsay remained a stickler for getting basic drills and procedures right, since he knew that what they failed to do in training would cost lives in combat. Sore feet or not, by the end of March the battalion had reached a high level of readiness. Few doubted that D-Day could be more than a few months or even weeks away, as the tempo of final preparations and exercises increased under the watchful eye of Lindsay's second-in-command, Major Terence Otway. The one man Otway watched in particular was his commanding officer.

Otway, like Lindsay, was a pre-war regular who had been commissioned into the Royal Ulster Rifles from Sandhurst. He had been overlooked for command of a company and having passed Staff College and served in the War Office on the prestigious Military Operations staff, he resented this and petitioned the Chief of the Imperial General Staff. Since Otway had served on Field Marshal Alan Brooke's staff, strings were pulled and he was offered the post of second-in-command of 9 PARA.

From the outset, it was clear that he did not get on with Lindsay and often cut across and contradicted his commanding officer in public. He made few friends among his fellow officers and he was equally aloof from the rank and file of the battalion, who considered him as a man who gave no quarter, but expected none in return.

However, he was a meticulous planner, paid great attention to detail and was respected for his ruthless professional drive. He was known as a man not to be crossed. But while not popular, the contribution he made to the preparation of the battalion, as the senior officer responsible for organizing training, was undoubted.

While the standards set by their commanding officer and second-in-command were unforgiving, 9 PARA's level of readiness for Overlord paid dividends and earned them the approval of Montgomery when he made an inspection of the battalion on 8 March. After visiting B and C companies training in the field, he spoke to the whole battalion, which had been drawn up in parade formation on the square at Kiwi Barracks. Wearing the newly issued Parachute Regiment cap badge next to his general's laurel badge on his beret, he stood in his open staff car, waved his swagger stick at them and, with a haughty lisp, told the assembled ranks to gather round him. No one moved. This may have reflected the mood of those who had done so much to earn the right to wear the winged emblem and who were irked to see it worn by someone who had never been through Hardwick or made a parachute jump. However, the compliments he paid them for what they had achieved in the space of just over a year came from a man who was free and harsh with his criticism. But the men of 9 PARA remained unimpressed by the senior Allied land forces general who would lead D-Day. To them, Montgomery was a distant commander and not one of their own. As far as they were concerned he was very different from Gale, who would stop and talk with any soldier on an exercise, or Hill, who would join a route-march at any given opportunity and lead it from the front.

The men may have taken a collective dislike to the commander of 21st Army Group, but the ranks who lined up to listen to Monty had swelled considerably from the nucleus of 156 former members of the 10th Essex who had formed up on the same spot fourteen months previously. The unit's monthly strength return for the end of February reported a full complement of thirty-three officers and a shortage of only twenty-three other ranks out of a total required strength of just over 700 men. The improvement in manning and the commendation from the most senior British file general was a positive indicator of 9 PARA's increasing readiness to take part in the invasion. The same could not be said for the RAF's new Dakota squadrons that would be carrying them into battle. The Albemarles and Halifax bombers of 38 Group had carried out the brigade drop on to Winterbourne Stoke rather than the Dakota crews of 46 Group which were still being worked up. But, as D-Day approached, the RAF's most recent addition to its order of battle was far from ready to conduct a large-scale drop of paratroopers.

During the winter of 1943 and 1944 many RAF crews returned to England from the Middle East and Far East. Some, like Flight Sergeant Bill Perry, were expecting a rest tour. Perry had flown over 700 hours in a DC-2 variant of the Dakota, dropping supplies to the 14th Army over the jungles of Burma and had been awarded a DFC for his steadiness under fire. Instead he found himself posted to 512 Squadron, which was forming up at RAF Broadwell in Wiltshire with thirty of the newly arrived DC-47s of 46 Group. Others were happy to volunteer to fly what they called the 'Daks'. Flight Lieutenant Alex McKee had always had a strong urge to fly since boyhood. He had flown Liberators in the Middle East and already held a DFC. He was serving as a flying instructor in England and wanted to return to 'ops', but having completed two operational tours was not allowed to return to active duty with Bomber Command. Instead he was posted to 233 Squadron at RAF Blakehill Farm. Also based in Wiltshire, the squadron was working up its Daks and he took over one of the squadron's three flights of ten Dakotas. He fell in love with the DC-47 as soon as he first flew it. To him it was beautifully designed and its twin Pratt and Whitney engines were powerful and reliable.

But not all the aircrew sent to fly the Dakotas were experienced. The majority of the pilots and navigators were straight from flying training schools in Canada, where the best students were selected to be sent to Fighter Command or frontline bomber squadrons. Unlike McKee, most newly trained pilots did not want to be sent to a squadron dropping 'brown jobs'. Even some of the ground crew were reluctant to be sent to 46 Group. Eighteen year-old Alan Hartley had just completed three months' air mechanics training on liquid-cooled

Sabre engines for the modern Hawker Typhoon ground-attack fighter bomber. Specifically picked from basic training to work on the Typhoon, he was dismayed to be sent instead to 217 Dakota squadron at RAF Down Ampney to service what he described as a 'bloody great monster' with old-style air-cooled engines. To him it was a step backward and to make matters worse the RAF bases for the Dakota squadrons were still being built. When Hartley arrived the station was a sea of mud and trenches and the unlined concrete walls of his thirty-man billet ran with condensation, which the single solid-fuel stove at the centre of the prefab hut did little to dry out. It was the start of a 'cold, miserable and muddy tour'.

With the coming of spring and an improvement in the weather, the Dakota aircrews' training intensified as they prepared for D-Day. They practised flying in 'V' or 'vic' formation, where two aircraft formed up wing-tip-to-wing-tip to a third lead Dakota; three 'vics' made up a flight. The three flights then formed up to make one large squadron V formation. As well as formation flying, they practised dropping paratroopers, first in single sticks of one aircraft at a time, then as flights and squadrons. Particular emphasis was placed on navigation and the crews learned to use Rebecca receiving equipment that picked up radio signals from a ground-based portable Eureka transmitter unit that would be carried by pathfinder paratroopers to bring an aircraft on to a drop zone.

The pathfinders would drop in advance of the main body from Albemarles flown by the more experienced crews of 38 Group. They came from 22nd Independent Parachute Company, which had been formed as a result of lessons learned from Sicily, where the DZ had not been marked and many paratroopers had been dropped wide of their drop zones. The pathfinders also carried Holophane lights, which were laid out on the DZ in the shape of the letter 'T', each light flashing a Morse code letter to the incoming aircraft. The orientation of the 'T' indicated the direction of the wind and would allow the aircraft to approach and line up for their run into the DZ so that their drop would be made into wind. This would allow the aircraft to slow down and dispatch their paratroopers just above stalling speed, which would reduce the shock of their parachutes opening in the slipstream. The

Dakotas also used Gee radar equipment, which would guide the pilot using navigational beams that led to the DZ, where the more precise Rebecca and Eureka system and Holophane lights could then be utilized to bring them on to the DZ with greater precision.

To give uninitiated crews operational experience, each aircraft conducted 'nickelling' ops to drop Allied propaganda leaflets over occupied France. For security reasons, drops were made along the entire enemy coastline, although many of the sorties were routed over Caen to familiarize the crews with the local topography and to get the Germans used to seeing large number of Daks flying over the area. At the end of March three squadrons of DC-47s flew units of 3rd Parachute Brigade across the Channel and into occupied airspace, then turned back towards England to drop their passengers over Salisbury Plain; 640 members of 9 PARA flew in Dakotas from 512 Squadron and, although they were provided with a fighter escort, many questioned the wisdom of testing enemy anti-aircraft defences and improving aircrew operational experience with live loads. However, there were no reports of German ack-ack fire and the Luftwaffe's failure to come up to meet them confirmed Allied air superiority over France.

The coming of spring brought an air of expectation; as the first green touched the trees and the blossom began to spot the hawthorn hedges around Bulford with a spray of white, few men doubted that D-Day could be more than a few weeks away. By the start of April the glass in the windows of garrison buildings rattled to the explosions of engineers using plastic explosive charges to practise blowing up glider poles and the days resounded to the crackle of gunfire from the surrounding rifle ranges. As the scenery around them began to change, hundreds of thousands of men and vast quantities of war-making materiel from all over the country, from the Mediterranean and from across the Atlantic also began to become drawn in to the final preparations and gathering of the mighty host that would open the second front in Normandy.

HMS *Arethusa* had been on bombardment duty off the Italian coast when she received orders in April to head for her home port on the Clyde. There she would refit her worn-out three twin six-inch guns before being assigned to the naval bombardment force, which would provide ship-to-shore gunfire support to the land units when they hit the beaches and jumped on to the DZs of Normandy. Other light cruisers, such as the *Mauritius* and the mighty First World War battleships, *Ramillies* and *Warspite*, each armed with huge fifteen-inch main armaments, would join *Arethusa* in the coming weeks. Four hundred miles to the south of the Scottish naval yards, fields and woods stretching between Devon and Hampshire were being stockpiled as pre-positioned ammunition dumps, equipment stores and vast vehicle parks of tanks, artillery pieces and trucks. Airfields across the south-west of England were being prepared as marshalling sites for thousands of aircraft and gliders, from which the invasion's mighty air armada would be launched across the Channel when the time came.

As the weather softened and the mighty host of the invasion force began to gather, sailors, airmen, soldiers and commandos knew that what they were preparing for could not be long off. While the precise date and location of invasion tasks remained a closely guarded secret, Lindsay knew that he would need every able-bodied man in 9 PARA for the coming battle. But the near full manning levels in the battalion at the start of the year had fluctuated. Some of the unit's reinforcements failed to meet its exacting standards and demanding training regime; those who did not make the grade were RTU'd or posted elsewhere. The hard nature of training also caused a higher degree of attrition of numbers through sickness and injury. During a large drop it was not uncommon for several men to suffer from concussion, sprains and broken limbs as a result of backward falls and landing in high winds. Keen to get as many men as possible fit for operations, Lindsay asked a local orthopaedic physician he knew to look at some of his injured paratroopers.

Whether the doctor enquired, or Lindsay offered the information is not clear. But as the two men discussed 9 PARA's medical facilities and equipment, Lindsay is alleged to have said to the doctor that the unit would be taking all the equipment he could see with them 'when we go over to France'. It may have seemed an innocent remark. Whether military or not, most people in England in March 1944 assumed that the invasion would take place in France. But while precise locations remained top secret, Lindsay's reference to the country of destination constituted an inadvertent breach of security. Two 9 PARA officers writing after the war maintained that Terence Otway reported his commanding officer to higher authority for making the remark to the doctor. Given the obsession with keeping any information about the coming invasion a secret, it was a breach of security that was to cost Martin Lindsay dearly.

On Saturday, 18 March the battalion was sent on a week's leave with the exception of Captain Bill Mills and Lindsay. That same day Martin Lindsay was arrested. Mills was told to report to the battalion orderly room where he met his commanding officer. Lindsay told him that he was under close arrest and he needed Mills to escort him to the officers' mess so that he could pack up his room. Lindsay spent the night in Bulford under Mills's nominal guard before leaving the next day to face the music at the Army's London District headquarters in Whitehall. Before departing after breakfast, Lindsay took one last look out of the windows of the anteroom in the mess. Lieutenant Alan Jefferson, one of his former platoon commanders, watched him unobserved from the far corner of the room. Jefferson should not have been there as he was meant to be on leave with the rest of the battalion, and had no idea of what had befallen his commanding officer, but as he watched Lindsay, his Sam Browne slung over his shoulder, gaze out over Bulford fields where jumping practice from a balloon was taking place, he had never seen a man 'so dejected and shattered'.

Lindsay saw one more of his officers as he left the mess. As he was leaving, Terence Otway was heading into the large redbrick building having been recalled from leave by Hill. According to Otway, Lindsay accused him of plotting his downfall and told him that 'you have got what you wanted'. Otway's response was not recorded as the two men passed each other, but it was the last time they would see one another. Martin Lindsay was never to return to Bulford and did not jump with 9 PARA on D-Day. Three months later he would be crossing the Channel in the demoted rank of major, to join a very different battalion that had already landed on the enemy coastline of Normandy.

Terence Otway always maintained that he had nothing to do with Martin Lindsay's removal from command and the War Office disciplinary records relating to the incident were destroyed in a fire in the Chancellery Office after the war. The circumstances surrounding Lindsay's departure have always been veiled in secrecy and details of the controversy submerged in rumour and speculation. Not least as to remove a CO of a new battalion after fourteen months in command and so soon before they were to jump as part of the vanguard of the invasion of France is a dramatic decision that could not have been taken lightly. Yet there is no official record of the event. Martin Lindsay's entry in *Who's Who* makes no mention of his having commanded the 9th Battalion of the Parachute Regiment and he himself never talked publicly about the incident. James Hill also refused to discuss the subject when asked about it after the war. What is fact is that in March 1944 Martin Lindsay was a lieutenant colonel commanding 9 PARA, but in July 1944 he was on his way to France to join 1st Battalion the Gordon Highlanders as their second-in-command in the rank of major. Additionally, the entry in the 9 PARA War Diary for 1944 records that at 1130 on 1 April, 'Maj TB Otway assumes command of the Battalion *vice* Lt Col MA Lindsay – relinquished'.

Writing to Lindsay's son in 1988, Major Allen Parry claimed that it was Otway who reported the incident either to Hill or directly to Gale and maintained that Otway was motivated by his desire to command the battalion. Parry also alleged that shortly before the incident, Otway had summoned him to his room in the officers' mess and asked him if he was prepared to go into battle behind Martin Lindsay. Parry replied, 'Most certainly. What prompts you to ask?' According to Parry, his answer left Parry in no doubt that Otway 'was determined to take command of the 9th Battalion before it went into action'. Parry also asserted that he subsequently discovered that Otway had approached all the company commanders in the battalion on the question of Lindsay's suitability to command, all of whom expressed having the same faith in Lindsay's ability to take them to war. Alan Jefferson, writing in 2006, also independently confirmed Parry's version of events although he was unaware of the precise circumstances surrounding his commanding officer's departure in March 1944.

It seems likely that Martin Lindsay did not know what was afoot regarding his ambitious second-in-command. But whatever the precise circumstances regarding Lindsay's breach, once it had been reported to higher authority Lindsay's fate would have been sealed. Gale and Hill, Lindsay's divisional and brigade commanders, would have been unable to ignore it once the matter had been brought to their attention. Although both men testified to Lindsay's impressive reputation and good character, the obsessive security surrounding preparations for D-Day was at an all-time high in the run-up to the invasion and any breach would have to have been dealt with severely. As a commanding officer, it could be argued that Lindsay should have known better and it is highly likely that the authorities wanted to make an example of him as a lesson to others. As Martin Lindsay's previous and subsequent war record was to attest, his qualities as a military commander in battle were never in doubt. Corresponding with Lindsay's son forty-four years after the incident, when asked what Lindsay had done wrong, Allen Parry replied: 'Nothing . . . it was a minor indiscretion. It has always been my view that success in Normandy was down to your Father.'

6

A Stinker of a Job

THE BATTALION RETURNED from leave a week later. After breakfast the following day, Otway assembled the officers in the mess and told them that he was now the acting CO, but made no mention of what had befallen his predecessor. Rumour and speculation were rife about what had happened to the commanding officer. The gossip was most marked among the officers and there was talk of an indiscretion about their D-Day mission and hints that Martin Lindsay had been escorted to London under arrest. But when Hugh Pond and others enquired what had happened to Lindsay, they were met by a wall of silence and told to mind their own business. Lindsay might have been a hard taskmaster and at times could be aloof, but he was popular, he had put his mark on the battalion and fashioned its spirit over fourteen months of tough training and the men had confidence in him as a leader who they had expected to take them into battle.

The unexpected loss of Polar Joe, so close to D-Day, provoked uncertainty and a drop in morale among the officers. The loss of a commanding officer was bad enough, but few relished the prospect of being commanded by Terence Otway, who had joined 9 PARA as the second-in-command in October 1943. Otway had served with the Royal Ulster Rifles protecting the international cantonment in Shanghai after the Japanese attacked the city in 1937, and a year later had served on the North-West Frontier where his battalion had been involved in skirmishing with Afghan tribesmen. In comparison to Lindsay, however, who had served in Norway, pioneered parachuting at Ringway, served on the Airborne staff in the War Office and commanded a parachute battalion in India, Otway had little airborne

or modern combat experience. Arguably, Otway had more operational experience, albeit on the periphery of empire, than the vast
majority of the battalion he now commanded, who had never heard
a shot fired in anger, but at the age of twenty-nine his command
experience was limited. Although he had served in the regular
army for nine years, he had not had the opportunity to command
an infantry company and had come straight into 9 PARA as its
second-in-command.

Like Lindsay's, Terence Otway's father had served in the Army
during the First World War and had died at an early age. His tuber-
culosis, brought on and exacerbated from being gassed in the
trenches, denied Otway the advantages he felt he might have had in
early life had his father lived. Like Lindsay too, he was brought up by
his mother in a home where money was in short supply. In Lindsay's
case it had bred a self-reliance and resilience to forge his own way in
life together with a strength of mind and body and a temperament
that could stand up to the stresses and strains of battle.

In Otway's case his early life bred a degree of resentment towards
those around him who were more fortunate, as well as a rather intro-
verted and brittle nature. This made him highly critical, overly ready
to find fault and lacking in empathy with the men he commanded.
However, Otway was a serious-minded officer and, despite his cold
detachment, in six months as the battalion's second-in-command he
had proved himself to be a first-class administrator who could absorb
a mass of detail and coordinate it into an operational plan. It was why
Hill selected him to replace Lindsay. The shock of Polar Joe's loss
would soon be replaced by the need to focus on their mission. It was
a reflection of the battalion's professionalism and testament to
Lindsay's legacy.

At the beginning of April 1944, Otway was called to see Hill. His
brigade commander told him that he had been promoted to lieutenant colonel and had been appointed as the new CO of 9 PARA. He
also told him that the battalion's D-Day objective was the toughest of
all the tasks allotted to the 6th Airborne Division. Hill confirmed that
the battalion was to silence the guns of a well-defended coastal battery before the main seaborne forces landed on the beaches. He also

described it as 'a grade-A stinker of a job'. Hill emphasized that it was a critical part of the divisional plan and was vital to the success of the landings. Hill did not tell Otway the location of the battery, but told him that he would be given access to all the other relevant intelligence on the objective and was at liberty to develop his plan to attack and destroy the guns as he saw fit.

Otway remained silent as he drove the two miles north of Bulford to Brigmerston House with Hill's brigade major, Major Bill Collingwood. When they arrived at the heavily guarded intelligence planning headquarters, Collingwood escorted Otway through the barbed-wire stockade that surrounded the Old Farm and showed him into a room on the first floor. Otway heard the door shut behind him and the key turn in the lock, as he was left alone to survey the mass of information laid out before him. On a table in the centre of the room a large-scale model captured every aspect of the gun position in intricate detail; based on aerial photographs it had been lovingly crafted in miniature by the divisional staff using Plasticine and plaster of Paris. Aerial photos showing the battery from different altitudes and angles, along with maps and diagrams, were pinned on the walls of the room. There was a host of detail about the village of Merville, its layout, population and topography; the only fact that was missing was its name and none of the associated information betrayed the battery's actual location in France. Otway lit his pipe and walked round the model and surveyed the surrounding data about his target.

The boundary of the position was octagonal in shape and about 400 metres across. At its centre were the four gun emplacements, each in bunkers under two metres of concrete and another two metres of earth, with steel firing shutters to the front and steel doors to the rear. The defending garrison and gunners were estimated to be between 150 and 200 men in strength. Otway counted up to twelve machine-gun positions and two 20mm anti-aircraft guns, which would be capable of being used in the direct-fire ground role. Together they covered every approach to the battery, which was surrounded by an internal double apron of concertinaed barbed-wire fencing; two to three metres thick and at least a metre high, it was designed to stop attacking infantry. Beyond the thick coils of high-piled wire was a thirty-metre-deep minefield, which was marked off by a single strand of cattle-wire fence. Beyond this on the north and west sides, 300 metres of an anti-tank ditch had been partially constructed and was four metres wide and three metres deep. A second entanglement of concertinaed wire filled the gap between the start and end of the ditch. Beyond the outer perimeter of the ditch and the second wire obstacle was a 100-metre-wide minefield that encircled the entire battery position. Hill had been right: on initial inspection the position looked impregnable. The level and layout of the defences meant that the battery would be an extremely difficult nut to crack and the cost of taking it was likely to be high.

Otway had become engrossed in the model and lost track of time as he absorbed the detail and his mind wrestled with how he might attack it. He felt the urge to relieve himself and glanced at his watch. He hammered on the door to be let out and when he got no response, he urinated out of a window. Any satisfaction he felt was not shared by the military policeman standing below him. Eventually released from the model room, he lunched with Collingwood who informed him he was now on the 'X List', which was personally approved by 21st Army Group headquarters and would give him access to the Old Farm whenever he wanted it. Otway returned to the battalion and shut himself away in the small mess flat he had inherited from Lindsay. He shared the information with only one man as he began to formulate his plan for attacking the battery.

Before the war, Captain Robert Gordon-Brown had been an architect. Balding and older than the majority of other captains in the battalion, he was one of the few officers close to Otway, which reinforced a perceived self-importance and did little to enhance his popularity with the rest of the mess. Gordon-Brown had already passed the entrance exam for Staff College, but he was a strange choice to bring into Otway's planning circle. It would have been more normal to include Allen Parry, who was not only a pre-war regular and the senior major in 9 PARA, but had also been appointed as the acting battalion second-in-command as a result of Otway's promotion; all criteria that should have made him an obvious and standard choice to be involved in the planning from the outset. The only other man in the battalion who was part of Otway's inner circle was his batman Corporal Joe Wilson, who had served Lindsay before him. Wilson was the classic officer's gentleman servant. With a reputation as a boxer, he was a tough soldier and a good marksman, but he was also discreet and quickly learned to manage Otway's temperament and mood. Although not directly involved in the planning, he was the only other man in the battalion who was party to what was afoot as Otway and Gordon-Brown spent a week locked away together poring over the detail gleaned from the model room at Brigmerston, which was constantly updated.

As more RAF reconnaissance flights were made over the area, even the appearance of new craters around the battery were faithfully added to its scaled-down replica as the most recent aerial photographs became available. Otway made repeated visits to the model room to study the details of the defences and the layout of the ground. Gradually, with input from Gordon-Brown, he formulated a plan. A parachute drop would allow the attacking force to insert behind the target and then march undetected under the cover of darkness and assault the battery from a forming-up point in its rear. However, he knew that the gun position had been constructed with all-round defence in mind and the model indicated that all likely approach routes were covered by the interlocking fire of several machine-gun positions. The attacking force would also need to breach the significant obstacles of the minefields and the thick wire barriers, both of which would be covered by fire. If his men were delayed by the barriers and caught in the crossfire of numerous machine guns that could be brought to bear against a single point of attack, he knew that they would be mown down before they could get into the battery. Consequently, he wanted to disrupt the cohesion of the defence by forcing the garrison to have to look several ways at once when the battalion attacked.

Between them, Otway and Gordon-Brown hit on the idea of landing an assault force by glider inside the defences of the battery at the same time as a main assault force breached the obstacles and attacked from the rear. They decided that the main assault would be made by C Company. Landing by parachute with the bulk of the rest of the battalion group two kilometres to the east of the position, they would then march to their forming-up positions behind the battery's perimeter defences. Once a path through the first outer minefield had been cleared, B Company would prepare to use explosives to blow gaps in the thick wire obstacles through which C Company would make its attack. As they did so, fifty men of A Company and a small party of engineers would simultaneously crash-land in gliders into the front of the battery. If the gliders managed to put down between the gun casemates, Otway and Gordon-Brown reasoned that the men they carried could then leap out and attack straight into the gun positions with Sten guns, grenades and flamethrowers.

Otway had still not briefed Parry on his intentions when he ordered him to assemble his company in the cookhouse a few days later. Gordon Newton sat with bated breath with the other 120 members of A Company while they waited for the commanding officer to address them. Newton was a big lad and since joining 9 PARA he had been sent to the battalion's Regimental Police (RP) staff with Private Ron Tucker, who was also well over six feet. Both he and Tucker hated putting their mates on petty charges for being late back from leave and guarding the poor unfortunates who had refused to jump. They felt sorry for them, especially under the strict regime of the NCO in charge of the 'Provo' staff, Corporal James 'Marra' McGuinness, who was also one of the battalion's expert Vickers machine gunners. The RP corporal insisted on the prisoners being handcuffed to their beds when they were not on fatigues, or being marched at double time round the battalion. Born in 1911, McGuinness came from hard West Cumbrian mining stock and was a good ten years older than most of the men in 9 PARA, who had an average age of twenty-two. His maturity and toughness made him an obvious choice for the RP staff. Apart from finding their duties distasteful, Newton and Tucker were conscious of the imminent approach of D-Day and did not want to miss out on the action; they wanted back into the rifle companies and what they considered 'proper soldiering'. The two soldiers put in a request to be posted and Newton went back to A Company and Tucker was sent to C Company.

The maxim of 'beware what you wish for' played on Newton's mind as he sat and listened to their new commanding officer. Otway told Newton and the others that he needed fifty of them to volunteer for a 'very special task'. He wouldn't tell them what it was, but he did say that it would involve gliders and that it would be dangerous. The air of expectation and excitement was palpable as Otway left the dining room to give the men time to reflect on what he had said. A buzz of animated conversation broke out as soon as he departed; people began to speculate that it was 'a German *coup de main* op' or a suicide job. Whatever it entailed, the fact that it involved gliders was not lost on the men. As paratroopers, they disparaged glider troops, whom they did not consider proper airborne soldiers, christening them 'the chair-borne airborne'; the antipathy was mutual, but they had joined the Paras to jump and now it looked as if some of them would be going in by glider. It made no difference. When Otway returned the whole company stood up to volunteer. It was a reflection of who they were. Even though they had no idea what it would involve, no one wanted to be left out of it. Otway thanked them and left Major Parry to select the fifty men he would require.

Otway had chosen Parry's company because he considered A Company to be the best sub-unit in the battalion. But he did not choose Parry to lead the glider assault element of his plan. Instead he chose Robert Gordon-Brown, who was not only considerably less experienced than Parry, but as the second-in-command of A Company he was also Parry's direct subordinate. Parry was bitterly disappointed to be passed over in favour of his non-regular junior. Otway was to claim later that he did not choose Parry as he was the only pre-war regular officer he trusted and he wanted him to land by parachute with the main body, so that he could call upon him if anything went wrong. Nonetheless it was a remarkably strange decision, not least as by 23 March a new battalion second-in-command had arrived, which allowed Parry to relinquish the acting role of 9 PARA's second-in-command and go back to focusing on his command of A Company. Major Eddie Charlton was a regular soldier from the King's Own Yorkshire Light Infantry and should have provided Otway with a sufficiently experienced soldier to call on should the need arise. Otway was later to claim that Charlton was an unknown quantity and that he had not asked for him to become his second-in-command. Regardless, it was still an odd call, especially as Otway did not bother to explain his reasoning to Allen Parry.

Parry did not take issue with his commanding officer. Instead he went about selecting the required men with a quiet professionalism and automatically excluded those who were married. Newton was unmarried and was one of those selected, as was Geoff Pattinson, although he had started stepping out seriously with a young clothes factory model called Audrey. Pattinson had been away on a fatigue duty when A Company collected in the cookhouse. On his return his section corporal, Jack Watson, told him that he had been selected for a job that was likely to be a suicide mission. Newton was chosen to fly in the same glider as Gordon-Brown. Even though he thought it was a 'bloody stupid idea', having asked to get back into a rifle company there was no way he was going to give up his seat to anyone else. Fred Glover would travel in the glider to be commanded by Hugh Pond. He trusted and respected his young platoon commander, but was disappointed not to be parachuting.

The chosen members of A Company were taken to the nearby airfield at Thruxton where they met the men from the Glider Pilot Regiment who would fly them. They were impressed by the easy manner of the pilots, but they were horrified when they first saw the gliders that would take them into action. The Horsa glider was a high-winged monoplane mounted on a tricycle undercarriage. With a sixty-two-foot wingspan, black painted canvas skin and blunt beaked perspex cockpit, it looked like a gigantic crow. Designed by the Air Speed Company in 1940 to meet the War Office's requirement for a troop lift glider, the Horsa was manufactured by furniture-making companies. It had begun to come off the production lines in 1942 and was made almost entirely of laminated plywood. To the uninitiated troops of A Company it seemed to possess all the robustness of a matchbox.

At a time when aircraft aluminium was in short supply, its wooden construction meant that the Horsa was light enough to be towed into the sky by a converted bomber from 38 Group and could carry twenty-nine fully equipped troops, or a combination of Jeeps, trailers and six-pounder anti-tank guns loaded by ramps just aft of the cockpit. It also had a troop door on the port side forward of the tail section, which in turn could be opened by means of four quick-release bolts to allow the Jeeps it carried to be driven out of its rear. The glider attached to its tug aircraft by means of a thick hemp Y-shaped towrope, which could be released in flight when it cast off to begin its glide into a target landing area. A telephone wire entwined into the towrope allowed the crews of the two respective aircraft to communicate with each other.

At least the pilots looked like they were made of sterner stuff than the aircraft they would fly into battle. The Glider Pilot Regiment had been raised in 1941 as part of the Army Air Corps to provide pilots and co-pilots for the Airborne troop gliders. They were also trained to fight as infantry once on the ground and had to pass a demanding six-week combat course as well as completing their flying training. The glider pilots were a unique part of the Army's order of battle as virtually every member of the battalions that made up the GPR's wings were either senior NCOs or officers. The pilots who would fly A Company on D-Day were specially selected, but like the men they would ferry into battle, had no idea of the location of their target.

Staff Sergeant Kerr, who would fly in Pond and his platoon, had to demonstrate his ability to make accurate spot landings in a marked white triangle 150 metres across by 150 metres long and use an arrester parachute deployed from the glider's tail to bring it to a dead stop, before he and his co-pilot were chosen with two other crews to take part in the mission. They needed to be good, as flying a heavily loaded Horsa glider and making a pinpoint landing at night was a dangerous business. It involved making a dive approach and pulling up at the last safe moment to slam the glider into a relatively small space and bring it to a dead stop. Carrying a full load without power and pulling up at low height just before the aircraft hit the ground risked a high-speed stall, the consequences of which were likely to be fatal. Landing the glider in such a small space required considerable skill. The pilot had to maintain a steep gliding angle to keep up his flying speed while keeping an eye on his target and judging just the right moment to commit to the landing by lining up his nose and pulling hard on the trailing edge of the glider's wings. If he committed too early or too late, he would under- or overshoot the landing site.

As the Stirling bomber pushed its throttles forward on the first training flight, it took up the slack of the towrope, which had been paid out in a zigzag pattern on the runway between the two aircraft. As the tug aircraft built up speed the Horsa lifted first and then slowly the four-engine bomber climbed up into the air in front of it. Pond was surprised by the smoothness of the take-off, although the roar of the tug aircraft's engines was deafening and the wind seemed to sigh through every tiny split and opening in the glider's canvas skin. However, despite the smooth take-off, flying as a passenger in a glider was a particularly unpleasant experience for the troops strapped in the back on the benches running along both sides of the fuselage.

Besides the normal pitch and yaw, the troops were subject to the ceaseless tug and surge of the towrope as the Horsa was buffeted in the slipstream of the tug aircraft. It induced a stomach-churning motion that few of the troops in the back could withstand, as the hemp rope slackened and tightened, slackened and tightened. Before long the sick bags were overflowing and the floor was soon awash with vomit. The stench was terrible. It was a blessed relief to cast off from the tug aircraft once the glider had reached its designated release point. As the pilot pulled the release lever, the shackles disengaged and the heavy hemp towrope dropped away from the front of the glider. The drone of the tug's engines faded into the distance and suddenly there was silence. The Horsa seemed to float for a moment, as if in suspended animation, then its nosed dipped and it dropped like a stone.

Both pilots pushed their sticks hard to the floor and used their feet to help keep them there. The Horsa was equipped with large barn-door-like flaps that meant it could be towed high over a target then swoop down on top of it. The steep dive would reduce the risk of anti-aircraft fire by minimizing the time spent in the air, but it made for a rollercoaster ride for the troops in the back. As the glider fell into the dive, the troops strained against the web safety belts, their stomachs heaving and their eyes bulging while the wooden aircraft plummeted to the ground. Just before it seemed that the glider would hit the ground nose first, Kerr shouted, 'Right!' Both pilots heaved back hard on the sticks and the mighty flaps dropped through the quarter, half and then full flap position. As the control panels bit into the slipstream, the air speed fell off and the glider came out of the dive at a ninety-degree angle a few hundred feet above the ground. Kerr kicked the wooden rudder pedals with his Army boots to pull the Horsa into line on to the target landing area. Now he and his 'oppo' (buddy) struggled to maintain flying speed to avoid the aircraft stalling as it hurtled in to land at seventy miles an hour. In order to pull it up short, Kerr landed with the brakes applied and immediately deployed the arrester parachute from the tail, which would help to bring the three tonnes of men and equipment to a dead stop within the white circle that had been painted on the grass to represent the battery perimeter.

Although impressed by the feat of airmanship, most of A Company were glad that their glider training flights would be kept to a minimum. The risks associated with this type of precision flying meant that most of the training flights would be made by the gliders carrying 500-pound bars, which would provide them with ballast and simulate the weight of a live load of troops. Geoff Pattinson was happy not to have to spend more time flying in the gliders. On his first glider flight from Thruxton the towrope between the tug aircraft and his Horsa snapped, forcing it to make an emergency landing; it was an inauspicious start.

The gliders continued to practise diving and flying a three-sided box of ninety-degree turns without A Company. They did it until they could land smack in the middle of the white painted circle. They practised by day, using blacked-out goggles and sodium marker flares, until they could do it by night with only one flare to guide them. They had to get within thirty feet of the flare by flying on a bearing and using time and distance. When not helping to wrestle with the control column, the second pilot used a hand-held compass and stopwatch to give the bearing to the pilot and would yell out to him when to turn. It was basic, but it worked.

By the beginning of April, Otway had been told that his target was the Merville Battery. Although he was not told the date, he knew that the invasion could not be far off. Having selected his glider force and set their training in motion, he was racing against the clock to bring together the other constituent parts of his plan. Otway also planned to use a number of small advance force groups jumping ahead of the main drop to cut the battery's outer wire fence, clear and mark four paths through the outer minefield for the assault party and recce the position before the main attacking force and the gliders went in. The recce group was codenamed the Troubridge Party, in honour of Admiral Troubridge who had recced the Spanish and French ship lines for Nelson at Trafalgar. Led by Major George Smith, with two sergeant majors, they would cut the outer cattle-wire fence on the edge of the minefield and observe the German sentry positions. A taping party under Captain Paul Greenway would then lift the mines and mark a clear lane through the minefield to the main coiled barbed-wire obstacle with white mine-tape.

The attack would be initiated by a bugle call as B Company blew gaps in the thick wire with explosive mines called Bangalore Torpedoes for C Company to assault through. At the same time the three gliders with fifty members of A Company would swoop out of the sky and attack the gun casemates from the front of the position. During the attack, Otway planned to use a separate diversion force of Bren gunners to draw the fire of the defenders' machine-gun posts. Four additional stores gliders carrying two six-pounder anti-tank guns to blow in the steel doors of the casemates and additional engineers equipped with 'General Wade' charges to destroy the German guns would also be flown in. The stores gliders would land on the main parachute DZ codenamed 'V' when the bulk of the battalion jumped in. The extra stores aircraft would also bring in two Jeeps for the medical section, its equipment and spare ammunition for the mortars and Vickers machine guns.

Otway's concept of operations was complex. With so many moving parts, he knew that it would have to be rehearsed in detail until his men were familiar with every aspect of the mission, their individual parts in it and the ground over which it would be executed. What he needed was his own life-sized model to train his men on that could capture the same detail of the defences and surrounding topography as the model in the Old Farm. When they reached the real thing he wanted them to feel as if they had been there before, by making them practise over it again and again, by day and by night until every single one of them could carry out the attack in their sleep.

Finding land to build a life-scale mock-up of the battery was not in itself a difficult task. However, Otway needed a piece of ground that would conform to the bocage countryside of thick hedgerows, high-banked lanes and ditches and orchards found around the Merville Battery. It also had to be big enough to mark out the large drop zone and two kilometres of track leading from it to the battery. Distances had to be precise in order to match the details and scale taken from air reconnaissance photos. With Hill's permission he got Bill Collingwood to use an Army light aircraft and scour the surrounding area for a suitable piece of land. Collingwood presented three options. Otway chose a forty-five-acre site in the vale of the Inkpen Ridge below the old Iron Age fort of Walbury Hill, near the village of Woodhay, four miles south-west of the Berkshire town of Newbury. The topographical features were similar to those at Merville and it was large enough to mark out the drop zone and the necessary battalion approach routes. The presence of the 100-metre-high ridgeline running along the southern side of the site offered the additional advantage of providing a bullet catcher for the use of live ammunition.

With the imminence of D-Day, Otway's requirements might have been considered a wartime priority, but although the war against the U-boats in the Atlantic had been won, Britain was still a country struggling to feed itself. The surrender of forty-five acres of prime agricultural land sown with summer crops estimated to be worth £20,000 would need the clearance of seven ministries. It took several days to cut through the red tape, as the bureaucrats protested about the short notice and cost, but Otway got his way. The entire area was sealed off with civilian and military police; no one got in or out unless they had a signed pass authorized by Otway. With the security blanket in place, engineering plant was brought from rubble-clearing duties in cities as far away as Liverpool and Plymouth. When they arrived, Otway worked the bulldozers and engineering party day and night for five days to get the site ready. They levelled the ground, dug a 300-metre anti-tank ditch, marked tracks, laid out the coiled-wire obstacles and staked out dummy minefields. At the centre of it all, the engineers built mock-ups of the four gun casemates using scaffolding poles and hessian cloth. In less than a week the dummy gun battery was ready, with each detail intricately reproduced to imitate the real thing at Merville. The dropping zone, various form-up points, tracks and junctions leading to the position were accurately marked out to reflect the distances the men would have to traverse when they made the attack for real. The site was then camouflaged to stop it being identified from the air by Luftwaffe reconnaissance aircraft.

In the early evening of 8 May, 9 PARA formed up on the square of Kiwi Barracks in full battle order. Even the sick paraded, unless specifically exempted by the medical officer. At 2100 hours the entire battalion stepped off to march through the night the thirty miles to the dummy battery near Woodhay. They arrived there the next day and bivouacked against the hawthorn hedges. They would live under their gas capes for the next two weeks, drawing water for their ablutions from the lake at West Woodhay House, built in 1635 to a design inspired by Inigo Jones. The grounds of the house would act as the battalion's administrative headquarters and a large briefing marquee, which doubled as a NAAFI, was set up on one of its lawns. On the first day of the exercise, Otway gathered 9 PARA together in the tent. He told them, 'Our final training for D-Day starts here. What I am about to tell you is top secret.' The men were briefed on every detail available save the precise location of the battery. With his intelligence officer, Captain Joe Worth, Otway went on to describe the critical nature of their mission and its relationship to the very success of the invasion. He told them that they would do by airborne assault what the RAF had failed to do by heavy bombing. He made it clear that the lives of many would depend on their success.

Over the next two weeks, in the words of Company Sergeant

Major 'Dusty' Miller who was part of the Troubridge party, they would 'eat, sleep and drink that bloody battery'. It was precisely what Otway wanted. His intent was to practise the attack continuously until his men could do it as brainwashed robots regardless of the conditions they would face when they did it for real in Normandy. First, platoons and parties tasked with specific missions talked over their role in the plan using sketch maps and models, then they walked and talked over the ground of the mock-up, each man and each group working out exactly how they would approach their task to nail down the synchronization of the individual and collective battle parts in detail. What they discussed they then put into practice as platoons and companies, before drawing the disparate elements together as a battalion group.

They rehearsed attacking the battery nine times, five times by day and four times by night; the last battalion attack was made using live ammunition. The troops of B Company practised placing and detonating Bangalore Torpedoes, which would blow gaps in the wire obstacles in four places to allow the platoons of C Company to assault through the wire and make their attacks on the casemates. The Bangalore came in 1.5-metre tubular metal lengths containing plastic explosives, which could be screwed together. When they exploded, the metal case would splinter into wire-cutting shrapnel to create a two-metre gap in the coils of wire. The taping parties became expert at lifting mines, including the lethal German S Mine, which jumped a metre in the air when triggered by a soldier's foot, then exploded into 360 steel ball bearings, which would tear into the flesh of advancing infantry at waist level.

The site had been stripped of turf and men toiled in the scorching heat, as a brilliant sun turned the dummy battery into a choking dust bowl. They rehearsed repeatedly until Otway was satisfied that each platoon, group and company could execute the attack to perfection. Over a period of two weeks the task of silencing the guns of Merville became ingrained into the soul of every man. After each attack, Otway held a post-mortem in the briefing tent on the well-manicured lawns of West Woodhay House. He was highly critical and every fault was highlighted and then put right in the next attack. Every man was questioned on his individual role and had to describe his tasks in flawless detail to his platoon commander. The only part Otway was unable to practise was inserting by parachute and landing the three Horsa gliders between the replica gun casemates. With the imminence of D-Day, the RAF was husbanding its aircraft and crews. In their absence 9 PARA had to make do with jumping from trucks across the drop zone and marching in column to the glider landing points.

With or without aircraft or gliders Otway's plan was complex in the extreme. Timings for each of its many moving parts were worked out down to the last minute and Otway was adamant about being precise in his calculations. The attack would start at 0430 on D-Day. As his men jumped into action at precisely 0050 hours, HMS *Arethusa* would be sailing into her bombardment position off the coast of Normandy. If she did not receive a signal from the naval fire control party attached to 9 PARA that Otway had successfully taken the objective by 0550 on the dawn of D-Day, she would rake the position with concentrated fire from her six-inch guns. It would be a final and last-ditch part of the insurance policy to prevent the battery from firing on the seaborne invasion troops as they came ashore. If the battalion's attack was delayed or became bogged down and the battalion had not withdrawn from the position by the appointed time, Otway knew that 9 PARA would be caught in the devastating gunfire and faced the risk of being killed by their own Navy.

With the flashes and explosions echoing back and forth across the fields at the foot of the Inkpen Ridge, the locals who had been kept out of the area could only guess at what was going on beyond the tight security cordon of checkpoints and policemen. Most would have had a hunch that it was something to do with the forthcoming invasion of Europe. But the CO of 8 PARA knew what it was all about, as he watched one of the practice attacks from the top of the ridge one fine morning in May. Lieutenant Colonel Alistair Pearson had a grandstand view and marvelled at the complexity of what he saw unfolding beneath him.

Pearson had more combat experience than anyone in 3rd Parachute Brigade. He was awarded a Military Cross for serving with 1 PARA in North Africa and went on to win three DSOs commanding the battalion after taking over from Hill. He had also jumped at Sicily, where he forced his US Dakota pilot to fly through flak to the DZ at the point of his pistol, only to watch three of the men who had jumped before him drop into the sea and drown. Pearson knew all about the frictions of war and the best laid plans of airborne operations. He doubted the complicated nature of Otway's scheme would survive the inherent chaos and dispersal of a parachute jump, or remain intact when in contact with the enemy. Collingwood was watching with him. Before driving off in his staff car Pearson turned to him and, referring to the attack, said, 'It's all too confusing to me.' Pearson would have favoured a looser plan, which he would have pulled together once he was on the ground, knew precisely what he was facing and how many men he would have available to him after the jump.

If Pearson doubted Otway, there is no record of whether the two men spoke about it. Terence Otway knew there was a risk of dispersion in any drop, but he had absolute conviction in his own plan. The men who rehearsed in the dust and the heat also had faith in Otway and his proposed manoeuvre. The repetitive drill of repeat attacks gave them confidence that it would work and brought a different psychological edge to their preparations for D-Day. After a year and a half of training, the scale and level of activity at Inkpen focused their minds that the big show was about to begin. As far as Fred Glover was concerned, 9 PARA had only been playing at soldiers up until then, but training on the life-sized replica of the target they would attack brought with it the reality of what they were being sent to Normandy to do. Even though they did still not know the location of the battery, now 9 PARA had a mission of the utmost importance to the success of D-Day and each man knew the critical part he would play in it.

Confident as they were, the vast majority of the battalion had never heard a shot fired in anger. As young private soldiers not long out of school, men like Glover, Geoff Pattinson and Gordon Newton had little real appreciation of the particular risks they would be facing. The nature of airborne operations is an inherently dangerous battlefield business at the best of times. The fact that they would be attacking by glider directly into the front of a well-fortified enemy position was bad enough. But also to land in the path of the oncoming friendly fire from their comrades attacking from the rear of the battery was something else. The risk of fratricide in the confusion and darkness would be acute and what they were about to embark upon would be a perilous undertaking. However, Gale and Hill had signed off the plan. Both men had combat experience, where the thought of two friendly forces attacking directly into one another at close range might have provoked them to think twice. But in the wake of Eben-Emael, something approaching a cult of the glider *coup de main* existed in 6th Airborne Division. Yet while it was one thing to conduct a single-direction assault landing straight on top of a Belgian fort or against a lightly defended bridge on the Orne or Caen Canal, it was quite another to do what Otway was proposing at Merville.

While the name and location of Merville remained a closely guarded secret from the men of 9 PARA, their detailed knowledge of the battery's layout and its significance to the success of Overlord was still an attendant security risk. But Otway knew that he could not keep the men cooped up inside the dusty cordon round the Inkpen and there was a risk of overtraining, which would dull the edge he was trying to fashion. Consequently, he was prepared to give them a break from the repetitive routine of constant rehearsals, allowing them the odd evening in the pubs and dance halls around Newbury. The importance of not uttering a word of what they were about had been drummed into every man, but if Otway was to let them out he also wanted an insurance plan in place to test their security, especially when under the influence of alcohol.

As the off-duty members of 9 PARA drank in Newbury's pubs teeming with other servicemen during one Saturday night in the middle of their training, few suspected that the numbers of pretty women in their best civilian clothes and nylons, wearing their rationed perfume, and who showed so much interest in them and accepted their drinks, were in fact deliberately chosen to seek out members of 9 PARA. Wearing their maroon berets and the distinctive Airborne insignia they were easy to spot. Otway had recruited twenty-two exceptionally attractive WAAFS from a local airbase to attempt to use their feminine charms to beguile the soldiers into revealing any of the top-secret information they possessed. The details of the tactics the women employed were not made known, but there were no reports of any sensitive information being divulged and the integrity, of the operation at least, was considered to have remained intact.

On 19 May the battalion returned from Woodhay and were sent on forty-eight hours' leave. Although they might have suspected it, there was no official mention that it was to be their last, or that D-Day had been set for Monday, 5 June. Like many young men, Newton and Pond were desperate to lose their virginity, especially as they knew that they would soon be going into action. They had not achieved their ambition with any of the pretty young undercover WAAFs sent against them around Newbury and they were to be equally unsuccessful during their last leave.

Saying goodbye would be harder for men leaving their wives or serious girlfriends. While they did not speak of it, most people in Britain knew that the young men who drank in their best uniforms or visited their homes were soon bound for battle. A heightened air of expectation hung over the whole country. On the evening of 21 May several hundred soldiers from 9 PARA gathered on the concourse of Waterloo station; they said their goodbyes to wives and sweethearts, then headed through the barriers to the train that would take them back to Bulford Sidings. For many it was a tearful farewell and many suspected it would be their last.

Everyone returned on time to Bulford and there was none of the occasional absenteeism. Though they had not been told, they knew the advent of D-Day was upon them. The final rehearsal for Operation Tonga started a day later and lasted for three days. It involved the whole of 6th Airborne and Polish paratroopers while the 1st Airborne Division provided the enemy. To avoid the risk of injury, the 6th Airborne did not jump. Otway needed every man; with 696 officers and other ranks, 9 PARA was still short of their officially established war strength of 733 men.

During the last night of the exercise they jumped from trucks that laid them out across the DZ in a simulated dispersal pattern that would come from a good drop. The containers with the Vickers machine guns and three-inch mortars were dispersed in between the middle of the sticks, where they anticipated they would land in a real jump. There was no moon as the men collected at the battalion RV, which had been set up by Parry thirty minutes before the main body arrived on the DZ. Once they were complete, Parry led them towards the battery where they met Major Smith who was in charge of the recce parties. Smith confirmed that paths through the mine-field had been cleared and neatly marked with white tape, just as it had been in numerous previous exercises.

The rest of the battalion crouched down in their attack positions, breathing hard as they waited for the bugle call that would sound the attack. They were tense and keyed up. Live firing exercises always bring a sense of excitement and realism, but they also knew that this was the culmination of their training. It was just before 0430 as the fuses of the Bangalore Torpedoes inserted in the wire fizzed. Then the rasping call of a bugle sounding reveille split the night air. Before the strains of the last note died, the darkness was rent with the bright light and the shattering crash of four lengths of Bangalore Torpedoes exploding in a blinding flash of scything fragments of wire and smoke.

The smoke was still clearing as Lieutenant Jefferson charged through one of the smoking gaps, blowing a small toy horn he had bought on his last leave. It played a single note and was the rallying cry to the men of his platoon who immediately followed him. Sid Capon shouted, 'Bastards, bastards,' over and over as he charged after him, firing his Sten gun from the hip as he headed for Casemate One. The other platoons of C Company fanned out on their left and made for their allotted bunkers, screaming and firing as they went. Overhead mortar shells thumped star-shells into the air, which was the signal for the glider force to land between the casemates. The fifty men of A Company broke from their imaginary landing positions and charged into their allotted mock-up bunkers. They hurled phos-phorus grenades into the steel-tubed structures and their hessian coverings began to burn. They continued to fire into the blazing dummy gun position until frantic shouts of 'Cease fire, cease fire,' brought a stuttering halt to the cacophony of sound. The temporary silence was shattered as the engineers were called forward to place their round cheese-shaped Wade charges against the barrels of the replica guns to ensure their destruction.

The men withdrew under the burning light of the dummy casemates and felt pleased with themselves as they marched the twenty-six miles back to Kiwi Barracks. The attack was a success; it had gone like clockwork. But apart from the lack of aircraft to drop them and the gliders to fly in the men of A Company, other features were missing. There was no enemy, no return fire and the mines were imitations, empty of lethal explosives and shrapnel. It was a one-way range, where the fire, danger and death only went in a single direction. The absence of a lethally armed opposition denied them a vote in the outcome and the butcher's ballot that they would have to contend with when the battle was joined for real. Jefferson had been in the theatre before the war and as he marched back to Bulford he wondered what it all meant. A bad dress rehearsal in a playhouse usually meant a good first night; now he speculated whether the converse was true. In twelve days' time he would find out.

At midday on 25 May 9 PARA climbed aboard a fleet of twenty three-tonne trucks. It was a perfect late spring day with a clear blue sky. Once the men and their kitbags were loaded, the vehicles' motors coughed into life and then headed out of the gates of Kiwi Barracks into the hawthorn-flanked lanes to start their journey to the transit camp, which would lead to Normandy. Those who sat in the back of the canvas-covered trucks as they lurched out of the gate, turned left and crunched their gears up the hill to the main road, had an average age of twenty-two. Most had never seen action before and for many it would be the last time that they would see Bulford.

7

The Gathering Storm

THE LATE AFTERNOON sun was still high in the sky when the convoy of trucks pulled into the makeshift camp of long rows of ten-man bell tents set up behind triple coils of Danet wire on the edge of RAF Broadwell. Situated between the Gloucestershire villages of Broadwell and Burford, the airbase was the home of 512 Squadron and the thirty-two DC-47s that would drop the battalion over Normandy. 9 PARA were just one small part of a mighty host that had begun to gather round airfields and ports towards the end of May, as southern England became one huge armed camp. All over the country hundreds and thousands of troops and vehicles moved to their staging locations, where they would receive their detailed D-Day briefings and complete their final battle preparations before boarding ships and aircraft bound for France.

At precisely one minute to midnight on 25 May all the transit camps and embarkation points were simultaneously sealed. No one would be allowed in or out of the staging areas unless they had a specially signed pass. Even the NAAFI staff in the camps had volunteered to be confined with the troops they served in mess tents and dining halls. Despite their common incarceration, the troops were forbidden to talk to them and the girls who came from the local villages to stare at the troops behind the wire were quickly chased away by military policemen patrolling the perimeter. Leave was cancelled, telephone boxes were locked and any mail was to be left unopened for the censor; it would not be dispatched until the troops had departed.

The invasion date was set for 5 June. Secured behind the wire and armed guards, and with all communications with the outside world severed, the 156,000 Allied soldiers, commandos and thousands of airmen who would take part in Operation Overlord could finally be briefed on the location of their D-Day objectives and the timings of the assault. Issuing the detailed orders set in motion the biggest combined operation the world had ever seen, one that would be difficult to stop once it had begun.

Arrival and incarceration in the staging areas was the culmination of nearly two years of training. As men stowed their kit, familiarized themselves with camp routine and sought out their mates among the tight-knit rows of canvas and guy ropes, the air buzzed with a palpable sense of imminence and expectation. 9 PARA shared their transit camp with the 1st Battalion the Royal Ulster Rifles who were one of the units of 6th Airborne Division's brigade of glider troops.

The only permanent structures in the camp were a wooden mess hall and a large briefing hut, which was under constant guard. The day after arriving in the camp, the battalion watched in eager anticipation as the company commanders and battalion staff officers of the CO's 'orders group' filed out of the briefing hut. They knew what it meant: the battalion's company commanders had been given their orders for D-Day. Parry, Smith, Ian Dyer and Harold Bestley divulged nothing of what they had been told when they returned to their company lines. The next day it was the turn of the subalterns to be briefed by their company commanders.

Hugh Pond remembered the drama of the moment, when a huge map of the Normandy coast was unrolled, and in the middle of it was a single red dot denoting the Merville Battery. Pond was impressed by the variety of air photographs on display; in one he could make out a Norman farmer waving at the aircraft as it made a low pass overhead. Alan Jefferson was struck by the detail of the large-scale model of the gun position and the surrounding countryside. The model makers of RAF Medmenham had created a work of intricate and detailed art, which captured individual bomb craters and trees. He later noted how it was kept up to date and new craters were dug out with a pin every time fresh reconnaissance photos were made available. Gazing at it for the first time was just like 'looking at the real thing from high in the air through a cloudless sky'. The platoon commanders drew confidence from the level of detail and effort taken to provide them with so much information, which surpassed anything they had seen during training.

Using the model and array of maps and photos, the topographical features of the ground over which they would fight were outlined. The marshy ground of irrigation channels and ditches along the line of the River Dives were reported as being deliberately flooded by the Germans to a depth of nine feet. It was not lost on the platoon commanders that the eastern edge of the cultivated fields where they would drop was worryingly close to the flooded area, while the southern edge of DZ 'V' was spotted with the leg-breaking hazards of orchards and buildings around the village of Varaville. They also noted the routes leading through the high-banked lanes and thick hedgerows of brambles and hawthorn of the Norman bocage, which spread across the Bréville Ridge to the village of Merville. From the model and photographs they were updated on the enemy and the damage inflicted to the battery by RAF bombing. Informed that none of the gun casemates had been penetrated, they hoped that the planned raid by 100 Lancaster and Halifax bombers against the battery, immediately prior to their own attack, might have more success.

The young officers scribbled furiously, noting down the details that they would re-brief to their men when they issued their own orders. The battalion's mission was confirmed and repeated twice, exactly as Otway had given it the day before to his company commanders.

9 PARA is to:
Capture and destroy the enemy battery at grid: 1556776 by P Hour minus 30 minutes.
  [then] Destroy enemy radar station at Sallenelles 132766.
  [then] Seize and hold the high ground area of the area of Le Plein at grid square 1375 until relieved by 1st Special Services Brigade.
  [then] Deny enemy movement on the roads Franceville Plage to Sallenelles and Franceville Plage to the road junction at Bréville.

It was a five-phase operation: drop, attack the battery, regroup, attack the radar station at Sallenelles as a secondary objective and then consolidate in the village of Le Plein on the high ground of the Bréville Ridge and hold the area against German forces attempting to attack towards the beaches. The critical task was to assault and silence the Merville Battery, which would have to be achieved thirty minutes before the coming of first light, or 'P Hour' which was calculated as being at 0525 hours on Monday, 5 June.

While the likes of Pond and Jefferson received their orders, the men enjoyed the glorious sunshine. Stripped to the waist, they played football, drew kit and queued for warm beer and tea at 9d a time in the NAAFI. They were issued with French francs, most of which were gambled away in the first few hours of receiving them. Every man's hair was cropped short as a precaution against lice and they were given three condoms as a precaution against VD, which was considered by the military high command to be rife among French women. They sewed parachutist escape kits, consisting of two brass button compasses, silk maps of France and a four-inch saw blade encased in a black rubber, into the lining of their smocks and battle-dress trousers. Unlike many of the transit camps holding normal units, they had no professional entertainers; the security risk was considered to be too great. Instead they performed their own skits, which parodied their officers, themselves and their predicament. In the film tent, movies were shown throughout the day and night. Fred Glover thought it incongruous that one film, which played repeatedly, featured the Delta River Boys band playing the song 'Dem Bones' as two skeletons danced in ominous rhythm across the makeshift screen.

There was a more serious edge to their final battle preparations, as they constantly cleaned, oiled and checked their weapons. The men had a degree of choice in how they armed themselves for the coming battle, as long as all main issued sidearms were carried in accordance with their individual roles in a rifle company or specialist weapons platoon. The officers, NCOs and those who crewed the Vickers medium machine guns or were part of the glider assault party carried Sten guns.

Although a platoon sergeant, Paddy Jenkins carried the standard rifleman's Lee Enfield. Heavier and longer than the Sten, and with a much lower rate of fire, he liked its reliability, greater range and the accuracy it afforded. Carrying a rifle was not an option for Newton. His height and weight meant he was one of six men in the glider assault party chosen to carry a Life-Buoy flamethrower weighing 117 pounds. With a gas canister igniter and fluid laced with petroleum jelly, it could shoot out a sticky flaming jet that could immolate a man at twenty-five metres. It could also eject a flash fluid to suck out the oxygen and burn out the defenders of an enemy bunker. It was a terrible weapon, but its lethal characteristics made it an ideal tool for G-B Force: the codename given to the glider troops in honour of their commander Gordon-Brown. Geoff Pattinson had been identi-fied as a marksman and had been sent on a two-week sniper course; now he faced the task of protecting his Mark 3.5x telescopic sniper sight so that it would not lose its zero during the shock of crash-landing in the back of a Horsa. The men supplemented their lethal array of weaponry with fighting knives, US .45 Colt pistols if they could get their hands on them, 36 Mills grenades and anti-tank Gammon bombs. Regardless of rank or role, every man carried a spare canvas bandolier of .303 ammunition and two slabs of plastic explosive.

Forty-eight hours after the company commanders received their orders and cascaded them to their young officers, each platoon com-mander was allocated fifteen minutes to brief his platoon using the model room and its maps and photos. The men were equally fascin-ated with the level of detail and measures taken to provide them with every conceivable aspect of information they would need about their target. Like their officers they drew comfort from it. Much conformed to the rehearsals at the Inkpen, which was a great advan-tage when Otway gave confirmatory orders to the whole battalion in the mess tent on 30 May. But despite the men's familiarity with the outline concept of operations, they hung on his every word. Utterly absorbed, they noted every detail: that the drop would be made from 500 feet, the arrangements of the lights on the DZ to guide them to the battalion RV and the passwords and codewords that would signify friend or foe and success or failure.

The challenge of 'Punch', to be replied to with 'Judy', might have been unimaginative, but it would stick in the minds of men as they stumbled around the DZ in the dark looking for their comrades. The codewords had greater significance. 'Hammer' would mean that the battery had been destroyed and would be sent to HMS *Arethusa* by the attached Royal Navy observation party. If they sent 'Hugh' it would mean that the battery had not been taken and would be raked by the ship's six-inch guns in a last desperate effort to silence it before the troops landed on Sword Beach. They were informed of the back-up signals of using yellow smoke to denote success and that a carrier pigeon would be on hand to send word if all else failed. Otway ran through the timings and stressed the importance of completing their mission by 0530, when the *Arethusa* would open fire if she had not heard from 9 PARA. He emphasized the need to concentrate quickly after making the jump and ordered that they were to make their way as fast as possible to the battalion RV and not to engage in private battles with any Germans they might encounter. As they filed out of the mess tent they were reminded about the lethal reality of what they were about to do.

Gordon Newton remembers hearing a loud explosion, followed by a quick succession of other ear-splitting cracks as a large black smoke ring rose above the tents of the Royal Ulster Rifles. The Irish soldiers had been priming grenades, someone had fumbled, a pin had been pulled inadvertently and the first explosion set off more grenades, killing an officer and wounding several others, as fragments shredded through canvas and flesh. The scene was one of pandemonium and devastation as smashed bodies lay among splintered tent poles and pools of blood. For men who had never seen death and injury it was a shocking sight, but veterans like William Cunningham had seen it all before. As the RSM and the senior soldier in the battalion, Cunningham was the rock that junior soldiers looked up to. He told the 9 PARA men around him to forget it, to go back to their tents and concentrate on their mission. But for men like Newton, who were not veterans, it was a sobering sight and engendered a sombre mood as they considered their own fragile mortality.

Whether through exuberance, negligence or pure random bad luck, such accidents were an inevitable consequence of mixing vast

quantities of ammunition with large numbers of men. Similar accidents were to occur throughout the Allied transit camps and 9 PARA
would not be immune. Shortly after the tragedy in the RUR lines,
Lance Corporal Edward Hull was hit in the neck by a stray 9mm
round that had been accidentally discharged by an officer as he
cleaned his Sten gun on the other side of the camp's sports field
during a football match. By weird geometry of chance, the bullet
missed all the players, but struck Hull as he walked along the touch-
line. He was to die from his wounds just after D-Day. The Sten's
propensity to discharge itself accidentally, if dropped or when being
stripped, was a concern to the authorities for another reason: any
soldier wishing to avoid battle through a self-inflicted wound could
claim that his Sten had gone off by chance while he cleaned it. Hugh
Pond had to work hard to convince the CO and adjutant that one of
his men should not be court-martialled when he wounded himself in
the leg; and the fact that the man was utterly devastated when he
realized that he would not be going to Normandy helped his case.

Tragedy and accidents were quickly forgotten as the tempo of
battle preparations – of briefings, drawing and packing kit – increased
as the days counted down. In the afternoon of 2 June 9 PARA was
addressed by the divisional commander. General Gale might have
struck an unusual figure with his ruddy face and Poona moustache,
wearing an open Denison smock, riding breeches and standard issue
Army boots, but what he said to the ranks of the battalion squashed
into the mess tent was inspirational. He pulled no punches about the
risks that lay ahead of them. Drawing on the intelligence reports
the men had already received, he made reference to the fact that they
would expect to face opposition from three enemy infantry divisions,
the 711th, 716th and 346th. Gale was also aware that it had been
reported that 21st Panzer Division had moved into the Caen area on
23 May. He reinforced the point that along with 12th SS Panzer
Division they would be within striking distance of two of Rommel's
premier armoured formations as well. He stressed the importance of
their role in stopping the panzers from reaching the beaches and
joked about killing German tanks on the receiving end of the 6th
Airborne Division's anti-tank guns. Gale was charismatic and played

to his audience's thirst for action and their collective self-confidence that came from being part of an elite band of fighting men. He finished by telling them, 'Only a fool would think of going where we are going. That's why I'm going!' The emphasis on the 'we', his use of humour and the fact that he would be with them at the heart of the action produced a rousing cheer from the packed ranks of the battalion. The men knew Gale, had confidence in him, and what he said to them that hot stuffy day inside the mess hall bolstered them enormously.

The station commander of RAF Broadwell also drew a cheer when he spoke to the battalion after Gale and told them that his Dakota squadrons had never missed a DZ. He omitted to tell them that making a mass parachute drop over enemy territory was something they had never done before. Nor did he tell them that many of his crews were inexperienced and had been drafted into his squadrons at short notice or straight out of flight school to develop an entirely new capability and reach operational standards with brand-new aircraft in just five months. A large number of the crews' operational experience was limited to the odd leaflet-dropping flight over France. But while the bulk of the unit would be dropped from the DC-47s of 512 Squadron based at Broadwell, not all of those parachuting in would do so from Dakotas. Parry and Smith's RV and reconnaissance parties would jump from an Albemarle aircraft from 295 Squadron based at RAF Harwell in Berkshire.

The Albemarles would also carry the divisional pathfinders, who would jump thirty minutes ahead of the main body, giving them time to mark the DZ with fluorescent Holophane lamps and Eureka beacons for the main stream of aircraft. While the pathfinders laid out the equipment, Parry would set up and mark the 9 PARA RV at the western edge of the drop zone. Simultaneously, Smith's small party would make their way to the battery, cut the wire of the outer perimeter and reconnoitre the position's defences.

The battalion spent the rest of the day and most of the night packing their equipment as they had been ordered to parade in full kit at 0900 the next morning, after which trucks would drive them to their respective airfields to draw their parachutes and pre-load forty

equipment containers into their aircraft. There would be no room for
sleeping bags, blankets and greatcoats, which would be handed in to
the quartermaster before they departed, but they would have to take
enough ammunition, water and rations to last them for forty-eight
hours. The heavier weapons, such as the Vickers medium machine
guns and three-inch mortars, would be packed in the containers
along with radios and extra ammunition, but much of what they
needed would have to be carried by the men when they jumped.
They worked into the small hours, as they debated the merits of what
to take, where to carry it and what to leave behind. Was it better to
take an extra couple of grenades, a Gammon bomb or a bandolier of
ammunition in addition to the kit, arms and ammunition they were
mandated to take?

Fred Glover set out his kit in his tent and made a mental inventory
of what he would need to carry. It consisted of: his Sten gun, chest
rig containing six magazines, extra boxes of 9mm ammo, two 36
Mills hand grenades, anti-tank grenade, two slabs of plastic explosive,
two phosphorus grenades, spare bandolier of .303 ammunition for
the Bren guns, gas mask, gas cape, toggle rope, double-edged
Fairbairn-Sykes fighting knife, entrenching tool, yellow ground-to-
air recognition panel, two twenty-four-hour ration packs, mess tins,
mug, knife, spoon and fork, water bottle, washing and shaving kit,
spare socks, torch, pocket knife, shell dressings, morphine, escape
kit, Denison smock, beret, jump helmet, spare underclothing, battledress jacket, webbing, large pack, French francs and French letters.
Officers and senior NCOs also had to carry map cases, binoculars, a
compass and a small black Bakelite bird whistle, which James Hill had
directed all officers to carry to be used to rally their men in the dark
and lead them to the RV.

Certain items had to be packed according to regulations: the small
toothpaste-like morphine 'tubonic' with its cork-capped needle was
carried between two shell dressings in the front of the Denison smock
and two additional shell dressings were carried in the back pockets of
the battledress trousers. Apart from the extra padding the dressings
provided to help protect backsides and morphine, every man would
know where his comrade's dressings were carried, should he need to

dress his wounds or administer pain relief. Each man took care of where he packed his phosphorus grenades; if hit by shrapnel or a bullet, they had a tendency to ignite and no one relished the prospect of being burned to death. Every item would also have to be stowed to avoid it becoming a snagging hazard in the aircraft or when they jumped. Rifles and Bren guns were sewn into felt-covered valises while Sten guns could be carried across the front of the chest under jump jackets. Back packs and webbing were squeezed into leg bags; rations were broken up and stuffed into pockets and down the front of smocks along with pistols, command kit and grenades. Each man carried over 100 pounds. Smaller men sagged visibly at the knees. When Gordon Newton first stood up carrying his kit as well as the Life-Buoy flamethrower, he immediately fell down under the combined weight of over 200 pounds. The next trial for the men would be to try to get their parachute harness to fit over all the kit they carried.

Dawn on 3 June was clear and cool, as the men shouldered their loads and made their way to the trucks that would take them to the airfields to draw and fit their chutes and 'bomb up' the aircraft with the containers. Most men could not help noticing that the breeze had freshened. It was D-Day minus one and the wind speed was important; anything over ten to fifteen knots would make for a hard landing and increase the risk of injury. At Broadwell, the men had a chance to meet their aircrew and were issued with a chute. Its acceptance was subject to superstitions prevalent among men who are about to go into battle. A worn or dirty chute could be rejected and some men refused to accept a chute whose number ended in a double zero and would ask to be given another one with a 'luckier number'.

It was a two-man job to extend and fit the four web straps over shoulders and between legs and then work each of them across bulging pockets and smocks to click them home into the quick-release mechanism on the front of the chest. Once they were done, each chute was taken off and placed on the parachutist's aircraft seat, twenty chutes to each Dakota, with the man's last two regimental numbers chalked on its canvas bag. It would be retrieved and refitted an hour before take-off when they emplaned for France on D-Day.

The one member of 9 PARA who carried no kit and thoroughly enjoyed the attention of having his specially designed chute fitted to him by his handler was a large black and tan Alsatian dog called Glenn. The dog was trained to sniff out explosives and Germans due to their distinctive smell. He also loved jumping and had been trained to stand still on landing, when a small red light on his collar would help his handler, Private E.S. 'Jack' Corteil, to find him on the drop zone. Nineteen-year-old Corteil had a reputation as a lovable rogue and had been caught poaching in Bulford. Parry was his company commander and recognized that young Corteil needed something to occupy him. As a suitable punishment he was tasked to look after Glenn. The two became inseparable, and in turn the pair found a place in the affections of the whole of 9 PARA.

With the chutes fitted to men and dog, the containers were loaded under the wings of the Dakotas and fitted into the bomb bays of the Albemarles. The stick commander or dispatcher would release each container by pulling on a lever located in the aircraft's fuselage after the first half of the stick had jumped. Each container carried a light to denote its contents that would glow on impact: red for heavy weapons, ammunition and explosives, blue for water and ammunition, and white for medical supplies. Parry was unimpressed by the Albemarle as he watched the containers being loaded into its bomb bay. The fuselage was cramped and uncomfortable and had to be reached by crawling on all fours under the belly of the aircraft through a small crew compartment; and there were no seats to stow the parachutes. The jump exit was a hole cut into the floor of the fuselage, albeit larger than the drop hole in a Whitley; it would be a pig of an aircraft to jump from.

If Parry was less than inspired at the prospect of having to parachute from an Albemarle, the glider pilots who would fly the Horsa gliders of G–B Force from RAF Brize Norton were also having last-minute concerns about the suitability of their aircraft. The six pilots from B Squadron of the GPR had also been incarcerated in the transit camp with 9 PARA. Like all the glider and transport pilots, they had been briefed in detail on their mission and had spent hours studying the models and air photographs in detail. But despite their best-laid plans, detailed preparation and weeks of specialist flying to perfect their pinpoint landing skills, a critical aspect of their part in the operation had been overlooked.

On 2 June the pilots were informed that the three glider aircraft that would carry the fifty-eight men of G–B Force had been modified to carry Rebecca transmitters/responders in order to pick up a signal from a Eureka beacon that would be positioned at the rear of the battery. The problem was that none of them had attended the necessary two-week course to learn how to use the equipment. Issued with a special pass to leave the camp, they completed a two-day crash course on the system only to discover that while the gliders they had been allocated for the mission had had Rebeccas installed, the arrester parachutes they would need to make a short-stop landing between the gun casemates had been fitted to different gliders. A series of frantic telephone calls to their battalion headquarters at Netheravon, using veiled speech to preserve the sensitivity of the issue, resolved the problem at the eleventh hour, but with D-Day almost upon them, there would be no time to flight-test the Horsas that they would fly into battle.

Before returning to the transit camp, the various elements of 9 PARA carried out aircraft dinghy drills and practised donning their Mae Wests in the event of having to ditch in the Channel. With their final preparations complete, the battalion regrouped to spend their final night in their bell tents. As the last vestiges of light drained from the western sky, the haggard face of fear stalked the lines of the transit camp. 9 PARA had been banned from drinking, but men about to go into battle find little difficulty in accessing alcohol. They played cards, recklessly gambling money that in a few hours' time could very well have little value or meaning. They wrote letters, or made another trip to the NAAFI for a weak cup of tea, but their minds kept drifting back to the model, that red dot on the map and what it would all mean when they attacked the battery. Each man dealt with his fear differently, but every man felt it: some became withdrawn and reflective, others grew more boisterous, cracked jokes and engaged in banter; non-smokers smoked, non-drinkers drank and non-believers started believing.

As the dawn of D–Day approached a collective dread settled over the transit camps across southern England. In many of the conscripted line units there was an air of impending doom as the hours counted down. The men of 9 PARA shared many of the emotions of those about to go into combat, but their collective ethos marked out para-troopers from the vast majority of ordinary soldiers. Men like Pond, Jefferson, Jenkins, Pattinson and Glover had all volunteered and put themselves through the mill of selection and testing in order to be there. It didn't stop them being scared, but no one wanted to be left behind, which engendered excitement mixed with trepidation. Where there was abject fear it was well hidden. Newton's biggest concern was of making a fool of himself and letting his mates down. Paddy Jenkins had similar worries as a junior leader. If his platoon commander was killed, he knew he would have to take over and was anxious as to whether he would measure up. Whatever their fears, when darkness gathered over the transit camp and the lights in the bell tents began to go out, all agreed that the waiting was the worst, as they glanced at their watches, waited for sleep to come and thought expectantly of the morrow.

In spite of their apprehensions, with take-off scheduled for the late evening of the next day, the battalion was primed and ready to go. But as 9 PARA sought a last night of rest, SHAEF's meteorological staff at Eisenhower's headquarters at Southwick House near Portsmouth were grappling with a very different enemy coming from an entirely different direction. Since the end of May they had been nervously watching an anticyclone forming up over the Azores that threatened to break up the fine weather that had prevailed through-out May. By Saturday, 3 June, it was obvious that the storm was about to break in the Channel, bringing high winds, a low rolling cloud base and heavy seas, which would preclude operations on 4 and 5 June. The weather conditions required for D-Day to be a success were precise. The Allies needed a low tide one hour before dawn to unveil the beach obstacles for the naval and air bombardment before the landing craft hit the shoreline at half-tide. The RAF needed a near full moon to conduct parachute and bombing operations during the preceding night, while Para operations needed a maximum wind speed of not more than fifteen knots. The ominous storm clouds that threatened to jeopardize the invasion were already visible in the distant horizon of the fading light of Saturday evening when Eisenhower decided to delay the operation by twenty-four hours.

When 9 PARA awoke the next morning the battalion knew nothing of the postponement as they paraded at the vehicle park in full kit. The first drops of rain were spotting the canvas of the bell tents while the men were preparing to head to the embarkation airfields when the decision to delay reached them at 0830 hours. Having been physically and mentally prepared to go, the news that the jump had been postponed came as a shock. For some it brought an immediate sense of relief: another day to live; but for others it meant another twenty-four hours of agonizing waiting: having got this far, they wanted to get the job done. But to Otway and his adjutant, Captain Hal Hudson, it was a blessed relief. As the principal staff officer in the battalion for the administration and movement of 750 men when all the battalion group's attached arms personnel were included, Hudson had worked himself to the point of exhaustion in the preceding weeks. His workload had been relentless as he organized equipment tables, logistics planning, air procedures and dealt with all personnel issues, from ensuring that every man completed his will on Army Form B2089 in the back of his pay book, to dealing with discipline matters, such as the wounding of Lance Corporal Hull. For once he had nothing to do, at least for the next twenty-four hours.

Otway, too, had also been under considerable strain and had been driving himself hard for weeks. He carried the heavy burden of responsibility for the lives of hundreds of men; not only those who would attack the battery, but also those who would die on the beaches if he failed in his mission. By the time he reached the transit camp he was shattered by his task, withdrawn and riven with self-doubt. He questioned whether he was fit enough to command the battalion, whether he had got the planning right and whether he had missed something. Although not popular, his officers nonetheless had great faith in him and the stress he felt was also a reflection of how seriously he took the lives of his men, which were in his hands.

As the weather grew steadily worse, Otway's men were in sombre mood, but they were to draw faith from their remarkable padre, the Revd John Gwinnett, who would be jumping into action with them, but as a man of the cloth he would be unarmed. He was a para-trooper's vicar with an empathy with the men, and often overlooked their waywardness and 9 PARA loved him for it. Many of the Paras would not have attended his church parades in Bulford by choice, but they packed into the drumhead service the delay now allowed him to hold that Sunday. Their attendance reinforced the fact that soldiers often find themselves closer to God on the eve of battle. During the service Gwinnett dedicated a battalion flag made from silk by ladies from the Women's Voluntary Services in Oxford. The coupons for the silk had been donated by some of the battalion's wives and Gordon Newton was nominated to carry it into action, which was testament to their faith that his glider would make it into the battery. But it was the words that Gwinnett had used when addressing his flock in the transit camp that imbued the men to whom he ministered with a moral strength. Part of his sermon con-tained the anonymous words:

> Fear knocked on the door
> Faith opened it
> And there was nobody there.

After the sermon James Hill addressed the officers; no doubt he detected their mood because, like the men they commanded, most had never been in action before and he needed to steel them against the unexpected. He told them, 'Gentlemen, in spite of your excellent orders and training, do not be daunted if chaos reigns. It undoubtedly will.' His words were to be prophetic.

Later that Sunday, the worst of the storm from the Atlantic broke in the Channel and across the southern coast of England. For the next two days the rain lashed down from low rushing clouds and the wind howled with a savagery that lifted tents from guy ropes and blew the briefing marquee over. The temperature dropped and the sprawling camp turned into a sea of mud, as men bailed out their sleeping quar-ters, dug makeshift irrigation channels and sat morosely inside their tents as the wind and rain battered against the canvas. More unfortunate were the thousands of troops already embarked on ships off the coast of Portsmouth and Southampton. Some had been on board for two or three days already, and seasickness was rife as two-metre waves hurled themselves against the landing craft and troop ships, making them buck and strain at their anchors. Codenamed Operation Neptune, the seaborne element of the invasion force now felt the full wrath of the sea god.

As HMS *Mauritius* rocked at her own anchor off the Isle of Wight, astern of her fellow light cruiser the *Arethusa*, Midshipman John Carlill marvelled at the huge armada of 5,000 ships, landing craft and escorts moored across the Solent as far as Spithead. He thought of the poor 'Army sods on the flat bottom boats', which lacked the deep steadying keel of a large naval fighting ship. It made him glad to be in the Navy, not least as it meant that he would not be wading ashore and fighting across the beaches into the teeth of German machine guns and artillery. With the *Arethusa*, HMS *Mauritius* formed part of the naval task force that would support the 6th Airborne Division with their six-inch guns. They had sailed to join the other ships in the task force on 2 June and Carlill, the signals officer, could not help noticing that they were close to D-Day, as he read the Morse code traffic, which spoke of mine-clear routes across the Channel and bombardment duties. But unlike the Army, the Navy were on operations the moment they put to sea and faced the constant risk of being torpedoed or attacked by enemy aircraft. Consequently, when news of the postponement was announced over the Tannoy by the captain, the crew simply went to breakfast.

In SHAEF headquarters the Supreme Commander fretted. If the Allies didn't attack in the next forty-eight hours the required tides and moon state would not coincide again until 19 June. He could not let the troops out of the transit camps, or back off the ships without compromising the secrecy of D-Day. But nor was keeping them bottled up for another two weeks an option and continued maintenance of the crowded staging areas would soon become a security issue in itself. At 2100 hours that Sunday evening he met his meteorological team and force commanders. The meteorologists predicted a small break in the weather on Tuesday, 6 June, when conditions were assessed to be marginal at best. Ike consulted his team; only Air Chief Marshal Sir Trafford Leigh-Mallory was pessimistic, but said his aircraft could operate in the forecast conditions. The Supreme Commander paused, looked at those gathered around him and quietly said, 'Okay, we'll go.'

Sid Capon had no idea of the decision Ike and his force commanders had taken in the library at Southwick House when he rose late on Monday, 5 June. It was still cold, but the rain had eased to a light drizzle and the wind that brought it across the sprawling camp had lost much of the fury of the day before. As he noted the improvement, he groaned inwardly and thought of the jump he still had to make. Oh God, it would have been over by now, he thought. Later that morning, Otway received the signal confirming that the invasion was on. Hill gathered the officers of his brigade together and told them, 'Gentlemen, the wind on the Continent is five to ten miles per hour, the operation is on; we go tonight.' The buzz went round the camp before the officers had officially briefed the men. Gordon Newton passed on what he had heard from Gordon-Brown's batman: 'Shit or bust; we go tonight!'

Enforced rest was ordered on the afternoon of the 5th, but for most men sleep proved elusive. Some wrote letters and drew on the words Gwinnett had used in his sermon to try to sum up to parents and loved ones how they felt and give them some form of comfort in what might be a last letter home. Sergeant Major Jack Harries lay on his camp bed and thought of his five-year-old daughter, his wife and the baby she was expecting. Doug Tottle, a medic in the field ambulance section, thought about a girl he had met in Crookham and the fights he used to have with the Yanks in the Rose and Crown on Salisbury Plain; he wondered whether he would ever drink there again. Like most men, Jenkins contemplated death. He considered filling in the will form in the back of his Army pay book, then thought better of it. He had a feeling that he would come through it and anyway, like the majority of his colleagues in 9 PARA, he didn't have much to leave to anyone.

A last meal was served at teatime in the mess tent, but few felt like

eating, although they collected flasks of warm water and jam sandwiches for the flight across the Channel, since they were thought to
guard against airsickness. The meal was also deliberately low fat for
the same reason, which did little to encourage its consumption. The
last few hours before the camp's assembly bell sounded were spent
dressing, making last-minute equipment checks, chain-smoking and
waiting. When the bell sounded, they once again shouldered their
equipment and weapons, lifted their leg bags and headed to the
motor transport park. It was 1900 hours on the adjusted D-1. The
whole battalion group formed up, minus the fifty-eight men of G-B
Force, who would depart an hour later for RAF Harwell with the
Jeeps and anti-tank guns that would be loaded into the stores-carrying
gliders.

The main body paraded, were counted off and then began loading
their equipment on to the trucks that would take them the short
distance to the airfields. Men made a dash to the long queues at the
latrines, then shook hands with mates in different platoons and companies and said they would see each other on the ground. As the
trucks drove out of the transit camp, they passed members of the battalion who would not be jumping. The men of Captain Bill Mills's
logistic group, which would move to France later by sea, stood to
attention with the members of G-B Force. They saluted as the trucks
passed. The Irishmen of the Ulster Rifles who had also gathered to
see them off cheered. The NAAFI girls cried as they waved and
wondered how many of the young men who waved back at them
would be returning. As the convoy turned into RAF Broadwell they
passed airmen and WAAFs walking out of the airbase gates in the
other direction; their day's work done, they were heading to the local
pubs and dance halls. It highlighted the gap between what they were
about to do and normal everyday life that continued around them as
they went to war.

The trucks took them straight to the Dakotas lined up along the
apron of the runway, where they met their pilots. The ground crews
had spent the last thirty-six hours painting the aircrafts' wings and
fuselage with black and white recognition stripes using paint mixed
from distemper powder and water. They were awestruck as they

watched the paratroopers climb from their trucks, each man a fearsome walking arsenal with close-cropped hair and blackened face, and marvelled at how they would be able to jump with all the kit they carried, let alone fight with it when the time came. They were also glad that they were not the ones who would be meeting them in battle. The aircraft engines had already been run up before the troops and aircrew arrived. The carburettors had been drained of condensation and the oil and cylinder pressure of each Pratt and Whitney engine checked. Each of the three flights of ten DC-47s was ready. The apron at the edge of the concrete runway now turned into a hive of activity as the troops prepared to emplane.

Otway moved among his men and wished them luck as they re-smeared their faces black with burned cork, drank tea, smoked cigarettes and completed six copies of their flight manifest list; twenty men to each of the thirty-two Dakotas. Everyone's mind was on the Met forecast and it attracted much comment as they waited to board. The evening sky had begun to clear, but as the last light of 5 June faded from the western horizon, the wind was still up and the men watched the tree branches swaying at the edges of the runway. Paddy Jenkins reckoned it was blowing twenty knots and gusting up to thirty; never before had he been so preoccupied with the weather. An hour before take-off they drained their last dregs of tea before searching out their chutes in the gathering gloom inside the Dakotas.

Men took a last chance to relieve themselves at the side of the aircraft then set about trying to refit their chutes. The harnesses had to be readjusted to fit over extra ammunition and items of kit that had been crammed into pockets, down the front of smocks and under jump jackets. The nervous tension was palpable and men cursed as they wrestled with the retaining straps to get their metal lugs to click home into the quick-release mechanism. Some could hardly stand, bent over like hags under the weight of kitbags, weapons and parachute packs and had to help each other climb up the thin portside metal steps into the aircraft. Hobbled by their leg bags, the Paras dragged themselves to their seats. Most were too heavily laden to strap into the benches that ran along either side of the fuselage and sat on the floor. Unencumbered, Glenn the Alsatian search dog scampered eagerly through the jump door followed by Jack Corteil who was so heavy that he had to be assisted by two other paratroopers. As the last of the paratroopers struggled aboard, the pilots completed their pre-flight checks; their minds were also on the weather and most thought that it looked marginal.

At RAF Harwell Allen Parry had a horrendous time getting into his harness beside his Albemarle, but he was in an exuberant mood. Having been evacuated from the beaches of Dunkirk four years before, he sensed that a moment of history was upon them and felt fortunate to be part of it. Although still bitterly disappointed not to be commanding the glider force, he was glad to be finally released from the incarceration of the transit camp. Parry gave up trying to fit his chute over the Aldis lamp he carried to mark the RV and managed to stuff the lamp into his leg bag. His mood soured as he struggled to get into the plane after crawling under its belly to the crew hatch where it took an enormous effort to climb the ladder and lever himself into the cramped interior with nine other men. They sweated and swore at each other as they tried to get comfortable. There was no room for Parry to attach his leg bag properly so he made do with tying one leg strap round his ankle. Smith also struggled to refit his chute. He dispensed with his leg bag and stuffed his respirator and large pack under his jump jacket. By the time he had finished he resembled a pregnant duck and only just managed to squeeze himself aboard the Albemarle by 2300 hours. Ten minutes later they taxied into line with six other Albemarle bombers carrying sixty pathfinders and began taking off into the coming darkness.

At Broadwell urine tins were passed aboard as the main body sat loaded and ready for take-off, although cocooned in harnesses and bulging jump jackets made fumbling open a fly during the flight a near impossibility. The atmosphere in the back of each aircraft was subdued, and the banter had died away as men withdrew into themselves. Paddy Jenkins thought of his men, his command responsibilities and one member of his platoon in particular, who sat further down the fuselage in the number four position. Paddy knew the young man had domestic problems; hardly the right frame of mind to make a jump into enemy territory. As a precaution, the corporal jumping immediately behind him had been briefed to watch him and make sure he went out of the door.

Two minutes after the Albemarle aircraft left Harwell, the Dakotas began to take off from Broadwell on a flight plan that would see them arrive over the drop zone thirty minutes behind the Albemarles. Inside the cockpit of the lead aircraft, Wing Commander Coventry completed his pre-flight check and flicked on two master switches; he watched the engine lights on his instrument panel illuminate and listened to the whine of the energizer button as it wound up. When it reached the right pitch, he pressed the starter button. The first engine coughed into life, the prop sputtered, feathered and then its propellers blurred into a single spinning disc as the cylinder engine caught and roared into life. The sequence was repeated to start the second engine, while the fuselage began to rattle and vibrate. He released the brakes and eased the throttle forward and began to taxi out to the end of the runway. When he reached the end of the long concrete strip he turned his aircraft into the wind and stopped.

The other twenty-nine Dakotas of 512 Squadron followed on behind, bumping and swaying as they adjusted their rudders to form up in line astern behind their squadron commander. At a signal from the control tower, Coventry pushed on the power. Private Ron Tucker noticed the increasing vibration as the aircraft strained against the brakes and he felt the definite pull as they came off and the aircraft surged down the runway. He looked around him. The blackened faces of the rest of his stick wedged tight among their kitbags and weapons sleeves were caught in the dim glow of the interior lights. He felt the tail wheel come up as the Dakota gained speed, and wondered whether they would get airborne with so much weight on board. As the main wheels of the first aircraft started to lift, the station personnel lining the edge of the runway waved and cheered. They watched the aircraft climb into the darkening sky one after the other and circle the airfield as they waited to form up in 'vics'. Flight Sergeant Bill Perry's Dakota was last to take off. Fifteen minutes after the first aircraft had lifted, he joined the rest of the squadron in formation. Those on the ground watched his aircraft until it smudged into obscurity in the blackness of the southern horizon.

The men of G–B Force would take off in their gliders two hours after the Dakotas from RAF Brize Norton. Having cheered and saluted the main body as it left the transit camp ahead of them, they were keen to escape the eerie stillness that had descended over the empty tent lines. They saw the Dakotas climb into the sky from the nearby airfield and watched as the interior lights were switched out one by one. It made them keener still to be on their way.

When they arrived at their airhead, they marched to their gliders and were met by their pilots who were also dressed for battle. Gordon Newton had shed some of his kit, so that he could carry his flamethrower, but his load was still well over 100 pounds and he wondered whether the Horsa would be able to lift with the weight of men and equipment it carried. Every space was crammed with extra ammunition and explosives. With his flamethrower between his feet, Newton couldn't help feeling that they were flying into battle in a wooden tinderbox. The luminous skull and crossbones symbol each man had been ordered to paint on the left breast of his smock as a last-minute recognition measure to avoid being shot by his own side, shone ominously. Pond thought it was a stupid act of bravado and his platoon rubbed dirt on them to deaden their glow.

As the troops sat facing each other along either side of the long canvas-skinned fuselages of their Horsas, they could hear the roar of the Stirling bombers' four engines as they built up power. The glider began to sway as the prop wash blasted back over the light plywood frame. Outside, the RAF tow master waved a flag from side to side as the slack of the towrope was taken up by the tug aircraft. As it became taut he lifted the flag above his head and brought it down in a single movement to signal to the pilot that he was clear and ready for take-off.

Those in the back of the glider felt the tug of the thick hemp rope as the bomber began to pull them forward. At eighty miles per hour, the sixty-two-foot wings of the Horsa bit into the air and began to lift above and behind the tug aircraft, which was still powering along the runway. Looking through the cockpit crew door, Newton could see the glow of the Stirling's exhausts. He didn't think it was going to lift before it ran out of runway. But slowly the cumbersome combinations of tug and glider climbed into the sky and the flight paths that would take them towards Normandy.

As the Dakotas, Albemarles, Stirlings and Horsa gliders that flew 9 PARA streamed across the unseasonably cold night sky of southern England towards the coast, they were only one small element of a mighty host that formed up and aligned in coordinated groups. The DC-47s of 512 Squadron joined two other Dakota squadrons, which carried the bulk of 3rd Parachute Brigade. Flying in 'vic' formations of thirty-second intervals they converged to form part of 430 RAF aircraft and gliders of the GPR that carried 4,255 men of 6th Airborne Division's first wave of airborne troops. As they headed for an air navigation beacon set up at Worthing the dark sky was a vast aerial carpet of thousands of winking navigation lights. Beneath them lay the sleepy towns and villages of a country not yet alive to the fact that D-Day had started, and a massive air armada droned overhead. When his aircraft flew over Southampton, Ron Tucker thought of his girl-friend, somewhere thousands of feet below him, where she and her family would just have gone to bed. To the west of 6th Airborne Division, 822 aircraft of the American transport groups formed up and flew on a heading that would take the US 82nd and 101st air-borne divisions towards their drop zones on the right flank of the invasion beaches. With the fighter escorts and bombers that flew ahead of them, it was the biggest air package the world had ever seen.

As the flower of youth from Britain and America spearheaded the liberation of occupied Europe, Eisenhower sat in his headquarters at Southwick House. He had spent the earlier part of the day with the US paratroopers and watched planes of the 101st Airborne Division take off with tears in his eyes. The airborne operation was critical to the success of D-Day, but it was the part of the invasion plan that concerned him most. His own air chief, Air Marshal Sir Trafford Leigh-Mallory, who had been reticent about the weather, had previously written to the Supreme Commander warning him against using airborne troops against a heavily defended enemy. With the invasion of France irrevocably launched, the burden of responsibility and worry was reflected in a note Eisenhower had pre-drafted in the event of failure. In it he stated that if failure came, the responsibility for it would be his alone. As the aircraft swept on towards France, the men of 9 PARA were about to find out how the planning, training, intelligence assessments and predictions about the weather would stack up.

8

Storm Front

T HE STORM THAT broke in the Channel on 4 June rolled inland
across the coast of Normandy. It rained all the next day. It had
begun to abate by the time General Wilhelm Richter's conference
broke up at his headquarters at Rue de Geôle in Caen at 1900 hours.
During the conference, the commander of the 716th Division made
a passing reference to the prevailing moon and tides and the need for
his unit commanders to be alert to the risk of an Allied invasion. But
he gave it no real emphasis; it was simply a general warning that all
German formations on the Channel coast had been receiving at the
start of each month since the beginning of April.

There was nothing specific to indicate that the Allies would attack
and the bad weather over the last two days was unfavourable for
operations in the Channel. Richter was more interested in discussing
training and the continued improvements of the Atlantic Wall
defences in his division's sector of the Normandy coastline. He also
wanted to finish paperwork in his office and then go to bed, as he had
an early start the next day to attend a 7th Army war game at Rennes.
Most of Richter's fellow divisional commanders were already there,
or would travel to Rennes later that night.

Like most of the 7th Army divisional commanders on the night of
5 June, the commander of Army Group B was absent from his headquarters. Erwin Rommel had left the Château de La Roche-Guyon
near Mantes at 0600 hours the day before to drive to his home in
Germany near Ulm so he could spend the night with his wife Lucie.
It was her birthday on 6 June, but Rommel's main purpose for being
away from the front was to have an audience with Adolf Hitler at his
mountain retreat at Berchtesgaden near Munich. The Führer's staff

had indicated that Hitler might be able to see the field marshal later on 6 June. Nor was Rommel overly concerned about being absent from the front. German meteorologists at Western Forces headquarters in Paris had predicted the approach of the storm from data they had received from U-boats stationed far out in the Atlantic, and the heavy seas and high winds they forecast were considered unsuitable for any Allied attempt at landing.

Rommel had expected the Allies to take advantage of the excellent weather in May to launch their invasion. Now he was optimistic that an invasion would not come until the middle of June, when the tide and moon would once again be favourable. He also believed the Allies hoped to time their operations to coincide with the Soviets' delayed summer offensive in the east, which could not be launched until after a late spring thaw in Poland in the middle of the month. The commander of Army Group B had other reasons to be optimistic too.

His tireless efforts and constant inspections of the Atlantic Wall had led to vast improvements in the defences all along the coast. Millions of mines had been laid and every beach was a mass of obstacles and explosives that would rip the bottom out of landing craft. Every potential landing site for Allied airborne troops had also been strewn with anti-glider poles hewn from the surrounding pine plantations and forests. But Rommel knew gaps remained and despite the improvements to the static defences, they formed only a thin crust that would delay the Allies getting ashore. To defeat the invasion on the beaches, he would still need armoured units positioned sufficiently close enough to the coast to attack the Allies as they struggled ashore and before they could establish a defendable beachhead. For that he needed more panzers and Hitler was the only man who could supply them.

In Rommel's view the key would rest with the location and command arrangements of the better equipped panzer and panzer-grenadier divisions. On 23 May, 21st Panzer Division, with its ninety Mark IV 'Tiger' panzers, had been moved from Brittany to the eastern outskirts of Caen, which put it within striking distance of the Normandy beaches. At the beginning of June, 12th SS Panzer

(*Hitlerjugend*) Division had been declared ready for operations and had moved to positions near Falaise.

With its 20,504 men and 185 panzers, 81 of which were the more capable Panther tanks, 12th SS Panzer Division represented a considerable reinforcement. But to Rommel, the positioning of the SS division was still too far back from the coast. It would take two days for it to move to a position where it could launch an attack on the beaches and he doubted that it would arrive in time to influence the battle and help defeat the Allies on the shoreline. Additionally, he feared that much of its armour would be smashed by Allied airpower as it attempted to move over long exposed distances to the coast. But the division could not be moved from its current location without permission from von Rundstedt. His superior continued to maintain that the armoured forces should be held back to launch a single massive counterstroke against the Allies once they had landed and once their main point of effort had been identified. Consequently, what Rommel wanted most from his visit to Berchtesgaden was Hitler's permission to move 12th SS Division and place it under his direct command.

Rommel had reason to believe that his plea would fall on fertile ground when he met the Führer. On 6 May German headquarters in the west had received a signal from OKW regarding Hitler's assessment of where the Allies would land. The message was conveyed to Rommel by von Rundstedt and stated: 'The Führer is of the opinion that an invasion along a 500km-wide strip is unlikely . . . attacks will occur primarily in Normandy and to a lesser extent at Brittany. The most recent information once more points in this direction.' Four days later OKW issued another communiqué from the Führer, which reinforced his opinion that Normandy would be the 'first and foremost' point of concentration. Hitler also predicted that the attack would include heavy use of airborne landings under the cover of darkness. His assessment agreed with Rommel's view of the likelihood of an Allied landing south of the Somme, although it ran counter to the prevailing orthodoxy of the German military high command that the invasion would take place in the Pas de Calais area. Hitler's judgement resulted in the movement of troops to 7th Army's sector, most significantly the movement of 12th SS and 21st panzer divisions to new locations around Normandy. The Führer's communiqué was also the reason why the commander of 7th Army, General Friedrich Dollman, called his corps and divisional commanders together at Rennes on 6 June. The purpose of the exercise was to war-game a table-top exercise based on an Allied landing in Normandy involving both seaborne and airborne troops.

Hitler's assessment was prophetic, but in reality it was little more than a personal hunch based on intuition. There was no 'recent information' that indicated that the Allies were planning to land in Normandy. OKW and von Rundstedt maintained that the Pas de Calais was still the intended area because of the advantages Calais provided to the Allies: the narrowest crossing point from England, a port facility and the shortest and most direct route across the north-west German plain to Berlin. Von Rundstedt discounted Hitler's theory. As far as he was concerned, Calais would remain the priority of the German defensive effort and in meeting it he would keep the majority of his panzers held back in reserve away from the coastal areas.

It was an appreciation that was reinforced by German intelligence failures and successful Allied deception measures. Since the beginning of 1944, double agents had duped the Abwehr into believing that the blow, when it came, would fall on Calais. The presence of dummy landing craft at the head of the Thames estuary and signals traffic relayed and re-broadcast from Kent, suggesting that 21st Army Group and Patton's 3rd Army were positioned to strike at Calais, supported von Rundstedt and OKW's view. It was an analysis that was enhanced by reconnaissance failures. Although German aircraft had detected the build-up of shipping at Southampton and Portsmouth in late April, Allied air superiority meant that the Luftwaffe's air reconnaissance was never comprehensive and after 24 May there was no successful penetration of Allied airspace. In reality the German high command remained blind to the true nature of Allied intentions. Even their assessment of the weather and its implications for operations in early June was flawed.

The U-boats that spotted the same trough of low pressure in the

Atlantic that had been identified by the Allied meteorologists failed to spot the brief ridge of high pressure coming behind it, which was forecast to bring a marginal improvement in conditions from 6 to 7 June for approximately thirty-six hours. While the gap in the weather had been picked up by SHAEF's meteorological planning staff in Portsmouth, the Germans' reliance on the U-boats gave them only one main source of meteorological information. In addition, the U-boat crews' primary concern was to sink Allied shipping and survive the onslaught of the British and American anti-submarine campaign, where the odds were increasingly stacked against them. Consequently they constituted only a rudimentary platform for gathering barometric data, especially when compared to the Allies' comprehensive weather-gathering capability, which could call on specially tasked aircraft, a huge array of maritime vessels and land-based weather stations on Greenland. The German reliance on the U-boats to predict the weather was a critical single point of failure.

As the generals gathered at Rennes or prepared to travel there on the night of 5 June, the soldiers of 7th Army went about their routine business. As commander of the 125th Panzergrenadier Regiment, Major Hans von Luck had spent the day in the rain watching his men conducting a training exercise with blank ammunition. One of 21st Panzer Division's two panzergrenadier units, equipped predominantly with half-tracks, some tanks and armoured assault guns, von Luck's unit were located near the village of Ranville on the banks of the Caen Canal and were the closest armoured unit to the Normandy coastline. The division's other panzergrenadier regiment and its one tank regiment were based further south on the other side of Caen. The division's reconnaissance battalion were based in the village of Troarn astride the River Dives. The 21st Panzer Division had once been part of the Afrika Korps and its units still bore the palm tree emblem as their insignia. It was also Rommel's favourite division.

Von Luck had served in North Africa where 21st Panzer Division had been all but destroyed. The division had spent the last eighteen months being reconstituted and re-equipped in Europe from a cadre of experienced officers and NCOs who had survived the mauling in the desert. Having reached a strength of 16,000 men, it was now at

70 per cent of its establishment and effectiveness, which made it of primary concern to the Allied invasion planners. Rommel had visited the division in May and had told von Luck's men to expect the Allies to attack in all conditions and not to rely on fine weather.

It was another prophetic assessment, but it was not uppermost in the field marshal's mind as he enjoyed the opportunity of spending a night with his wife at his home in Germany. Von Luck was glad of the bad weather. The heavy leaden grey clouds above him meant that he could train his men without having to worry about the presence of 'Jabos', the term given to the prowling Allied fighter bombers. For once his air sentries could ease their vigilance and their commander could exercise his tanks and half-tracks without the fear of having them shot up from the sky.

Leutnant Raimund Steiner was less impressed by the meteorological conditions. The change in the weather had come too late to prevent his battery from being attacked by heavy high-altitude RAF bombers. The first raids had started at the end of May. None of the 1,000- and 4,000-pound bombs that had been dropped on the Merville Battery had hit and penetrated the casemates that protected his guns. But over fifty had landed within the perimeter of the position, hundreds more had landed outside it and the surrounding area resembled a lunar landscape of deep pitted craters, each several metres across and several metres deep.

The ones that landed on the position hurled up tonnes of earth, collapsed trenches and destroyed machine-gun nests, as well as tearing large gaps in his minefield and wire defences. While the men inside the four-metre-thick concrete and earth bunkers were safe from anything but a direct hit, anyone caught above ground during a raid would be blown to pieces, as each Halifax or Lancaster bomber unleashed up to thirteen tonnes of death and destruction. On 28 May, at 0158 hours, fifteen Lancaster aircraft of 100 Squadron RAF attacked the battery. Their time over the target would have been measured in seconds, but in that brief period they delivered eighty-three tonnes of high explosive on to the ground below them.

Each time the bombers came the survivors of his garrison would set about rewiring the position and re-laying the gaps in the minefield. They also had the grizzly task of digging out the men who had been buried alive in collapsed trenches that entombed them. Others just disappeared. Anyone caught above ground ran the risk of being vaporized by the massive overpressure of the bombs. Unless recognizable body parts could be found, the missing were simply identified by their failure to answer the roll call at the end of an attack. The last raid on the night of Friday, 2 June had been the worst and the atrocious weather made the task of repairing the bomb damage all the more unpleasant, since the rain lashed the three-hectare site for two days and turned the explosively rent earth into a quagmire of churned mud, splintered wire and body parts. But there was another bigger problem to deal with, which went beyond fixing the defences and finding the dead.

As his men set about clearing up the position the next day, as they had done on over twenty previous occasions, they had to work round an unexploded 4,000-pound bomb delivered during the raid. It had failed to detonate on impact and had drilled itself at an oblique angle into the foundations of one the casemates. The RAF had started using the 4,000-pound high-capacity impact-fused 'Cookies' when bomb damage assessment from Spitfire reconnaissance revealed that the more standard 1,000-pound bombs were having little effect on the thickly protected casemates. Each Lancaster could carry one Cookie, which was a cast steel cylinder of massive destruction. Filled with RDX/TNT and measuring just over 2.79 metres in length, the 4,000-pound ordnance could increase the destructive power a bomber could unleash when carrying a standard bomb load by a factor of two and a half.

On Saturday, 3 June a platoon of twenty pioneers arrived at the battery to begin the delicate task of extracting the unexploded bomb. The battery sergeant major, Hauptwachtmeister Buskotte, met the platoon when they arrived and was informed that they were from a 'Death Battalion'. The German Army penal units were made up of prisoners of war captured on the Eastern Front, political prisoners and Wehrmacht soldiers under sentence. To the men who sent them there, they were already dead and their expendable nature meant that they were given the most dangerous jobs, such as clearing minefields under fire and bomb disposal. Their dishevelled appearance betrayed their fate, which Buskotte saw reflected in their sunken features.

He accommodated them in the casemates and as they began to excavate a shaft to access the buried bomb, he noticed that many of them were Russians. While the condemned men started to dig, Buskotte and Steiner oversaw the repair of the battery's perimeter. Steiner repositioned his remaining machine guns to make up for those he had lost during the air raid. The single 20mm flak gun was also moved from the top of the cookhouse bunker. It was the only integral air defence weapon at the battery, but it also doubled as an effective ground-role weapon and Steiner wanted to make sure it could contribute to defending against a ground attack.

The two men worked well together and had developed a mutual respect since Steiner's appointment as the commander of the battery on 20 May. As a lieutenant, Steiner was a relatively junior rank to be commanding a battery, but as far as Buskotte was concerned, the young Austrian mountain gunner officer was a vast improvement on his predecessor. Hauptmann Karl Heinrich Wolter had been killed on 19 May, during an air raid when the local mairie where he was sleeping with his French mistress took a direct hit. Buskotte did not mourn Wolter's loss.

On Steiner's posting to Normandy he had been shocked to discover the general degree of fraternization between the officers of the 1/716th Regiment and the local women, their high consumption of alcohol and the numbers willing to abuse the compassionate leave system to visit their homes in Germany if they had been damaged by Allied bombing. Steiner had made a difference when he arrived at the battery, particularly to ensuring it was properly defended. As his men toiled through the rain and the mud to dig out trenches, fix the gaps in the perimeter of coiled barbed wire and bury fresh S mines, the young lieutenant's intent was to have the position back in defendable order by the evening of Sunday, 5 June. Given his family background and the death of his father as a result of being sent to Dachau, Steiner may have been no Nazi, but he was a professional soldier and the equally professional Buskotte liked and respected him for it.

With the exception of the unexploded bomb under Casemate Three, at least Steiner and Buskotte did not have to worry about their four guns, which remained safe inside the casemates whose construction was now complete. Rommel's arrival had made a difference to the tempo of work that had first started constructing Casemate One in June 1943. Following his first visit to the battery in January 1944, the field marshal had made a subsequent visit on 6 March where he exhorted the engineers and workforce of 200 conscripted labourers to work faster.

Built to the specific regulated dimensions laid down by the Todt Organisation, the work was often conducted under floodlights, especially when pouring concrete into wooden moulds when it was still dark, and which would be stripped off five hours later once the concrete had set. A local farmer called Jules Le Grey brought up the sand for the concrete from the beaches; his horse and cart were captured in some of the photographs taken by reconnaissance sorties; Alan Jefferson had seen him waving at one of the low-level Spitfires in one of the shots in the transit camp at Broadwell. Using an anti-earthquake technique, the four-metre-deep foundations were laid with gravel before the concrete was poured to create a shock-absorbing layer that would reduce the risk of subsidence caused by bombing, although the depth of the foundations meant that a pumping system also had to be installed to keep them dry.

By the end of March Casemates One and Two had been completed, but work on the other two continued. Casemates One and Three were more elaborate and had accommodation built into them for the gunners and underground storage areas for the gun ammunition. Thick steel doors sealed the rear entrances through which the guns could be manhandled, and large steel shutters shielded the firing ports. Each bunker had an air filtration system to guard against poison gas attack. Casemate One also had a machine-gun position cast into its roof. Known as a 'Tobruk stand', it was designed to interlock with the arcs of fire of the machine-gun sites around the perimeter of the position and was capable of sweeping the rear of the casemates with fire. Each of the individual machine-gun positions was dug in with sandbags and connected by communication trenches, which also linked the separate command bunker and underground cookhouse to the back of the casemates. The final casemates were cast and topped with two metres of earth by the time the RAF bombs began to fall in May.

The labour brought in to work on the battery were not drawn from the thousands of slave labourers transported from the other occupied territories to work on the Atlantic Wall defences by the Todt Organisation. Instead they were local French males, cobblers, hairdressers and former French Army soldiers from Caen and the surrounding villages. Although they were paid for their labour, none had any choice in whether or not they wanted to work for the Germans.

Claude Ridel had been mobilized on 16 April and did eight days' work at the battery filling a concrete mixer until he was able to feign illness and get a sick note from a sympathetic doctor in Caen, who was willing to alter the dates so that Ridel could avoid being sent back to work. There were other small acts of defiance too, such as the removal of shovels and picks, which would cause a delay until replacements could be found. Allegedly the foreman, Jason Fiont, added over 200 kilos of sugar to the concrete mix in the belief that it would help make the concrete crumble. Such minor non-compliance and sabotage typified the general extent to which the majority of civilians in France were part resister and part collaborator, depending on their personal circumstances. Although most local people hated the Germans and longed for the liberation, until it came they had little option but to coexist with them. Others were more active in their resistance.

Rommel made one final visit to the battery, when he inspected the defences along the boundary of his two armies, which was centred on the Orne valley. On 9 May he visited 716th Division at Ouistreham, which gave him a chance to inspect the deliberate flooding of the marshes and low-lying fields along the banks of the Dives. He noted that the depth of the water had fallen as a result of the dry weather, but the deep irrigation ditches, which were now beneath the surface of the water, would still constitute a significant hazard to any parachutist unfortunate enough to land in one. As would the hundreds of thousands of glider poles that had been erected across every identified potential landing site along the entire Channel coast. Some 170,000 poles had been erected in the Orne valley area, although Rommel observed that many were still to be strung with wire and linked to mines and recycled French artillery and naval shells, which would make them particularly deadly.

Five months had passed since Rommel took command of the 7th and 15th armies in Army Group B. The Atlantic Wall defences had improved considerably during that period. In his own words, his constant round of visits showed 'an extraordinary amount had been accomplished' since the start of the year. But even though he would still need armoured formations to break the Allied onslaught on the shoreline before they could establish a beachhead, the defensive crust had an important part to play in slowing the enemy until the panzers arrived. After dinner Rommel inspected 716th Division's positions along the Orne, which included the battery at Merville. Steiner was at his observation post (OP) bunker position in the sand dunes at Franceville Plage when the field marshal's party arrived at the gun position. A telephone call was put through to him and he was out of breath by the time he reached the battery. Rommel talked of the invasion and the importance of defeating it at the beaches, but appeared satisfied with Steiner's preparations and the progress that had been made since his last visit. The only part of the defences that was incomplete was the anti-tank ditch, which still needed to be extended round the north-eastern part of the battery.

Even with its partially completed anti-tank defences, the garrison of 160 men, solid casemates, wire, trenches and machine guns made the battery a formidable defence position. But it was an isolated strongpoint amid the scattered remainder of 716th Division's other units. The division's lack of manpower meant that they were thinly spread across its area of responsibility. As a result the defence of the area as a whole lacked depth and the distance between positions meant that the mutual support they could offer each other if attacked was limited. The nearest unit to the battery was the 3rd Company of the 736th Infantry Regiment stationed three-quarters of a mile away on the other side of Merville.

As the infantry's forward observation officer, equipped with a radio and signaller, Warrant Officer Timpf's job was to call for fire from the battery to support the company. In turn, it gave Steiner the means of calling on limited infantry support from the 100-plus grenadiers that made up its ranks. Steiner could also use the radio and landline in his OP to call on artillery fire from 716th's other gun batteries located across the Orne, in the Riva Bella area around Ouistreham.

Another company of the 736th Infantry Regiment manned a blockhouse and bunkers in the sand dunes around Steiner's OP bunker in Franceville Plage overlooking the Orne estuary. In addition a single platoon of the 736th Regiment guarded the bridges over the Orne and the Caen Canal more than seven kilometres away, but it was too small and too distant to offer any support to Steiner's position. The headquarters of the 642th Ost Battalion and one of its companies was based three and a half kilometres to the south at the village of Le Plein. However, the battery was beyond the effective range of any of the battalion's weapons systems and, since the battalion was made up of Russians, it was considered to be of dubious quality and reliability. The dispersal of 716th Division's units therefore meant that, if attacked, Steiner and his men would be largely on their own.

Although he did not visit the battery again, Rommel returned to the Ouistreham area once more on 30 May; it would be his final visit to Normandy before departing for Germany on 4 June. After watching a demonstration of multiple-barrel mortars and smoke generators he visited 21st Panzer Division. He was pleased to learn that its commander, General Edgar Feuchtinger, had completed time and distance appreciations for the movement of his division along routes leading to the coast across the Cotentin Peninsula, but both men knew that none of his armour would be able to move until they received authority from von Rundstedt. On his way back to his headquarters near Mantes, Rommel stopped on the high ground of the Bréville Ridge. With his back to the Dives valley, he surveyed the panorama laid out before him to the west. The weather was perfect and he could see for miles as his practised eye took in the details of the terrain.

In the valley below him the double water feature of the Orne and Caen Canal glistened in the sun as they ran north from the ancient city and flowed out to meet the sea through the mouth of the estuary and the lock gates at the seaside town of Ouistreham. With its distinctive red and white lighthouse, the gates were a registered target, which was covered by the guns of the Merville Battery, stationed across the estuary on the higher ground of the east bank. Rommel could just make out the red tiled roofs of the village of Merville and the yellow-grey Norman stone of its church and farm buildings. Beyond Ouistreham, eight kilometres of flat sandy beaches spread out in the hazy curve of the Cotentin Peninsula as it swept towards Cherbourg. If the Allies landed south of the Somme, as Rommel increasingly predicted they might, he was convinced that the area stretched out before him was where they would come.

If they did, he knew that the ground on which he stood would be the vital terrain in the coming battle. The wooded landscape, with its sunken lanes and thick hedgerows was ideal terrain for infantry to defend against armour. Whoever dominated it would control the only two bridges over the Orne and the canal a few kilometres below him between the villages of Bénouville and Ranville. The combination of holding the ridgeline and the bridges would decide the security of the eastern flank of the invasion force. If the Allies seized and held the ridge, it would allow them to open up a route to Caen and the flat tank country beyond it around Falaise, from which a mass armoured breakout could be made. A breakout that he knew the German Army could not stop once it had started. Consequently, he was convinced that the ridge was the key, not only to taking or losing France, but also to Germany. Reading the ground strengthened his belief that if he was to stop the Allies he had to defeat them on the beaches and prevent them taking the ridge and seizing the route to Caen, but to do that he needed more panzers.

Five days later, on the evening of 5 June, Rommel was back in Germany, Steiner's men were completing the final repairs to the battery's defences at Merville, and as the light faded the pioneers also halted work for the day. The access shaft behind Casemate Three had not yet reached the unexploded bomb beneath it. The pioneers retired to their accommodation in the sleeping chambers of the larger gun bunkers where they sought room to bed down for the night. The space inside the casemates was cramped; since the bombing started most of the gunners had been moved from their billets in the village to sleep under the protection of reinforced concrete and to be closer to the guns. If they were lucky, the pioneers would be able to find one of the naval-type metal-framed cots that hung from the bunker ceiling to sleep on; if not they would have to find room in the narrow corridors or ammunition chambers.

The members of 1/716th Battery had little enough space for themselves as they repaired for the night to their musty-smelling quarters. Some men prepared for bed, while others waited their turn to go on sentry duty or man the machine guns guarding the perimeter. The air reeked of body odour, stale tobacco, damp clothing and drying leather, as the soldiers drank ersatz coffee made from chicory, and played cards while smoking and listening to the radio playing popular songs, such as 'Lili Marlene' by Marlene Dietrich. Many just thought of home, as the last vestiges of light slipped from the gathering grey gloom of the western horizon and the Merville Battery settled down to its usual night-time routine.

In the gathering gloom, Steiner was preparing to leave the battery and return to his own accommodation at the OP bunker two kilometres away at Franceville Plage, which he shared with two signallers. He would remain in contact with Buskotte, who would stay on at the battery, by means of radio communications and landline. The sentry at the guard position saluted Steiner as he left. Other sentries manned posts along the perimeter wire or chatted idly with their companions in the machine-gun posts that were manned during the hours of darkness. Although the weather had eased, the sentries were glad of the thick clouds above them and the drizzle that came with the wind as it blew off the Channel. They hoped the weather might spare them from another air raid, although the sound of bombers droned high overhead as the RAF headed inland towards Caen; they hoped that some other poor devil would be getting bombed instead of them.

Steiner was thinking of sleep as he headed towards Franceville

Plage, but others around him were preparing for action. At 2215 hours British Double Summer Time, the BBC began transmitting its usual series of coded messages to the Resistance across the airwaves from the other side of the Channel. Normally 'The Voice of SHAEF' transmitted for no more than five to ten minutes, but on this occasion it took over twenty minutes. The local time was 2115 hours when Frenchmen all over France began picking up pre-designated phrases on their home-made Galène radios. Listening to foreign broadcasts was forbidden and possession of the small crystal radio sets risked imprisonment and deportation to a labour or concentration camp in the east. André Heintz hid his radio in a small bean can. Heintz was a student from Caen who lived with his mother on Rue de Geôle and had been working for the Resistance since 1940. Most of his time was spent gathering information on German defences and troop movements, which would be sent back to London via the western intelligence headquarters of the Resistance based in the city.

On 5 June he sat, his headphones on, tuned in to the BBC World Service evening news broadcasting from Bush House. Heintz listened intently as the newsreader announced, '*Et voici quelques messages personnels*,' which he knew meant coded messages for the Resistance. He heard two messages that he recognized: 'the dice are on the table' and 'it is hot in Suez'. The first was the trigger word for the Resistance to activate its plan to sabotage railway lines, and the second meant that they should initiate plans to cut telephone wires. Heintz was excited; he had been told to listen out for the code words and he knew they meant that invasion was about to begin. His own allotted task was to observe movements at the headquarters of 716th Division. As other members of the Resistance slipped out into the night to begin their D-Day missions, Heintz did not have far to travel. The German divisional headquarters was located in the house next door to his mother's.

The German signals intelligence section of 15th Army, which had been monitoring the coded traffic from the French Service of the BBC for months, picked up the coded messages too. The abnormal length of the transmission was considered a possible indicator of an

Allied invasion, and was duly passed to Army Group B and von Rundstedt's OB West headquarters in Paris. As a precaution a message was sent back to 15th Army ordering them to change their readiness state from Alert State I to Alert State II.

But the message was not passed to 7th Army headquarters. The failure to pass on the warning to the higher headquarters of 716th Division was a result of the prevailing military orthodoxy that Normandy was not the threatened sector. The German meteorological assessment that the weather was unsuitable for an invasion also militated against informing 7th Army. The combination of strategic bias and inaccurate weather forecasting was to have fatal consequences, as it engendered a false sense of security in the very sector of the Atlantic Wall where the blow would fall.

As Steiner arrived at his low, squat, diamond-shaped observation bunker among the sand dunes of Franceville Plage, the 7th Army remained on Alert State I. The rain had abated to occasional squalls that were blown across the estuary by a gusting wind that drove the dark empty sea into choppy waves. Behind him in Merville, the men of his battery were engaged in their normal night routine of sleep and guard duty. Major Hans von Luck had also returned to his own accommodation at his regimental headquarters near Caen after watching his regiment complete their training exercise. The tanks and half-tracks of 125th Panzergrenadier Regiment had been re-camouflaged in their shelter areas in the surrounding woods. They still carried the blank rounds they had used for training and there seemed to be no pressing imperative to reload them with live ammunition.

On the night of 5–6 June, while the mighty Allied armada of over 5,000 ships and 2,000 aircraft approached over the horizon, German units across the Normandy sector bedded down for the night and remained at the lowest level of readiness. With the exception of Richter, virtually every other senior commander responsible for defending the threatened coastline was absent from his post. Rommel was in Germany, the 7th Army commander and four of his five front-line divisional commanders were either travelling to Rennes or were already there, ironically to war-game the very scenario that was about to unfold upon the formations under their command. Unaware that anything was amiss and that his headquarters was under observation, Richter went to bed at 88 Rue de Geôle. Next door, André Heintz watched and waited.

9

Chaos Reigns

TERENCE OTWAY WAS asleep before the wheels of his Dakota left the concrete runway at Broadwell. The soporific rhythm of the drone of the engines and the vibrations of the aircraft combined with nervous tension to induce acute drowsiness. Otway was also mentally exhausted. The extra night's sleep at the transit camp caused by the twenty-four-hour postponement had given him a brief respite from the fatigue that came with his heavy burden of responsibility. But it had returned with the move to the airfield and the loading of the aircraft. Now once again he could doze in the dark confines of the Dakota with nothing to do until his aircraft reached the drop zone in Normandy. His fate and that of his men, at least for the next hour or so, would be entirely in the hands of the RAF and the vagaries of the weather.

The thirty-two DC-47s of 512 Squadron flew a course that took them east from Oxfordshire towards London. They then turned south to begin streaming with the rest of the Allied air armada towards Worthing, where a navigation beacon flashed 'V' for 'Victory' in Morse code as the aircraft converged and passed overhead. Otway woke just before his Dakota crossed the Sussex coast. He passed a flask of whisky round the men in his stick. But there were few takers and he made his way over piled kitbags and slumbering bodies towards the open door on the port side of the aircraft; the exit panels of all the Dakotas had been removed and left at Broadwell to ease jumping when the time came. Otway stood in the open frame and braced himself against the blast of cold air from the slipstream.

The night sky was full of scudding clouds, their edges gilded by the silver rays of a slowly rising moon. Spread beneath him in the darkness was the invasion fleet. Every inch of the wave-capped water from the Solent to the far side of the Isle of Wight was crammed with ships. Some were already steaming out into the swell of the Channel and the barrage balloons fixed to the decks of some of the ships shone dimly in the pale glow of the ambient light. It was an awesome sight, as the biggest naval force ever assembled lay ready for war. Otway sensed he was witnessing history and looking upon the likes of something that would never be seen again. Ten minutes after crossing the coast, the pilots switched off their navigation lights, but by the time the twinkling carpet of thousands of wing and tail bulbs suddenly disappeared, Otway was already asleep again.

The sky reverberated to the sound of thousands of aircraft, imperceptible save for the occasional sparks of burning carbon spent from the exhaust stubs of their engines. The pilots reported 10/10ths cloud, which obscured the moon intermittently and made map-reading difficult, as well as placing more reliance on the low-intensity blue lights on the topside of the aircraft, invisible save to the pilots following in formation behind. They had to work hard to maintain station within their 'vics'. Set at a distance of only 100 metres between wing tips, the pilots had to constantly adjust their throttles as they jockeyed to keep position with the leaders of the V-shaped formation.

For those not asleep in the back of the aircraft, the noise of the engines made it difficult to talk. Most sat in silence, alone with their thoughts, their coal-black faces blending into the blackness of the fuselage's interior. The glow of the odd cigarette, cupped in hands to shield its glow, illuminated features briefly, but betrayed nothing of what men were thinking or feeling. Some thought of loved ones, how they might perform and what awaited them; what the jump would be like, how strong the wind would be and whether the enemy would be ready and waiting for them. Some felt relieved that they were finally on their way; some men prayed. Corporal 'Marra' McGuinness had been praying ever since take-off, when the first knot of fear tightened in his guts. He kept repeating his Hail Marys throughout the flight. He was glad to have his mate Sergeant Sammy

McGeever with him; two of the battalion's Vickers machine-gunners, they were an inseparable team and the best gun crew in 9 PARA.

Others thought of those with whom they had a closer bond and who were also bound for battle. On another Dakota, medic Lance Corporal Terry Jepp made himself comfortable among the leg bags and thought of his younger brother Ron. Private Ron Jepp looked up to his elder sibling and had followed him into Airborne Forces to be like him. He was part of the machine-gun platoon and flew on the same aircraft as McGeever and McGuinness. Terry felt a strong sense of fraternal responsibility for Ron; he also felt guilty for the role he had played in influencing him to join the Paras and the predicament he felt he had placed him in as they both now flew towards Normandy. At that moment in time, Ron Jepp wouldn't have wanted to be anywhere else, although the Jepp brothers were never to see each other again.

Regardless of how they felt, or what they thought about, no one ate the dry butter-less jam sandwiches or bothered to use the urine tin. If they needed to urinate, they would have to go into battle damp. The smoothness of the flight across the Channel meant that on most aircraft the sick bucket was also under-utilized, although on McGuinness's aircraft Albert Richards made good use of it throughout the flight. Richards was a war artist, not a soldier, he was unaccustomed to flying and was visibly nervous. As the Normandy coast neared, McGuinness continued to make his acts of contrition with God, faintly aware of Richards spewing up next to him in the gloom as the cold slipstream blew in through the open door, a harsh reminder of their purpose.

Thirty-four minutes ahead of them the invasion had already begun. At 0016 hours three Horsa gliders of the reinforced D Company of the 2nd Ox and Bucks Light Infantry crash-landed into the low barbed-wire perimeter of the steel swing bridge over the River Orne. Having landed within fifty metres of their target, the men quickly overwhelmed the German platoon of the 736th Infantry Regiment and by 0040 hours the bridge and the second structure over the Caen Canal 600 metres away had been secured. Codenamed

Operation Deadstick, it was the most amazing feat of airmanship, skill and daring. The bridges were the first of 6th Airborne Division's objectives to protect the left flank of the invasion against Rommel's panzers and block their most direct route to the beaches. They were also the first places where men had started to die; the battle to secure the high ground above the bridges was about to begin.

As the short, sharp action around the bridges began to unfold, seven kilometres to the north-east the division's pathfinders and men of 9 PARA's advance and reconnaissance parties were preparing to jump ahead of the main body of the battalion on to DZ Victor. In the cramped confines of the Albemarle there was no room for a dispatcher. Consequently, Smith and Parry's parties would have to 'self-dispatch' from a type of aircraft that none of them had ever jumped from before. Company Sergeant Major Dusty Miller struggled to open the jump hatch of the aircraft as it ran into the drop zone. He hooked himself up on the dispatch cable that ran over the large coffin-shaped hole in the bomber's belly and faced Smith while they waited for the jump warning light to turn red.

Both men placed their feet on the thin metal sills either side of the hatch and braced their legs across the black rushing void beneath them. Steadying themselves with their hands against the side of the fuselage, the two men looked like contorted acrobats of a circus troupe about to conduct some macabre crowd-pleasing stunt. Smith focused on the red light as it came on, but in the periphery of his vision he could see the flashing tracer of anti-aircraft machine gunfire as it arced up through the night sky towards them. The red light came on for four seconds and then changed colour. As it burned green, Smith snapped his legs together and dropped smartly through the hole. An instant later, Miller followed him out into the rushing blackness.

Parry was only too eager to get out of the Albemarle. He had travelled in acute discomfort in the back of the aircraft crammed up tight between the legs of the man behind him. Jumping further back in the stick, his exit was less than perfect and his poorly secured leg bag caught on the edge of the hole as he fell through it. His exit caused severe twists as he tumbled earthwards, so Parry was relieved to feel the tug of his harness as his parachute snapped open above him. Kicking out violently against the entwined rigging lines, he was still wrestling to release his leg bag when he landed on the ground thirty seconds later with his feet wide apart. Sprawled in an ungainly heap on the ground, it was a far from textbook landing, but he was down, uninjured and mightily relieved to be out of the Albemarle.

Parry's poor exit meant that he was widely dispersed from the rest of his stick. There were no other jumpers around him and no one responded to the birdcalls he made from his Bakelite whistle. Alone in the dark, Parry set a bearing on his compass, shouldered his troublesome leg bag and set off to try to find the battalion RV.

As unorthodox as it had been, Smith and Miller's acrobatic jumping technique resulted in both men landing close together. They had been dropped accurately and Smith orientated himself quickly and collected the rest of his three-man recce party. The ground conformed exactly to the air photographs and the model they had studied in the transit camp and they set out to start their reconnoitre of the battery two and a half kilometres away to their north-west. They had hardly got off the DZ when they heard the bombers coming.

Suddenly, the air was rent with a harsh tearing sound, as the first of 100 RAF Halifax and Lancaster bombers began to unleash 4,000-pound 'Cookies' on the ground beneath them. Smith had been anticipating the raid that had been planned to hit the battery at 0030. The bombers were dead on time, but their aim was not. Smith's party were already in a ditch beside a hedgerow when the first bombs exploded. Observing their fall, Smith made the decision to use the cover of the bombing to make a dash for it across a large field in front of them. They were halfway across the open ground when Smith heard what he thought was the approach of several express trains descending upon them. As they threw themselves flat, arms covering their heads, the earth ahead of them began to heave up skywards leaving smouldering craters twenty feet deep. Trees were uprooted and thrown into the air like chaff, as mud and debris rained down on the three prone figures. The deadly shower seemed to go on for an eternity. Then there was silence and it stopped as quickly as it started, leaving the air thick with dust and the caustic tang of burned high explosive. Dusty Miller took his arms from his head and uttered one word: 'Fuck.'

Parry was scared witless by the violent storm of the bombardment. But when it was over he was relieved to find that he was no longer alone. As the silence returned he heard a rustling in a hedge. He had given up on his bird whistle and issued the password challenge 'Punch'. He got the reply 'Judy' and relaxed as two paratroopers from the 1st Canadian Parachute Battalion emerged from the shadows. Both men had lost their weapons in the drop. Parry handed over his own Sten gun, as he still had his pistol and was more intent on getting to the battalion RV before the rest of 9 PARA arrived over the dropping zone. He looked at his watch; it was nearly 0050 hours and he knew that he would have to sacrifice stealth for speed as he thrashed through hedges and ditches with his two new-found companions to try to get there on time. Separated from their own unit, the Canadians weren't complaining; at least they had an officer to follow who seemed to know what he was doing. Having also survived the bombing, Smith was equally intent to get to the perimeter of the battery, cut the cattle fence and scout out the sentry positions. To his east he could hear the steady drone of approaching engines. It was 0050 hours and he knew the approaching aircraft were bringing in the rest of the battalion.

Fifteen minutes out from the coast, Basil Coventry and his crew of Dakota KG 392 had seen the orange flashes of the bombs light up the underside of the thick bank of cloud that had formed on the horizon ahead of them. Sitting in the cockpit behind him, Flight Lieutenant Williams monitored the series of shortwave megahertz blips that danced on the small oscilloscope screen on his instrument panel. The Gee navigation system received radio signals from ground-based transmitter stations in England and allowed Williams to make dead reckonings on the air chart on his lap. The navigator then called out directions to Coventry who adjusted his control column in response to the headings that Williams gave him. They had used Gee to take them across the Channel towards Ouistreham. Three minutes out from the French coast, Williams instructed Coventry to turn to port and set a new heading due east towards Le Havre. As Coventry made the turn, he flicked on the switches to the subdued interior lighting running along the floor of the fuselage. When he did so, Flying Officer Lee unbuckled himself from his seat and made his way through the crew door of the cockpit into the amber glow of the back of the aircraft.

The other DC-47s adjusted their position to conform to their leader's aircraft. The formation would parallel the shoreline briefly, then make a wide banking turn to starboard to make landfall between a 'flak gap' that existed between Ouistreham and Cabourg. Once they made the turn and crossed the coast, the Dakotas would be seventy-five seconds' flying time from the DZ, a patch of cultivated ground, measuring just over one and a half kilometres long by half a kilometre wide. Accuracy was now important and Williams switched his attention to the Rebecca transceiver that would receive and respond to the ground-based Eureka transmitters the pathfinders had set up on the DZ. The small portable radar sets would bring the aircraft into line for their final run into the drop zone. Their radar beams would also allow the pilots to pick up the visual markings of the Holophane lights set up in a 'T' shape, which would confirm the direction of the wind and the dimensions of the drop zone. Williams searched frantically for the signal on his Rebecca set, but his screen was blank.

Flying Officer Lee was already in the back of the aircraft and had made his way to the tailplane when the small single red jump light by the door of the aircraft came on. As KG 392's radio operator, he would also act as the dispatcher during the jump. He faced the paratroopers sitting along the length of the fuselage, who were already nudging sleeping men awake as soon as he appeared. They had watched him in the eerie half-light as he fixed his belt-strop to a strongpoint near the dispatch exit. Lee had to roar to make his voice carry over the noise of the engines and the blast of the slipstream coming in from the open door. 'Get ready! Stand up! Hook up! Check equipment!'

Although he gesticulated with his hands to emphasize the commands, there was no need, as the men responded instantly to the drill they had practised so many times in training. Every man felt a nervous dread as they struggled to their feet and began clipping the snap links of their static lines into the inboard cable running the length of the roof of the aircraft. There was a spasm of nervous fumbling, grunts and swearing as men fought for enough space to fit leg bags and make any last-minute adjustments to their harnesses and equipment. The interior of the aircraft rang to the metallic jangling of twenty steel links being rattled home to ensure that they were properly secured into the dispatch cable. The men had already turned to face the door and were pressed up tight against each other, when Lee bellowed his next word of command: 'Sound off for equipment check!'

Each man checked his own equipment one last time, running through the familiar top-to-toe routine of snap link, helmet, chin-strap, harness and leg bag fastenings, then checking the man behind him and turning back to face towards the tailplane. The last man in the stick just behind the cockpit shouted, 'Twenty okay!' and slapped the man in front of him on the shoulder, then the next man confirmed that he was okay and ready to jump. The acknowledgement cascaded down the plane: 'Nineteen okay!' . . . 'Three okay!' . . . 'Two okay!' until the last man confirmed that he and the rest of the stick were okay and ready to jump by shouting out, 'One okay! Stick okay!' As a final act of confirmation, he gave the thumbs-up sign to the dispatcher. Lee gripped Number One by the arm and manoeuvred him smartly into the open door. The drill was repeated in thirty-one other aircraft as the Dakotas paralleled the enemy coastline and readied to make the turn into the drop zone.

The men with the heavier and specialized loads, such as radios and Bren guns, would jump first. In his aircraft, Jack Corteil pushed his left leg forward to feel for the edge of the jump-step with his foot. It was part of an instinctive drill to ensure he was in a good position to push off from when he jumped. One hand steadied himself against the frame of the door, the other gripped Glenn's lead tight to his side. As soon as the light turned green, he would let the Alsatian leap into the slipstream and then he would follow the dog out of the door. In Alan Jefferson's aircraft, his stick were already up and ready to go. At

Broadwell the young lieutenant had agreed with the pilot to reduce the normal five-minute warning to one minute before the green light came on.

Cutting the time down meant that his men would have to get ready to jump quickly. As Jefferson urged them to haste he shouted at them to check that their static lines ran free from their parachute packs to the dispatch cable and were not caught up under their arms. But in his excitement and his own hurry to hook up he had forgotten to check his own static line, which lay undetected under his left armpit. Around him, heavily encumbered men shuffled forward to press up close against the man ahead of them, as they formed up like a tense coiled spring behind the first man in the door. Those closest to the exit stared intently at the red light glowing ominously in the darkness; every man was focused on the jump, getting the drill right and making a clean exit through the open door where the wind howled in. Like the men in the other thirty-one aircraft, Jefferson's stick of twenty were pent-up, excited, nervous and ready to go.

At the head of the formation, Coventry touched the rudder bar with his feet and started to make a slow wide starboard turn into the coast. Without the signal from the Eureka transmitters his pilots would have to rely on the visual landmarks of the River Orne and the Caen Canal. The two silver ribbons of water would help set them up for the run into the drop zone and the lights they expected to see marking out the DZ. Still out at sea, but good for line, Coventry adjusted his flaps, reset the pitch of his propellers and began to throttle back.

To make a successful drop, he needed to slow his Dakota down to 100 miles per hour. This was just above the stalling speed of the aircraft, but slow enough to allow the paratroopers to make a clean exit and minimize the risk of inducing twists in their rigging lines as they hit the slipstream. With his flaps adjusted, his fuel mix set from fully rich to fully fine, he altered his trim to bring up the tail wheel to avoid the danger of a parachute becoming caught up in it. Coventry kept the plane steady as he began his run in to the coast; to his starboard side he noticed some light flak coming up to meet another stream of aircraft approaching the DZ. These were the Dakotas carrying Brigadier James Hill's 3rd Parachute Brigade and the men of the 1st Canadian Parachute Brigade, which were also making for DZ Victor.

McGuinness felt the tail wheel come up on his aircraft and the knot is his stomach tightened. The slight change in the attitude of the DC-47 and pitch of the engines were clear indicators that they were about to jump. He prayed that he would make a good clean exit. It was the focused determination of every man on the Dakotas as they thundered towards the coast at 500 feet above sea level. No one wanted twists, especially not on a combat jump. Those standing by the door could see the flashes of bombs exploding inland and caught a glimpse of the white surf breaking on the pale shadow of the beach beneath them before being replaced by the darker shadows of fields and hedge lines as the aircraft swept over the coastline and headed towards the DZ.

All attention was fixed on the jump lights at the side of the open door. The dispatcher in each plane tightened his grip on the first man in the stick, his eyes intent on the small bulb below the red light, ready to dispatch his human cargo as soon as it turned green. Suddenly, the changing pattern of the rushing landscape below them was blotted out when they hit a bank of thick cloud, mixed with the dust and smoke caused by the bombing. Red ribbons of tracer came up to meet them through the murky haze as the German anti-aircraft gunners opened up. Those standing in the open doors ready to jump could see the bright dashes of incendiary bullets stream upwards. Those behind them could hear the rattle of shrapnel against the fuselage as anti-aircraft shells burst around them, as things started to go wrong.

Alarmed by the sudden loss of visibility and panicked by the flak, the more inexperienced pilots began to take violent evasive action. What had been a tight V formation disintegrated as panicked aviators pushed forward on their throttles and yanked on their control columns in a desperate bid to escape the tracer and get through the anti-aircraft fire that slashed and burst around them. The effect on the paratroopers standing in the back of the aircraft was catastrophic.

The centrifugal force of the pitch and yaw of the evading aircraft as they suddenly pulled upward and banked sharply threw men carrying nearly their own body weight in kit and equipment to the floor and pinned them against the side of the fuselage and seats. The interiors of some aircraft became a thrashing mêlée of arms, legs and tangled equipment loads, as men swore and fought to get back on their feet and back in line to jump.

The risk of a mid-air collision was also extreme, as pilots lost their points of reference in the turbulent bank of cloud and smoke. When they broke through it, visibility improved and the rising moon shone brightly through the gaps in the cloud. But any semblance of an ordered formation was gone and planes passing perilously close to one another added to the sense of chaos and panic. More experienced pilots held their nerve. Bill Perry in KG 324 had been under fire before and made his 700 hours of operational flying in the monsoon over the jungles of Burma count. He held his line, but still could not see the 'T' shape of lights that were meant to be marking the DZ.

Flying half an hour ahead of the main stream of aircraft, only one of the two sticks of 22nd Independent Parachute Company had been dropped accurately. To make matters worse, many of the fragile Eureka beacons and DZ marker lights they carried had been broken during the jump and most of those that survived proved to be unserviceable. Lacking time and functioning equipment, the pathfinders only managed to put out two sets of green Holophane lights, but in their haste they set them up in fields of high standing crops where they were invisible to the pilots desperately looking for them. Without the aid of the Rebecca and Eureka homing system and unable to see any lights on the DZ, Perry used time, speed and distance calculations to work out his position. When he estimated that he was over the drop zone, he flicked on the jump light. As the red warning light went blank, the bulb beneath it burned green in the back of the aircraft and the wireless operator began dispatching his stick of paratroopers into the night.

Other pilots made a random guess as to their position and switched to green regardless of their speed, height or location. On McGuinness's aircraft the dispatcher bellowed, 'Go! Go!' as he slapped the first man on the back and helped push him through the open door. Even before he had been whipped away from the aircraft by the slipstream, a second man immediately filled his place and tumbled out behind him. If they were on their feet, the shuffling chain moved like a jointed caterpillar, shedding its segments through the door into the night. It gained momentum and began to move faster and faster in the frenetic rush to get out of the aircraft.

For men who were still on the floor, it was a very different matter. The well-rehearsed drill had broken down and men on their backs or forced hard down on their knees struggled against the force of gravity and heavy loads to stand up. All had one thought on their mind: to get out while the light was still green. In their haste to get to the door some men tripped and fell, as metal-studded boots lost their purchase on the smooth metallic floor of the aircraft, impeding those behind them. Haste also caused outsized loads and weapons sleeves to get stuck in the door. It took less than thirty seconds for a Dakota to fly across the 1,500-metre length of the drop zone. If a fall or wedged obstruction caused a sufficient delay the aircraft would overshoot the DZ before jumping could resume and the rest of the stick could get out.

It happened in Coventry's aircraft when a leg bag became wedged in the door. By the time the obstruction was freed, the aircraft had flown over the drop zone, forcing Coventry to switch off the green light and flick the red back on. On his second pass a man fell and only half the stick got out. He had to make three passes before Otway, who was jumping in the middle of the stick, was ready to jump at the door and by then KG 392 was off the eastern edge of the drop zone. Otway was on the point of jumping when the blast of an anti-aircraft shell rocked the fuselage and he fell through the door.

In some aircraft there were refusals. As the stick commander in his aircraft, Paddy Jenkins would jump last. He hated the final moments before a drop, but he was keyed up, every muscle in his body tense and ready to push forward as soon as the green light came on. But he was still concerned about one of the men in his platoon jumping number four in the stick. Others in the platoon had overheard the individual talking about refusing to jump when the time came.

Jenkins knew that a refusal over the drop zone would be a disaster, because it would break the chain of momentum and a single hesitation could become infectious. He also needed every man. Jenkins's aircraft was still flying straight and level and when the green light blinked on the first man was away through the door, followed immediately by the second, as the others behind them pushed forward ready to make their own exit.

The third man was leaping from the step-plate when the fourth man faltered. His hands came up to brace himself against the frame of the door to prevent him going through it. The corporal behind him had been well briefed by Jenkins and in an instant he chopped the defaulter's arms away and used the momentum of his own forward body weight to heave him out over the step and into the slipstream. The chain continued unbroken and they were almost all out, with the eleventh man about to jump when the plane suddenly pulled up and banked hard to starboard as the pilot reacted instinctively to a stream of tracer directed at his aircraft. The floor of the plane tilted sharply and the man ahead of him crashed back into Jenkins. The two men collapsed into a tangled heap and had to struggle to get back to their feet, the dispatcher yelling at them to get out.

Then the plane banked hard to port and the fulcrum effect of the counter-movement tipped the first paratrooper out of the door; Jenkins followed him. The relief of his chute cracking open above him was short-lived. They had got out well below 500 feet, so Jenkins had only just enough time to release his leg bag before the ground seemed to be rushing up to meet him. He saw that he was heading for a road flanked on either side by tall thick hedges and he pulled hard on his lift webs while raising his legs in an attempt to clear the obstacle. Jenkins landed on the other side of the road, his knees forced hard into his chest, knocking the wind out of him. He lay motionless on his back, struggling for breath as he watched the aircraft cross the sky in all directions above him.

Jack Corteil's dog was initially more successful in his refusal. Frightened by the flashing tracer and crack of the anti-aircraft shells, Glenn lost his usual enthusiasm for jumping and retreated under the jump seats just as the green light came on. Private James Baty and

Corteil dragged the large terrified Alsatian out of his hiding place and threw him bodily out of the door. Corteil followed straight after his hound and was immediately whipped away from the aircraft as he fell through the door, but as Baty was about to jump, the plane banked sharply and the floor of the plane came up like a seesaw. Baty was thrown back hard against the starboard side of the fuselage. The number three and the dispatcher had to haul him up and push him out of the door and by the time Baty got out he was well off the drop zone.

Even if they still had paratroopers on board who had been unable to get out in the first pass, many pilots were deeply reluctant to go back round again. To turn back into the crowded airspace over the DZ, where 100 aircraft blundered through the clouds and the flak required courage; some only found it thanks to the forced insistence of men who were adamant that they were going to jump. In several cases, they were willing to use their pistols to make the point. Some men were so desperate to get out that they didn't care whether they were over the drop zone or not. There was a pause in dispatching in Terry Jepp's aircraft to release the under-wing containers carrying bundles of Bangalore Torpedoes. As number thirteen in the stick he was in the door and ready to resume jumping when his rifle valise and leg bag became wedged tight in the doorframe. He and the dispatcher cursed and kicked to try to release them, but by the time the obstruction had been freed they were well past the drop zone and the red light had come back on. Jepp jumped anyway.

Jefferson's stick managed to get out in a single pass over the DZ. He glanced at the face of the dispatcher as he followed his men out and momentarily resented the fact that in two hours' time the RAF crews would be back in their messes in England having breakfast. His antipathy was quickly replaced by the shock of the slipstream hitting him in the face, which was followed by his left arm, as the static line caught under his armpit wrenched it smartly upwards. Jefferson felt a sharp pain as his shoulder dislocated.

Some aircraft were flying too fast. In a desperate attempt to clear the chaos that the airspace above the DZ had become, pilots had pushed their throttles forward. The shock of jumping into the slipstream at speeds approaching 150 knots tore heavy leg bags and weapons away from the body when parachutes snapped open. When he jumped, McGuinness swore, as he felt his leg bag and rifle valise ripped from his grip. The weight and the force of his exit snapped the retaining rope and he watched them plummet into the blackness below him.

Even if their exit had been bad, most men were relieved to feel the reassuring tug at their shoulders and the crack of silk as their chute opened and deployed into a fully functioning canopy above them. But the initial relief was soon replaced by the pressing urgency of what was going on in the air around them and the ground below rushing up through the darkness to meet them. Marra McGuinness had closed his eyes when he jumped, but when he opened them the sky seemed to be filled with the lethal dashes of red burning tracer. He watched it come up in lazy ribbons of light that looped over in a curved arc as the trace element burned out. After he had been blown out of his aircraft, Otway glanced up to catch sight of rounds punching holes through the silk of his canopy. But he had other things to think about as he came in to land.

The wind was gusting hard and Otway's late exit carried him off the eastern edge of the DZ towards the village of Varaville. In the light of the moon and searchlights that criss-crossed the sky, he could see the structure of a house looming out of the darkness below him. Otway pulled hard on his lift webs to avoid hitting the house, but knew that he was fighting a losing battle against the forces of wind and gravity so he prepared for a hard landing into the side of the building. Ahead of him the air was filled with the sound of breaking glass as his batman landed on top of a greenhouse in the garden at the back of the house. Private Mead's landing was harder still. His pilot had held his nerve and he made a good jump, but his leg bag was full of radio batteries and was swinging wildly below him. As he looked down and tried to bring it under control, he realized that he was going to land in a wood. Despite his desperate attempts to steer away, he knew that he was not going to be able to avoid the leafy canopy of a large tree. He brought up his legs and hands to protect his body. As he crashed through the foliage a branch snapped and the splintered end penetrated his gut; he screamed in agony.

Mead pulled the quick release strop to drop his kitbag to the ground and managed to shrug off his parachute harness before he climbed down from the tree. He was in great pain and could feel the blood running down his trouser leg and collecting in his boot. But he was adamant that he was going to try to make it to the RV and set off with his hand held tight against his wound. Men also broke legs and ankles as the gusting wind caught their chutes and slammed them down on uneven ground. At twenty-five to thirty knots, the speed was three times what had been forecast for the drop. Some of the injured managed to make their own way towards the RV; others lay moaning in the darkness with shattered limbs hoping that someone would find them.

Although they didn't know it, the men landing on firm ground were lucky. In the chaos of the broken formations, failed guidance systems and inexperienced aircrew, several pilots became disorientated and mistook the mouth of the River Dives for the River Orne and used the wrong river line as a point of reference to make their drop. At its widest point, the floodwaters of the Dives extended for two kilometres and had become a deadly catchment area for a large number of 9 PARA who were dropped off the DZ. Private John Speechley knew he was in trouble when he saw the surface of the water reflected in the moonlight and heard the urgent cries of men below him. Initially thinking that he was about to land in the sea, he went into the water-landing drill by activating the quick release on his harness and inflating his Mae West. Just before he hit the water he let go of his harness and dropped below the surface of the water. Unencumbered by his parachute and attached leg bag, he was able to stand up. The water came up to his neck. As he waded through the flooded fields and ditches in search of dry land, he listened to the frantic appeals of men drowning in the darkness around him.

Speechley's presence of mind ultimately saved his life, but most men only knew they were landing in water when they touched down in it and suddenly found themselves fighting for their lives. If a man landed in the shallower areas of the floods or waterlogged marshes and could stand up quickly, he had a chance of surviving. But if a man landed in one of the many submerged irrigation ditches that criss-crossed the surrounding water meadows of the Dives valley he stood little chance. The ditches were over a metre and a half deep and were often several metres wide. The kit the men carried almost doubled the weight of each jumper and those landing in the deeper water, or who were unable to stand up quickly, found their lungs filling with water as saturated clothing, entangled parachute gear and heavy equipment dragged them down to die a lonely death in the stinking and oozing mud that lay beneath the floodwater.

Whether they landed in the water or on dry land, the accuracy of the drop had fallen disastrously short of the overly confident predictions of the station commander at Broadwell. A combination of poor visibility, exacerbated by the thick clouds of dust and smoke generated by the RAF bombing raid, high gusting winds, the failure to mark the drop zone properly and the inexperience of many of the aircrew led to the battalion being scattered over an area of twenty miles. Subsequently, many were to put most of the blame on the overreaction of some of the crews to what has been described as 'light' to 'moderate' flak. However, these are relative terms to the men at the receiving end of tracer and exploding shells, especially when most of the airmen had never experienced anti-aircraft fire before.

The cause of their predicament was academic to the men who had been dropped too fast, too low or in the wrong place. If they had one thought on their mind, it was to get to the RV. The mission depended on being able to rally at the battalion RV quickly after the jump, but few men knew where they were and many landed alone. Doug Tottle found the silence of solitude unnerving. After discarding his chute, he looked around; the ground didn't resemble any of the photographs or the model he had studied so hard in the transit camp. As he crouched by his parachute, alone and lost, all he could hear was the wind blowing through the waving tops of wheat. Then he heard the birdcall from a Bakelite whistle. He crawled through the field towards the sound. Suddenly, his ankle was grabbed and he hastily shouted 'Judy! Judy!' in response to the challenge 'Punch' issued by a black-faced corporal who now covered him with his Sten. He was directed to a small copse where he found the unit medical officer, Captain Harold Watts. Watts should have had thirty men with him; Tottle's arrival brought the numbers of his medical section up to six.

Ron Tucker came down near the Dives. He had the good fortune to land on a dry track above the waterline, but his leg bag and rifle valise caught on the other side of a thick hedge. Before he had a chance to recover them he saw four German soldiers approaching down the track. He took cover in a ditch on the other side of the hedge and pulled the pin on one of the Mills bombs he had in his smock. He waited with bated breath, his grip maintaining tight pressure on the fly-off lever of the grenade. Once released it would go off in three seconds. Tucker wanted to kill Germans, but he also wanted to survive his first encounter with them; the odds of three to one, with no rifle, weren't great. They had seen him land and it was obvious that they were looking for him as they pushed themselves into the hedge line. The Germans came near enough for Tucker to smell them and he froze when the toe of a jackboot came close to his face. He remained deathly still, scarcely daring to breathe until they gave up the search and moved on. Replacing the pin, Tucker heaved a sigh of relief. He had no idea where he was, but he suspected that it was a long way from the RV.

Similar experiences were happening all across the area as men stumbled through the darkness, trying to orientate themselves, find their comrades, their equipment and somewhere to go. Between the hedges and the ditches men were meeting up and forming into small bands, while the German patrols began stalking the hedgerows looking for them. There were jagged flashes in the darkness and the staccato sound of intermittent small-arms fire, Bakelite birdcalls and urgently whispered challenges and responses to the passwords uttered from the shadows of bushes and ditches. Numerous other close encounters with the enemy took place, but the orders of their commanding officer were ingrained into every man: 'No person will return fire unless directly attacked by the enemy at close quarters.' Getting to the RV remained paramount and there were to be no private battles.

Otway's own encounter with the enemy occurred almost immediately on landing. The house he struck was the headquarters of a

100-strong Wehrmacht company based at Varaville. As he slid down the side of the building, an enemy soldier threw open a window to see paratroopers landing in their midst. Otway might have become an early casualty had it not been for the quick reactions of one of his men who had landed nearby who picked up a stone and lobbed it through the glass. Thinking it was a grenade, the Germans took cover and the pair were able to make their escape from the grounds of the house. His batman, Corporal Wilson, also used the diversion to make his escape from the back of the house and he was able to catch up with his CO. Otway headed north-west towards the RV and soon discovered the difficulty of traversing the thick tangled hedgerows that bordered every field. He also came across the horror of the flooded ditches and struggled in vain with Wilson to pull a paratrooper from the water, only to watch him slip beneath the stinking black surface. The commanding officer's close brush with the enemy and watching one of his men drown were ominous portents of what was to come.

Otway's adjutant, Captain Hal Hudson, was dropped accurately on the DZ, although he landed unharmed in a tree. Releasing himself from his harness and climbing down to the ground, he recognized a prominent ditch from aerial photographs and the model, which he knew would lead him to the RV. He had jumped last from his aircraft and expected to find the place teeming with the battalion, so was horrified to discover that there was nobody else there. Hudson convinced himself that his navigation must have been faulty and set back out along the ditch to retrace his steps. Had he stayed he would have seen the first of Parry's marking party arrive at the RV. Their commander didn't get there until 0100 hours. It had taken Parry forty minutes to cross the DZ. He had seen the main body of 9 PARA jump at 0050 hours and he had watched the tracer slash up through the night air to meet them. But as the engines droned off into the distance he had no idea of how bad the drop had been. Conscious that men would soon be arriving, he scrambled up a tree and began signalling out on to the DZ with his red Aldis lamp that he had carried in his troublesome leg bag. Out on the DZ, men spotted the light and slowly began to trickle in, as individuals and in small groups.

Otway arrived at the RV at approximately 0130 hours after a brief encounter with two fat Germans on bicycles, who were disarmed and sent on their way. He had no time for prisoners and pressed on to link up with the rest of the battalion. Otway anticipated that they would already be forming up in numbers under the direction of Parry. He was shocked by what he found. There were no more than a handful there and no sign of the heavy equipment from the store-carrying gliders, which should have landed on the side of the DZ. Jefferson spotted the red light and made his way into the RV, his left arm hanging uselessly at his side. He couldn't see his company commander, Ian Dyer, or any of the other officers of C Company. In their absence, he reported to Otway, who told him that he was now the officer commanding C Company. Jefferson looked at his CO incredulously, thinking, Where the hell were all the others? Otway snapped at him, 'Don't just stand there, go and take over your company!' He found his new command in a ditch, all eight of them. Many of them were without their helmets or weapons, but he was relieved to see Sid Capon among them.

The CO also snapped at Hudson, when he eventually made his way back to the RV. Otway demanded to know where he had been, his annoyance exacerbated by the presence of several French civilians Hudson had with him, including two women. Hudson had apprehended them as he returned along the ditch having re-checked his navigation. Otway told him that their presence on the DZ suggested that they were Nazi collaborators and ordered his adjutant to take them away and shoot them. Hudson was not in the habit of disregarding the orders of a superior officer, but he could tell his CO was stressed and had no intention of committing murder. He escorted the bewildered civilians from the RV, placed them in a deserted barn and told them that if they came out they were in danger of being shot.

Just after one and a half hours since making the drop, only 110 men had made it to the rally point. The discarded kitbags and abandoned weapons Paddy Jenkins noticed as he made his way across the drop zone, having been dropped well away from it, gave him a sense that things were amiss even before he reached the RV. His worst fears were confirmed when he arrived to see just how few men had made it in ahead of him. The disaster that had befallen 9 PARA was not lost on the rest of the rank and file. When Marra McGuinness arrived at the RV he met Hudson and when he asked him what had happened to the rest of the battalion, Hudson replied, 'God knows, McGuinness.'

It wasn't just men that were missing. The high winds and poor visibility had also taken their toll on the five Horsas carrying in the Jeeps with the engineer stores, medical equipment and anti-tank guns. None of the gliders had made it to their designated landing zone on the edge of the DZ Victor. One had broken its towrope over the Channel and had gone down in the sea with all on board. The others made landfall, but crash-landed short of the LZ. Seven of the men they carried were killed or severely injured when trees and anti-glider stakes turned their fragile wooden aircraft into matchwood. With the loss of the stores gliders there were would also be no engineers, no metal detectors to clear the minefields or Wade charges to destroy the guns once they had been captured. The company of Canadian paratroopers who were tasked with securing 9 PARA's flanks during the attack on the battery had also failed to report to the RV.

Only one of the Vickers medium machine guns and none of the three-inch mortars had been recovered from the equipment containers that had been widely scattered by the Dakotas. The lack of mortars would not only deprive the battalion of integral fire support, but would also mean that Otway had no means of illuminating the battery with star-shells to bring in the Horsa gliders carrying the men of G-B Force, which were due to arrive as the main assault force went in. Otway was also desperately short of the Bangalore Torpedoes he would need to blow gaps in the belt of wire obstacles that surrounded the battery. Only twenty lengths of the explosive tubes had been recovered in two bundles from the drop zone. Additionally, the naval gunfire party and their radios, who had jumped in with 9 PARA, were missing. Their absence meant that the battalion would have no means of signalling HMS *Arethusa* to confirm whether the attack on the battery had been a success or failure.

Otway was in no doubt about the disaster that was unfolding around him, as the prophetic words James Hill had uttered in the transit camp became a reality. Kneeling in a position not far from Otway, Jenkins noticed his commanding officer's highly agitated state. Otway snapped at those around him as he glanced anxiously at his watch and demanded to know where his men were. He cursed the RAF and his misfortune, his meticulously crafted plan in ruins before the attack had even started. Otway was beside himself with rage and also riven with self-doubt. His orders were clear: nothing was to prejudice his mission to silence the battery at Merville. If he failed to take the position before first light, thousands of British soldiers would die under the guns when they landed on Sword Beach. But to attack the battery with only 20 per cent of the men he should have had available was madness.

Military wisdom dictated that to have a reasonable chance of success in an assault, an attacking force should expect to have a ratio of superiority against a defending force of three to one. But with only 20 per cent of his men present, the German garrison, which would be fighting from well-prepared defences, would now outnumber them. Otway would have to attack without fire support and without the ability to communicate his success or failure to HMS *Arethusa*. If the ship did not hear from Otway by 0530, she would rake the battery with fire from her six-inch guns and there was every chance that 9 PARA would be cut to pieces by their own naval gunfire. With the odds stacked against him, Otway was racing against the clock and the onset of daylight when the landing craft would begin to hit the beaches. He knew that he could not wait any longer in the vain hope that more of his men would arrive at the DZ. He had to decide.

The men at the RV looked to their commanding officer, while Otway took stock of his reduced strength and meagre resources and struggled to control his emotions. Instead of seeking the counsel of men such as Allen Parry, he turned to his batman and said, 'What the hell am I going to do, Wilson?' The reply was blunt and to the point. Wilson told him there was only one thing he could do and that there was no need to ask him. Otway thought of his reputation, the regiment and how he would face his superiors, friends and family; he knew that he had to attack with what he had and that he could not wait any longer. It was 0245 hours; he told Wilson to order the men to be ready to move in five minutes. As the remnants of 9 PARA picked up their kit and prepared to move, another group of forty paratroopers arrived at the RV bringing the total strength of Otway's force to 150 out of a total of the 640 men who had jumped. The arrival of the gliders carrying Gordon-Brown's force due to crash-land into the battery would add another fifty-eight desperately needed men to the assault. The odds had just improved marginally. The question was whether Otway could get there in time and whether his force would be enough.

10

'Get In!'

T HE MOON CAST eerie shadows among the hedgerows and
tracks as the depleted ranks of 9 PARA set out from the RV.
They moved off exactly as they had rehearsed during their training in
England: the remnants of A Company led by Parry, followed by
Otway and his headquarters group. Behind them came the other
groupings, B Company with the twenty lengths of Bangalore
Torpedoes and C Company, the rear being brought up by Captain
Watts and his six medics.

It was a pathetic paltry vestige of the full complement of 750 men
who had practised forming up to attack the dummy battery near
Newbury. The column of paratroopers extended for little more than
the length of a football pitch as they set out to traverse the two-
kilometre route that would take them to their forming-up point
behind the battery. They had just over an hour and a half to get there,
meet up with Smith's recce party and then shake out into assault
formation and await the arrival of G-B Force. But as the thin snake
of men tramped through the darkness, the three Horsa gliders Otway
was depending on to even up the odds were having problems of their
own.

Staff Sergeant Arnold Baldwin's concerns about the flying-
worthiness and the overloading of his battered Horsa glider were
coming home to roost as he struggled to maintain a good tow position behind his tug aircraft while it pulled him towards the south
coast. The powerless Horsa was a ponderous aircraft to fly at the best
of times, but as far as Baldwin was concerned his was the dud of the
three plywood gliders allocated to the 9 PARA assault force of fifty-
eight men who would crash-land into the front of the battery. As he

wrestled with the controls, he could just make out the two glowing exhaust ports of the Albemarle bomber slightly above them in the darkness ahead, which he used as a point of reference to try to maintain station. If he flew too high above the tug aircraft, the additional strain on the towrope risked snapping it. If he flew too low, there was a risk that he could stall the bomber ahead of him and the tug pilot would be forced to cut the glider loose to save his own aircraft.

The last of the three gliders to take off at 0237 hours, the weight of his Horsa was so great that Baldwin had only just managed to lift from the airfield at Brize Norton. Initially the weather was clear, but as they gained height and headed for the coast he was alarmed to see a bank of monstrous black tumulus clouds building on the horizon in front of him; they were headed straight for it. Baldwin felt the claw of fear in the pit of his stomach as he lost sight of the Albemarle and the glider began to buck and shake in the severe turbulence of the cloud. Then he felt a sickening jerk as the towrope parted and his nose dropped. No longer under tow, Baldwin knew that he had to get his Horsa down quickly, because a fully laden glider drops at 400 feet per minute. He searched the blackness beneath him.

To his relief Baldwin saw the lights of a runway just off his starboard wingtip. He glanced at his air speed indicator; it read 140 knots and he knew that he had enough height and speed to make it. Geoff Pattinson was aware that the glider was lumbering violently, but he was lost in his own thoughts until the shout went up to brace for landing. He heard a bang when the Horsa touched down and thought that they must be in France as the aircraft slewed along the runway and then came to a halt. There was none of the anticipated haste to get out and Pattinson thought it strange that they were told to stay put by their platoon commander, who climbed out of the glider with the two pilots. When Lieutenant Hugh Smythe returned, he told them that they had landed at RAF Odiham. It was only then that Pattinson realized they were still in England.

Staff Sergeant Stanley Bone's glider had made it over the coast and the pilot of their tug aircraft had managed to avoid the tumulus clouds, but halfway across the Channel the Albemarle's airspeed suddenly dropped and it struggled to maintain height. The pilot knew something was badly wrong with the glider he was towing and he frantically communicated with Bone. Gordon Newton knew there was a problem when the co-pilot rushed into the back of glider and asked if anyone had a knife. The Horsa's arrester mechanism had broken and the parachute now trailed in its wake, catching in the slipstream and threatening to drag the glider and tug aircraft into the sea. It was cut away hastily into the choppy waves not far below them. The tug and the glider regained height and continued their flight towards France.

In Normandy, Smith's party were already cutting the outer perimeter wire and starting to reconnoitre the battery. Using a thick apple orchard as cover, they cut more cattle wire, then stole on their hands and knees into the surrounding minefield in front of the thick barbed-wire obstacle belt that formed the inner perimeter of the gun position. They could see the mounds of the casemates looming out of the darkness like four gigantic mushrooms 200 metres ahead of them beyond the wire. They moved slowly, feeling with their hands for anti-personnel mines and trip wires. When they found a wire, they cut the strands and moved forward cautiously, occasionally pausing to listen for sounds in front of them.

It was deathly quiet. For a moment Smith wondered whether the battery was occupied. As he and Miller moved closer to the wire, they heard the low murmur of human voices on the other side and caught the smell of tobacco smoke in their nostrils: Germans talking and smoking as they waited for their shift of sentry duty to end. The smell of the drifting smoke provoked Miller's own craving; he desperately wanted a cigarette.

The presence of the enemy confirmed, Smith motioned to Miller to head back while he crawled forward alone. He wanted to see more, but if he failed to return he also wanted Miller to be able to take the information back to Otway. He reached the wire; fixed with metal piquet stakes, it was over a metre high, four to five metres thick and more than capable of stopping an infantry attack. Smith began cutting carefully into the wire, a strand at a time, slowly making a hole to crawl into. He cut deeper as he pushed further into the tangle of barbed strands, bending each one back to avoid becoming snagged.

It was methodical and tedious work; he was two and a half metres into the wire when the battery stirred.

From the other side of the wire he heard excited voices and shouted orders. Smith froze, and then he saw the glider and tug aircraft approach over the battery from the west, as four machine guns opened up. Their muzzle flashes cut the darkness with angry bright flashes, stitching the night sky around the aircraft with tracer rounds. Fifteen metres from where he lay prone, a light anti-aircraft gun opened up, thumping 20mm cannon shells upwards as the tug and glider passed overhead. The firing ceased as the intruders disappeared into the night and Smith decided to take advantage of the defenders' preoccupation to crawl out of the nest of wire and make his way back to Miller. He had got the information he wanted: the battery was occupied, well defended and its garrison was alert.

As Smith edged back through the wire, Hauptwachtmeister Johannes Buskotte had already put a frantic call through to his battery commander at his OP bunker in the sand dunes on the edge of the Orne. The battery sergeant major's tone was urgent and excited as he told Steiner that a glider had crash-landed in the minefield on the edge of the battery and that his men had engaged it and killed its occupants. He also reported that before the glider caught fire and burned out, it had been searched and found to contain explosives, flamethrowers and pneumatic drills. Steiner was convinced that it must be part of a commando raid on the battery, or even the beginning of the invasion itself.

One solitary glider meant that more were to follow or a larger attacking force was already forming up in their midst. Steiner left his small squat bunker to liaise with the infantry commander stationed in a large blockhouse further back in the dunes. Before he called his divisional headquarters, he wanted to make sure the German grenadiers located on the other side of Merville were tasked to conduct a clearance patrol behind the rear of the battery where the anti-tank ditch had not yet been completed and his defences were most vulnerable. He also told Buskotte to double the sentries and stay alert.

Unaware that any glider had landed, Smith arrived back where he had left Miller. As he began telling Miller what he had seen, the taping party under Captain Paul Greenway arrived ahead of the rest of the battalion. Greenway informed Smith that the drop had been a disaster; he had only half his mine-clearing and taping party with him, no metal detectors to clear the minefield and no white marking tape. They would have to find and lift the mines by hand and would use the heels of their boots and entrenching tools to mark a cleared path to the inner perimeter of wire, which Smith had begun to cut into. Smith quickly sketched the layout of the position, leaving Miller to fill Greenway in on the rest of the detail. He was keen to get back to a crossroads to the south of the battery where he would meet Otway and the rest of the battalion and brief his commanding officer about what he had seen. He set off at speed to the meeting point, conscious that time was running out.

The depleted column of 9 PARA moved in single file to where they would rendezvous with Smith. The tracks and hedge lines they followed mirrored the features that had been replicated faithfully on the ground over which they had trained and the air photographs they had studied. While navigation was easy, the going was difficult. The landscape was rent with twenty-foot-deep bomb craters, the result of the numerous RAF raids that had missed the battery. The huge fissures gouged into the earth were too large and too many to go round and slowed their progress. As they made their way through the churned fields and orchards, Parry skirted the village of Gonneville that lay a kilometre to the west of the drop zone, since intelligence reported that the Germans occupied the small group of houses nestled round the church, but there was no sign of life.

It was quiet save for the braying of wounded and dying cows hit during the bombardment. Still several hundred metres short of where they would meet Smith, the file went to ground when the machine guns opened up on the lone glider and tug that Smith had seen fly over the battery, causing the tormented cattle to stampede through the fields around them. Jefferson looked up to see a bomber hit by the anti-aircraft fire and watched as two parachutes appeared, but the rest of the crew plunged to earth in their stricken plane. They moved off as the firing ahead of them in the distance died down, only to freeze again as they advanced up a sunken lane that ran west through some orchards on the other side of Gonneville. Ahead of them another file of men moved across their path. Parry held his breath as the German patrol passed by less than a few metres to their front.

Peter Timpf had no idea of the presence of the enemy paratroopers kneeling undetected in the shadows of the sunken lane as he passed close by with a platoon of the 3rd Company of the Wehrmacht's 736th Infantry Regiment. The German warrant officer had been attached to the platoon as its artillery observer in response to the mystery glider that had landed at the battery. The glider in fact had nothing to do with 9 PARA and subsequent speculation suggested it was carrying stores for 3rd Parachute Brigade and came down short of LZ Victor. However, its origin was immaterial; the battery was alert to the potential for some form of ground attack and Timpf and the platoon of German infantry had been sent out to help guard against it. Equally unaware of the background to its dispatch and oblivious to the danger it posed, Otway now had a mobile element of the enemy that would be operating in his rear as his attack went into the battery.

Smith arrived at the rendezvous point ahead of the battalion to see the front of the column loom out of the darkness in single file along the track, Parry at its head. It halted and the men went down on one knee, while Otway pushed up the stationary file to confer with Smith. He listened to his report and then called a hasty orders group. Otway delivered his plan for attacking the battery calmly; the basic outline would conform to what they had practised numerous times before, modified to accommodate their depleted numbers and lack of support. Instead of attacking through four breaches in the wire, B Company would blow only two gaps. What remained of A and C companies would be amalgamated into one assault party, fifty men split into four groups, one for each casemate. Jefferson would attack Casemate One; Lieutenant Mike Dowling would take Casemate Two and Company Sergeant Major Ross and Colour Sergeant Long Casemates Three and Four respectively.

Sergeant Knight and six men would use their Bren guns and grenades to attack the gatehouse and cause a diversion just before the main attack went in. The left flank would be secured by the solitary

Vickers medium machine gun under the command of Sergeant McGeever and would provide fire support. Parry was elated that Otway appointed him to command the main assault. Otway would retain overall command with a small reserve and what remained of the medical section, which would be held back to deal with casualties. The signal for the attack would be a single blast on a whistle given by Parry. Time to cascade the orders to the rest of the men was short. Otway still wanted to coordinate the assault with the arrival of the gliders, which were due to crash-land into the front of the battery at 0430 hours. He also wanted to attack under the cover of darkness and was acutely aware that at 0530 the *Arethusa* would open up on the battery. It was 0400 hours and the first trace of dawn was already making its appearance in the western horizon.

Ambient light conditions made no difference to the crew of HMS *Arethusa*. Inside the confines of the steel superstructure, most of the ship's complement lived and worked in the artificial red half-light of inboard illumination and had little idea of whether it was night or day. Those on the bridge had seen the flashes ahead of them in the darkness as they steamed across the Channel at the head of Task Force D of the Royal Navy. The two battleships, five other light cruisers and one monitor bombardment ship would guard the east bank of the invasion fleet and provide naval gunfire support to the troops ashore. The six-inch guns of *Arethusa* and her sister ship HMS *Mauritius* would fire in direct support of 6th Airborne Division, and the *Arethusa*'s first task would be to try to neutralize the Merville Battery if 9 PARA's mission failed. The ship sailed under blackout conditions and radio silence; she had no way of knowing that the ability to communicate with the unit by radio had already been lost.

As in all operations the *Arethusa* put to sea ready for war. Her magazines had been restocked with six-inch rounds and charge bags, guns refitted and projectile hoists and shell cradles checked. Although they were aware that the landings were imminent, the crews had only been briefed on their D-Day mission over the Tannoy system by their captain once they had set sail from the Solent. Making a steady twelve knots at the head of the column, *Arethusa* was less than an hour away from her bombardment station.

Knight moved off with his Bren gun group along the track that ran parallel to the rear of the battery. He would then peel off to the west and make his way round the perimeter to the gatehouse. B Company followed on with the Bangalore Torpedoes. Two guides from the taping party would lead them to the start of the two paths that had been cleared through the minefield adjacent to the battery. Parry moved behind B Company with what remained of A and C companies to head to their start line position in the tall grass of the orchard, where the cattle wire had been cut by Smith and where more guides waited to mark the routes into the minefield. As Smith had already proved the route to be clear of Germans, they moved at speed along the track. Otway brought up the rear with his small reserve, the medics and the medium machine-gun crew carrying the split-down Vickers. McGuinness carried the gun, McGeever humped the canvas belted .303 ammunition and Private Fenson, the third member of the crew, sweated behind them with the heavy metal tripod for the gun.

The underpowered Albemarle bombers bringing in the two surviving gliders of G–B Force were also labouring hard. Weather conditions had made the flight across the Channel difficult, and a low cloud base of less than 1,000 feet meant that the tug aircraft would have to take the Horsas all the way in to the target, instead of releasing them at 5,000 feet as soon as they crossed the coast. Having made the commitment to cut them away directly over the battery, the next challenge was to confirm that 9 PARA were in position and ready and waiting for them. There were none of the marker flares, or mortar star-shells they had expected to see when they made landfall just before 0430 hours. The Rebecca transceiver sets, which the glider pilots had made so much effort to train on just before they left England, were also worryingly silent.

The Albemarle towing Gordon-Brown's men prepared to circle the battery in an attempt to pick up any signal from 9 PARA on the ground. The pilot of the tug aircraft kept his navigation lights on so that Staff Sergeant Bone could follow the bomber through the murky darkness. While the twinkling lights would make it easier for the glider pilot to maintain station with the tug they would also provide the Germans with an ideal target marker. As the bomber started its orbit, below them the breaching party was crawling through the hastily cleared paths in the minefield to place their Bangalore Torpedoes in the thick-coiled wire of the inner perimeter. Behind them and further to their right, Sergeant Knight had just passed a track junction that led round the edge of the battery and would lead him to the gatehouse facing the village of Merville. It was still quiet and he could just make out the piled wire coils of the obstacle belt and the shadows of the casemates beyond it, outlined against the slowly lightening skyline. Then the blackness in front of them turned into a blazing world of light and noise, as several machine guns opened up.

The eruption of sound and muzzle flashes spewed from several weapons pits inside the perimeter on the other side of the wire, as German sentries manning the MG 42 'Spandau' machine guns detected movement along the hedges and orchard to their front. The guns' distinctive burring sound when they fired split the night air and came from several locations across the rear of the position as the defenders engaged the attackers in their midst. Men instinctively dived for cover just as a frantic shout went up from Otway to 'Get those bloody machine guns!' One of Knight's Bren gunners fired a return burst from the hip at three muzzle flashes on the right flank of the battery, and the rest of his section then joined in.

The Vickers crew had been caught in an open field and were nearly hit by a beaten pattern of rounds fired from enemy automatic weapons on the left, which drove them back into the shelter of a large crater. McGeever swore at his team and ordered them to get the gun into action and Private Fenson responded with great courage. He leapt out of the bowl of the crater, flipped the tripod off his shoulders, kicked its legs open and pushed them hard into the ground to provide a firm base for the gun. McGuinness followed him and mounted the Vickers, locking it home as Fenson slapped a canvas belt of 250 .303 bullets into the gun's feed tray and slammed the cover down. McGuinness was already cocking the weapon when McGeever shouted the range and gave the order to fire. He gripped the spade handles, pressed the thumb trigger and the Vickers barked back at a rate of 600 rounds a minute at the bright enemy muzzle flashes less than 300 metres away from them. The German machine guns were firing on fixed lines and at that range they were easy for the expert gun crew of McGuinness and McGeever to silence.

The Bren gunners and Vickers teams duelled with the German machine gunners on the flanks, while Parry urged his assault force into their start line positions. The breaching party had already crawled through the minefield and were placing their Bangalore Torpedoes in the wire, leaving one man behind ready to detonate each of the long line of connected explosive tubes when Parry gave the order. He was almost set to begin the attack when the first glider appeared overhead. The men on the ground were riveted as the glider swooped in low over the top of the casemates at a few hundred feet. Then the German 38 Flak gun joined in the cacophony of sound, pumping glowing red 20mm cannon rounds skywards in five-round bursts. The Horsa was still under tow and seemed to hover and shudder when the anti-aircraft gun's tracer began to find its mark. Jefferson watched it taking fire and thought of the men on board the thin plywood-covered aircraft.

Gordon Newton had heard the crunch of flak as the gun fired. Then projectiles of burning tracer punched through the floor, splintering wood and metal before exiting through the roof of the glider. The flashes of the automatics on the ground and the red arc of anti-aircraft fire confirmed the fix of their target, but without the flared illumination of star-shells there was insufficient light for Bone to discern where to put down his glider. Taking fire and running out of fuel, the tug pilot gave the Glider Pilot Regiment airman a choice: he could either cast off and take his chances, or he could return with them to England. Bone made his choice. Reaching forward, he pulled on the towrope lever and the glider was in free flight. The fully laden Horsa immediately started to bleed altitude as Bone pushed the nose into a forty-five-degree angle; it dropped like a stone in the direction of what he thought was the battery. At 500 feet he realized that he had miscalculated and was about to land among the buildings of the village of Merville. Bone pulled hard on his flaps and banked away into the darkness to the east of the battery, taking the commander of G–B Force with him, where he would play no part in the attack on the battery.

Flying two minutes behind Bone, the arrival of the second glider over the position provided the anti-aircraft gunners with a replacement target. Staff Sergeant Dickie Kerr and his co-pilot Sergeant H. Walker were still under tow when the two men stared hard through the square Perspex panes of their snub-nosed cockpit looking for a place to land. Lieutenant Hugh Pond stood between the bucket seats of the Horsa searching for recognizable landmarks as they cast off. They were already under fire and the crack of passing rounds suddenly became much louder and more real when the noise of the tug aircraft's engines droned into the distance. Pond was certain that they were over the battery when they started to get hit. Machine-gun fire mixed with the shells from the cannon found their mark in the fragile wooden fuselage and wings. Kerr felt the Horsa lurch as fire punctured the wings, while the men in the back were hit by rounds. Private Fred Glover felt his legs lift involuntarily as cannon fragments struck the back of his thighs, bullets passed through the hand and knee of another paratrooper and the gloomy interior at the back of the tail end of the aircraft began to burn.

Pond could hear the screams of one of his men. He looked back in horror to see one man on fire, but there was little he could do since the glider was coming in to land. Kerr had caught sight of a red recognition light and pulled the glider round hard to make his approach. He could not see the battery and focused on the glowing red marker. Behind him, Pond's men linked arms and braced themselves for the landing. German tracer fire followed the glider down and Kerr felt the impact of the bullets slap the fuselage sideways. The glider was coming in too fast.

Approaching at over 100 miles an hour, Kerr glimpsed a flat area of ground between him and a hedge line. He pulled on his flaps and pushed the nose down and prepared to land. Then he saw the white wooden signs that told him he was about to put down in a minefield at the front of the battery. His forward air speed suddenly became an advantage; he heaved on the horseshoe-shaped wheel of his steering column, the ailerons bit into the air and the glider lifted again. It crested the casemates and swooped low over the heads of the troops waiting to begin their assault. As the gun position passed away behind them, Kerr shouted at Walker to release the arrester chute mechanism, kicked his rudder bar hard right and banked the Horsa round on full flaps. He was making for a small field on the other side of an orchard next to the sunken lane leading up to the battery from Gonneville.

It was still 500 metres away, but they had just enough height to make it. With the outsized flaps and drag parachute acting as airbrakes, the glider turned sharply and sank. The tailplane scuffed the top of the branches and the canopy of the chute caught in the apple trees as the glider slapped down. The front undercarriage buckled and the nose piled into the soft leafy Norman soil, skidding to a halt in a shower of splintering plywood, earth and sparks, and came to rest in a dense line of hedging and brambles. The force of the landing smashed open the tail section and broke Kerr's restraining straps, catapulting him from his wooden bucket seat through the Perspex squares of his cockpit. He landed in a bomb crater ten metres away from his broken aircraft. There was silence and then the firing started.

With no sign of the third glider Parry knew that he could wait no longer. He looked at his watch; it was 0445 hours, forty-five minutes before the *Arethusa* would rake the position with her guns. He gave one shrill blast on his whistle. The two men from B Company pulled the small detonator cords at the ends of the two lengths of Bangalore Torpedoes and pushed themselves backwards from the wire. The men of the assault party pressed their faces into the dirt. As the fuses fizzed, Jefferson psyched up his men, telling them that they were cold-blooded killing machines and their job was to deliver death to the Germans. Sid Capon muttered, 'Bastards, bastards,' over and over to himself as he prepared to do his young platoon commander's bidding.

Off to their right, Knight's diversion party loosed off everything they had at the gatehouse, emptying the magazines of their Bren guns and hurling grenades at the wooden sentry post and gatehouse guard hut. The rattling crescendo of their fire was a kinetic drum roll to what was about to unfold, as the men on the start line held their breath and prayed. The thin strip of light in the western sky was growing brighter. Otway was anxious and nervous; he was about to find out how fate had stacked up the odds.

Bright flashes lit up the night and the air split with two almighty cracks when the Bangalore Torpedoes detonated. The sky filled with smoke and dust and the mass of wire and stakes blew into thousands of spinning metal fragments as the explosives cleaved ten-metre paths through the thick obstacle belt of the inner perimeter. The dust and debris had hardly settled when Otway yelled, 'Get in! Get in!' Jefferson was already on his feet blowing his toy horn, his damaged arm tucked limp into his webbing, as he made for the two smoking gaps in the wire. Hearing cursing and shouting behind him, he was aware that his men were with him as they charged through the minefield.

The hastily scuffed paths cleared by the taping party became indistinct as men spread out and zigzagged to avoid the defenders' fire that zeroed in on them from the other side of the wire. The enemy sent up flares to illuminate their targets, their machine guns no longer firing on fixed lines, and automatic weapon butts kicked back into German shoulders as foresights beaded on the dark running figures converging on the gaps in the wire.

Under the effective crossfire of the defenders, any sense of lane discipline broke down in the frantic scramble to get through the breaches and the shout of 'Mines! Mines!' went up as unwary feet strayed from the path and initiated trip wires attached to mines buried just beneath the surface. Jefferson could clearly see the monolithic outline of Casemate One ahead of him when he felt something bite him in the back, as an 'S' bounced up behind him to explode at belly height, sending a lethal spray of hundreds of steel balls in all directions. Then a piece of shrapnel slashed him across his left thigh and he stumbled and fell. Unable to get up, he cursed and exhorted his men forward. Capon was vaguely aware that his officer was down, but rushed on firing his Sten gun from the hip as he went.

There were other detonations and more went down; Jefferson's batman Private Smith lost an eye to an exploding mine and men fell to bullets as well as shrapnel. Caught up in the moment of the charge, Hudson had pushed himself forward. As he approached one of the breach points, he was punched backward. He felt no pain and thought he had been struck by a piece of debris, but when he lifted up his hand he was surprised to feel that it was sticky and wet. Unable to stand, he crawled forward. Weak from the loss of blood that ran from serious wounds in his stomach, he was still desperate to take part in the action. He could see German figures silhouetted through the wire ahead of him in the dying light of the flares. He forced himself up on his shoulders, drew his pistol and took careful aim at the enemy. He squeezed off a round and felt burning agony as his own round smashed through the top of his left foot.

Those not hit in the minefield broke through the wire and made for their allotted casemates as fast as they could. But the churned earth of deep craters impeded their momentum. They were too numerous to go round, so men ran down into them and then struggled up the loose soil sides to continue forward. Although it slowed the assault, the scarred ground provided a degree of cover and did nothing to abate its fury. Parry attacked through the right-hand gap in the wire, determined that he would take the first casemate. The German machine-gun fire grew more accurate and the area between the concrete bunkers and the perimeter wire became a deadly killing zone.

Rounds began striking those around him and then Parry was hit. Private Fred Milward watched him go down. Struck high up in his thigh, Parry's left leg gave way and he tumbled into a crater. Above him the area was a confusion of noise and death. Private Mead found cover and returned fire with one hand, while the other grasped the weeping wound in his gut where it had been penetrated by the branch of the tree he had landed in. Suddenly he was hit and flung to the ground. Fred Milward paused on the lip of each crater to provide a point of fire with his Sten gun to cover those in the open, then dashed for the next crater. He traversed several more of the deep depressions before jumping into a trench; he saw enemy figures illuminated in the moonlight at the other end and fired a long burst along its length. He heard shouts of '*Paratruppen, Paratruppen!*' as the enemy fell or fled and 9 PARA began to gain the initiative against the defenders.

Jefferson had dragged himself into cover and heard the heavy crackle of small-arms fire start to abate, to be replaced by the dull thud of grenades exploding. It indicated that his men had closed with the bunkers and were bombing their entrances. On the left hand of the position Sergeant Major Ross and Colour Sergeant Long had reached the third and fourth casemates. Of the fifteen men in Ross's party only four had made it across the murderous ground to reach the large bunkers. The steel doors at the back of the casemates were partially open and the attackers stuffed Mills bombs and 66 phosphorus grenades through the gaps in an attempt to get at the defenders.

The 36 Mills fragmentation grenade, with its distinctive pineapple-grooved surface, was deadly in confined spaces. Its chunky cast-iron shrapnel fragments tore round the inside of the concrete structure, lacerating flesh and splintering bone, the concussion of the explosions bursting eardrums. Combined with the burning phosphorus and suffocating fumes of the 66-type grenades, it was enough to drive the defenders out of their bunkers. The enemy came rushing out of the steel doors and paratroopers covering the entrance immediately picked off the first ones out. Those behind them discarded their weapons and threw their hands up, shouting, '*Kamerad! Kamerad!*' indicating their desperate attempt to surrender. Some were pioneers of Russian origin and shouted '*Russki, Russki!*' in an attempt to save themselves. Others were near-Germans of Polish extraction who had been forcibly conscripted into the ranks of the Wehrmacht and were equally keen to distinguish their nationality from that of the Germans.

Not all of the enemy came out. Fred Milward pushed into the first casemate; it was dark and the only light came from jagged muzzle flashes and exploding grenades. Sensing motion in an internal side chamber he fired a burst through the entrance and the movement stopped. With the casemate subdued, Milward was ordered to hand over all his Gammon bombs; all that mattered now was destroying the guns and getting out before the Arethusa opened up on the battery.

Similar scenes were being repeated in the other casemates, as the surviving members of the assault teams forced out the defenders and took their surrender. More Germans died in the fourth bunker, because it lacked the internal side shelters that offered a degree of protection from grenades in the other casemates. One lone enemy machine-gun position continued to fire until persuaded by Sergeant

Knight's section to surrender. Mopping up continued around the battery, in numerous isolated close-quarter actions, as the remnants of the garrison were winkled out of bunkers and trenches. With the paratroopers close among them, most Germans chose to give up. A few, however, were more determined to resist the invader.

Paddy Jenkins had been held back at the wire during the main assault, but he moved forward to reinforce the depleted assault teams when they reached the casemates. At Casemate Four an explosion from a German stick grenade felled three paratroopers who were caught between the sloped buttresses that flanked the entrance, its effect amplified by the concrete walls. Private George Hawkins was riddled with shrapnel, lethal fragments penetrated the head of the Bren gunner next to him and Private Alan Mower was struck in the back of his legs. Jenkins rushed up behind them and levelled his rifle against the lone German at the top of the casemate. He squeezed the trigger of his Lee Enfield and then finished him off with the point of the bayonet as the man rolled down the steep banked sides of the bunker.

But even as the last isolated attempts at resistance were eliminated, the operation was not over. Although the battery was in their possession, the guns still had to be destroyed before what remained of 9 PARA could withdraw from the position; and the British insurance plan in the event of failure was still being ranged against them from the naval bombardment gun line in the Channel. Parry, lying at the bottom of a crater, was in no doubt about the importance of completing the job of spiking the guns and getting off the battery position before they were raked by fire from the *Arethusa*. He had tied a makeshift tourniquet above the wound in his thigh to stem the blood using the lanyard from his whistle, then climbed painfully from the bomb crater. In the increasing light of early morning, the scene the greeted him was one of carnage and horror.

The position was littered with the debris of battle and the caustic tang of burned cordite hung in the air and assaulted the nostrils. German and British dead and injured lay scattered across the battery, dishevelled prisoners were being formed up in small groups and the medics had set about collecting and tending the wounded. Doug

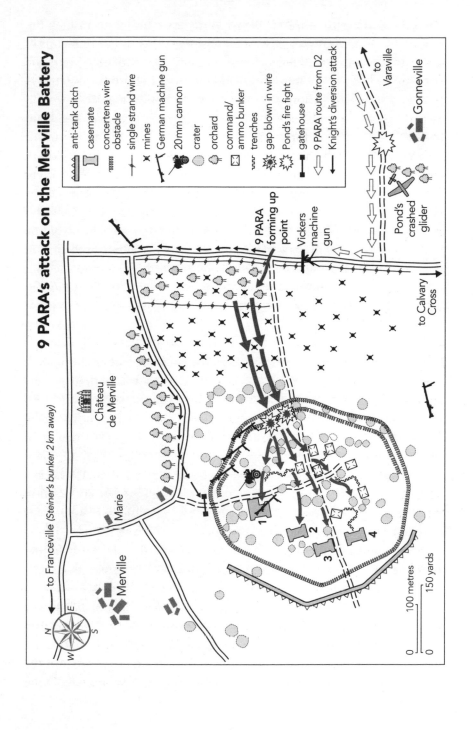

9 PARA's attack on the Merville Battery

Legend:
- anti-tank ditch
- casemate
- concertena wire obstacle
- single strand wire
- mines
- German machine gun
- 20mm cannon
- crater
- orchard
- command/ammo bunker
- trenches
- gap blown in wire
- Pond's fire fight
- gatehouse
- 9 PARA route from D2
- Knight's diversion attack

to Franceville (Steiner's bunker 2 km away)

Merville

Château de Merville

Marie

9 PARA forming up point

Vickers machine gun

to Calvary Cross

to Varaville

Gonneville

Pond's crashed glider

1
2
3
4

0 ___ 100 metres
0 ___ 150 yards

N
E
S
W

Tottle puked in shock and revulsion at the scene as he moved among smashed bodies, dismembered limbs and men crying out in pain. He heard Hudson moaning from the minefield and went back through the wire to help him. Hudson was still conscious and sufficiently alert to hear Tottle's sharp intake of breath as he lifted his smock to look at the terrible wounds to his gut. His lower stomach had been penetrated in several places and he had exit wounds in his backside.

From his position near the wire, Otway had seen that the battery had been taken. But he had received no reports that the guns had been destroyed, so he went forward to investigate. Moving down the cleared route through the minefield, Otway stopped next to Hudson, who was lying prone on the ground and managed to exchange a few words of comfort with him before his wounded adjutant slipped into delirium. Otway continued through the wire into the centre of the position to confirm the destruction of the guns. By then the firing had ceased but, although he was unaware of it, not all the Germans had surrendered.

In the confused nature of the fighting and in their haste to reach the casemates on the western side of the battery, the assault parties had bypassed a submerged command bunker that lay in the south-east corner of the position. It was indiscernible from the nearby cookhouse and administrative bunkers that lay next to it. Since the structure had no firing points, it had been unable to return rifle or machine-gun fire at the British paratroopers when they attacked. Instead Buskotte had watched the action through a periscope. By the end of the attack he had twelve men with him, six of whom were wounded and had managed to crawl into his command headquarters undetected.

It was already getting light by the time that Buskotte could communicate with Steiner in his own command bunker and by then the battery had been taken and Otway's men were reorganizing on the position. Steiner had attempted to get to the battery during the night when he heard the outbreak of explosions and small-arms fire coming from the other side of the village as the attack started. But the fighting had been too fierce and he was forced to return to his small observation bunker in the sand dunes on the other side of Franceville.

He tried to raise the 716th Division headquarters to appeal for assistance, but since making his original call to General Richter four hours earlier he was unable to get through. The telephone lines had been cut through a combination of RAF bombing and Resistance activity. As a result he was unable to communicate with the other batteries of his regiment situated on the west side of the Orne.

On the east bank of the river the telephone lines were still working. Part of the network depended on a small exchange located in a requisitioned house in the village of Merville which belonged to the Yvonne family. Twelve-year-old Lucien Yvonne would later watch his father bury the bodies of British soldiers who had fallen round their home earlier that morning. The paratroopers had been sent to cut the wires to the telephone exchange, but their failure meant that the lines to the battery were still open. When Steiner got through to the battery, Buskotte was able to report that the position had been taken and that they had 'suffered many losses'. He was unable to confirm the state of his guns, but he told Steiner that the British parachutists were still on the position. Steiner ordered Buskotte to stay where he was and to make sure that all his surviving men were under cover.

As a result of their failure to neutralize the small telephone exchange in Merville, the lines to the neighbouring 711th Division, based four kilometres to the east in Cabourg, were still intact. Since Steiner was unable to raise his own division headquarters in Caen, he put through a call to the 711th Division and requested artillery support. When he was asked where he wanted it, he told them to drop it right on top of his own battery. As his OP bunker faced out to sea he would be unable to observe the fall of shot and send corrections to adjust its accuracy, so the barrage would have to be map predicted. He told the headquarters to hold their fire until he called for it. The Merville Battery was already beginning to come under intermittent German mortar fire from the 3rd Company of the 736th Infantry Regiment based on the other side of Merville. But it was sporadic and would be nothing compared to the combined shoot of several much larger calibre artillery batteries. The target data was sent to every available German gun within range in the 711th Division area.

Out to sea on the naval bombardment line the crew of the *Arethusa* were also making preparations to fire on the battery. On the bridge the ship's captain was watching the minute hands of his fire control clock count down. Since arriving on station at 0455 hours, the target coordinates for the Merville Battery had been fed into the ship's electromechanical fire control system and the three double gun turrets of her six-inch guns were trained broadside towards the direction of the battery. In the red half-light her gun crews waited by their shell trays, while above them on the bridge Captain Hugh Dalrymple-Smith fretted; he had still not heard from the naval shore party attached to 9 PARA and his orders stated that he was to open fire at 0530.

As the close-quarter infantry battle around the position subsided, Parry had managed to limp to Casemate One. He felt a profound sense of anticlimax when confronted by an ageing 100mm calibre gun mounted on wooden spoke wheels. He had expected to see a modern 150mm artillery piece; he wondered whether taking it had been worth the cost of so many lives. He ordered the paratroopers inside the casement to destroy it with sticks of plastic explosive. Once the charges were set the party took shelter outside the casemate and hugged the walls, and a thick pall of black smoke, dust and shot blasted through the entrance as the sticks ignited. Parry returned to inspect the damage and was as satisfied as he could be, given that the gun chamber was choked thick with acrid fumes. He coughed and wheezed in the suffocating atmosphere. When a mortar round exploded outside the entrance of the casemate he steadied himself against the embrasure sill of the gun chamber and caught a bomb splinter in his wrist.

Being wounded a second time was a reminder that the battery was still a dangerous place to be, but before they could withdraw they had to be sure that all the guns had been spiked. Lacking the semicircular Wade charges designed to cut through metal, paratroopers in the other casemates were also having to improvise with plastic explosives, Gammon bombs and grenades in their attempts to blow barrels and wreck breeches. Parry checked on the guns in the third and fourth casemates, where officers or NCOs assured him that they had been disabled, either by explosives or by removing parts of the breech blocks. Otway was equally keen to ensure that the guns' destruction had been completed. Lieutenant Mike Dowling reported to the commanding officer that he thought that the gun in Casemate Two had been disabled. Otway told him to go back and 'Bloody well make sure those guns are out of action'. Dowling returned to the bunker, but was killed outright by a mortar bomb before he got there.

In the confusion of trying to reorganize on the position, deal with their casualties, and collect prisoners while under intermittent mortar fire, the manner of checking that the guns had been made inoperable was less than systematic. Neither Otway nor Parry personally inspected the damage caused to every gun, nor did the two men confer. In truth, without the hollow-shaped cutting charges and engineers trained in specialist explosive demolition, which had been lost with the gliders, 9 PARA's attempts to disable the guns to prevent them firing again could only be rudimentary. They were not gunners and efforts to destroy the guns by double-loading them and firing them, with a round in the breech and loading one down the barrel, would have had little effect unless the shell in the breech was correctly primed. Removing the breech from a LFH 15/19(t) Czech howitzer was also a complex and time-consuming process and no one in 9 PARA would have known how to do it properly.

Time was pressing, dawn had broken and 9 PARA needed to get off the position before HMS *Arethusa* opened fire. The risk of being blown to bits by their own Navy was on everybody's mind. Without a radio link to the *Arethusa*, they lit yellow candle flares in the hope that they would be spotted by Allied reconnaissance aircraft. A carrier pigeon, which had been transported in a cardboard container in the smock of the signals officer, was released with a message that the battery had been taken. But these were desperate measures with no guarantee of success. The imperative now rested with gathering their wounded and getting clear of the battery.

Although delirious with shock and the effects of morphine, Hudson did not relish the prospect of being caught by the naval bombardment. He asked to be moved to the orchard at the rear of the position. With the assistance of some of the German prisoners, Hudson was carried to a bomb crater on the edge of the battery on the only stretcher 9 PARA had recovered from the DZ. The rest of the wounded were being gathered there on planks of wood or ammunition sledges. Paddy Jenkins and Sid Capon assisted Alan Mower from the side of Casemate Four, but they had to leave Private Hawkins, who was too badly injured to carry without a stretcher. The twenty-three German prisoners were initially reluctant to move through the minefield with the withdrawing paratroopers, until a burst from a Sten gun into the ground behind them made them see the wisdom of moving with their captors.

As what was left of 9 PARA began to withdraw through the gate-house position, Parry shouted at the remaining stragglers to get moving. He was weak from loss of blood and had to be towed from the battery on a soapbox trolley. Jefferson was assisted out of one of the bomb craters after the shrapnel wounds to his leg had been bound by the medical officer and limped off the position. The British and German wounded, who had been collected together under Corporal Tottle, were loaded on to an old farm cart from a nearby barn. German prisoners helped him push it as they followed the thin column of those who could still walk south to the designated rally point. They had just short of a kilometre to travel to a lonely stepped Calvary cross at a track junction on the slopes of the higher ground above the village of Gonneville.

Those too seriously wounded to be moved or who had been presumed dead were left behind. It was an agonizing decision, but 9 PARA now had only a vastly depleted medical section; they hoped that the injured would stand a better chance of survival by being picked up and cared for by nearby German forces.

Through the periscope in his command bunker, Buskotte watched the remnants of the 9th Battalion withdraw and reported their movements to Steiner in his OP position. His battery commander then put in a call to 711th Divisional headquarters in Cabourg. By the time Steiner had put down the receiver, the shells from every gun battery on the east bank of the Orne within range were already on their way to the Merville Battery.

As they moved towards the Calvary cross, Parry looked back at the battery. The air seemed fresher, no longer pervaded by the stench of death, cordite and freshly churned earth; he felt the renewed optimism that so often comes with the break of dawn and the start of a new day. Stragglers were still making their way through the wire behind him, some limping; the dead lay where they had fallen. It seemed strangely quiet and he felt a pang of guilt about the men who had been left behind.

Suddenly there was a tearing sound as shells split the sky above them. Parry saw the first round hit in a momentary flash of orange flame before it heaved up a fountain of earth; the screaming whistle of more artillery rounds followed, as the Germans plastered the ground in and around the casemates. Private Hawkins, badly wounded, hugged the inside of the bunker where he had been left, while the 'stonk' of incoming metal rained down outside. Anyone not off the position and not underground was vulnerable to the Germans' final protective fire mission. Parry saw a paratrooper passing through the wire at the back of the strung-out column double up like a clasp knife when a shell's shrapnel struck him. The killing at the Merville Battery was not yet over and the battle to protect the east flank of the invasion was only just beginning.

11

Scattered

THE FIRST RAYS of daylight were breaking through the band of grey murk that hung over the coastline and a low mist hugged the surrounding fields when the thin bedraggled line of what was left of 9 PARA arrived at the Calvary cross. It was just before 0600 hours and the desolate group of survivors moved like ghosts as they collected round the tall battered black timber crucifix at the side of the track junction. It was an ironic symbol of their degradation and sacrifice. They had diced against the mathematical odds, but the butcher's bill had been high: of the 150 men who had attacked the battery, 75 men had been killed or wounded.

The men were dirty from the shock of battle, their faces smudged black with grime and sweat; their smocks had been torn by the wire as they fought their way into the position and their boots were caked with the churned Norman mud of the battery. Some were without weapons; others carried captured German arms in lieu of their own that had been lost during the drop. The German prisoners were pushed into a bomb crater under the watchful guard of Sergeant Knight, who covered them with his Sten gun. But there was little other semblance of military order, as the Paras gathered in small groups around the cross. No sentries were posted and no orders were given.

The trauma of the morning's fighting with its shocking baptism into the violent realities of warfare and its associated planning miscalculations, intelligence failures, confusion and fatigue, formed a collective malaise of loss and bewilderment. All had lost friends and conversation was limited to muted enquiries about what had happened to their mates. Sergeant Major Miller pulled on a cigarette and as he exhaled looked at the desolate band of men and asked, 'Is this all that is left?'

None felt the effects of their ordeal more than their commanding officer who sat alone on the steps of the cross in a catatonic state, his head in his hands. As the figure of Christ gazed down upon him, Otway was overcome by exhaustion and emotion, consumed by an inner turmoil of remorse and anger. As the man in charge he felt a dreadful responsibility for the decisions he had taken and the loss of so many men. He cursed his misfortune and what he considered to be the incompetence of the RAF for the disastrous drop that had forced him to attack a well-defended location with the odds stacked so cruelly against them. Otway's demeanour was not lost on his men who were caught in their own post-combat trough and needed his leadership now more than ever. They were isolated behind enemy lines and extremely vulnerable to an enemy counter-attack. Lance Corporal Wilson recognized his commanding officer's condition and the brandy-laced tea he proffered slowly induced Otway out of his trance of self-reflection and ire.

Allen Parry was in a fundamentally different frame of mind when he was towed into the RV location with his bloody leg resting on the edge of the box cart he had commandeered. The man who felt he had been passed over by Otway had played a seminal role in the attack. Despite his wounds, he was buoyed up by his own perform-ance and those of the men around him, and his arrival and cheery salutations to his colonel acted like a tonic and helped Otway snap back into the reality of the situation around him. Otway told Parry to seek medical treatment, then ordered a headcount and instructed Knight to get the men into all-round defence while he took stock of his losses.

Fifty per cent of the force that had attacked the battery had been wounded or killed. With the arrival of twenty men from Pond's glider that had crash-landed in the orchard, his numbers at the RV rose to approximately 100 men. Welcome as the reinforcements were, Otway's total strength still amounted to only just over 10 per cent of the total battalion group force of approximately 750 men who had landed in Normandy. As Otway got a grip and began reorganizing the shattered remnants of his battalion, he had little idea of just how close he had come to being counter-attacked during his assault on the Merville Battery, had it not been for the fortuitous crash-landing of Pond's glider.

Amid the crash of splintering wood and the cries of the wounded, Pond had screamed, 'Everyone out!' as the glider landed and came to an abrupt stop. Fred Glover didn't need any encouragement; the back of the Horsa was in chaos and had begun to burn. Pond was already out when his platoon sergeant warned him that a German patrol was approaching up the road leading to the battery where firing could already be heard as Otway's attack went in. He split his men either side of the road and an immediate firefight broke out. Glover bolted from the broken tail section when German rounds smacked through the thin canvas skin behind him. He felt no pain from the cannon splinters that had penetrated his legs and tumbled into a bomb crater from where he immediately returned fire at the muzzle flashes that cut through the darkness less than twenty-five metres away.

The sudden arrival of the glider and the instant reaction of Pond and his men had taken Timpf by surprise as he and his men hastened back from the clearing patrol Steiner had ordered the instant they heard the firing at the battery. They had been caught at the bottom of the sunken lane and the weight of enemy fire was impressive and effective. Every man in the glider carried a Sten gun and a five-magazine chest rig, which meant they could blaze away on full automatic. Glover now put into practice the firing drill he had run over in his head again and again as he flew across the Channel. He kept the butt pressed tight against his shoulder, tilting the weapon slightly to the right to allow the empty rounds to eject cleanly without jamming the breech. He tried to count the rounds, so that he would know when to change the magazines and prevent the dread of a 'dead man's click' as he squeezed the trigger. Twenty men were doing the same thing on both sides of the lane.

The short, sharp exchange of thousands of rounds lasted only a few minutes, but Pond's men bested the grenadiers from 3rd Company, 736th Infantry Regiment convincingly. The Germans took several casualties, while none of the paratroopers was hit, which forced them to withdraw back down the lane. The two sides hurled insults at each other in the darkness, until the Germans melted away. The unintended consequences of the glider landing behind the gun battery and Pond's impromptu action ultimately saved Otway's depleted force from being attacked in the rear at the very moment when they would have been crossing the minefield and bunching at the perimeter wire to the battery.

After the gun position had been taken, Miller had gone to link up with Pond's men whom he hailed from a meadow marked as a minefield. Pond yelled at him not to come any closer, but Miller insisted it was a phoney minefield and motioned them to follow him. Regardless, Pond ordered his men to move through it in single file, each man glad of the daylight as they stepped gingerly in the footprints of the man in front. Pond had been surprised to see Otway sitting beneath the Calvary cross with his head in his hands, but he was shocked by how few of the battalion had made it through both the drop and the attack. He had expected to see a company of the 1st Canadian Parachute Battalion securing the RV, but of over 120 men assigned to the task, only five had made it to the allotted location in time; the rest of the Canadian paratroopers having been as badly scattered as 9 PARA.

The battalion's secondary objective had been to take a German naval radar station on the banks of the Orne at Sallenelles. But even with the few Canadians and the arrival of Pond's men, the total strength 9 PARA could muster amounted to less than a company. Attacking a defended location with such depleted numbers was a task that Otway was not prepared to undertake; the risks were too great and Hill still expected the battalion to join his brigade's defensive line on the higher ground of the Bréville Ridge. Consequently, Otway made the decision to move straight to his third objective of occupying the village of Le Plein on the northern end of the ridge. His mission was to hold the village until relieved by Lord Lovat's 1st Special Service Brigade of commandos, which was due to land over the beaches with the main seaborne assault force later that morning. Otway had to take a harder decision concerning his wounded.

Twenty-two wounded had been placed in a nondescript house on a stud farm called the Haras de Retz close to the Calvary cross track junction. As well as Parry, they included Jefferson, Alan Mower and Private Mead, who despite his punctured intestine and being hit at the battery had managed to walk to the RAP unaided. Hal Hudson had been carried there on the battalion's only stretcher, clinging grimly on to life despite the terrible wounds to his stomach, but only just. He was in agony and lapsed in and out of consciousness. His forehead was marked with the letter 'M' from a chinagraph pencil to indicate that he had been given morphine, but there were no more of the Tubonic Ampoule Syringe monojets to give him. In normal circumstances, a serious battlefield casualty needed to be in a field hospital for surgery within two hours of his wounding if he was expected to have a chance of survival. But 9 PARA had no transport and there was no hospital to evacuate Hudson to. The nearest 6th Airborne Division Advanced Dressing Station was at 3rd Parachute Brigade headquarters at Le Mesnil, but that was seven kilometres away and not yet set up. His prospects looked grim.

Hudson's only hope was that the Germans would pick him up before he died. Harold Watts did what he could for the wounded, but he and his medics were required to move with the battalion. Instead the injured men were left in the care of two Wehrmacht medical orderlies. Jefferson was still mobile and went round those lying on the bare boards of one of the downstairs rooms. He tried to console his batman, Private Smith, whose eye had been removed by the blast of a mine; he chatted to a soldier shot through both legs by a German MG 42 machine gun, and noted Hudson's deathly white complexion. Talking to the wounded he discovered that Mike Dowling, his best friend in the battalion, had been killed at the battery.

Fred Glover, who was still desperately trying to make his way to the RV, had struggled to keep up as Pond led them through the minefield. The adrenalin of the crash-landing and the firefight had worn off, and he was feeling weak from the loss of blood, which had begun to pool in his boots. He stopped to look at his wounds. His legs were peppered with shrapnel and one of the gashes in his thigh was particularly deep. A lone pathfinder came across him and helped him up the sunken lane to the junction with the main track behind the battery. What he saw across the short stretch of field before him 'shocked him to his core'. The battery was a scene of utter devastation and carnage, The position was still littered with bodies. Palls of black smoke hung in the air and he smelled the stench of cordite, which meant that the battalion could not be far away and so he struggled on towards Calvary cross.

Fred Glover was not the only paratrooper struggling to re-join his unit. All over the Calvados region of Normandy, individuals and small bands of airborne soldiers widely scattered in the drop were evading Germans – and sometimes fighting them – as they searched for their parent formations or made for where they thought they might be. Brigadier James Hill, jumping number one from his aircraft, had landed in four feet of water. It took him several hours to wade back to the DZ. By the time he got there he had collected a disparate group of other paratroopers, including Jack Corteil with his dog Glenn and the naval bombardment party, who had also dropped into the flooded marshes.

Terry Jepp had been dropped into the submerged fields to the east of the DZ. In the darkness he had joined up with three others and struggled through the floodwater until a Norman farmer called Adrien Vermughen rescued them and sheltered them in his barn near Cabourg. He was eventually to give shelter to twenty-two paratroopers until the Germans attacked his farm. The British soldiers were taken prisoner, while Vermughen and his farmhands were tortured and summarily executed.

Some paratroopers remained alone. Private James Baty, who had been pitched out of his aircraft after helping Corteil push his Alsatian out, would spend three days evading capture before he got back to the battalion. Soaking wet and covered in the thick slimy mud of the Dives, he hid by day and moved at night. Without a compass or map, he simply followed the sounds of the fighting. Padre John Gwinnett found the silence of being alone in the darkness and the water unnerving. He wanted to be with his flock when they opened the door of fear at the battery, but it took him nearly fourteen hours to make it out of the swamps and reach the brigade at Le Mesnil, where 3rd Brigade headquarters were located.

Having survived the landing in the marches, Ron Tucker found his platoon and company commander leading other members of C Company. They spent the first night evading the Wehrmacht patrols by avoiding the roads and moving through water-filled ditches. By daylight they had made it to a small crossroads half a kilometre from an old brickworks in Le Mesnil. They joined up with some paratroopers from the Canadian battalion who were tasked with protecting the brigade's headquarters established in a farm on the other side of the brickworks.

As the men dug in along the side of a hedge, they spotted a truck carrying six Germans approaching them on the main Cabourg to Caen road, which ran across the top of the ridge. The Paras ran the vehicle off the road in a fusillade of fire from their concealed position in the hedge line. Tucker advanced up a ditch to make sure they were all dead. One of the prone bodies spilled from the truck pulled a pistol; Tucker shot him in the face, blowing a hole 'the size of a fist' through the back of the German's head. The vehicle he had been thrown from was an old British Army four-hundredweight Austin Morris that had been pressed into service by the Wehrmacht after its capture at Dunkirk four years before. The ambush party started the truck and sent it back to brigade HQ, where they thought it might be put to good use.

After his pilot had mistaken the Dives for the Orne, Corporal Mick Corboy had been dropped beyond the floodwater and landed twelve kilometres away near Dozulé. He joined up with fourteen other mis-dropped members of 9 PARA and took the risk of following road signs to Troarn, where they knew 8 PARA were meant to be. It took them two days, but on the first day they shot up no fewer than four German vehicles, killing some of their occupants and taking others prisoner. During their second encounter, two cars overtook them on the road to Troarn. The first car was past them before they could react, but they raked the second car with a hail of small-arms fire that forced it to crash. Corboy went forward to investigate and found three dead senior German officers inside the bullet-ridden vehicle.

As the rest of 9 PARA began their advance on Le Plein, they were unaware of these events, but Otway would have been pleased with his men. Although cut off and isolated they were following their training, using their initiative and guile to make their way, as best they could, back to where they thought their own lines would be. Despite his orders that the men were to avoid their 'own private battles', with the battery taken Otway could be quietly satisfied that they were killing the enemy whenever they encountered them. But as men fought and died to return to their units, the battlefield remained porous. In those first few hours of D-Day there was no front line and no clear geographic delineation of who was friend or foe. 9 PARA were behind enemy lines and until they managed to link up with the rest of 6th Airborne and the troops that would land from the sea, they would be on their own.

It was a fact not lost on Otway, as he moved his small force three kilometres across country towards the small village of Le Plein on the northern edge of the Bréville ridgeline. With Major Smith leading the remnants of B Company, the battalion moved cautiously. They kept below the skyline, moving along the edges of sunken lanes and hugging the hedgerows. The wheat in the surrounding fields was an early summer green and the undergrowth and trees were abundant with leafy cover. It was ideal infantry country, where the close nature of the terrain and thickness of the seasonal foliage offered advantage to both attacker and defender depending on their tactical ability to read and use the ground. The sun was coming up and beginning to burn off the thin veil of mist that persisted in the corners of the fields they traversed.

The arrival of daylight also signalled the start of the seaborne invasion. Out to sea 5,000 ships prepared to launch the Allied assault divisions on five beaches along sixty miles of Normandy coastline. The 8th Infantry Brigade would land on Sword Beach as part of the first wave of the 3rd British Division, which had orders to capture Caen by the end of D-Day. Before the first troops hit the beaches a massive bombardment from both the sea and the air was about to be unleashed against the thin coastal strip of the Atlantic Wall defences. The naval guns would fire first and be followed by over 700 British and US heavy and medium bombers that would target German defences along the Cotentin Peninsula from the mouth of the Orne to the western edge of the invasion area where the Americans were landing.

Three kilometres out to sea, the mighty fifteen-inch guns of the battleships *Ramillies* and *Warspite* were elevated towards the shoreline. A smokescreen had been laid by the RAF and combined with low hanging cloud to obscure the coast. It meant that the ships would be firing blind and the fall of shot would have to be adjusted by naval firing parties attached to the airborne troops already ashore. The smaller six-inch guns of the *Arethusa* and *Mauritius* would join in the bombardment too. The two light cruisers were given the specific tasks of providing naval gunfire support to the 6th Airborne Division. Aboard both ships there had been considerable anxiety about the progress of the paratroopers; but none more so than on the *Arethusa*, where concern about 9 PARA's progress at the Merville Battery had been acute.

At 0550 the gunnery officer, Lieutenant Commander H.T. Burchell, made his first entry in the ship's fire log, as the *Arethusa*'s long six-inch gun barrels belched fire and engaged her first shore-based targets. But she did not bring her salvos down on the battery. By 0530 Captain Dalrymple-Smith had not heard from 9 PARA and had been about to open fire. He had no way of knowing whether the battalion had taken the guns, but he also had his orders. On the bridge next to him his gunnery officer stood poised by a voice pipe ready to pass the command to fire to the crews manning the three gun turrets of the ship. Had Burchell done so, a tonne of high explosive would have caught 9 PARA while they were still on the position. At 0525 the ship received a frantic message from their liaison officer stationed on the task force bombardment control ship HMS *Largs*; he reported that a reconnaissance aircraft had spotted yellow smoke coming from the battery. To his enormous relief Dalrymple-Smith gave the order to cancel the fire mission.

The ships had plenty of other targets to engage and 9 PARA heard the harsh rasp of metal tearing through the air as the first heavy naval rounds ranged over their heads towards German positions further inland. The defences of the Atlantic Wall on the coastline behind them were also taking a pounding, which gave the depleted units of Airborne Forces and the isolated stragglers a sense of comfort that they were not alone. It also meant that seaborne troops would soon be hitting the beaches and fighting their way inshore to link up with them. But the screaming trajectory of metal objects the size of dustbins shooting high above them soon gave way to an altogether more ominous sound, as the sky filled with hundreds of Allied bombers headed towards them. Smith was attempting to flush out some German snipers when he heard them.

He could not see the enemy in the orchard ahead of him, but they had slowed 9 PARA's progress, forcing the men Smith commanded to fire and manoeuvre forward in an attempt to draw their fire and outflank them. As the drone of the approaching aircraft engines grew louder, Smith could not help thinking that they might be on 'the wrong side of the bomb line'. His worst fears were confirmed when he saw masses of US Flying Fortresses in formation high above him. His men sprinted for a ditch and pressed their faces into the dirt. The rest of the battalion were doing the same thing. The American aircraft were too high up to see the yellow smoke candles and marker panels the Paras had put out and their bomb bay doors were already open.

The huge wave of bombers had been sent to soften up the German beach defences, but the thick bank of cloud and the smokescreen laid to cover the Allied ships, now hung over the coast forming an impenetrable mist, which caused the aircraft's bomb aimers to release their deadly cargos too late and too far inland. Suddenly, the air was filled with the high-pitched scream of thousand of bombs, as the bombers spewed their loads over a large swathe of the Norman countryside. The men caught underneath them listened horrified to the jarring sound of high explosive destruction, as the aerial bombardment crashed down around them and the ground shook as if it were jelly. Pond was 'truly terrified', as large trees were uprooted and thrown upwards as if 'propelled by rockets'. The bombing seemed to stop almost as soon as it had started. The deep ditches the men had sheltered in had saved them from a stick of bombs that had bracketed either side of the track they had been moving along.

Hill's party was not so lucky. The brigadier was leading his disparate band in an effort to link up with 9 PARA and was less than two kilometres to their east when they heard the 'horrid noise' of the approaching bombers, but there was nowhere to run to. His party was strung out along a farm track flanked on either side by impenetrable thick hedges. Hill shouted, 'Get down!' and threw himself flat across the already prostrate body of Lieutenant Peters, the 9 PARA mortar officer. The track erupted in shattering explosions and fountains of earth and scything shrapnel, as a stick of 500-pound bombs plastered the ground, obscuring everything in a cloak of dust and smoke. As the air cleared, Hill could smell death all around him. He knew that he had been hit and thought that the severed leg next to him must be his. Only when he managed to stumble to his feet did he realize that it belonged to George Peters, who lay dead beneath him.

Over half of the other men also lay dead, including young Jack Corteil and his dog Glenn, still linked to his lifeless master by the lead wrapped round his hand. Most of those who had not been killed instantly lay mortally wounded. Only three got up when the sound of the bombers faded into the distance. Hill had had his left buttock removed by a bomb splinter, but he could manage to walk. He and his defence platoon commander took the morphine from the dead and administered it to those still living, then resumed their search for 9 PARA. Unbeknown to Hill, Captain 'Robbie' Robinson had also survived, but believing everyone else was dead, set off alone in the direction of Varaville. The cheer that the wounded gave Hill as he left them stayed with the brigadier for the rest of his life, made more poignant by the fact that none of those he left behind were to survive their wounds.

The spread of the bombing extended to the RAP at Haras de Retz and the falling bombs rocked the house to its foundations, covering the wounded in a film of white plaster dust. The blast of the explosions assaulted Alan Jefferson's senses; he was petrified and found the experience far worse than being under artillery fire. He noticed how the two German medical orderlies simply shuttered the windows and seemed to take the bombardment in their stride, no doubt having become well used to it from their time in the battery. The bombers came in three waves, each bombardment seeming more intensive than the one that had preceded it. Each time Jefferson covered his vitals with his small pack. As the bombs rained down outside the building, he tried to make himself as small as possible, imagining himself squeezing into the joins of the floorboards; he cursed the airmen overhead while he wept for his dead friend Mike Dowling.

Out in the Channel, the horizon was alive with the thousands of ships of the invasion fleet lying off the beaches. From their midst, hundreds of landing craft forged through the swell of a choppy sea, their passengers hunkered down beneath the gunwales as the coast ahead of them erupted in a barrage of explosions. Sword Beach received the heaviest naval bombardment of D-Day. Lasting two hours, the battleships, light cruisers and destroyers of the British naval task force pulverized the shoreline defences with ten tonnes of high explosives a minute. H-Hour, the time when the first troops of the British 3rd Division would touch down on the beach, was set for 0725 hours and came ninety minutes after the first American landing at the western end of the invasion area had already begun. The time discrepancy was because of the need to land at half tide and took into account the difference in sea conditions between the five Allied beaches.

At 5,000 metres short of the beach the Duplex Drive, or DD, amphibious tanks of the 13/18th Hussars nosed their way cautiously down the ramps of their tank-landing craft into the water. The DD tanks were American-built M4 Shermans that had been fitted with a canvas flotation screen and propellers. The modifications meant that the tanks could swim ashore from their launching craft and drive straight on to the beach. They would not only provide the infantry landing behind them with direct armoured support, but they would also help protect other converted tanks designed to deal with the Germans' defensive beach obstacles and concrete emplacements. Known as 'Funnies', a variety of converted tanks crewed by the 22nd Dragoons had been fitted with flails to detonate mines, fascines made of bundles of logs to fill anti-tank ditches, bridges to cross sea walls and outsized guns and flamethrowers to blast bunkers and burn out their occupants.

The levels and types of armoured support took the Germans by surprise and were a significant contribution to overwhelming the beach defences. But it was the men of the 8th Infantry Brigade landing behind them who took the brunt of the enemy's resistance. Much of the bombing had missed their targets and the heavy gunfire from ships and tanks could not neutralize every position. While the tanks duelled with German 75mm guns and bunkers, Wehrmacht soldiers, stupefied by the bombardment, dug out weapons from collapsed trenches, cleared out the clogging sand from breeches and barrels and readied machine guns and mortars against the wave of incoming infantry.

Landing thirty men each, the assault craft were under fire before they hit the narrow strip of beach. But the real devastation started as the ramps came down and the ranks of tightly bunched infantrymen were disgorged into the water to make their way up the slope of the beach. The German mortars and machine guns found their mark when the men plunged off shifting ramps carrying sixty pounds of equipment and struggled up the sandy shingle. In those first few minutes, the men of the 1st South Lancashire and 2nd East Yorks regiments were horribly exposed. The DD tanks continued to fire in the infantry, despite their engines being swamped by seawater, but when their crew compartments flooded, the tankers were forced to bail out, which meant that the majority of Shermans were unable to accompany the infantry up the beach. Lacking intimate armoured support, soaking-wet soldiers began to fall amid the hail of bullets and shrapnel that greeted them.

On the left of the thin strip of the assault sector of the beach, the East Yorks took 200 casualties and were held up at the sea wall in front of Ouistreham by a troublesome 75mm gun until a flail tank eventually knocked it out. On their right the South Lancs took ninety-six casualties in as many minutes, including their CO. But impressive as the forward defences along the beach line were, they lacked depth and the leading assault companies of both battalions cleared the foreshore relatively quickly and then set about attacking the isolated German strongpoints immediately behind it. Just before 0800, the first commando units of Lovat's 1st Special Service Brigade landed behind the infantry. Wearing their distinctive green berets, they disembarked precariously from larger landing craft down double gangplanks slipped either side of the bows of their assault vessels. By then the storm of bullets that had met the leading infantry had abated.

As Lovat's men waded ashore they passed the bodies of the infantry drifting in the waves and littering the shoreline. As the 8th Infantry Brigade advanced directly inland, the commandos swung east into Ouistreham and began fighting in the narrow Norman streets of the town. By 0900 hours they were under heavy fire from a 20mm flak gun mounted on a belvedere overlooking the seafront. It was knocked out by two rounds from one of the few Shermans of the 13th/18th that had managed to get off the beach. By 1000 hours Number 4 Commando had reached the Ouistreham lighthouse and the lock gates of the Caen Canal, and swung south to advance down the west bank of the River Orne to the bridges at Bénouville and Ranville that were held by the 6th Airborne Division. In the race to build up the strength of British forces holding the vital left flank of the invasion, they were making good time.

Although the canal gates were one of the registered targets covered by the guns at the Merville Battery and the top of the lighthouse was visible from Steiner's OP bunker nestling in the sand dunes on the other side of the Orne, the battery had remained silent. Not one round was fired against the men of the 8th Infantry Brigade fighting their way off Sword Beach or at the commandos who landed behind them. 9 PARA may not have been able to destroy the guns effectively, but their contribution in taking the battery lay in the killing of the gunners who would crew them. By the time the first waves of British assault troops hit the shoreline, Buskotte could not muster a single gun crew that was capable of firing the howitzers in support of the German defences at Sword Beach.

To the men pushed tightly together as they came off ramps and down gangplanks on to the beach, the false intelligence about the calibre of the guns was academic. Although smaller than the 150mm artillery type they had been reported to be, the effect of four 100mm guns firing from heavily protected bunkers, impervious to naval counter-battery salvos, would have been devastating. In a matter of minutes, their combined rate of fire of twenty-four rounds a minute would have covered an area the size of several football pitches in a blizzard of lethal shrapnel. By preventing the guns from firing on men bunched closely together on the thin strip of shoreline, 9 PARA's attack on the Merville Battery, as risky and costly as it had been, undoubtedly saved the lives of hundreds of British soldiers coming ashore that morning on Sword Beach.

As the infantry and commandos fought their way inland, 9 PARA were about to fight their next battle. Having been warned by French civilians to avoid the neighbouring village of Hauger, due to the presence of over 200 Russians fighting for the Germans, the battalion approached Le Plein along a main road leading into the village from the north-east. Sergeant Major Dusty Miller and Private Fred Milward were part of the advance guard and immediately engaged in a brief skirmish with several Germans mounted on bicycles coming in the opposite direction. They were continuing their advance along the hedgerows towards the houses when the German machine guns opened up on them.

Pinned down in the road along their main axis of advance into the village, three soldiers of B Company broke into an adjacent farmhouse. They engaged the MG 42, firing from the upstairs windows, and forced the crew to withdraw towards a road junction in the village. The rest of the company then attacked them, killing fifteen of the enemy and capturing two machine guns. As the men of B Company advanced forward to close on the junction, a counter-attack was launched into their left flank. McGeever, McGuinness and Fenson saw it coming. Their Vickers was already set up and they waited until the leading elements of the enemy counter-attack were twenty metres away, then they opened up. Canvas-belted .303 bullets chewed through the gun's receiver as McGuinness traversed the Vickers from left to right. When he ceased firing, the attack had been broken and a pile of field-grey figures lay dead on the street.

Split on either side of the road, the advance into the northern end of the village continued with the men taking cover in ditches and behind walls. The village was crawling with the enemy and it slowly dawned on the Paras that the majority of the men they were fighting were Russians not Germans. Miller made a dash across the street and was winged by a bullet in the shoulder. A large walled farmhouse on the southern edge of Le Plein seemed to be the focus of the enemy activity and dominated the open green at the centre of the village. Otway ordered Lieutenant Tom Halliburton of B Company to take a patrol and flank the building to establish its strength. Approaching the building from the rear, they came under small-arms fire from a walled enclosure. Halliburton made for an open wooden gate, but in his haste he didn't see the sandbagged machine gun stationed inside the walled courtyard. It dropped him as he charged through the gate.

The weight of fire forced back the men who were with him. They returned fire and sought to probe an alternative entrance into the courtyard through adjacent outbuildings in an attempt to get to Halliburton. Private Joe Milward had been hit in the face, but he continued to fire his Bren while his mates worked their way through the outbuildings. Another of the Paras took a round through his windpipe as bullets fired from the first-floor windows splintered through the wooden outbuildings. In the face of such overwhelming fire, there was no chance of getting to Halliburton; the farmhouse was too strongly held and the patrol pulled back and reported to Otway. Behind them Halliburton lay bleeding to death from the burst of MG-42 fire that had riddled his stomach and another of their number struggled for his life, breathing through bubbling blood and the bullet hole in his neck.

The failed attack convinced Otway that the Hiwis were not going to give up Le Plein without a fight and that he lacked the strength to take the village by force. But if 9 PARA remained in the open streets they ran the risk of being defeated piecemeal by a stronger enemy. Otway decided to occupy a château on the north-west side of the village. With its stout walls of Norman stone running along three sides of the property and an iron railed fence and gate to its front, the Château d'Amfreville would provide him with a strongpoint. If he held the château, he could prevent the enemy from driving him out of the village and it would allow him to retain a foothold from which to await the arrival of Lovat's commandos. 9 PARA entered the château from the rear and set up a hasty defence position along its walls and outbuildings. Otway placed a section on the nearby junction of the road to Hauger, while McGeever and his Vickers crew were left in a separate house covering the north-east flank.

The Paras dug slit trenches in the grounds to strengthen the defensive perimeter. The tennis court was used as a makeshift stockade for the German prisoners from the battery and those taken when entering the village. The wounded were placed in a makeshift RAP in a dug-out vehicle scrape in one of the barns. The château had been used as a billet by the Russian troops and was strewn with the debris of their occupation. The sour smell of ammonia, unwashed bodies and sweat pervaded the rooms, which were littered with smashed furniture, soiled clothing and foul-smelling blankets. But the château was well stocked with German rations of sausages, cheese and bread. It was 0930 and for the first time 9 PARA had somewhere to shelter, a chance to brew up, eat and consolidate. Outside the walls of the château, the enemy began to dig in at the crossroads in the centre of the village and the German commanders of the Hiwis laid their plans to move against them.

The firing at Le Plein provided Hill with a point of reference to head for and he arrived at the château at around 1000 hours. He looked dreadful, having lost half his backside during the bombardment on the track, but his mental stamina and inner fortitude came to the fore when the battalion's medical officer insisted on treating his wounds. It led to an altercation when Captain Watts suggested that he looked bad for morale and should take a sedative, but Hill had no intention of being taken out of the battle. The shot that put him to sleep for two hours had to be administered surreptitiously by the doctor during his examination. As Hill slept, the Germans and their Russian lackeys probed the position. Domination of the southern half of the village gave them possession of the church and the château was soon brought under rifle fire from its belfry, while other enemy sharpshooters moved into fire positions in the surrounding houses and trees.

Any unconcealed movement inside the perimeter attracted a fusillade of shots from the Hiwi riflemen using the Wehrmacht's standard K98k bolt-action Mauser rifles. Although they were not trained snipers, their fire was effective and Otway saw one of his men fall back from the château wall with a bullet through his head. He matched the threat with his better equipped and better trained snipers. Using their specially converted Number 4 Lee Enfield rifles and Mark 3 telescopic sights, the snipers took up positions inside the perimeter and covered likely firing positions beyond its walls. Their superior skills began to count against the enemy, as individual Hiwis who exposed themselves were picked off. But the enemy were more numerous and had greater freedom of movement than the paratroopers confined within the château walls; they also had a plentiful supply of ammunition. 9 PARA had only what remained of the supplies they had jumped in with. As the morning progressed it was beginning to run out.

While the snipers concentrated on making every round count, Hill woke from his involuntary sedation to find that his leg had seized and he could not walk. Nonetheless he was insistent on making his way to the headquarters of 6th Airborne Division three kilometres away at Ranville. A ladies' bicycle was procured from an outbuilding and a paratrooper was detailed to wheel Hill down the slopes of the ridge. It was a risky undertaking, as the ground between Le Plein and Ranville was not yet under the Allies' control, but it was a risk that he had to take. 9 PARA had no radio communications and Hill had been away from his brigade since landing in the marches and out of contact with his superior commander since leaving England. Before he made his way to his own headquarters at Le Mesnil, he needed to report to General Richard Gale that the Merville Battery had been taken.

Balancing precariously on his unorthodox chariot, Hill passed DZ 'N', the main dropping and landing zone for 6th Airborne Division headquarters and the 5th Parachute Brigade. In the fields large strips of unripened wheat had been scythed flat by scores of Horsa gliders. Like gigantic black prehistoric birds of prey they now lay broken in a mass of splintered wood, torn canvas and sheared wings. Some had ploughed nose down, while others lay with their cockpits raised up when their undercarriage had snapped off on landing. The tail sections lay open, either broken off on impact or unbolted by their crews to unload Jeeps and heavy weapons. Soldiers were still unloading stores as Hill passed, while engineers dismantled the remaining anti-glider poles and used an air-portable bulldozer to clear new strips for more gliders, which were due to land later that evening.

Hill arrived at the Château du Heaume in the Bas de Ranville without incident. The grounds were a hive of activity, as operations and signals staff of the division established themselves in the stables, which were a mass of stores, tents and radio masts. Hill found Gale in the château, wearing his unzipped Denison smock and jodhpur riding breeches, in buoyant mood. The ruddy-faced general welcomed the news Hill brought him about 9 PARA's activities and in turn was pleased to inform Hill that in his absence, and although widely dispersed during the drop on to DZ Victor, 3rd Parachute Brigade had achieved all its objectives. Hill learned that 5th Brigade's drop on to DZ Nick had been far more successful and they had dug in a solid defensive position with anti-tank guns around the Orne and Caen Canal bridges. The landing zone was defended and being prepared for the rest of 6th Air Landing Brigade to fly into later that night. Gale also told Hill that Lovat's brigade of commandos had begun to cross the bridges and his lead elements were preparing to progress towards Le Plein to relieve 9 PARA.

Despite the good news, Hill looked dreadful and the senior chief medical officer at the division seized upon him and told him that he was taking him to the main dressing station for an operation. Hill protested but then relented on condition that the doctor would personally take him straight to his headquarters after the operation. The division's main surgical facility had been set up in a nearby town house and had been open since 0500. By the time Hill arrived there its gravel driveway buzzed with Jeeps, as wounded were stretchered off the vehicles' backs and bonnets and taken in through the front doors. As Hill began to succumb to the effects of the chloroform, he heard 'a tremendous concentration' of artillery fire coming down around Ranville. It was 1300 hours and the first consolidated German counter-attack against the Allied invasion was about to be launched.

The German reaction to the invasion had been fatally slow. Since Steiner had put his first call in to General Richter, when he received the report of the glider crash-landing at the battery, 716th Division had received fragmentary reports of further glider and parachute landings throughout the night from other positions. But the dispersed nature of the drop had helped to confuse the enemy. Without a clear picture of the airborne troops' precise objectives, it was difficult to coordinate a consolidated response. Richter also lost communications with the Merville Battery shortly after midnight.

The early counter-operations, such as Timpf's patrol and the counter-attacks by the company of Hiwis from the 642 Ost Battalion at Le Plein, had been local affairs, taken on the initiative of individual commanders on the ground reacting to events around them. Richter's inability to act was exacerbated by the fact that 716th Division was spread thinly over an area of forty kilometres. His only troops not committed to defending static locations were the two companies of the 642 Ost Battalion, which were fighting against 9 PARA. The only definitive decision Richter made that night was to cancel his planned move to Rennes to participate in the map exercise to war-game an Allied landing in Normandy. But he still had little idea that he was about to be playing it for real.

The commander of the one significant mobile reserve available to the 716th Division was in no doubt about what was happening; Major Hans von Luck had put his regiment on standby after receiving the first series of reports at the headquarters of 125th Panzergrenadier Regiment in the early hours of the morning. By 0300 hours, his men were mounted in their tanks and half-tracks and ready to go, the blank ammunition in their magazines and gun racks, which they had used for training on the previous day, replaced by live bullets and shells. Stationed around Caen, his unit was only a few kilometres away from where it was reported that Allied airborne troops were landing and the routes to potential forming-up positions to attack them had all been reconnoitred. Von Luck knew the advantage of counter-attacking at night and while the British paratroopers were vulnerable and disorganized. He was beside himself with frustration, but he received no orders to begin moving his unit.

German confusion was further hampered by the Wehrmacht's complex command and control structure and the predominant belief that, if any attack came in Normandy, it could only be a diversion to detract attention away from the Allies' main objective of the Pas de Calais. The reluctance to commit armoured reserves amounted to a paralysing paranoia. Richter would not act unless he had the sanction of several commanders above him, all of whom were equally uncertain and unwilling to use their initiative without the express permission of their own superior headquarters. Consequently, little more than limited probing attacks by German self-propelled guns and Panzer Mark IVs were made against the 6th Airborne Division perimeter round the bridges, until Von Luck finally received orders to launch his complete unit later that afternoon. But once again the attacks were local affairs and by the time they came, the paratroopers of 5th Parachute Brigade had dug in. By first light the glider-borne six- and seventeen-pounder anti-tank guns were also in position and were able to help the more lightly equipped parachute troops fight off the German armour.

Had the full weight of von Luck's regiment been committed in the first few hours of remaining darkness, there is little doubt that the under-gunned airborne troops, still in the process of rallying and digging in, could not have withstood his armoured onslaught. Additionally, there would have been carnage if the gliders had been caught on the LZ while their troops struggled to offload their equipment and anti-tank guns. Once they had retaken the Orne and Caen Canal bridges, 125th Regiment's tanks and mobile grenadiers would have been poised to launch against the beaches and drive the amphibious force back into the sea as it landed. Had this happened, it would then have been a matter of mopping up the more isolated units of 6th Airborne Division. Cut off and alone behind the château wall in Le Plein, the 100-odd men of 9 PARA would have stood little chance. The fact that the panzers did not come in those first few critical hours gave the Allies landing on the eastern flank of the invasion area a chance, but as far as Terence Otway was concerned, with his ammunition running low and a more numerous enemy pushing against his thin perimeter, it was still an extremely slim one.

Hal Hudson's chances of survival were also looking grim, as he hovered between life and death at the Haras de Retz. Alan Jefferson noted how he had turned a ghastly yellow colour. It was Jefferson who heard the vehicle first. The shadows of late afternoon were beginning to lengthen when John Gwinnett returned to the 3rd Brigade's headquarters, which had been set up in a farmyard among a leafy glade of trees on the opposite side of the road from the brick factory at Le Mesnil. When Gwinnett discovered the fate that had befallen 9 PARA and the wounded from the battery, he knew exactly what he would do with the old bullet-ridden Austin truck Private Tucker had helped recapture from the Wehrmacht. Driven by Allen Parry's batman, he took the battered vehicle and made his way down the road that ran along the crest of the Bréville Ridge to the makeshift RAP at Haras de Retz, where the two German medical orderlies were tending the wounded.

There was only room in the back of the truck for four men and Gwinnett made one trip back up the ridge to prove the route, then returned for the more seriously wounded. It was 1800 by the time Gwinnett arrived to pick up Hudson. Parry and Jefferson thought he was too seriously wounded to move, but Gwinnett insisted that it was his only chance and he was loaded on to the back of the truck. Parry and Jefferson went too, as did Private Smith with his missing eye and mangled face. It was the second of a total of four return trips that Gwinnett would make through unsecured territory to collect all the wounded from the Haras de Retz and deliver them to the field ambulance dressing station at the 3rd Brigade's headquarters at Le Mesnil. The barely conscious Hudson seemed to feel every bump in the road during the journey. Jefferson had reached out to hold his hand as they placed him in the truck, but the terribly wounded captain clenched on to it when he tried to withdraw it. At each jarring jolt, Jefferson felt Hudson grip his fingers more tightly, as if clutching on to his one tenuous link to the living.

Narrowly avoiding a meeting engagement with a German half-track en route to Le Mesnil, Hudson was taken straight into the advanced dressing station when he arrived at 224 Field Ambulance. The ADS was located in an outbuilding used by the farmer to slaughter his livestock across from the farmhouse where the brigade HQ had been established. The butcher's table had been set up as the main operating table, since the medic's own folding tables had been lost in the drop, along with other vital essentials such as clamps, sutures, scalpels and anaesthetic. The first incisions into Hudson's stomach would be made by Gillette razor blades from someone's wash kit, but his operation would have to wait until the first light of morning. Without much of his medical kit and with darkness gathering, the surgeon was not prepared to attempt a procedure until he had daylight to work in.

Had Fred Glover stayed at the Calvary cross, he too might have been picked up by John Gwinnett. But Glover had attempted to follow the battalion as they set out for Le Plein and the men of G-B Force later discovered him at the side of a road. But Gordon-Brown was keen to catch up with Otway, having missed the assault when their glider landed beyond Merville, and, to the chagrin of his men, he was unwilling to take Glover with them. Instead he left him with a wounded German officer and enlisted man. One of Gordon-Brown's party suggested spreading out playing cards behind them for Glover to follow, but it was an empty gesture, because Glover's legs were too badly damaged for him to be going anywhere. Glover hoped that he would eventually be picked up by British troops landing on the beaches and his spirits rose when a lone Para medic happened upon them. But although he carried medical satchels, he could do little for either Glover or the German lieutenant who had serious stomach wounds and suggested that their only chance was to surrender. They did not have long to wait.

In response to the sound of guttural shouts in a field, the medic used his recognition panel to attract a passing patrol he spotted across a field. The Germans broke into extended line and headed towards them, as Glover hastily dismantled his Sten gun and threw away the various parts. Things looked ugly when the enemy soldiers broke through a hedge and searched him. In his haste to get rid of his side-arm, he still had his fighting knife strapped to his leg and a Gammon bomb in one of his smock pockets. The presence of the Fairbairn-Sykes commando dagger caused consternation, since the German troops had a particular loathing for what they considered an under-hand and inhuman weapon. As they roughed him up, Glover heard a Schmeisser machine pistol being cocked and was convinced he was about to be executed. The mood of his captors changed markedly when the wounded German private told the NCO in charge of the patrol that Glover had given his own morphine to the young German lieutenant to ease his agony.

Wounded, vastly outnumbered and virtually on his own, Fred Glover had little choice but to surrender, and, although his circumstances at Le Plein were very different, Terence Otway was also considering capitulation. 9 PARA had continued their sniper duel with the Russian marksmen throughout the morning. Their fire was accurate and effective; a few well-aimed shots through telescopic sights, especially at the wooden slats in the belfry of the church tower, were usually enough to silence an enemy marksman until another took his place. But the battalion's .303 ammunition had run desperately low. Foraging parties had been sent out to recover containers from the surrounding fields, but they yielded nothing more than three-inch bombs for mortars that 9 PARA didn't have. The news from the returning parties sent Otway into a spiral of despair. With Hudson wounded, Captain Paul Greenway had become his acting adjutant and found Otway alone in a room of the château contemplating his fate. Otway looked up and said he considered their situation to be hopeless and was thinking of surrendering. The younger officer was incredulous; he rebuked Otway sharply, reminding him that he was the commanding officer and telling him, 'We've got to go on.'

Later that afternoon, Otway's gloom was broken by the sound of heavy firing in the centre of the village as the commandos probed into the centre of Le Plein. Their arrival prompted Otway into action. He and Wilson left the château, took an abandoned German motorcycle and sidecar and linked up with Lovat in the low ground on the western side of the village. At 1530 Number 3 Commando put in a deliberate attack and, while the Paras provided fire support, Lovat's men cleared the Russians and their German commanders out of the village. As the commandos consolidated their position at Le Plein, Hill was being delivered, as promised, to his headquarters at Le Mesnil. He had made the trip standing in the chief medical officer's

Jeep with a bottle of penicillin strapped to his thigh to help fight off infection to his wound.

Hill's personal quarters were located in the main farmhouse across the courtyard from where Hudson was waiting to have his stomach wounds treated. He had been allocated an upstairs room at the end of the house, which was accessed by its own external staircase. It served his purposes ideally. Unable to sit on his cleaved buttock, Hill used the wooden steps as a seat for his one good buttock, while his injured cheek hung over the edge. It meant that he could sit while he received updates and gave orders to his staff. Being outside was also helpful, as his wound was weeping and beginning to smell. As he sat there, he listened to the reports and took stock of his brigade's situation.

Under the temporary command of Alistair Pearson, the depleted units of the brigade had a tenuous hold on most of the Bréville Ridge. Pearson's own battalion had destroyed the bridges over the Dives at Troarn and Bures on the southern edge of the ridge. 8 PARA now held the high ground in the thick woods of the Bois de Bavent, which overlooked the demolished structures. They had repulsed one attack by six half-tracks of the reconnaissance battalion of the 21st Panzer Division and were dominating the southern end of the ridge by aggressive patrolling. The 1st Canadian Parachute Battalion had successfully blown the Dives bridges at Varaville and Robehomme and were now dug in and defending the Le Mesnil crossroads. One attack by 200 German infantry against the crossroads had been beaten off with heavy casualties inflicted on the enemy.

But all Hill's units were under strength. From a total of 2,200 men, fewer than 1,000 were fighting as part of the brigade's three parachute units. By the evening of the first day, the Canadians could muster 300 men, 8 PARA some 280 and 9 PARA's numbers had dropped below 100 with the casualties taken at Le Plein since the morning. Having been badly dispersed, some men had managed to find their way back to their battalions or, like Ron Tucker who was with the Canadians, had joined up with other units in the brigade line. Some, like Fred Glover, had been taken prisoner. Others, like Mick Corboy, were holed up, hiding or fighting the

Germans in isolated skirmishes and doing their best to find their way in.

Hill's defensive line was not only thin, but there were also gaps in it. While the southern half of the ridge was held from Troarn to Le Mesnil, the high ground between Le Mesnil and the village of Bréville, which Gwinnett had driven across during his mercy mission in the battered Morris truck, was still a no-man's-land. Bréville itself remained in German hands. After handing over Le Plein to the commandos, Hill would use what was left of 9 PARA to plug the gap between his own headquarters and Bréville. But he would lack the strength to do anything more than contain the enemy in the village of Bréville itself, until they could be driven out by other units in 6th Airborne Division. Until that happened, Bréville would remain a dangerous thorn in the thin Allied line and Hill would have to hold seven kilometres of the forward edge of the British left flank with what he had.

In the fading light the drone of engines grew steadily louder and the sky began to fill with hundreds of bombers. As if a mighty flock of birds, the air above the beaches became thick with aircraft. Carrying in the rest of 6th Airborne Division's air landing brigade and its heavy equipment, the 250 Horsa and gigantic Hamilcar gliders cast off from their tugs at 6,000 feet and headed for the LZs around the Caen Canal. Above them the sky buzzed with fighter escorts and below them men cheered. On the ships in the Channel, sailors came up on deck and watched in awe as the towropes fell from the gliders' noses and the bombers turned to starboard. The gliders seemed to float for a moment; then they banked to port, applied their flaps and dropped their noses to begin their run in to the cleared fields of corn. To Midshipman John Carlill, stationed on the quarterdeck of HMS *Mauritius*, it was 'one of the most magnificent moments of his life'.

To the paratroopers up on the ridge, it meant reinforcement, relief and resupply. Gordon Newton watched the gliders land from the brickworks at Le Mesnil, where he had arrived with G-B Force an hour earlier. He also saw the sky bloom with hundreds of coloured silk parachutes, as containers delivering desperately needed ammunition and medical stores fell earthwards. Down to their last few rounds of ammunition, the men in the Château d'Amfreville were elated. They stood and cheered as the black-winged wooden aircraft swooped in across the LZ and scythed the crops flat when they slapped their long canvas-framed bodies down on the ground. As soon as they stopped, men disgorged from the gliders and began unbolting tail sections. The landing zone became a frenzy of activity, as men unloaded guns and stores, anti-tank guns were hooked up and Jeeps and men streamed out of the fields to their forming-up points; all the time more gliders landed among them.

The Germans were also struck by the magnitude of what was unfolding around them. Steiner felt the ground shake and watched the sand at the top of the dunes round his bunker crumble when the streams of departing bombers passed overhead. Behind him on the other side of Franceville his guns at the Merville Battery lay neutered. There was nothing he could do to bring the mass of gliders, men and vehicles in the fields a short way to his south under fire. Other enemy units within range fired their mortars and anti-aircraft weapons, and some of the gliders were hit in the air and others already on the ground began to burn. Major von Luck, still licking his wounds from the failure of his attack on Ranville, also watched the mighty host come in and knew that the limited fire that came in against it was too little, too late.

As the light of 6 June began to fade on the western horizon and D-Day drew to a close, Hill had every right to feel pleased with what the men of his brigade had achieved and the role they had played in the first day of the invasion. With most of the ridge held, the bridges on the double water feature taken and the success of the seaborne landings behind them, the Allies had won the first round in the battle of the beaches and had penetrated up to ten kilometres inland. By the time the dark blanket of night folded over Normandy, 28,845 soldiers had been put across Sword Beach out of a total 156,000 troops landed on D-Day across all five Allied beaches. The British losses on the shoreline amounted to 683 men and there is no doubt that if the Merville Battery, as the most difficult task allotted to 6th Airborne, had not been taken early that morning by 9 PARA, the casualties would have been considerably higher.

The German reaction had been slow; the opportunity to achieve an early victory and evict the Allies from the shoreline had been lost due to hesitancy and a paralysis of command. But the German response was consolidating and the Allied lodgement ashore was precarious. By the end of the day the enemy had begun to recognize what was unfolding against them. Absent commanders had returned to their headquarters, including the commander of Army Group B. Rommel realized that the battle of the beaches had been lost, but knew that he now had to focus on containing the Allied beachhead, prevent it from expanding and fix it for a decisive counter-attack by the as yet uncommitted German divisions. One aspect of his strategy was to take the Bréville Ridge and the battle for the high ground was about to begin.

12

'D+1'

JUNE 7 DAWNED bright and clear, but when he first opened his eyes Terence Otway thought it was raining. But the spots that fell on his face were grains of sand worked loose from the side of his slit trench by his batman as he shook him awake. Otway had managed to snatch a few hours of exhausted sleep wrapped up in a foul-smelling blanket Corporal Wilson had found discarded in one of the rooms of the Château d'Amfreville. The rest of 9 PARA were already up and standing to in their positions behind the wall of the château. Otway climbed out of his slit trench and walked between each of the fire positions in the grounds to chat to his men. It did not take him long.

With the arrival of the commandos the previous afternoon, 9 PARA had had a relatively quiet night. 3 Troop of 3 Commando of Lovat's 1st Special Service Brigade had dug in on the southern side of the village facing towards Bréville further along the ridgeline, 6 Commando held the remainder of Le Plein and 4 Commando had occupied the nearby hamlet of Hauger and driven out the Ost troops. The presence of so many British commandos gave Otway's men a respite from attack and a chance to reorganize, although there was little opportunity to sleep. The hours of summer darkness were short and easily consumed with the field routine of sentry duty, servicing kit and the need to 'stand to' in their positions an hour after dusk and before dawn. A precaution in the event of a surprise attack under the cover of darkness, this was a standard military procedure that also delineated day- and night-time routine. Before the light faded each man would have cleaned his weapon, and donned his equipment and helmet to take up his alert positions. The process would be repeated again before first light, when re-cleaning their weapons, shaving and breakfasting on their meagre twenty-four-hour ration packs would herald the start of another day.

Though sleep had been limited by the seasonally short hours of darkness and defensive routine, the lull in the fighting and the coming of morning brought a renewed sense of optimism. Having taken the battery at such cost, many believed the idle talk made over their mess-tin breakfasts that they would be withdrawn from the beachhead and sent back to England where they would be brought up to strength and held ready for future parachute operations behind enemy lines. Given their selection and specialist training, few thought they would remain employed in a general infantry role in Normandy for long. Sid Capon was one of them. As far as he was concerned they were too valuable for that and they had done their bit, so he was eager to believe any rumour that they were about to be pulled out of the line. But he was wrong.

In the lower ground at the bottom of the Orne valley two kilo-metres from where Capon ate and talked of the prospect of being sent home, the rest of 6th Airborne Division were also 'standing down', brewing up and preparing for daylight operations. The battalions of 5th Parachute Brigade remained dug in around the battered town of Ranville, where they had held out against the attacks of 21st Panzer Division. During the night, the units of the 6th Air Landing Brigade had reinforced the bridgehead protecting the routes over the River Orne and Caen Canal and were preparing to expand the perimeter round the crossings. Daylight bore witness to the preced-ing day's fighting: burned-out hulks of tanks marked where the attack by 125th Panzergrenadier Regiment had petered out, broken up by a combination of 6th Airborne's anti-tank guns and the storm of fire from six- and fifteen-inch naval shells that had delivered hun-dreds of tonnes of explosive into the path of the German armour.

It was part of the only serious German counter-attack on D-Day. The enemy's assault had been fragmented. While one battalion of tanks had supported von Luck's attack against the British Airborne Forces holding the bridges, the rest of 21st Panzer Division's three tank battalions had been diverted to the west bank of the Orne to attack the Allied troops landing on the beaches. Without control of the crossings over the double water feature, they had been forced to make a long detour around Caen.

The rubble in the streets of the city had delayed their movement and the battalions were constantly strafed and rocked from the air by RAF Typhoon fighter bombers, which left a trail of burning German armour in their wake. By the time the surviving tanks were in their attack start positions at 1630 hours, the seaborne landings had been in progress for over eight hours and the leading brigade of the British 3rd Division had already linked up with the 6th Airborne Division. At 1900 hours, panzergrenadiers of the 192nd Regiment of 21st Panzer Division had managed to reach the sea at Lion-sur-Mer, where a section of the Atlantic Wall defences was still intact in the gap between the 3rd British Division landing on Sword Beach and the Canadian 3rd Division landing on Juno Beach. But it was too little and too late. By last light the panzers pulled back to avoid being cut off between the two Allied divisions.

As the second day of the invasion dawned, the Allies' high command could reflect on the remarkable success of D-Day. Churchill cabled Stalin and reported that he was well satisfied with the situation, reporting that 'we got across with small losses. We expected to lose about 10,000 men.' Eisenhower would not need the note he had scribbled in the event of failure, which now lay superfluous in his jacket pocket. The landings had certainly been far less costly than most had predicted. Success lay in surprise and deception combined with the Allied ability to bring overwhelming air superiority into play. The belief that Normandy was only a diversion to distract German attention from the Pas de Calais was critical, as it bred a disinclination to commit reserves. Even Rommel, who had arrived back at his headquarters at La Roche-Guyon from Germany late in the evening of 6 June, was still uncertain as to the scale and intent of Allied operations in Normandy.

The Germans dysfunctional command structure and confusion regarding the true significance of the landings meant that 21st Panzer Division, the one armoured division immediately available to 7th Army, was committed piecemeal and was unable to bring its full weight to bear against any decisive point. OKW did not grant

authority to release the next most readily available armoured formations, 12th SS *Hitlerjugend* Division and Panzer Lehr, until the late
afternoon of D-Day, despite repeated requests from Rommel's headquarters since the early hours of the morning. The SS division was
not ready to move until 1700 hours and was still 120 kilometres from
the front line. The 229 tanks of Panzer Lehr were even further away
at Chartres, which lay 160 kilometres from the battlefield.

Prevarication and distance meant that neither of these two powerful divisions was able to participate in battle on the first day. Even as
the 12th SS and Panzer Lehr advanced to the front, the bulk of
German forces would continue to be held in 15th Army's sector
north of the Seine by the deception of the Allied Operation Fortitude,
which still convinced the German high command that the decisive
Allied push would fall in the Pas de Calais. The progress of those
divisions OKW was prepared to release to support 7th Army in
Normandy was severely hindered by the ground attack aircraft of the
Allied Second Tactical Air Force. The Luftwaffe was a spent force
mustering only 500 aircraft and could do little to counter them,
allowing the Allied fighter bombers to roam unmolested over
Normandy and ravage the slow-moving armoured columns at will.

But while the Allies could bask in the success of Fortitude's use of
double agents, technical deception techniques and their air and naval
superiority to cause German indecision and disrupt the impact of
what limited forces they sent to Normandy, they were not without
problems of their own. Caen was the one D-Day objective that had
not been realized. The slim chance of capturing it on the first day by
pushing hard inland had been blunted by 21st Panzer and squandered
by a marked tendency of conventional British infantry units to pause
and dig in once the main defensive points of the Atlantic Wall had
been taken. Their mental and physical energy had been dedicated to
getting ashore rather than rapid exploitation inland. It was a psychological disposition born of a lack of combat experience among the
majority of troops, who were conscripts who had spent their war
training in England. It would also be exacerbated by the nature of the
terrain over which they would have to fight.

The British drive on the city of Caen on the west bank of the Orne was about to descend into a bitter contest for the tight hedge lines and stoutly built stone villages of the Norman bocage, where the landscape favoured the defender and his anti-tank weapons. Although Rommel had failed to defeat the Allies on the beaches, their foothold in France was precarious and it would take weeks before the full materiel of the Anglo-American armies could be landed. By 7 June Rommel had begun to recognize the significance of the landing in Normandy and the implications of the fall of Caen, which would allow Allied armour to exploit the relatively open tank country beyond it.

But only one day into the campaign the race to build up the ratios of the opposing sides still hung in the balance. The lack of British combat experience and their initial want of dash would give Rommel one potential opportunity to exploit the slight advantage restricted Allied space to manoeuvre, low aggressive drive and limited numbers offered him. Although the bulk of German forces would remain allocated to 15th Army around Calais, he still had a chance of checking the Allied advance inland with 21st Panzer Division, the Hitler Youth of the 12th SS and Panzer Lehr. And OKW's decision to release one division from 15th Army would provide him with forces to attack the 6th Airborne Division on the Bréville Ridge. Rommel knew that the high ground and the bridges that they dominated were vital to unlocking the right flank of the invasion. He also knew that the destruction of the bridges and the floodwater in the adjacent Dives valley, combined with the close bocage country astride the ridge, made it unsuitable ground to assault with mass armour. Consequently, the one division reallocated from the 15th to 7th Army was an infantry division.

The decision to dispatch the 346th Infantry Division from its defensive location at Le Havre was made at 2300 hours on 6 June. It reflected the importance Rommel attached to recapturing the higher ground. While the Allies held it, his panzer units would continue to have to make a lengthy detour to the south of Caen to attack the beachhead. Retaking the ridge and recapturing the bridges would allow the Germans to attack directly into the British left flank from the east and would offer the opportunity to disrupt their advance along the Orne valley. Consequently, while his panzers fought in the lower ground of the valley to blunt the Allied drive on the city, he was determined to use the 346th Division to wrestle the ridgeline from the British paratroopers and retake the bridges. It was a decision that would have profound consequences for 9 PARA and the brief lull in the fighting they enjoyed was not to last for much longer.

The surgeons at the main dressing station at Le Mesnil went to work on Hudson early in the morning. They still lacked scalpels and sutures from their medical kit that had been lost during the drop, but Hudson had been lying wounded for over twenty-four hours and they could not afford to wait any longer. At 0500 hours the medics lifted him from the grass beside the outbuilding where he had spent the night on a stretcher, took him into the slaughterhouse and placed him on a tile-covered butcher's table. Once the Pentothal anaesthetic took effect, the incisions into Hudson's stomach were made with the Gillette razor blades found in someone's washing kit. The first cuts were made to clear away the congealed tissue and debris that had been carried into Hudson's mangled intestines when he was wounded. As the surgeons worked, his blood ran in dark pools over the white tiles of the table and dripped on to the grooved redbrick floor, where it mixed with the dried gore of butchered cattle.

In Le Plein the wounded from all sides were collected in the old post office on the north side of the open village green. Paratroopers, commandos, German and Russian casualties were treated alike in the regimental aid post set up by Number 6 Commando. During the morning Otway visited his wounded and took the opportunity to walk round the village to survey the aftermath of the previous day's fighting. The ground was strewn with enemy dead and the bodies of horses that had been caught in the crossfire, their bellies already beginning to swell in the sunshine. The warmth brought a plague of flies to swarm over human and animal remains scattered beneath the lime trees. Otway found the local priest and, convinced he was complicit in allowing the Germans to use his church to engage his Paras from its tower, forced him at gunpoint to show him the belfry of the Roman-arched building in the centre of the village. The tall slatted windows of the tower were holed and splintered by the accurate fire of his snipers, and on the floor below them lay the bodies of six enemy sharpshooters.

The dawn also gave those who were still scattered a chance to find their bearings, as they tried to make their way back to their units. Mick Corboy was with the other twelve men from C Company who had also been dropped east of the Dives and had spent the night holed up in an empty farmhouse near Robehomme. After shooting up several German vehicles, they had seen the glider train arrive before last light on D-Day. Corboy knew they were on the right track when he watched the great mass of wooden aircraft swoop in and drop behind the ridgeline a few kilometres to their west. Cut off on the other side of the River Dives, they had waited until daylight before resuming their journey, as no one wanted to be shot by their own side while trying to make it in to British lines during the hours of darkness.

Corboy's party took advantage of the early morning tide to ford the river. The deeper sections of the Dives were made passable by what remained of one of the bridges that had been blown by the Canadian paratroopers. The banks of the river were quiet as they waded between the demolished posts of the bridge. Close to the bridge a twisted and broken Horsa lay half submerged in the water. It had overshot the landing zone; lacking height and power, the river line offered its pilot the last best option of somewhere to put down the glider. The muddy water flowed through the smashed plywood structure and Corboy could see a Jeep still inside the fuselage, but there was no sign of the crew or passengers and Corboy wondered what had become of them as he pushed his legs through the steady drag of the current and made for the opposite bank.

On reaching the other side, Corboy and his group set out for the crossroads at Le Mesnil, where the intersection of the Cabourg-to-Caen road cut across the main route running north to south along the top of the Bréville Ridge. Bound by thick woods on three sides, with open meadows to its front, it made an ideal defensive position. The troops holding the crossroads were an eclectic mix of individuals and groups separated from their units when they had landed in Normandy on D-Day. When Corboy arrived there, other members of 9 PARA, including elements of C Company, already held the intersection. The men of Gordon-Brown's glider, having missed the assault on the Merville Battery, had also reinforced them. Their numbers had been bolstered further the previous evening when Lieutenant

Smythe's troops, whose glider's towrope broke over England, were flown into Normandy in a replacement Horsa during the second wave of gliders that landed just before last light on 6 June. The mixed force dug in around the crossroads was under the overall command of Major Ian Dyer from C Company and also included Canadians, the odd paratrooper from 8 PARA and a section of engineers.

Captain Robbie Robinson arrived at the crossroads a few hours ahead of Mick Corboy. Having survived the bombing of Hill's party, he had been captured by a German patrol and taken towards Troarn with a number of other prisoners. After an arduous march, his captors dropped their guard and he made a run for it. He broke through a hedge line with bullets cracking in the air around him and ran for his life, then submerged himself in a pond to evade recapture and was eventually hidden by French civilians in the crypt of a church. In the early hours of the morning he set a bearing on the small escape compass he had concealed in the collar of his smock and headed north towards the ridgeline until he came into the wooded area of the Bois de Bavent held by 8 PARA. They sent him on to 3rd Brigade headquarters from where he was duly dispatched up the road to the crossroads. When he got there, Robinson was still soaking wet. He had been dropped in the Dives, bombed by his own side, captured, escaped, hidden in a pond and spent a freezing night among the bones of the dead. On meeting Dyer at the crossroads, the first thing he asked for was 'something to shoot with'.

The importance of holding the crossroads meant that Hill sent every spare fighting man there, but his brigade headquarters at the farmyard had become a collecting point for a motley collection of other individual stragglers. Those who could not fight, the wounded, shot-down aircrew and glider pilots would be held there until they could be evacuated across the beaches to England. Although trained to operate on the ground as infantry, each member of the Glider Pilot Regiment carried a chit that exempted them from being used in a general combat role. Even though 3rd Parachute Brigade was short of men, the War Office considered glider pilots too valuable to risk losing in fighting on the ground. Consequently, 21st Army Group had issued orders that once they had landed their gliders they were to be sent back across the Channel so that they could be used for future airborne operations. Having flown in on the second lift of the previous day, men such as Staff Sergeant Arnold Baldwin and the other glider pilots waited in the woods that surrounded the farmyard to be evacuated. But for the moment they would be going nowhere, as Hill was preoccupied with his own problems of manning his headquarters and filling his gaps in the line.

Across the courtyard from Hill's headquarters, Alan Jefferson lay among the wounded on the grass outside the main dressing station where the medics of 224 Field Ambulance worked on Hal Hudson. As the sun came up and climbed high into the sky, he welcomed the warmth of its rays. When he sought information about how Hudson was doing, the news about his severely wounded comrade was less welcome. The surgeon's investigation with razor blades had revealed deep perforations into his lower intestines, which had lacerated his abdomen and exited through his pelvis. The lesions had been closed, but Hudson had lapsed into traumatic shock and had not responded well to the infusion of plasma that had scarcely kept him alive during the operation. He was very weak and suffering from gas gangrene brought on by the dirt in his wounds and the length of time he had had to wait for his operation. The surgeon spared Jefferson the details, but a barely perceptible shake of his head was enough to indicate that he was unlikely to survive.

Private George Hawkins did not see the sun come up and doubted his own prospects of survival as he lay wounded in one of the casemates at the Merville Battery. One of Jefferson's team, he was badly wounded by shrapnel in the assault and had spent all day lying in the darkness until the Germans found him, bandaged him and put his leg in a cast. He was then left undisturbed in one of the thick concrete bunkers.

Since the Paras' attack there had been little activity at the battery, but at noon two of the howitzers started firing. The gunfire was slow and desultory. In the wake of 9 PARA's attack, Hauptwachtmeister Buskotte had managed to get only half his guns working again and most of his battery personnel were dead, missing or wounded, but he was doing his best to respond to the fire mission that his young battery commander had sent him.

Steiner heard the solitary rounds of his own guns split the air as they passed over his OP bunker looking out across the River Orne. Beyond the mouth of the estuary stood the British fleet and its support vessels, which, caught in the sunlight, looked to Steiner like 'a golden city' of ships. He could not see the fall of the shot, as their target lay beyond the opposite headland that obscured the shoreline in front of Ouistreham. But he knew they were destined for the beach where Allied troops continued to stream ashore. The battery's rounds were too few to have much impact on troops of the 51st Highland Division, which landed on Sword Beach in the afternoon of D+1. Obscured from his vision, Steiner could not tell what impact the shells were having, or adjust the fall of shot. But the furious response they provoked from the floating city of sun-gilded warships was not long in coming.

The weight of fire put back by the battleships and light cruisers of the Allied task force dwarfed anything the surviving guns of Merville had directed towards Sword Beach. For the every one 100mm round the battery fired, the British put back twenty times the number of heavy naval shells, each of which was three times the size of those fired by the German howitzers. Buskotte and his men cowered in their bunkers while the ground shook as tonnes of high explosive rolled and blasted across their position. Buskotte was later to remark, 'It's all very well for Herr Leutnant to give orders from down there, but it is here where we will always catch it!' But the men inside the thick concrete and earth casemates, including Hawkins, lived.

Two hours after the storm of steel had subsided, two-inch mortar rounds began popping on the southern edge of the battery. The sound of the smoke rounds was superficially unthreatening compared to the crashing cacophony of the naval shells that had raked the battery. As the small mortar bombs landed, they fizzed a curling column of thick pungent grey smoke; then the crackle of small arms could be heard in the distance. It was 4 Troop of 3 Commando providing covering fire to their comrades in 5 Troop who were using the smoke to mask their movement, as they went right-flanking to assault the battery from the north. It was a classic hasty infantry attack launched in response to the battery opening up on Sword Beach.

The commandos' attack was as hurried in its execution as it had been in its conception. The fact that the Merville Battery was firing again had come as a surprise to the troops landing on Sword Beach and the British commanders. But unequal as it was, the British knew that the backlash of the naval counter-bombardment could only suppress, not destroy the battery; if was to be silenced, it would have to be attacked again on the ground. Once more the task fell to 6th Airborne Division, but it was beyond the capability of the badly depleted airborne units, which were now committed to the defence of the bridgehead around Ranville, so Gale turned to the commandos. Lovat's 1st Special Services Brigade had come under Gale's command and 45 Royal Marines Commando with 4 and 5 troops of 3 Commando were preparing to push along the east bank of the Caen Canal to clear Franceville. Lovat gave brief orders to the commanding officer of 45 Commando to detach the two troops of 3 Commando to attack the guns as part of his advance. The instructions they received were equally brief.

As far as Fred Walker was concerned there was 'no planning whatsoever' and Walker had seen a few battles in his time. He had been a commando since volunteering at seventeen and was already a veteran by the time he landed on the beaches on D–Day. Walker had participated in the disastrous raid at Dieppe and survived the Allied landings in Sicily and Italy, where he had been taken prisoner and made a daring escape. He found the experiences in Italy far more hairy than anything he had experienced when landing on D–Day and his troop had suffered very few casualties, but their test was about to come. Unlike Walker, Herbert Beddows had no combat experience. He had been a corporal in the Norfolk Regiment but had become disillusioned by the low standards of his fellow conscript infantrymen. As well as having to pass the commandos' gruelling selection course, he had also had to give up his tapes and revert to the rank of a private soldier in order to win the right to wear their coveted green beret.

The commando ethos was very similar to that of the paratrooper, but the orders and preparation they received for attacking the guns at Merville stood in stark contrast to the months of planning and training 9 PARA had undertaken before being launched into the assault. After the most meagre of verbal briefings, Walker and Beddows found themselves trudging in the direction of Franceville as part of 45 Commando's advance on the village. The two troops of 3 Commando peeled off and headed towards Calvary cross, where they left their heavy packs and shook out into their assault formations. There was no time to prepare artillery support, they had no engineers with them to blow the guns and their numbers were limited. With each troop consisting of seventy-five men they were about to attack the battery with precisely the same number of men as had 9 PARA. However, unlike the British, the Germans had profited from their experience and Buskotte had developed a drill in the event of infantry attack.

Some of the German wounded had not survived the night in the command bunker following 9 PARA's attack, but Buskotte was still alert. As he scanned his position through his periscope, his men were already hunkered down in their casemates and trenches. Suddenly the image of the ground above him was full of advancing enemy infantry. He stepped back involuntarily as a bullet shattered the optics into a kaleidoscope of broken images. His words to Steiner were crisp and to the point: '*Herr Leutnant!* We are under attack again! I am putting our drill into force; bring down fire on to our position when you hear from me again.' By the time he had replaced the receiver, the heavy steel doors to the gun emplacements had been sealed shut and the defenders' machine guns had already begun opening up on the men of 5 Troop.

The imperative of speed meant that there was little finesse in the commandos' assault technique as they advanced on the position 'two sections up'. The bomb craters afforded them a degree of cover, but the defenders' fire was intense. The industrial buzz-saw of the German MG 42s drowned out the slower methodical stutter of the Bren guns, as their belt-fed bullets churned through their receivers at three times the cyclic rate of fire of the magazine-fed light automatics. Walker saw the men of the section in front of him scythed down in the murderous fire that chewed the lips of each bomb crater. Twenty men went down in Beddows's section; Trooper Abrams, the Bren gunner beside him, took thirteen rounds in his arm, almost severing it to the shoulder. The first assault stalled, but the second made headway and Germans began to fall too as the commandos closed with their positions. As the British came on, the surviving defenders retreated along their trenches back into the safety of the bunkers and casemates. Then Buskotte made the call to Steiner.

The fire from other Wehrmacht gun batteries to the east raked the position sending up fountains of earth as red-hot shrapnel splintered the ground around the concrete structure. More commandos fell as they tried to force entry to the casemates and force the doors to grenade the occupants. Pinned out in the open and unable to winkle the Germans out of their bunkers, the attack lost its momentum. The commanding officer of 3 Commando had watched in dismay as his men had been cut to pieces fighting their way into the battery. Lieutenant Colonel Peter Young was another experienced combat veteran and he had been against the attack from the start. Now his senior major who led the assault lay dead, having been shot through the head by a determined German gunner in the Tobruk stand of Casemate One. The best part of two of his troops had also been badly mauled and he had nothing to show for it.

German self-propelled guns had been brought up to help defend the battery. The bomb craters limited the armoured vehicles' manoeuvrability and their tracks squealed in protest as their gunners braked hard to avoid the deep fissures and slew their chassis into position where the main 75mm gun they mounted could be brought to bear. Unable to get into the casemates and with the appearance of German armour, Young knew his position had become untenable. He gave the order to pull out. Buskotte watched the commandos withdraw and put the next part of the garrison's new defensive drill into action. As the British picked their way back through the minefield more men fell to the deadly 'S' mines still buried beneath the surface. Then German gunners in the first and third casemates added to their misery. Buskotte had ordered that the steel shutters should be opened and the howitzers manhandled into position outside the casemates where they could engage the commandos in the direct fire role over open sights.

Still lying wounded in one of the casemates, Hawkins had thought that the arrival of the commandos had been his salvation. Young's men had managed to get into the casemate where he was lying, as its gun was still out of action and the doors had not been sealed. Hawkins was desperate not to be left behind and he pleaded to be taken with them. But the commandos got him no further than the battery's anti-tank ditch. The enemy fire was too great and the commandos' own wounded were too many; once again British casualties were left on the position. Hawkins's chance of rescue had died in the incompetence of conducting a hasty attack on a well-defended position without any of the requisites of reconnaissance, planning or supporting artillery fire.

The sounds of battle at Merville carried across the high ground along the eastern side of the Orne valley. At Le Mesnil, Gordon Newton heard what he thought was the distant crack of field artillery. He thought it strange, especially as it seemed to be coming inland from the direction of the battery; since landing in Normandy most of the shellfire he had heard had come over the beachhead from the Allied ships. But he thought little more about it, because his position around the crossroads was beginning to attract attention.

Before last light the Germans made a series of probing attacks against the crossroads. Small groups of the enemy attempted to infiltrate the paratroopers' positions, but they were beaten back by Dyer's mixed force of stragglers who had been banded together to defend the critical junction. Although the position at the crossroads had held firm, the German attack exposed the seriousness of the gap in 3rd Brigade's line, which extended for almost two kilometres from Le Mesnil to Le Plein, where the men of 3 Commando had consolidated after their disastrous assault on the Merville Battery. Bréville lay in the middle of the gap between the two locations held by the British and intelligence reported that the Germans were reinforcing it, as more of the 346th Infantry Division began to arrive from Le Havre.

Hill lacked the strength to push the enemy out of Bréville, but he could attempt to contain them if he was able to hold a château located 800 metres to the south of the village. Situated on the crest of a small knot of higher ground on the northern side of a large wood, the Château St Côme was the dominant feature between Le Mesnil and Bréville. It overlooked the lower ground on the southern side of the ridge, across which any attack from Bréville on Hill's position at

Le Mesnil would have to be made. If he held the château, he would also be able to threaten a crossroads junction on the edge of Bréville where the main route across the ridgeline intersected with the road running down the western side of the ridge towards Ranville, which was the shortest and most direct route to the bridges over the canal and the Orne. The rest of what remained of 9 PARA were still at Le Plein, but despite their limited numbers, Hill knew that he would have to use them to try to plug some of the hole in his line. At 2130 hours he sent a radio message to the commando headquarters at Le Plein. It was for Otway and it ordered him to move to the Château St Côme and hold it 'at all costs'.

Two hours later, the small 9 PARA column snaked silently out of Le Plein into the darkness. Otway knew that there were Germans at Bréville, but he did not know whether the enemy held the Château St Côme or not. He decided to bypass the village and approach the château by an indirect route from the south-west as a precaution. Lieutenant Hugh Pond was ordered to lead the column and Otway sent Major Eddie Charlton ahead in an old battered Renault to conduct a reconnaissance of the area in advance of the battalion's arrival. The men stalked cautiously along moonlit hedgerows, ears cocked for the sound of the enemy as they kept to the shadows. Behind them, two white horses pulled a brewer's cart, which carried McGeever and McGuinness's single Vickers machine gun and spare ammunition. With the exception of the occasional barking dog in the farmyards they passed and the dull rhythmic clopping of the horses' muffled hooves, it was unnervingly quiet.

At the head of the column, Pond checked his map. Heavily encumbered men attempting a tactical move in the darkness do not move smoothly. Each time Pond halted to get his bearings the stop-start effect, as if they were queuing traffic, rippled back through the column. Men cursed as they bent down on one knee, at the very moment when the man ahead of them started to move again. As is inevitable with dog-tired infantrymen moving at night, gaps opened up between men as some nodded off during halts, only to wake with a start to see no one in front of them. Oblivious to the concertina effect he was having, Pond knew he had blundered when he smelled stale tobacco and unwashed bodies around him; bodies that he could hear snoring in the positions on either side of the road. Instead of skirting to the west of Bréville, he had led the battalion straight through it. He held his breath as he pushed on through the sleeping enemy and the men behind him followed suit. As he moved through the village he heard movement ahead of him and went to ground. He froze as he saw a large formed body of men approaching in the moonlight. They marched in column of route, which suggested that they were not expecting an encounter with the enemy. Behind him men eased the safety catches off their weapons and McGuinness stroked the noses of the two horses to keep them quiet. The Germans numbered at least 200 men. Although they outnumbered 9 PARA by two to one, they made for a tempting target for an ambush. However, Otway's orders were clear: he was to take and hold the château, not to engage in impromptu skirmishing with the enemy before he got there.

Having avoided the German unit and successfully extracted themselves from Bréville, Otway decided not to go straight to the Château St Côme. Not knowing if it was in enemy hands or not, Otway wanted to reconnoitre the château first. Having studied it on his map, he also doubted that he would have enough men to dig in around it and hold it properly. Instead he had decided to occupy a villa located 250 metres away on the other side of the road from the château that ran across the ridgeline. The building was boxed in by 200 metres of thick woods on two sides, with a large stand of trees and dense hedging to its front and rear. Lying on the western side of the road, immediately across from the château, the grounds of the villa lay on a reverse slope from the highest point of the ridgeline. Combined with its natural perimeter of trees, it would help make it a tight defensive position, which Otway could hold with the limited numbers of men available to him. It also had the added advantage of being bounded on its north-eastern side by a deep sunken lane enclosed by the stout branches of trees that grew on either side of it. Its depth, width and cover meant that it provided a ready means of natural shelter for a large body of men, as well as a good route up to the road in front of the château.

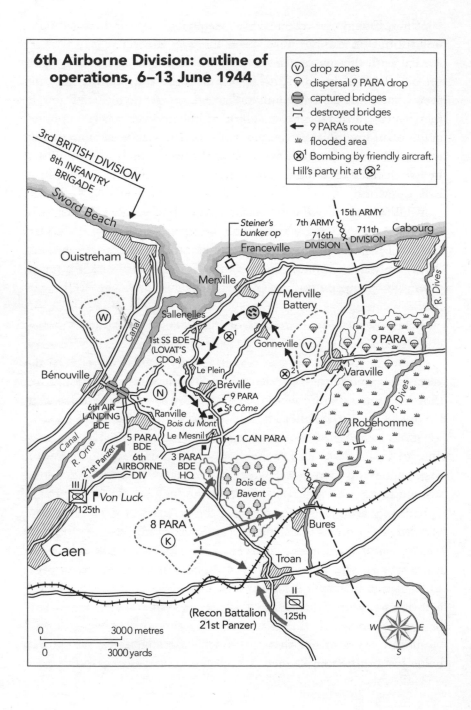

6th Airborne Division: outline of operations, 6–13 June 1944

Legend:
- Ⓥ drop zones
- dispersal 9 PARA drop
- captured bridges
- destroyed bridges
- 9 PARA's route
- flooded area
- ⊗¹ Bombing by friendly aircraft. Hill's party hit at ⊗²

3rd BRITISH DIVISION

8th INFANTRY BRIGADE

Sword Beach

Ouistreham

Steiner's bunker op

Franceville

15th ARMY

7th ARMY

716th DIVISION

711th DIVISION

Cabourg

Merville

Merville Battery

R. Dives

9 PARA

Sallenelles

1st SS BDE (LOVAT'S CDOs)

Gonneville

Ⓥ

⊗¹

Le Plein

⊗²

Varaville

Bénouville

Ⓦ

Canal

Ⓝ

Bréville

9 PARA

St Côme

Robehomme

R. Dives

6th AIR LANDING BDE

Ranville

Bois du Mont

Le Mesnil

← 1 CAN PARA

21st Panzer

R. Orne

5 PARA BDE

6th AIRBORNE DIV

3 PARA BDE HQ

125th

Von Luck

Bois de Bavent

Bures

8 PARA

Ⓚ

Troan

Caen

(Recon Battalion 21st Panzer)

125th

N
W   E
S

0   3000 metres

0   3000 yards

When Otway got to the top of the sunken lane, he gave Pond a bollocking for leading the column through Bréville. He was more cordial with the owners of the one-storey villa when he banged on the door and informed the occupants that he was about to requisition their home. Initially Madame Magninat suspected that Otway and his men were Germans, until a search of the house revealed a photograph of an English relative who had attended Sandhurst with Otway in 1936. He also learned the name of the small patch of ground that he had decided to defend. The owners told him that it was called the Bois du Mont.

While Otway spoke with Madame Magninat and her husband, the area immediately outside their home was a hive of activity, as officers and NCOs positioned their men in all-round defence. Regimental Sergeant Major Cunningham undertook the overall coordination, placing B Company in the sunken lane and the men of A Company in the hedgerow running along the road at the front of the villa. C Company were kept in depth at the rear of the position and would help A Company cover their additional task of holding the wood line on the right flank. In truth the men had become mixed up and the companies were little more than strengthened platoons. The position they held was no more than a box of 200 square metres, but it would have to do. The men began digging two-man slit trenches eight to ten metres apart. Excavating among trees made for exhausting work with the inadequate short lightweight entrenching tool they carried; the ground was thick with roots and had been baked hard by the summer sun.

Paddy Jenkins paused and wiped the sweat from his brow. He glanced up, noting that the moon had disappeared. He listened to the sounds that echoed in the darkness around him: the dull clinking of metal striking chalk and the low cursing of men as they struck roots had a certain finality to it. After the jump, being scattered, taking the battery and fighting through in Le Plein, he knew that the small piece of ground on which the survivors of the battalion dug and cursed would be where 9 PARA would make their stand in the coming battle for the Bréville Ridge.

13

Digging In

By the time they stood to, an hour before dawn, the men of 9 PARA who had arrived at the Villa Bois du Mont on the night of 7 June were less than two feet down into the hard Norman earth of tangled roots. They had spent the night digging and for most it was their third twenty-four-hour period without sleep. As they stood down, Lieutenant Dennis Slade was ordered to conduct a reconnaissance patrol of the Château St Côme. Otway wanted to confirm the presence of the enemy. Slade collected seven men to accompany him, and left the position through the emerging perimeter of shell scrapes, which were beginning to form in a rough defensive line round the leafy boundary of the villa's garden.

As the patrol departed, other paratroopers 'brewed up' in shifts at the bottom of their shallow slit trenches and cooked breakfast on small folding stoves. They shaved and cleaned their weapons as tea, made from powdered tea leaves, milk and sugar consolidated into a single cube, boiled in mess tins above the pale purple-blue flame of a solid fuel tablet. The tea was known as a 'monkey block' and it was a vile concoction, but men who were already beyond the limits of fatigue cared little; at least it was wet and warm. The rest of the men manned the Bren guns or continued to dig with their inadequate tools until it was their turn to fix a meagre meal, clean their weapons, shave and eat.

The gates to the château were almost immediately opposite the entrance to the villa on the other side of the hedge-banked country lane and the building was just visible 300 metres away at the end of a yellow gravel driveway lined with manicured trees and a grass verge on either side with a ditch cut into it.

The tree-lined avenue cut between white railings that fenced in two paddocks on its flanks. The paddock on Slade's right ran to a thick line of woods that curved round to the side of the house on its southern end. Beyond the railings in the paddock on his left, he could see an imposing collection of large stone stable blocks surrounding a courtyard. The solid outbuildings and wood offered ideal positions for any waiting Germans to hide. If they were there and decided to open fire, he and his men would be caught out in the open on the drive and risked being cut to pieces. Slade made a mental note of the ditch; it would provide him with the only cover available if the enemy was present and decided to engage them.

The patrol moved with their safety catches off, nervously scanning the ground around them as the château loomed ahead. The crunch of their boots on the gravel reverberated in their ears and made them wince as it served to negate any sense of stealth in their approach. The bottom of the drive split into a stirrup-shaped bend, one side running to the front entrance of the château and the other looping round to take in the stable blocks. Slade followed the fork in the drive leading to the front door of the house, but was accosted by a local civilian before he got there. In broken English the Frenchman indicated that the Germans had left the château and that two British gliders had landed in the fields to the rear of the house. The lieutenant split his force in half and ordered four men to peel off and search for the gliders while he took the remainder of his party into the château.

As dawn began to break at the Le Mesnil crossroads, Geoff Pattinson cradled his Lee Enfield sniper rifle and looked out over an expanse of unripe green wheat rustling gently in the morning breeze. Having originally broken their towrope, he had arrived in Normandy the previous evening with the rest of Smythe's men as part of the second lift of gliders. Now concealed in a ditch at the bottom of a stout hedge, he drew comfort from the fact that his position was bounded on two sides by a thick leafy line of trees and a dense orchard on his right flank. It gave him a good field of fire across the 350 metres of open fields to his front. To his right he could cover the road running up from Cabourg, which was the enemy's most likely approach to the crossroads. Moving up to the Bréville Ridge under the cover of night, he had heard the sound of gunfire and had seen distant flashes of explosions in the darkness around him. He had expected to be launched straight into battle, but as first light chased away the darkness from the fields to his front, the road from Cabourg was ominously quiet.

Back at the Bois du Mont, Paddy Jenkins wanted to rest the young privates in his platoon, but he knew that they had to dig deeper. He cursed the small picks and spades, which were made for carrying rather than digging. Jenkins ordered half his men to clean their weapons and cook their breakfast of awful-tasting tea and oatmeal blocks, which made a mean gruel of porridge when mixed with water and heated. Meanwhile the other half continued to pick and dig or man the sentry positions. Jenkins would swap them over to give them a chance to eat and clean themselves and their kit as best they could; it wasn't much of a rest, but at least they could ease their blistered hands and aching backs while they got something warm in their stomachs.

Hard living and a shortage of rations had not been an issue for the German officers who had once occupied the Château St Côme. The house was a three-storey oblong-shaped building of yellow-grey Norman stone similar to that found in the Cotswolds, with a short, squat, roofed tower at its northern gable end and sizeable rooms. Built in the nineteenth century, the château belonged to the Haras de Bréville stud farm, whose owners had left for Paris when the Germans arrived in 1943, and had made a comfortable headquarters for their new occupants. The remnants of an unfinished evening meal and fine wine on the dining-room table, the reek of perfume and half-packed suitcases of women's luxury clothing suggested that they had lived well during its occupation. It also suggested that they had departed in a hurry. In an upstairs office, Slade found a large cash box stuffed with 50,000 francs sitting on the desk. Light streamed in through the window, which gave him a commanding view of the village of Bréville less than a kilometre away to the north. Slade decided that the Germans would not be requiring the money, so appropriated it along with a German officer's ceremonial parade sword, which he thought would make an ideal souvenir.

Other loot from the château included German rations and two MG 34 machine guns, which would supplement both the defences of the Bois du Mont and the stomachs of the men defending it. The discovery of the crashed gliders in the fields at the rear of the château also yielded two Jeeps and an additional quantity of ammunition. But while the supplies and vehicles were welcome, they would not make good Otway's main deficiency in manpower. As well as establishing the absence of the enemy, Slade's patrol confirmed that Otway lacked the necessary forces to hold it. Located on the highest point of the ridgeline at sixty metres above sea level, the Château St Côme dominated the immediate area and provided a commanding view over Bréville to the lower ground 800 metres to its north. Its situation and stout walls of Norman stone made it an ideal defensive position, but it would take a complete battalion to defend it properly and 9 PARA's strength was scarcely that of a single company.

Observing the ground in daylight, and based on the information from Slade's patrol, Otway decided that his limited numbers could be used to best effect by enhancing their current position at the Bois du Mont into a tight defensive box. Locked in by greenery on four sides, the clearing round the villa was a relatively compact area, smaller than a football pitch, but he had just enough men to hold it. The wooded edges of the property also offered concealment and its reverse slope position would provide a degree of protection from German artillery firing from the other side of the ridgeline. More importantly, the nature of the surrounding bocage of small fields, hemmed in by thick woods, tangled banked hedges and ditches, fashioned by centuries of farming, would funnel the advance of oncoming enemy towards the villa. Any German force attempting to cross the ridge from the château would have to traverse the open ground of the fenced paddocks on the other side of the road immediately in front of the Bois du Mont. If they pushed up the road from Bréville they could be brought under fire from the sunken lane on the left flank of the position.

Otway adjusted the disposition of his trenches to cover both approaches and maximize the effectiveness of his men's weapons. A Company had already begun digging into the roadside hedgerow facing the Château St Côme, but they were ordered to extend their position across the road and an under-manned platoon were sent to start digging into a ditch along the edge of the thick line of trees that ran towards the southern end of the château. Taking extra Bren guns with them, they would form the slim finger of a salient from where the drive and fenced paddocks could be covered with enfilade fire, which would take any enemy attempting to cross it in their flanks. Their trenches would also help protect the right flank of the Bois du Mont from Germans attempting to infiltrate in small groups through the thick overgrown undergrowth inside the main body of the wood. Otway placed Sergeant McGeever's single Vickers in an old dried-out pond on the north-east corner of his defensive box, which provided the machine gun with a good field of fire across the front of A Company's trenches. Firing from defilade positions, the interlocking fire of the Vickers gun and the Brens of the men placed along the wood line turned the open area in front of the château into a lethal killing zone.

The forward defences of the position around the Bois du Mont were enhanced by the limited anti-tank capability that Otway had at his disposal. He sited Sergeant Knight and his Projector, Infantry, Anti-Tank weapons at the top of the sunken lane that ran from east to west on the left flank of the property. They would offer some protection against tanks approaching along the road from Bréville or across the open ground in front of A Company. However, with a range of only 100 metres, the PIATs would not be able to engage any German armour until it was almost on top of the position. The sunken lane itself was a natural defensive feature. Its wooded banks were topped by a mass of dense undergrowth and it became steeper as the submerged track sloped down to its western end. The branches that interlocked in a verdant canopy above it enhanced its benefits for concealment. B Company continued to dig into the sides of the sunken track, but they had insufficient numbers to cover more than 100 metres.

Otway reinforced them with the captured Wehrmacht MG 34 machine guns, which were mounted on sandbags to allow them to fire over the thick mass of brambles that grew atop the sides of the lane. The German weapons covered open fields to the north, which rose round a gentle spur of ground at the top of the sunken lane, and then dropped down gently to the crossroads at Bréville. The slight rise of ground flattened out as it sloped down in front of the last of B Company's trenches on the north-west corner of the position. It provided some dead ground to an enemy approach from Bréville, but beyond the rise and to its west, the ground was open and exposed, except where it was cut by two thick hedge lines. The topography meant that a German advance from the crossroads would have limited cover if they attempted to outflank the position and attack it from its rear.

With A and B companies digging in to cover the most likely enemy approaches with the support of the battalion's few crew-served weapons, C Company were tasked to cover the rear and right flank of the position. They also provided a reserve in the event of having to launch counter-attacks against any German penetration of the other companies' positions. C Company sited their trenches on either side of the line of trees that formed the western and southern boundary of the property. From where Private Ken Walker dug his slit trench on the other side of the trees along the bottom of the villa's garden, he had a commanding view of the Orne valley. Across the rolling fields of green wheat that stretched out below him he could see Ranville and its surrounding hamlets and beyond them the double water feature of the canal and river that ran south towards Caen. A pall of black smoke hung above the city, a result of the first of many Allied bombing raids that had begun to pound its streets to rubble. The main divisional LZ, on the other side of the road down the ridge from Bréville, was much closer and was a mass of broken gliders, their wings tipped dark above the green of the fields and the bright blue of the sky. But Walker would not enjoy the view for long, as daylight brought a reorganization of the unit's manpower.

As a signaller, Walker was part of HQ Company. Having spent all night digging, he was ordered to abandon his trench and start digging all over again in a new position with the other members of the signals platoon, who were located with A Company at the front of the position. Although they were still without radios, they would be closer to battalion headquarters, which Otway had located in the villa at the centre of the clearing. The building was small and had one upper-storey room between two front-facing eves of the roof. The RAP was situated downstairs in the kitchen, where the kitchen table, readily available water and the means to heat it, would prove useful for treating casualties. Extra space for the wounded was found by turning a nearby wooden tool shed into an overflow dressing facility.

With the position adjusted, Otway discussed his defensive strategy with his commanders while his men continued to dig. During the morning he had managed to link up with Hill. His brigade commander endorsed his decision not to hold the Château St Côme, in preference for turning the position around the Bois du Mont into a bastion against German attempts to cross the ridge from the open ground to its front, or if they tried to push up the Bréville road towards 3rd Brigade headquarters at Le Mesnil. By the time 9 PARA had arrived to take their place in the line at the Bois du Mont, Hill's units held most of the southern end of the ridgeline. Alistair Pearson's 8 PARA dominated the Bois de Bavent forestry block by aggressive patrolling and the 1st Canadian Parachute Battalion had moved to Le Mesnil to reinforce the hold on the crossroads there and the brick factory opposite Hill's HQ. 9 PARA defences round the villa would help extend the brigade line northwards, but a large gap still existed between Otway's position and the commandos in Le Plein and Hauger. The Germans' hold on Bréville in the middle of the gap constituted a serious threat not only to Hill's position, but also to the bridges in the lower ground of the Orne valley held by the rest of 6th Airborne Division.

9 PARA's position would form a hard shoulder against the southern side of the gap. The flank of any German attempt to attack through the hole in the British line towards the bridges at Ranville would be exposed to the fire of Otway's men. However, Otway wanted to conceal his positions and hide his limited strength from the enemy. If they discovered how few his numbers were, he ran the risk of inviting a large-scale assault, which might overwhelm his defences. Consequently, he ordered his men only to fire if directly attacked when the enemy advanced within close range of the position.

As 9 PARA enhanced their defences around the villa, the 346th

Infantry Division began to arrive in the area in strength. Consisting of nine infantry battalions, the German division had been raised as a static defence formation and sent to St Malo in France in September 1943. Under the command of Generalleutnant Erich Diestel, it had relocated to 15th Army and had been stationed around Le Havre in the spring of 1944 as a result of Rommel's concern about an Allied invasion in the bay of the Seine. In response to the landings in Normandy it had moved south in a mixture of its own limited integral military transport and commandeered civilian vehicles. The 857th Regiment of three battalions of infantry had made the journey to Bréville on bicycles towed behind trucks, while much of their heavier equipment and artillery support had been brought in by horse-drawn transport.

While its operational mobility may have been limited, the 346th was nonetheless a formidable division. Its order of battle fielded another two German infantry regiments, the 858th and 744th, and an Ost regiment of Russians. The division also had its own artillery regiment and armoured support in the form of Panzer Mark IVs and StuG IV self-propelled guns. Its armour was yet to arrive, but in terms of infantry, the 346th Division outnumbered Hill's units by a ratio of three to one, while 3 Brigade had no tank support or long-range anti-tank guns. The decision not to hold the château gave the Germans another advantage, as they could use the cover of the house and its stable blocks to mask their approach from the low ground to the south and east side of Bréville. In order to give himself advance warning of German movement behind the house, Otway sent more patrols across the road from the Bois du Mont, with orders to get out fast if they encountered the enemy.

Sid Capon found himself part of a patrol led by Lieutenant Parfitt. The young officer had a reputation for being out to make a name for himself; Capon did not relish the thought of helping him make it, when he and three other men followed him down the drive to the château. For speed of movement they had left most of their equipment behind. Parfitt carried only a revolver, but Capon lugged a Bren gun to give them a degree of firepower, while the others carried their much lighter Sten guns. They passed the main house on their right to scout out the fields at the back of the stable buildings, where Parfitt halted his small patrol. From the stable block, he moved forward alone, pistol in hand. As he entered the edge of the fields, he stopped in his tracks; it was full of Germans resting on the other side of a hedgerow. The pause of mutual surprise was brief, as the enemy fumbled for their weapons; Parfitt beat a hasty retreat back into the stable yard. Shouting a warning to his men, they bolted for the drive while the first shots cracked in the air around them.

The extra weight of the Bren was slowing Capon down and he struggled to keep up as the patrol headed at full pelt back towards their lines. He felt a loud metallic thwack when a German round struck a glancing below against his helmet and the force of the bullet knocked it off his head. Capon didn't give it a second glance but pumped his legs harder along the drive towards the gate. When he reached the safety of his own lines, he bent double, fighting for breath as he gripped the barrel of the upright Bren to steady himself against the urge to collapse in a heap. The fleeting encounter was enough to confirm that the Germans were aware of their presence in the vicinity of the château and at midday the assault began.

The first attack came from a fighting patrol of platoon size and, as Otway had suspected, it was designed to probe his positions and discover 9 PARA's strength and defensive layout. It came in across the fields along the road from Bréville on the right flank covered by B Company. The paratroopers dug in along the bank of the sunken lane held their fire as the first field-grey-clad figures of German infantrymen crested the small lip of higher ground immediately to their front. They were less than 150 metres away. The men of B Company nervously fingered their triggers as they let the enemy come on.

Sergeant Len Daniels was at the top of the lane manning one of the MG 34s. He ghosted the advancing Germans in the 'V' notch of the weapon's vertical leaf sight as he pushed forward the safety catch with his thumb. His index finger rested on the lower part of the double trigger beneath it to select automatic fire. To his left, and further down the submerged track, the crew of the second captured German machine gun was mirroring the process. The men in between them, armed with Sten guns and rifles, sucked in the air and sought to control their breathing while the enemy came down the forward slope of the rise towards where they lay concealed in the dense undergrowth beneath the trees.

No one can remember who shouted it, but when the Germans were within fifty metres the shrill order to 'Open fire!' suddenly broke the tension, and the line of foliage erupted in bright flashes of automatic and rapid rifle fire. The interlocking arcs of the MG 34s firing at a rate of 900 rounds a minute did most damage, as the cross-fire of their 7.92mm bullets tore up the turf and ripped into human flesh. At almost point-blank range the Germans at the front of the advance didn't stand a chance. Daniels could see his rounds strike the chests of the enemy infantrymen and the air behind them hued into a pink mist. Bodies fell and there were shouts of alarm in German, but it was too late; most of the enemy were caught on the wrong side of the slope. There was no cover and those who did not fall immediately were cut down as they tried to retreat behind the crest. A few survivors further back managed to get down and return fire, but their Schmeisser machine pistols and bolt-action rifles were no match for the stunning volume of fire that greeted them from the brambles and thorn bushes before them.

The first attack was easily beaten off by overwhelming firepower. The second came just over an hour later across the paddocks in front of the château. Like the first attack it was made without artillery or mortar support and, although it came from a different direction, the Germans' tactic of a direct frontal assault was unchanged. However, some of the enemy who were not mown down on the open ground by A Company and McGeever's Vickers machine gun managed to get into the woods to the east of the position where A Company's small platoon had formed their thin salient.

After the initial assault had faded, Jenkins looked to his left from his position in his trench in the bottom of the sunken lane, and saw a section of Germans crawling through the bushes only two metres away. They were attempting to infiltrate through the thick under-growth to the villa on the other side of the bank. One of his men posted a grenade through the foliage. The paratroopers dropped into the bottom of their trenches to shield themselves from the close proximity of the blast as a bright flash momentarily lit the under-growth and shrapnel scythed the immediate area, forcing those Germans not hit to run back through the woods. Jenkins's men scrambled from their holes to take the wounded survivors prisoner and escort them under arms to the RAP.

At the Le Mesnil crossroads the day had already started with German probing attacks. During the hours of darkness the engineers had laid a protective minefield. They had completed it just before first light and were about to begin marking it, when the air was filled with a dreadful shrieking sound. Seconds later six fat German rockets screamed through the sky one after the other. The sappers abandoned their mine-tape and marking stakes and scrambled for the safety of their shell scrapes. Seconds later, the world around them erupted in a storm of shattering explosions as the projectiles smashed into the earth and detonated into spinning shards of fragmented metal, blast and dirt. It was Airborne Forces' first encounter with the 'Moaning Minnie'.

Firing 30cm high-explosive rockets, the Wehrmacht's Nebelwerfer rocket launcher was capable of hurling six ninety-pound explosive projectiles over four and a half kilometres. The frightful noise was caused by the rocket motor as the incoming missile shrieked through the sky towards its target. The sound had a psychological effect on troops at the receiving end who developed a particular loathing for the weapon, although compared to artillery and mortars, which tended to be fired in simultaneous salvos, the actual lethal effect of a single Nebelwerfer was limited. It could only launch its six rockets one at a time and the noise preceding the arrival of the first one usu-ally gave enough warning to allow troops to get under cover before the rest of the incoming projectiles landed. While it packed a heavy weight of explosive, its thin metal casing also fragmented ineffect-ively into several large pieces of shrapnel compared to the hundreds of smaller lethal jagged fragments produced by an artillery round or mortar bomb.

Regardless of its ballistic characteristics, the bombardment was an overture to the opening of a full-scale German infantry attack on the crossroads. Ron Tucker saw them come and his finger had already taken up the first of the two pressures on the two-stage trigger of his rifle. His instinct was to engage them as soon as he saw them, but Dyer ordered his men to hold their fire. Tucker ghosted one of the advancing figures in the iron sights of his Lee Enfield, which were set to their minimum range of 200 yards. The man he had selected to fire at loomed larger and larger in the small circular metal frame of the rifle's rear eyepiece. It seemed like an eternity until Dyer gave the order to fire. Tucker squeezed through the second pressure of his trigger, taking care not to snatch the trigger, which would send his round high. He felt the butt kick backward into his shoulder. He didn't observe the impact of his shot, as he was already instinctively working the smooth action of the bolt backward and forward to load, aim and fire a second round. A trained British rifleman could fire an average of fifteen well-aimed rounds a minute from a .303 Lee Enfield and they added to the devastating near point-blank fire of Brens, Stens and Vickers machine guns, which stopped the initial German attack across the open ground dead in its tracks.

The weight of the defenders' fire caused the enemy to adjust the focus of the assault away from the fields, which had become a bloody killing ground. The lone high-walled house on the edge of the Cabourg road provided an obvious piece of cover from which to work their way forward towards the British position. Dyer spotted the movement towards the house and ordered Lieutenant 'Jock' Lepper to occupy and hold it before the Germans could take posses-sion of it. Lepper took Tucker and four other men. The crack of German bullets split the air as they dashed forward, keeping as low and moving as fast as possible, at any minute expecting to be hit by the volume of fire directed against them. They got to the house just ahead of the enemy and slammed two large green doors in the sur-rounding walls shut behind them, then legged it into the house and took up fire positions at the upstairs windows.

The Germans were already in a ditch across the road and poured fire at the upper storey of the house and hurled stick grenades over the walls. Lepper sent out a Bren gunner in an attempt to flank their assault with automatic fire, but he was cut down as soon as he left the confines of the house. Inside, plaster dust and chipped masonry rained on top of the defenders as bullets came in through the windows and struck the ceiling. While the assault on the house continued, the rest of the German force pushed along the roadside ditch and made for the crossroads. The Moaning Minnie opened up again, but this time it was dropping smoke on the Paras' position to mask the approach of the attacking infantry. Supporting mortars and MG 42s added to the mix in an attempt to suppress Dyer's men, while the forward German assault troops took advantage of the smoke to close on the position with machine pistols and stick grenades. The assaulting fire was intense and there was a danger of being overrun. Visibility was down to less than 100 metres and the defenders shot frantically at the shadows of advancing Germans as they emerged from the smoke only a few metres in front of them.

Captain Robbie Robinson now had a weapon to shoot with and he ordered his men to fix bayonets and prepare for hand-to-hand fighting. But the German attack was running out of steam, as a steady chatter of fire from the Bren guns shot down the Germans when they emerged through the smoke, or tried to thrust through the surrounding hedgerows and ditches. The nature of the fighting meant that the accuracy of the Bren guns and their swift repositioning were made to count. Consequently, the critical focus was placed on keeping the Brens firing by providing them with charged magazines. These were loaded with all the spare .303 rifle ammunition and tossed over hedges and across ditches to the gunner's number two, who was responsible for ensuring that the machine gun had a ready supply of ammunition and fresh barrels to prevent it from overheating. The Germans began to pull back from the crossroads along the ditches on either side of the road, but while the pressure on the main defensive position had eased, Lepper and his men still held the solitary house and were now cut off from the rest of Dyer's force.

Since treating the casualties at the Merville Battery, Doug Tottle had been working at the ADS set up at Hill's headquarters. The lull in the fighting at the crossroads afforded a chance to start collecting Dyer's casualties and he and a fellow medic from 224 Field Ambulance were driving a Jeep along the road between the brick factory and the crossroads to collect the casualties. They had already made several trips, but with the German attack broken, they could now get further to the front of Dyer's position. The Jeep was already loaded with six wounded paratroopers and was doing nearly seventy miles an hour when it struck the mines laid by the engineers earlier that morning. Robinson saw the vehicle suddenly lift upwards and somersault through the air in an almighty explosion and a gout of flame as the petrol tank ruptured and spewed burning fuel.

The scene was one of carnage and pandemonium. Men on either side of the road thought they were under attack and started firing, while men ran between the ditches burning like oily rags and screaming for help. Robinson managed to pull one man from the mangled wreckage and put out the flames that engulfed him. The man pleaded to be shot, but the captain pushed his ampoule of morphine into his arm. Robinson offered soothing words to the horribly injured man, who managed to utter a brief thank you before he passed out. Doug Tottle was also ablaze and staggered into a ditch where he ripped off his clothes to escape the flames. He was in agony, his skin hanging in folds from his scorched body. He was conscious of the firing around him, but he couldn't see a thing as the heat had sealed his eyelids shut. Other men did what they could for the survivors and arranged for their transport back to the ADS.

The incident at the crossroads highlighted the danger of vehicle movement along the ridgeline road between the British positions. However, that afternoon 6th Division had managed to get supply vehicles forward to 3rd Brigade's headquarters. They brought in much needed medical supplies including plasma and proper surgical instruments. Hal Hudson had survived his razor blade operation and now that the medical Jeeps had arrived he and the other wounded, including Alan Jefferson, could be moved back to the divisional MDS and subsequent evacuation to England. Supplies could be driven forward to 9 PARA too but the porous nature of the front line meant that the journey to the brigade and its units was a precarious undertaking. In the late afternoon, Staff Captain John Woodgate survived the trip to get two Jeeps to the Bois du Mont.

The priority for resupply was ammunition and medical supplies. Most importantly, Woodgate brought in two three-inch mortars and three Vickers machine guns to replace some of the crew-served weapon systems that had been lost in the drop. But like the weapons they replaced, the majority of the men who were trained to man them were also missing. McGeever set about training new crews for the Vickers from scratch with men selected from the rifle companies. Sergeant Hennessey, a trained mortar man, did the same to ensure each of the three-inch barrels had a team of three paratroopers to fire it: one man to sight the weapon, another to prepare the mortar bombs and set their fuses, and one man to slide the projectile down the barrel. The bomb would self-fire when the detonator at the base of the round struck the firing pin at the bottom of the barrel. But the crew also needed to know how to strip and assemble the weapon, as well as getting it back into action if it had a misfire. All were drills that were usually taught over several weeks' training in England, but urgent necessity provided ample motivation to learn quickly.

Although the crews lacked experience, the additional machine guns and mortars significantly boosted the defences around the villa. Otway placed the three-inch mortars at the rear of the position where the garden sloped down. The mortar had been the standard close infantry support indirect-fire weapon for the British infantry since the 1920s. Its single metal barrel was mounted on a square heavy metal base plate, which absorbed the recoil as the mortar fired and bit down into the ground to give it stability. Made to provide high-angle fire, its simple design made it ideal for use at the Bois du Mont, where it could be dug in half a metre below ground and fire a four-kilogram bomb over the tops of the trees. With a range of 1,500 metres and a rate of fire of fifteen rounds per minute, it could be used to break up attacking enemy infantry and bring 'danger close' protective fire down in front of the trenches.

Sergeant McGeever was elated to have a machine-gun platoon to command once again. He sited one of the new guns with Corporal McGuinness on the south-west corner of the position, across the road from where the isolated A Company platoon position stretched along the line of woods towards the château. It would cover the approach from Le Mesnil, as well as being able to fire across the front of A

Company's positions and interlock with the original Vickers gun in the dried-out pond covering the drive from the north-east corner. The second gun was mounted in one of the Jeeps recovered from the gliders in the fields behind the château. The tripod of the gun was weighted down with sandbags to create a mobile firing platform that could be driven wherever the need for additional fire was greatest. The final gun was unmanned and was kept in reserve at the villa.

The additional weapons were not in operation when the next assault came in against the position. This was another probing attack across the open ground in front of A Company. McGuinness had spent most of the afternoon linking German ammunition into the non-disintegrating fifty-round metal machine-gun belts for the captured MG 34s, and he and McGeever put his work to good effect when they rushed one of the guns to a forward position opposite the drive and began engaging the enemy. McGeever rested the front legs of its tripod on the edge of the ditch in the road and fired, while McGuinness handled the belt so that the rounds fed evenly through the receiver as the fire of the weapon traversed the open ground in front of them.

Beaten back by McGeever and McGuinness's use of the MG 34, it was the last significant attack of the day against 9 PARA's position around the villa. However, another attack was forming up against the Le Mesnil crossroads.

From his well concealed position in the hedge line, Geoff Pattinson had taken little part in fighting off the earlier assaults made against Dyer's mixed force. As the light faded in the early evening, the fields to his front remained quiet. Pattinson was smoking a cigarette when Gordon Newton came up to relieve him. He tossed his butt away casually, telling Newton that there was nothing going on. Then they heard shouts coming from the far side of the unripened wheat, as grey-clad figures began breaking from the greenery of the distant line of woods. A German officer barked curt commands at his men and they shook out into extended order along the opposite edge of the field. They were only visible for a moment, then they disappeared into the waist-high crop. Some of them bobbed up briefly then dropped down again out of sight, only to pop up once more, each time coming a little closer as they 'pepper-potted' forward towards them.

Newton was incredulous for a moment and questioned what he had seen, as he tried to point out the advancing enemy to Sergeant Albert Woodcock. There was no incoming mortar fire and initially Woodcock could not see the advancing enemy. By the time he did they were running towards them. An MG 42 began its buzz-saw bark, providing covering fire from the corner of the wood behind the advancing enemy. Newton and Woodcock set about knocking them down with their rifles, but as the enemy fired and manoeuvred they were not easy to hit. An advancing man at 200 metres requires no lead, although the firer needs to aim low as the trajectory of the round is likely to climb upward. However, if the target moves from side to side, the firer has to lead off his target by one body width, so that he will move into the shot if he is moving slowly, two if he is running. The hours they had spent on the Bulford ranges now began to pay off as they applied the marksmanship principles against the Germans moving through the wheat. But the enemy were many and while some fell others continued towards them.

Geoff Pattinson puffed air into the side of his right cheek as he pushed it out against the wooden cheek-piece on his modified Mark IV version of the bolt-action rifle. The sights of his Mark 3, 3.5x telescopic sight were set for 400 yards. He saw the muzzle flash of the MG 42 in the corner of his optics and steadied his breathing. When he exhaled he became perfectly still, took up the first pressure of his trigger and squeezed through the second. The slick oiled rattle of his bolt chambered another round as the German machine gun stopped firing and he searched for another target. He didn't have long to wait: more MG 42s opened up from the other side of the field, but at least Gordon-Brown had moved up to assist him.

The captain had brought up a Vickers gun and ordered Pattinson to load tracer and spot out the German machine guns for its Canadian crew. The arrival of the additional fire support was timely, because some enemy were already closing in on the position. Newton picked up a Schmeisser and cut one down as he appeared in a ditch on his flank. But as Pattinson's rounds found their mark, the Vickers gun was following up with a much higher rate of fire that started to break the momentum of the attack. The Germans faltered and began to withdraw, leaving their dead and wounded behind them where they had fallen.

As the shadows lengthened across the ridge, the Germans retired for the night to lick their wounds. Their attacks had been hasty attempts either to rush the paratroopers' positions or to probe them to determine their strength. Like the men they fought, many were inexperienced in the art of war and had paid a high price for their greenness. But similarly, like the men of the British Airborne Forces, they were rapidly becoming combat veterans and would learn quickly. When darkness fell, men on both sides across the porous front settled down to improve their positions, eat their rations, reflect on a day of battle and marvel that they were still alive.

At the Bois du Mont, Sid Capon had finished the last of his twenty-four-hour pack, but he had procured a tin of German sardines, which he ate with milk still fresh and warm from the udders of a cow tethered in the clearing round the villa. In the sunken lane, Jenkins started a roster to rest his men in shifts, with one man on sentry duty in his trench while the others slept the sleep of the dead at their oppos' feet, wrapped up in a gas cape. Jenkins stayed awake, having told those who slept, 'I will wake you if I need you.' Ron Tucker watched the shadows from one of the upper windows of the lone house. The stout walls and the defenders' fire from the windows had kept the Germans out, but the enemy still probed the perimeter and any movement they detected brought a fusillade of shots. Lepper and his men remained cut off and isolated and their ammunition was beginning to run out.

14

Incoming

PADDY JENKINS WOKE each of his men in turn with his finger held to his lips. 'Wake up. Stand to; we've got company,' he whispered, in a manner that left them in no doubt about the urgency of his instructions. All over the position, men were rolling themselves out of gas capes and fumbling for their weapons. Each man fought to shake off the fuddle of sleep and blinked hard into the darkness as they took up their positions next to those already awake. Jenkins heard the distinctive *thwump, thwump* of mortars popping in the distance. They could not be far away and Jenkins estimated that the time of flight would be brief. He told his men to get down and stay down.

Seconds later a barely perceptible soft wushing sound split the quiet of the night air. Almost immediately the silence was shattered by the resounding *crump, crump*, when a score of rounds landed among them in a series of short, sharp, ear-splitting cracks. The mortar bombs burst on impact in a momentary flash of bright light and threw up fountains of earth, as their high explosive shattered their steel casing and blasted out a myriad of red-hot jagged fragments in deadly circles of shrapnel. Some of the incoming rounds detonated in the branches of the trees, causing a shower of metal sparks and wood splinters to rain down on the defenders.

Men curled themselves into the bottom of trenches and pushed themselves against their walls. They kept their mouths open to minimize the effects of overpressure, while the blast and storm of shrapnel from the mortar bombs ripped across the tops of the dugouts like a hurricane, showering the occupants with dirt and debris. The hessian sandbags reinforcing the parapets of the trenches were shredded by sharp metal and fine earth poured out in thin streams on top of them. With a lethal radius of up to 100 metres, anyone above ground would have been maimed or killed. But unless they took a direct hit, or shrapnel entered from above and hit someone, the men were relatively safe as long as they stayed pressed into the earth at the bottom of their holes. Although most of the men had never been under a stonk before, they all knew that the heavy concentration of mortar rounds could only mean one thing: it was the prelude to a heavy German attack.

The bombs were landing close enough for men to taste the caustic tang of burned explosives. Over the crashing noise of the landing rounds, Jenkins yelled at his men, 'Keep your heads down and your eyes open! Hold your fire! It will lift soon.' Then it stopped. Men pushed themselves up, brushed the dirt off their weapons and rested forward at the alert position on the front edge of their slit trenches. Rivulets of dirt continued to run from the punctured sandbags on to their feet, as the men strained their eyes into the darkness in front of them. Daylight was not far away, but it was still too dark to distinguish friend from foe. However, when they saw it, they knew that the phalanx of dark shapes moving at the periphery of their night vision could only be the enemy. They held their fire while the blue-black figures advanced towards them.

The attack came in across the fields in front of the château against A Company and along the roadside hedge line on the left flank of the position held by part of B Company in the sunken lane. At fifty metres the defenders let them have it, the brambles on the banks of the sunken lane and lines of trenches on two sides of the fenced paddocks turning into a blaze of stabbing muzzle flashes. 9 PARA's own three-inch mortars added to the mix. Ignoring all normal range safety limitations, Sergeant Hennessey's newly trained crews dropped their rounds 'danger close' just in front of their own trenches. The backsplash of shrapnel nicked some of the paratroopers in the forward companies, but the impact among the Germans was devastating.

McGeever's replacement gun on the south-east corner of the position interlocked with the Vickers machine gun in the dried-out pond to criss-cross the ground with a deadly stream of fire, which made mincemeat of the enemy. Even though the machine gun was fitted with a water-cooled jacket, McGeever fired killing bursts to avoid overheating the barrel. Then the gun stopped. Without missing a heartbeat, McGeever carried out the stoppage drills as if he were on a training exercise in England. He flipped open the feed tray cover, cleared the breech of a mal-ejected cartridge, realigned the canvas belt and snapped shut the cover, then re-cocked the weapon and depressed the thumb trigger; the Vickers kicked back into life again.

The paddocks and fields astride the château driveway and along the road from Bréville were consumed in a deadly ensemble of direct and indirect fire. The coordination of 9 PARA's small arms and support weapons turned the open areas in front of the trenches into the lethal killing zones that Otway had intended. No one was sure how long it had lasted, but when the order to cease fire was given, daylight had broken and revealed the carnage on the ground in front of the position. Clearance patrols were sent out into the corpse-strewn fields to search for intelligence. An unfinished letter was discovered on the bullet-ridden body of a Hauptmann who had been hit no fewer than eight times. The young German captain told his wife how his company would drive the British paratroopers back across the Orne. In another pocket they found a bloodstained copy of Adolf Hitler's infamous Führer order, which dictated that no mercy was to be shown to captured airborne soldiers.

The pungent stink of burned propellant still hung in the air as the men stood down. They had defeated a major enemy attack, which bred a new confidence; they had been tested and they had prevailed. For most it had been their first experience of coming under a sustained concentration of indirect enemy fire with nowhere to run to. Some men had been hit when shrapnel entered the top of their trenches, although overall their casualties had been light. However, there were lessons to be learned. It was one thing to be trained to react to enemy mortar fire, but it took the real thing to make men realize the importance of having properly dug positions with overhead cover. The elation of post-combat success and the reality of experience washed away their fatigue, and men set about improving their fire positions with a renewed vigour. There was no longer any need for NCOs to chastise their men about the depth of their slit trenches.

The second attack came about an hour after first light. Preceded by another heavy mortar concentration, the brunt of it fell on the men of A Company in the edge of the wood on the château side of the road. As soon as they heard the tell-tale signature of enemy mortars firing in the near distance, men stopped digging and piled into the trenches cut into the side of the ditch. The salient caused the Germans a particular problem, as A Company's forward position threatened any enemy advance from the château across the open ground of the drive and the fenced paddocks. If the Germans could winkle out the paratroopers in the wood, it would remove the threat of withering enfilade fire from the ditch on to the flanks of any attack. The attention the enemy focused on their position soon led the men who held it to nickname it 'Bomb Alley'.

McGeever yelled at his driver as he crunched the gears of the Jeep and sped out of the villa's entrance to respond to the enemy threat forming up against the woodline. McGeever loved the Vickers; he thought it was the best machine gun in the world and he was in his element as he traversed it over the top of the roadside hedge and fired at the ranks of advancing Germans less than 200 metres away. Pinned to the floor of the Jeep by weighted sandbags, the gun rocked back and forth with the recoil as its thick water-jacketed barrel pumped hundreds of bullets across the field. McGeever braced his legs against the sides of the Jeep as it raced along the road and the breech stripped rounds from the canvas belt. He fed with his left hand, while he depressed the trigger with the thumb of his right. Empty cases spewed from the gun and made a metallic ringing sound as they cascaded on to the floor at his feet. By the time he stopped firing, it had begun to rain lightly and the drizzle hissed as it vaporized into steam on the hot metal of the gun.

The use of the Vickers mounted on a vehicle had taken the Germans by surprise. Its effectiveness could be measured by the large numbers of enemy dead littering the ground in front of the A Company salient. The defence of the ditch and the use of the Jeep as a mobile platform for firing over the top of the hedge demonstrated the daring and imaginative use of the bocage terrain, which tended to favour the defender. But the tight-knit nature of the landscape also offered advantages to the enemy. With the mass assaults of the early morning broken, the Germans attempted to use the hedges and ditches to crawl up to within grenade range of 9 PARA's positions.

After the first attacks, Colour Sergeant Len Graham had moved forward from battalion headquarters to relieve Sergeant Daniels on the Vickers gun on the north-east position. Daniels had been manning the gun since the first attack and he welcomed the chance to slip back into the grounds of the villa and get a brew from behind the hedge line running along the front of the property. He had just left the dried-out pond and crossed the road when he heard the thump of a grenade detonate behind him. As he turned, he saw another stick grenade come spinning over the top of a hedge to the left of the gun position and explode next to Graham. Daniels grabbed a Bren from a nearby trench. He sprinted back across the road and loosed off a complete thirty-round magazine through the hedge, but not before two more grenades had landed and peppered Graham with shrapnel. Peering through the bushes, he spotted a pair of jackboots pointing to the sky. Daniels crawled through the hedge and found a dead German NCO lying on his back with a Schmeisser strung across his bullet-riddled chest and more stick grenades tucked into his belt.

German infiltration techniques were not limited to individual acts of bravery by lone enemy soldiers. Frustrated by the failure to dislodge Dyer's men and the force of Canadians from the Le Mesnil crossroads, the Germans attempted to take advantage of the porous nature of the brigade line. Later that morning, Otway received a radio call from Hill who reported that a force of the enemy had outflanked the defences at the crossroads and was infiltrating along an undefended line of woods to the north of his position. The incursion threatened the security of his headquarters at the farm opposite the brick factory. 3rd Brigade's depleted defence platoon was holding them off, but was in danger of being overrun. Hill needed 9 PARA to come to his aid.

Otway gathered thirty men under the command of Lieutenant Murray Christie from C and HQ companies and ordered Major

Smith to form a fire section of two captured German MG 42 machine guns to support them. It was all he could spare from the defence of the villa, but if he moved quickly along the low ground of the ridge he hoped to flank the enemy and dislocate their attack. Smith was ordered to set off independently, find the enemy and fix them, while Christie's group moved on the higher ground of the slopes and attacked into their rear. The Germans were less than a kilometre away and Smith and his party of three privates and two sergeants armed with the machine guns moved at speed. As they advanced along the right-hand side of an orchard, they were spotted and engaged by a larger force of Germans in buildings on the outskirts of Le Mesnil. As they attempted to return fire, both MG 42s jammed. Smith yelled at his men and he and the three privates bounded forward firing their Stens and lobbing grenades ahead of them, while the sergeants behind them tugged at the working parts of their useless captured German weapons.

When Christie heard the crackle of small-arms fire on the lower ground to his right he manoeuvred his force into a hasty firing line. Smith's sudden charge unhinged the Germans and eighteen of them broke and fled north, straight into the guns of Christie's men who shot them down like rabbits. Smith continued to move forward in bounds to deal with the Germans still in the buildings. He advanced up a ditch, but was forced back behind a wall by accurate enemy fire. Captain Tony Wilkinson, a bespectacled brigade intelligence officer, witnessed Smith's assault and saw the opportunity to take a German prisoner for questioning. He was eager for action and ran over to join Smith. He got ahead of him in the ditch and pushed himself up to the edge of the wall. Smith shouted a warning, but Wilkinson's blood was up and he took a bullet in the stomach as soon as he exposed himself. Smith reached him and told him to lie still, but there was little he could do as he watched the young officer's life-blood drain away in front of him.

Wilkinson's lifeless body blocked the ditch and Smith's party retraced their steps and attempted a flanking manoeuvre from a different direction. They caught the Germans behind a high-banked hedge and lobbed grenades over its top. Smith's men waited for the blasts of the Mills bombs to go off before skirting round the hedge. On the other side two Germans were left standing; six others lay on the ground lacerated by shrapnel. Smith's gallant action and Christie's quick thinking disrupted the German attack and removed the threat to 3rd Brigade headquarters. But by the time Otway's party had returned to their own positions, a new threat was unfolding against the men in their isolated salient.

Intermittent mortar fire had continued against the Bois du Mont throughout the day. The post-combat high of the morning had dissipated and the sporadic bombardment began to fray the nerves of the men. They built up overhead cover in an attempt to protect themselves from shrapnel, scurrying rapidly underground each time more bombs came in. Men avoided hanging around unnecessarily in the open. If they had to move across exposed ground, they did so quickly, their eyes fixed on the nearest trench, their ears cocked for the sounds that would herald the imminent arrival of the next stonk. Sid Capon marvelled at how the battalion second-in-command, Major Eddie Charlton, carried himself erect as he walked about the position, offering words of encouragement as he went. Seeming to care little about his own personal safety, his example was not lost on the men and helped boost their confidence.

They needed no encouragement to try to excavate their trenches a little deeper every time the mortaring stopped. The men in the A Company salient used the lull in the firing to try to get a brew on in the bottom of his slit trench, but every time they lit their stoves and got the water to boil, a new stonk would come down and interrupt their efforts to make a cup of tea. But making a brew was the least of their problems. Later that afternoon the weight of the mortar fire against Bomb Alley intensified. When it stopped, they could detect movement in the thickness of the dense foliage behind them and suspected that the enemy were trying to outflank the salient and infiltrate through the wood. The suspected enemy movement was reported on the field telephone that connected their isolated outpost to battalion headquarters back at the villa.

Otway was concerned about a German attack being made through the wood and he ordered Charlton to conduct a fighting patrol to counter the threat. The battalion second-in-command took Lieutenant Parfitt and ten men with him. They crossed the road through A Company's main position along the hedge in front of the villa and pushed into the thick undergrowth of the trees behind Bomb Alley. The men back in the Bois du Mont heard the distinctive sound of German MG 42s and the brief crackle of Sten guns. Ken Walker heard it as he sat in his trench and thought of his mate Harry Courtney. It was Walker's twentieth birthday and the two men had flicked a coin to decide who would accompany the patrol. Those dug into Bomb Alley heard it too. Then there was silence. Minutes passed until the silence was broken by the sound of someone running through the bushes. Private Harold Walker tried to burst through the bushes at the rear of the position, but in his panic he got tangled in the brambles and had to be pulled into their trenches, where he managed to blurt out what had happened.

Charlton's patrol had been ambushed as they reached a small glade in the centre of the wood. The Germans had fired first from both sides of the clearing with two MG 42s. Charlton, Parfitt and two others lay dead, including Sergeant Rose who had had the top of his head removed by a Spandau bullet. Another five men had been wounded. Aware that there were men still out there in the woods behind them, A Company lay down covering fire through the trees. They could not see what they were firing at, but it allowed some of the survivors to crawl back and flop into the trenches along Bomb Alley. News of what had happened soon spread round the rest of the position. The losses were felt keenly, but none more so than by Ken Walker who lamented the slaughter of his comrade Harry Courtney and reflected bitterly on the weird geometry of chance, where fate had been decided by the flick of a coin.

At the lone high-walled house near the Le Mesnil crossroads, Ron Tucker was also contemplating his destiny. After a restless night, Jock Lepper and his men had spent the day in an uneasy stand-off with the Germans in the ditches on the other side of the road. Lepper had lost his hearing to the blast of a grenade and two of his party of five were wounded. During the afternoon, a German medical officer had arranged a temporary truce so that an enemy stretcher party could evacuate one of Lepper's more seriously injured men. It was an indication of the desperateness of their situation: they were cut off and down to their last few rounds of ammunition;. they believed that their comrades at the crossroads had already been overrun and they expected to be next.

Tucker sheltered behind the remnants of smashed furniture and eyed the gates in the perimeter wall nervously. He kept a single primed grenade at his side; he was determined to take as many of the enemy with him as he could when they burst through the gate. Around 1700 hours they heard the sound of heavy firing beyond the walls. Lepper and his men braced themselves. Tucker fingered his grenade and prepared himself to meet the rush of the enemy through the gates. But when the gates burst open, the men were British and Canadian paratroopers not Germans. Robinson was at the head of the mixed relief force, which had fought its way up from the crossroads to the house. Lepper fell into his arms as the two men greeted each other and wept tears of joy.

With the relief of the lone house and the defeat of the Germans' attempt to flank 3rd Brigade's headquarters earlier in the day, the situation at the Le Mesnil crossroads had stabilized. With mounting enemy pressure around the Château St Côme, Hill decided to send Dyer and the men from A and C companies back to re-join 9 PARA. Doug Tottle still lay in the ditch that he had crawled into to extinguish the flames of his burning clothes after his Jeep had run over the landmine the day before, drifting in and out of consciousness, his eyes sealed shut by the fire. He heard the 9 PARA men preparing to move off on the road above him and cried out. Some of Dyer's men discovered him and took him with them to the Bois du Mont, where he was delivered into the care of Harold Watts's RAP in the kitchen of the villa.

Dyer's composite force of forty men arrived in the clearing round the villa at 1900 hours. Sid Capon saw them come in across the lower slope of the field beyond the trees at the back of the position. He had not seen the members of his own company since they had boarded their Dakotas in England, but he had been expecting them. Before Charlton had taken out his forlorn patrol, he had walked round the position and had helped bolster Capon's spirits by telling him that the battalion was soon to be reinforced by Dyer's men. They shuffled in dirty and dishevelled, their faces and uniforms caked in the filth and grime of three days of fighting round the Le Mesnil crossroads. The battalion were equally taken aback by the appearance of their comrades who had squatted in the trenches at the Bois du Mont. Capon stood up in his slit trench to greet them. As they came into the position he asked them, 'Where the fuck have you been?'

Dyer reported to the commanding officer in his headquarters in the villa. Otway gave him a drink of fresh cow's milk laced with Calvados, then he ordered him out on patrol. Dyer broke the news to Robbie Robinson and Jock Lepper that they were to form part of a fighting party to wipe out the enemy mortars firing from behind the château.

The light was fading by the time the twenty men of C Company gathered in front of the villa, their faces blackened against the night and their equipment stripped down to the bare minimum. They took their weapons, as many grenades as they could stuff into their pockets and extra magazines for the Bren guns; anything surplus to the requirements of the specific task of killing the enemy was left behind. Each man was checked to ensure his kit didn't rattle; no one wanted to die for the sake of a poorly packed ammo pouch. Then they were ready to go.

The sudden flash and angry crack of a mortar bomb momentarily lit up the darkness just as the fighting patrol was about to leave the villa. It sent men scurrying for the nearest slit trench as more rounds came in. Twenty minutes later the bombardment was over and the patrol crossed the roads and set out into the woods behind Bomb Alley. Taking two stretcher-bearers with them, they followed the route Charlton had taken, as Dyer planned to use the cover of the trees to get close to the château undetected.

The inky blackness of the night was almost as impenetrable as the wood itself as they pushed slowly through the thick undergrowth. With no points of reference the party marched on a compass bearing, each man holding on to the jump flap of the smock of the man in front to avoid becoming separated. Placing their feet carefully, to avoid snapping twigs that might give away their presence to a waiting enemy, became an intense act of concentration. Halfway into the wood, Dyer heard murmuring in the blackness ahead of him and could detect a slight difference in the darkness as they approached the small clearing in the middle of the wood. The patrol went to ground and Dyer motioned for his men to be quiet. He cocked his ear and listened hard. The noise was still there, a soft groaning in the dark.

Advancing, the men came across one of the wounded from Charlton's forsaken patrol. The bodies of its commander, Parfitt and Sergeant Rose and one of the other men cut down by the German machine gun lay nearby. Before pushing on, Dyer sent the wounded man back with the stretcher-bearers to the Bois du Mont with orders to arrange for the subsequent recovery of Charlton and the other dead. The patrol became separated in the tangle of undergrowth and trees but managed to RV at the edge of the wood where it protruded towards the southern edge of the Château St Côme. They could make out the enemy mortar line in one of the paddocks beyond the rear of the house and shook out ready to begin their assault.

As they moved out of the wood a barrage of mortar bombs forced them to take cover. It was a brief engagement. The German mortar teams did not stay around to see the effects of their final protective fire mission. Instead they used it to cover their withdrawal towards Bréville. The sudden appearance of Dyer's men from the edge of the wood had achieved their objective, but Dyer wanted to make sure that there were no more enemy lurking in the buildings around the château. Satisfied that the main house was empty, Dyer ordered the Bren gunners to fire through the doors and windows of the stable block. Ron Tucker fired in short killing bursts. Some of his rounds chipped the Norman stone, while others struck tethered horses and foals inside their stalls. Thoroughbred animals thrashed wildly and neighed in terror as tracer slashed at them through the darkness. There were no Germans inside, but rifle shots were soon engaging Dyer's men from the shadows. They moved back to the villa position in haste, the sporadic fire making it too dangerous to hang around. But their night's work was not yet done.

On returning to the Bois du Mont, Dyer was informed that he had to mount a standing patrol out on the ground he had just traversed in front of the battalion position. His mission was to catch any enemy patrol who decided to follow them up and to keep any marauding Germans from getting within grenade-throwing range of the forward trenches. Already dead on their feet with exhaustion, his men received the order with dismay. They took Benzedrine tablets to try to help them stay awake. The amphetamine drug was designed to increase alertness and reduce the effects of combat fatigue, but it seemed to have little effect on men whose bodies were already functioning on the edge of human endurance.

Their eyes burned and felt full of grit as they strained hard into the darkness. They stretched their limbs while they lay on the damp grass in an effort to fight off the demand for sleep that their minds and bodies craved. Only half awake, Sergeant Daniels found himself hallucinating. Bushes suddenly seemed to take on the shape of men, which loomed weirdly towards him. He would shake his head, rub his eyes and they would be gone. Necks lolled and men woke up when their heads dropped forward and their chins bumped off the butts of their weapons. Around them they had the company of the dead, because the ground was thick with German corpses from the morning's attacks.

As Dyer's men struggled to stay awake, Gordon-Brown and Lieutenant Smythe's men arrived at the Bois du Mont to reinforce 9 PARA with an additional thirty men from Le Mesnil. Despite the dark, Gordon Newton could see that every open space between the trees seemed to be scored with slit trenches; it was obviously a place where nobody stayed above ground. As the new arrivals filed into the position, they passed the recovered bodies of Charlton's patrol laid out in a line on stretchers by the villa, which was a grim and ominous welcoming party. Half the men moved into A Company's roadside trenches running along the front of the villa, while the other half reinforced the isolated salient in Bomb Alley. As Newton began digging in, a heavy stonk of bombs came in. The German mortar teams were back in action.

15

Close Quarters

THE STRENGTH RETURN for 10 June 1944 records that the arrival of Dyer and Gordon-Brown's troops from the Le Mesnil crossroads brought the total number of 9 PARA up to 170 men. With the exception of Dyer, all Otway's original commanders and key battalion officers were now either dead or wounded. Captain Paul Greenway had already stepped up to command B Company in the sunken lane. Gordon-Brown was given A Company, which had been without a senior officer since Allen Parry had been hit at the Merville Battery.

Within Otway's headquarters, Smith replaced Charlton as the battalion's second-in-command and Dennis Slade had filled the vacancy of the adjutant left by Hal Hudson. Many of the unit's SNCOs, such as Paddy Jenkins, had also stepped up as platoon commanders to make good the loss of young officers such as Jefferson and Mike Dowling. The replacement of so many command positions by junior men reflected a grim statistic that the average life expectancy of an officer in a front-line unit in Normandy in 1944 was on a par with that of an infantry officer serving on the Western Front during the First World War.

Individual stragglers had continued to trickle in to reinforce the battalion. Private James Baty arrived at the Bois du Mont on 9 June. He had not seen another member of 9 PARA since helping Jack Corteil heave his dog out of his aircraft. Landing wide of the drop zone in the flooded area of the Dives, he had spent the three days holed up by day and moving at night. Baty did not have a compass or map and found his way back to the unit by following the sounds of the fighting. He was still plastered head to toe in the foul-smelling mud of the waterlogged marshes when he was ordered to report to his company sergeant major, who proceeded to give him a bollocking and demanded to know where the hell he had been. He could only reply that he had 'never been so relieved to see anyone as you, sir'.

Baty was famished, having had nothing to eat but apples plucked off the trees in the orchards he passed through as he searched for the battalion, but he would remain hungry, as there was precious little to eat at the Bois du Mont. Unlike the line infantry who rarely operated far away from their vehicles, which carried surplus kit, spare ammunition and rations, 9 PARA continued to survive on what they had carried on their backs since jumping into Normandy. The supplies brought in by the Jeeps that managed to run the gauntlet of the Bréville to Mesnil road had kept them replenished with just enough small arms ammunition to fight off the German attacks, but rations and three-inch mortar bombs remained in short supply.

German mortaring had continued through the night and for the new arrivals it was their first experience of being under a sustained enemy bombardment. The lack of ammunition for their own mortars meant that 9 PARA had to husband their bombs, which prevented them from returning counter-battery fire. Consequently, they could do little more than hunker down in their trenches and take the incoming fire, hoping it would lift. In the early hours of the morning it stopped. The men stood to, expecting an imminent attack. But the position remained silent; the enemy were about to focus their attention elsewhere.

At 0730 the Germans brought down a heavy concentration of mortar and artillery fire on the crossroads at Ranville. Fifteen minutes later a battalion of the 857th Grenadier Regiment moved down the slopes from Bréville and advanced across the graveyard of smashed gliders on the LZ. It was the start of a concerted attempt to exploit the gap in 3rd Parachute Brigade's line and capture the Orne bridges to open up an attack route into the left flank of the Allied bridgehead around the beaches. German attacks were also launched by other units of the 346th Division against the commandos' positions around Le Plein and Hauger. By mid-morning the attack had been stopped by units of the 5th Parachute Brigade and Lovat's men. But Otway was concerned about his own position and feared that another attack against the Bois du Mont was only a matter of time and he anticipated it would come from the direction of the Château St Côme.

Two sections of A Company led by Sergeants Doug Woodcraft and Jimmy Frith were ordered to conduct a reconnaissance patrol to check for enemy activity around the château. They took a signaller from HQ Company with them so that they could stay in contact with battalion headquarters and send situation reports every fifteen minutes. Frith's section was tasked to check on the stable buildings while Woodcraft took his section to clear the main house. The patrol picked their way along Bomb Alley, then broke out across the open ground to the right-hand side of the château. Frith's men peeled off and headed for the stables, while Woodcraft took his section into the house. The ground floor was empty and Woodcraft hugged the edge of the staircase wall as he made his way cautiously upstairs.

Corporal Jack Watkins and Geoff Pattinson pushed through one of the archway entrances of the L-shaped stable block on the western side of the buildings, which took them into the fields facing Bréville. Watkins took point as the two men kept low and worked their way north along the outside of the building. Beyond the stable block they could see a high Norman stone wall running along the far side of an open paddock. Suddenly Watkins stopped and held up his hand. 'When I say run, you run,' he said to Pattinson in a hushed voice. Watkins had spotted an enemy patrol moving on the other side of the field, less than 100 metres away. When he saw the first German crest the end of the wall he shouted, 'Run!' and all hell broke loose, as the Germans saw them and opened up on them with machine-gun fire. Watkins tore back along the edge of the wall heading for the archway. Pattinson was fast behind him, as bullets chipped the stonework around them.

When the bullet fragments hit him, it felt as if he had been slapped across the back of his legs with an axe. Pattinson staggered, but managed to make it through the entrance back into the stable yard. The pain in his upper right thigh and left leg burned like a red-hot poker and he was swearing blindly. In a mist of all-consuming rage,

Pattinson began climbing a large mound of straw and horse dung stacked up against the inside of the stable wall. He wanted to get on to the roof and shoot back at the bastards who had wounded him, who were now racing across the fields behind them. Watkins pulled Pattinson back and told him that they needed to get the hell out of it, as Frith was already running back towards the main house to warn Woodcraft that they were about to be flanked.

Woodcraft heard the burst of automatic fire from inside the château and pelted down the stairs, where he met his fellow section commander at the front door. Watkins was behind Frith and shouted, 'Look out, Jerry's here and they have hit Jock!' Through the open doorway he could see the diminutive figure of Pattinson cutting across the drive and heading towards the safety of A Company's trenches along Bomb Alley, the backs of his trousers stained dark with the blood that pumped from his wounds. Frith had already set up a point of fire with his Bren gunner and was putting rounds back at the Germans who were coming through the stable block. Woodcraft told his signaller and Frith's men to make a run for it and watched rounds kick up the gravel in their wake as they sprinted across the drive and headed after Pattinson. Woodcraft was about to follow them when the door frame disintegrated into a blizzard of splinters and stone fragments and a storm of bullets beat him back into the house, as the Germans switched their fire to the men still in the château.

Their exit blocked, Woodcraft acted on instinct and rushed down the entrance hall to the opposite side of the house. He and one of his men crashed through a set of French windows and landed in a heap in the kitchen garden in a shower of broken frame and glass. They could hear the enemy entering the château behind them. They picked themselves up and ran round the back of the house and into the nearby wood, at which point the Germans emerged through the shattered French windows and fired after them as they disappeared into the undergrowth. In their desperation to get away, they almost ran into another German position on the east side of the trees but managed to correct their mistake and use the cover of the wood to get back to the trenches in Bomb Alley.

Pattinson was the only casualty from the reconnaissance patrol. He was sent to the RAP, where the MO dressed the deep lacerations in his legs and prepared him for evacuation. On the low ground below the Bois du Mont, the Germans were about to launch a fresh assault across the LZ towards Ranville supported by tanks and anti-tank guns. However, the close encounter with the enemy at the château indicated that the Germans had not forgotten about 9 PARA. Otway's suspicions were confirmed when an unsupported attack was launched from across the fields against A Company in Bomb Alley. It was broken up by the Vickers manned by McGuinness, which was dug in at the end of the ditch where it formed a junction with the road on the south-eastern corner of the position. The Germans withdrew and resorted to making a series of unsuccessful attempts to infiltrate through the woods in a bid to neutralize the machine gun.

Although the main weight of the enemy effort still appeared to be concentrated on attacking Ranville, Otway expected the enemy to make a more concerted effort against the Bois du Mont. He therefore pushed a platoon of A Company with two Vickers guns into a ditch along the Bréville road on the left side of the drive leading to the château. His intention was to give his forward line more depth as a precaution against future attacks; it was a timely move. Just before noon, the new outpost spotted half a company of Germans moving along a hedge from the direction of Bréville. They stopped, stacked their weapons and began digging fire support positions facing across the LZ in the fields below them. The enemy detachment had been tasked to support the German attack in the lower ground and they were oblivious to the imminent threat further along the hedge line. The fire from the two Vickers and additional Bren guns rushed up to support them took the startled Germans by surprise as it cut them down from their flank.

Any survivors quickly surrendered, but fifteen minutes later a platoon of enemy were spotted approaching from the direction of Bréville, also unaware of the presence of the new A Company positions in the roadside ditch. The paratroopers let them come to within ten metres of where they lay concealed before opening fire. Some of the German soldiers rushed forward and were shot down close enough for their bodies to fall into the ditch on top of the men of A Company. The remainder fled back towards the château and were able to report the redisposition of Otway's defences. Their escape meant that the next German advance, when it came, would be better prepared and better supported. The defenders did not have long to wait.

The attack came less than two hours later. As the Germans began to reoccupy the area from the east side of the château in strength, the ominous sound of engines and squeal of metal tracks indicated that they had tanks with them. The men in the forward positions crouched low in their trenches and held their fire. As they watched, a Panzer Mark IV Tiger tank and two StuG III self-propelled guns emerge round the side of the stable blocks across the open fields in front of them. The lumbering armoured vehicles stopped less than 200 metres away. The paratroopers could hear the whirr of the panzer's electronic turret motor as it traversed its gun towards them. The StuG IIIs were low-silhouetted close support infantry weapons. Like the Tiger, they were equipped with 75mm guns, but lacking turrets they slewed their tracks to bring their guns to bear on the men in Bomb Alley on the other side of the paddocks.

There was a momentary pause while the self-propelled guns moved into line and pulled the brakes on their tracks. Then the muzzles of all three armoured vehicles flashed and barked out loud retorts. Travelling at over 2,000 metres per second, the rounds arrived an instant later, cracking the sound barrier as they sliced into the trees running along the edge of the ditch. Some of the tree trunks were cleaved clean through. But the tank and self-propelled guns were firing solid anti-tank shot, rather than high-explosive shells designed to kill dug-in infantry and the rounds were only lethal if they scored a direct hit. Paratroopers pressed themselves into the bottom of the trenches, while the high-velocity steel shot slashed into the trees above them. 9 PARA's mortars brought a short barrage of bombs down on top of the vehicles, but their rounds were running low and Sergeant Knight ordered his men to engage with their PIATs from the top of the sunken lane.

The German armour was beyond the effective range of the crude

Heath-Robinson-looking anti-tank weapon, so Knight instructed his men to improvise by firing the PIATs at a high angle which increased the reach of their short fat pointed projectiles and made them drop round the stables. The unorthodox use of the PIATs was enough to cause the armour to back off. But the commander of one of the StuG IIIs was braver than the rest and he engaged his tracks and manoeuvred forward along the driveway.

Knight's men wrestled with the huge metal springs of the PIATs in a desperate effort to re-cock them. Suddenly, McGeever's Jeep-mounted Vickers gun burst out of the entrance of the Bois du Mont and fired a sustained burst of .303 rounds at the advancing self-propelled gun. The unarmoured Jeep and the steel-clad self-propelled gun were less than 150 metres apart at opposite ends of the drive when they began their unequal duel. The rest of 9 PARA looked on in amazement as rounds bounced off the StuG III's armoured plate and McGeever took on the German in a David and Goliath-type engagement. Completely unexpectedly, the StuG burst into flames and began to withdraw back down the drive to the wild whoops of delight from the men in the trenches. McGeever's bullets had either set off ammunition or fuel carried on the exterior of the vehicle, but fire is a major fear of any armoured crew and it was enough to force the self-propelled gun's commander to back off.

The stables around the château had also started to burn. The exploding PIAT bombs, which had helped drive off the other two armoured vehicles, had set the buildings alight; the place was as dry as tinder and was soon ablaze. From his position at the top of the sunken lane, Company Sergeant Major Beckwith saw the flames and heard the terrified neighing of the horses trapped inside. He took advantage of a lull in the fighting to race up the drive and cut as many of the animals loose as he could, but he was courting his own death as the fire took hold and the enemy remained close at hand. The horses he managed to save would roam the battlefield; some would later be collected and cared for, but others would die in the crossfire and shelling.

The respite in the fighting caused by the withdrawal of the latest attack allowed another act of human decency to be performed. For three days, the majority of German dead and many of their wounded had been left in the killing zones of the paddocks and fields in front of the battalion's position. For the most part the weather had been warm and the corpses bred a terrible plague of flies that swarmed among the carcases of dead cows, horses and men. Rigor mortis stiffened limbs and the putrefaction of death distended bloated bellies as they filled with the gasses of corruption. The pungent stench of death pervaded the ditches and the hedge lines and was indescribably appalling. For the sake of humanity and reasons of health and hygiene, John Gwinnett asked Otway to arrange a temporary truce with the Germans, which allowed the padre to lead out a work party under a white flag to begin its grisly task.

While Gwinnett supervised the collection of the dead from both sides and oversaw the evacuation of the enemy wounded to the RAP, the fighting across the LZ in the lower ground of the Orne valley below 9 PARA continued. The final attack against Ranville had been defeated, but a remnant of the German force had withdrawn to a line of woods on the outskirts of the village, which effectively severed the 6th Airborne Division's forward supply line and cut off 3rd Parachute Brigade on the ridgeline above them. In response, Gale brought tanks across the Orne and B Squadron of the 13/18th Hussars and the regiment's recce troop cleared the truculent enemy from the wood.

The first use of Allied armour to support the paratroopers was not without cost. The Hussars lost two of their Stuart light reconnaissance tanks and four of their main battle tanks. Bigger and better than the British tanks it had replaced, the American-made M4 Sherman had proven itself in the North African campaign. But while the Sherman remained out-matched by the heavier Panther and Tiger tanks fielded by the Germans, the nature of the bocage terrain also made it particularly vulnerable to infantry anti-tank weapons, and it had an alarming propensity to catch fire almost immediately when hit, as the crews of B Squadron discovered. It was a vulnerability that was to breed a marked nervousness among tank crews about close country that had not been cleared by dismounted troops, but in the

early days of the Normandy campaign, infantry-armoured cooperation was in its infancy and the Allies still had much to learn.

The support of the British armour did not extend as far as 3rd
Parachute Brigade on the ridgeline that day and the men of 9 PARA
felt the logistic impact of being cut off from the rest of the division.
They had used the last of their mortar rounds fighting off the German
panzer and self-propelled guns. A scarcity of rations meant they
would continue to go hungry and water was in short supply too.
Their throats were parched dry by a combination of acute thirst and
the caustic tang of burned cordite in their mouths. The men felt the
lack of water keenly and for many it was one of their most enduring
memories of the rigours of living and fighting at the Bois du Mont.
Combined with the near constant attention of the enemy, it made it
difficult for the men to brew up at the bottom of their dugouts, so
runners were used to try to get a bucket of the foul-tasting compo tea
to the forward trenches when there was a lull in the action.

This task fell to the company clerks. Although Ron Phelps had
passed parachute selection and training, he had been made A
Company's clerk on passing out of Ringway. He was given the rank
of acting lance corporal, but while he wore the single white stripe of
a junior NCO he did not get the pay. He was still expected to parachute, but most of his time in England had been spent in the company
office filing paperwork. In Normandy, his job also entailed taking
messages to the forward positions and keeping them resupplied with
ammunition and the small amounts of food he managed to scavenge
from around his own position near the rear of the villa. For the rank
and file, whose worldview was limited to the immediate horizon
beyond their trenches, Phelps fulfilled a vital role in keeping them
informed of what was going on.

Phelps's job was a dangerous one. Moving about the position
above ground exposed him to mortar bombs and artillery fire and by
the third day of the fighting he sported a fat swelling on the side of
his head, the result of being caught in the blast of an incoming round.
Phelps also had to run the gauntlet of German sniper fire, especially
when he crossed the open road between A Company's positions to
keep McGuinness's Vickers machine gun and the rest of the troops in

Bomb Alley resupplied. One sniper, concealed further up in the edge of the wood as it curved towards the château, caused him particular concern.

The German marksman was well camouflaged and he changed his position each time he fired. The men across the trees from him in the salient of Bomb Alley drew most attention and the sniper used a prominent tree at the far end of the ditch as an aiming marker. It made crossing the road especially dangerous for Phelps, who had to make repeated journeys across it in a fast and low running dash. Each time a bullet smacked into the trunk, Phelps counted his blessings that he had made another trip unscathed. But others were not so lucky.

On one occasion Phelps made it safely across the road to find a private from A Company sitting in a lotus position in the bottom of the ditch with his rifle resting across his legs. Phelps shook him gently, thinking he was asleep but when he slumped forward, Phelps saw the neat bullet hole in his forehead and realized that another member of the battalion had fallen victim to the sniper.

Despite the threat of the concealed German marksman, the fatigue of constant combat made men complacent. Corporal 'Lofty' Wingrove shared a trench with Gordon Newton. As evening approached, he informed Newton that he was going to take the opportunity to complete his ablutions before the next German attack came in. He took off his helmet and smock below the cover of the parapet, then climbed out of the trench to take a crap. Newton heard the crack and thump of the high-velocity bullet fired by the sniper from the opposite side of the trees. As he looked upwards, Wingrove fell backward into his arms, gravely wounded. He had been hit in the head, but he was still alive and Newton shouted for a medic. As the stretcher-bearers worked their way along the ditch to get Wingrove back to the RAP, Sergeant Doug Woodcraft decided to try to do something about the troublesome sniper.

Woodcraft had a rough idea of the German's location. When the sniper's next round smacked into the marker tree, Woodcraft waved a mess tin tied to a stick using the butt marker drills of a rifle range to indicate the accuracy of the round. The sniper took the bait and fired more rounds; each time Woodcraft responded with the mess tin to signal the prowess of the shot. As he did so a team of Bren guns crept along the ditch and set up a fire position. The German's own complacency allowed him to be drawn into the game, but each time he fired in response to Woodcraft's signalling he gave the waiting gunners a better idea of his location. His next shot was met with the three Bren guns firing on full automatic as they poured ninety rounds of .303 ammunition into where they had seen the merest hint of rifle smoke among the foliage. The sniper was not heard from again.

As Woodcraft and his men dealt with the sniper, B Company was preparing to face a much bigger problem from a different quarter. The first German shells began to land in the sunken lane at around 1900 hours. It was the first heavy stonk of the day and indicated that the Germans had shifted their efforts away from Ranville back to 9 PARA at the Bois du Mont. The men in B Company hunkered down and held their fire, while the enemy moved up behind their barrage across the sloping fields to the west side of the Bréville road. The mortar line had been replenished and metal scraped on metal as the three-inch rounds were fed down the barrels. The crews turned away momentarily to shield their ears from the blast when each weapon fired, then dropped in another primed mortar bomb in a fast-paced rhythm of fuse setting, sight checking, loading and firing. The rate of fire was prolific and the barrels started to overheat so the mortar men had to urinate on them to cool them. Even Otway lent a hand, but, as his urine steamed on hot metal, he knew it was not enough.

Paul Greenway watched the effect of the mortar rounds landing among the Germans. They were killing some of them, but the enemy were making good use of the dead ground and dropping off their own points of covering fire as they skirmished forward. Greenway knew that he needed something more if his company was to hold them. Otway was alive to the danger of B Company being overwhelmed and the signallers at battalion headquarters were already working their wireless sets calling for additional fire. The forward observation officer at 3rd Parachute Brigade heard them and fed the coordinates to a naval signaller, who manned a direct link to the fire control officer on the bridge of HMS *Arethusa* stationed out on the bombardment line in the Channel.

Inside each of the ship's three cramped steel gun turrets, the boiler-suited crews worked a slick, well-oiled drill of manhandling the large six-inch shells from their hoists, ramming them home and snapping the large metal breeches of the guns shut. The advancing enemy were less than 500 metres away from B Company's trenches and there was no time to fire single ranging shots. With the bearings and elevations set, the crew commanders reported 'Ready.' When they received the order to fire, the gunners depressed the foot trigger of the firing mechanism and the *Arethusa* shuddered. The six guns belched flame and smoke as they launched a heavy weight of death and destruction shoreward and the water around the ship was lashed into angry ripples by the overpressure. With the deck of the ship shrouded in smoke, the flash-masked ratings repeated their rhythmic cycle of swabbing the barrels of their guns, reloading and waiting for the next order to fire.

Greenway's men knew the rounds were on their way and pressed themselves tight into the bottom of their trenches as the air vibrated with the incoming shells. They landed with an almighty crash of orange flame and thick black smoke among the forward edge of B Company's positions. Greenway exposed himself on the top of the bank of the sunken lane and shouted corrections 'to add 200' back through the trees to Otway who relayed the adjustment to his signallers in the villa. The normal safety range for naval gunfire support was 1,000 metres from one's own troops, but the bombardment had missed the enemy who were now only 150 metres away and Greenway still needed the next salvo danger close. Less than a minute later, the signals officer on the bridge of the *Arethusa* sent a message back to brigade to confirm that the adjusted salvo of rounds was on its way. The message was passed to 9 PARA and Greenway stayed out of his trench, ready to correct the fall of shot to ensure that it fell on the enemy.

This time the shells fell further forward of his trenches and tore a pattern of devastation across the field. Each round landed in a flash of flame and heaved up huge geysers of earth. The German infantry twisted and fell, as jagged splinters of metal scythed through their formations, tearing limbs from torsos and blowing bodies through the air like rag dolls. Some men simply disintegrated in the enormous blast of high explosive. The enemy line faltered. As smoke drifted over their depleted ranks, the cries of the wounded mingled with the harsh orders of commanders shouting themselves hoarse to keep their men moving. The impact of the *Arethusa*'s shells was horrifying, but it had not broken the momentum of the attack and the Germans were too close for another salvo of naval rounds.

Hand-to-hand fighting broke out among the brambles and the undergrowth when the remaining enemy broke into the forward edge of B Company's positions. Men threw themselves at each other like animals. They fought at close quarters with short-range bursts of sub-machine guns, rifle butts, grenades and bayonets. Germans fell among the trenches and piled down the steep banks of the lane. But their numbers were too few and the weight of their attack, which might have carried the action, had been bled white by the heavy shellfire from the *Arethusa* in the fields behind them. Otway was able to restore the position by sending in reinforcements from C Company, who managed to kill or capture the few Germans who broke through B Company's line of trenches. The courage and determination of the German assault was undoubted and the commander of the 857th Grenadier Regiment, who had led the attack from the front, lay wounded on the banks of the sunken lane.

Throughout the day there had been a steady trickle of casualties into the RAP, as Dr Watts and his team of medics treated men wounded in previous actions, such as Pattinson and Wingrove. By the time the battle around the sunken lane had finished the RAP was working at full tilt. The 9 PARA medical post was overflowing and the small rooms of the villa were reminiscent of a butcher's shop. British and German wounded lay side by side, as every spare room in the villa was brought into service as part of the makeshift clearing station. Each man was treated in accordance with the severity of his injuries and the colour of his uniform made no difference. Watts and his medics worked swiftly, concentrating on those he had a chance of saving. Medical necessity meant that the RAP operated a strict policy of triage. The less seriously wounded waited on the villa terrace among the dying; the medics did what they could for them and administered morphine to relieve the pain for those to whom the RAP offered no salvation.

Some men moaned and cried out in pain, while others waited patiently to be treated, their faces a greenish pallor from the shock of trauma and the loss of blood. The rooms stank of a heady mix of stale body sweat and urine. The villa was strewn with used field dressings and discarded bandages soaked with body fluids, while pools of dried blood stained the floor brown. Watts administered plasma, debrided mangled flesh, clipped arteries and bound wounds tight in an attempt to stop the bleeding. The RAP was not a surgical facility and his job was to try to keep his patients alive and ready them for evacuation by Jeep to the ADS at brigade headquarters. Whether a seriously injured man lived or died often depended on the quality of first aid he had received at the point of wounding and whether Watts could stabilize them for onward movement to the medical facility. It then depended on how fast they could be taken there.

With the German attack broken, the Jeeps from brigade were already arriving to begin evacuating the wounded. Men were lifted on to stretchers and strapped across the fronts of bonnets as well as placed on the rear of the vehicles, while sitting cases were crammed in between them for the short journey to the farmhouse at Le Mesnil. Gwinnett supervised the loading. He wanted to get the living away before he turned his attention to the dead. The rows of rough-hewn wooden crosses at the side of the villa were already growing in number, but the padre wanted to ensure that every man received a Christian burial and he knew that there would be time enough for that.

Geoff Pattinson had spent most of the day in the RAP, lying in the corner of a room that he shared with a gravely injured German. His wounds had been dressed and the bleeding from the deep lacerations in the backs of his legs had been stopped. But he doubted that the enemy soldier next to him would make it. The German colonel who had led the assault was also being treated in the RAP. The medics bound a painful wound to his head and cut away his bloodstained tunic; he winced but made no sound. Otway came into the RAP to question the officer about his dispositions and strength. He commended him for his bravery and noted the Iron Cross at his throat. The German grunted a reply at the compliment. He was the acting commander of the 857th Grenadier Regiment, and although he would not reveal the location of his headquarters he told Otway that most of his unit had been wiped out during the afternoon's fighting around Ranville and at the Bois du Mont.

While the medics in the RAP worked on the British and German wounded alike, small groups of enemy were attempting to infiltrate back up the slopes of the ridge in an effort to return to their own lines. Eight survivors of the Wehrmacht colonel's battalion were working their way along the edge of a field at the rear of the Bois du Mont when C Company opened up on them. The front man was hit in the face and a brief firefight broke out when the remainder tried to make it to the cover of a hedge line. Three more were wounded before they got there. They were taken prisoner and brought into the position to add to Watts's growing workload.

Further along the ridgeline at Le Mesnil, Hill was watching another line of German stragglers working their way through the fields below his headquarters, when he heard the piston-throbbing growl of a Typhoon's engine. The RAF fighter swept out of the sky with its guns blazing, and Hill and his brigade staff scattered and ran for the cover of their slit trenches dug in on the edge of the farmyard. With a porous and ill-defined front line, where the distance between friendly and enemy forces could often be measured in metres, the difficulty of delineating the forward line of one's own troops from the cockpit of a fast-moving aircraft made close air support a hazardous business. Allied air planners had established a restricted fire line east of the Orne, in order to reduce the risk of air-to-ground fratricide to the units of the 6th Airborne. But they were little more than chinagraph lines drawn on a map and to the pilot of the Typhoon the opportunity of engaging the remnants of the withdrawing enemy force was too good to miss.

The fighter bomber roared in at low level travelling at 230 miles per hour, while its four wing-mounted cannons spat a stream of 20mm shells that chewed up the ground when they converged on the target below. But the pilot had miscalculated. He was not only engaging on the wrong side of the 'no-fire' line, he was also shooting up his own side and could not see the friendly forces' air recognition panels, as four neat lines of exploding cannon bursts stitched the ground across the farmyard. The pilot pulled up and banked away into the sky oblivious to his error and how lucky he had been not to kill anyone on his own side. But it was a mistake that would be repeated again in the coming days with fatal consequences.

The withdrawing parties of Germans were not the only ones moving on the lower slopes on the western side of the ridgeline. The commanding officer of the 5th Battalion the Black Watch and his recce party had spent a frustrating afternoon trying to link up with 3rd Parachute Brigade. As part of 51st Highland Division, Lieutenant Colonel C.M. Thompson's battalion had been ordered across the Orne. The German attacks against Ranville had caused the British concern. While Montgomery's main effort remained focused on capturing Caen, he also wanted to ensure his left flank was properly secured. By using infantry units from the Highlanders to expand 6th Airborne Division's bridgehead on the east bank, the British hoped to remove the threat the German occupation of Bréville posed to the paratroopers' hold on the high ground once and for all.

At 1230 hours Thompson had been ordered to detach his unit from the 51st Highland Division's 153rd Highland Brigade. He was told to report to 5th Parachute Brigade at Ranville, but their commander was absent. After two hours of hanging around at his headquarters the orders for the Black Watch were changed and Thompson was told to report instead to 3rd Parachute Brigade. Thompson's move to Le Mesnil was then delayed by the fighting in and around Ranville and he did not manage to report to Hill's head-quarters until the late afternoon. It was agreed that his battalion would fill in the line between the Château St Côme and Amfreville, which would necessitate taking the village of Bréville by attacking from 9 PARA's positions the next day. His orders finally confirmed, Thompson set off for the Bois du Mont.

Otway only became aware of the Black Watch's mission after he spotted a group of British officers huddled over a map in the fields below the villa. As he approached them with an escort, he noted that they all wore the distinctive tam-o'-shanter bonnet, which marked them out as Scottish troops. He also noted the red tabs of cloth on the battledress collar of the senior officer with them. Although the 5th Black Watch was temporarily no longer under his command, Brigadier Nap Murray had accompanied the reconnaissance party and was deep in discussion with Thompson when Otway approached. Otway introduced himself and enquired what they were about. He was incredulous when the brigadier informed him that the Black Watch were planning to attack across the open fields from the south-west side of the sunken lane and take Bréville.

A heated exchange ensued. Otway informed Murray of the presence of the Germans in the thick hedges around the crossroads beyond the dead ground where they stood. He argued that the nature of the terrain over which they intended to advance would not only impede their movement, but would also expose them to deadly enemy machine-gun fire. Otway pointed out the direction of known enemy positions and recommended that the battalion launched their assault from the north side of the crossroads. Murray, a former CO of the 5th Black Watch and veteran of the North African campaign, Sicily and Italy, did not take kindly to being given a lesson in tactics by a subordinate officer, from a junior regiment, who had never commanded in action until D-Day. When Otway told him that he would take no responsibility for the results if he chose to ignore his advice, Murray told him to 'fuck off'.

On returning to his headquarters in the villa, Otway put in a call to Hill and remonstrated with his own brigade commander. Hill told him that there was nothing he could do; General Gale had made taking Bréville a priority and how the Black Watch intended to do it was a tactical matter for Murray and Thompson. But he asked Otway to use his own men to secure the Château St Côme to protect the Black Watch's right flank during the attack. Otway also agreed to send a patrol to Bréville to assess the presence of the enemy, as Thompson's unit was still in the process of moving to the Bois du

Mont and would not have time to conduct their own reconnaissance of the German positions before the attack.

At 2300 hours, Dyer led his men up Bomb Alley towards the château, taking additional Bren guns with them. They waited at the edge of the woods as the moon broke through the clouds and cast shadows across the dark structure of the château. From the back of the Bois du Mont they heard the pop of mortars as a supporting stonk was fired to cover the ground in front of them. When it lifted they assaulted forward from the trees with the supporting fire of A Company. The main house was cleared with grenades. It was empty and they took up an all-round defensive position to prevent the Germans from attempting to reoccupy it. For Sid Capon, it would be another sleepless night spent among the corpses of the enemy that still lay on the field of battle. The darkness was punctuated by the crack of shots and short bursts of automatic fire as the Germans harried Dyer's men and ensured that they would not have a quiet night. To add to their misery, it started to rain.

The rain was still falling when the main body of the Black Watch arrived at the bottom of the sunken lane two hours later. As the Highlanders settled themselves along the bank of the lane, Thompson called his company commanders together to give them their orders for his plan of attack. His intent remained unchanged from the plan he had discussed with Murray that afternoon, although he told them he would reappraise it in the light of anything significant reported by the 9 PARA reconnaissance patrol led by Lieutenant Smythe when it came back in. The battalion would 'advance to contact' over the fields towards the crossroads and they would start their assault once they made contact with the enemy's forward positions. A Company of the Black Watch would lead the attack, with their B and C companies moving in echelon behind each other on the left flank. The unit's D and HQ companies would take over from Dyer's men in the château before the attack started.

The operation would be supported by the sixteen 5.5-inch guns of 63rd Medium Artillery Regiment, who would bring down fire on the crossroads for ten minutes just before first light, as A Company started their advance. Thompson's intent was that the gunners would suppress the enemy and cover his men while they advanced, lifting when they reached the German positions. Once his lead company broke into and breached the enemy defences, his two other companies would then be echelon forward and could exploit the gap made by his leading sub-unit.

After his orders group split up and his officers had briefed their men, the Jocks of the Black Watch rolled into blankets and gas capes and hunkered down in the mud and the wet between the banks of the lane, trying to get what sleep they could. Although subsequent information from the recce patrol led by Lieutenant Smythe suggested that Bréville might not be strongly held, his paratroopers had not managed to penetrate into the village itself. Consequently, the information they were able to gather about the exact disposition of the Germans in Bréville was scant and inconclusive. But the lack of certainty did not result in any change in the plan of attack.

16

Breaking Point

THE FIRST LIGHT of a grey dawn was already creeping in from the east when the crush of troops gathering in the sunken lane picked up their weapons and kit. As they began to move to their start positions for the attack, Company Sergeant Major Beckwith was organizing his own men to shift right to the bottom of the submerged track in order to give the Black Watch room to shake out. A line of Scottish soldiers trudged past him, the rain dripping through the canopy above them and their feet churning the earth into a thick porridge of mud. The party of Jocks was heading up the lane to take over from Dyer's men at the château before the assault started. The Highlander lieutenant at their head looked at Beckwith. In the gathering light the subaltern could see that the NCO's face was grubby and strained after six days of constant combat.

'It's okay, Sergeant Major,' he said to Beckwith. 'The Ladies from Hell are here. You can go home now, we don't need you any more.' The officer's remark was a reference to the fearsome reputation the Black Watch had gained when they had fought in kilts during the First World War. Although they now wore rough serge battle-dress trousers, their nickname had been reinforced by the fighting prowess the contemporary regiment had shown at the battles of El Alamein and the Wadi Akarit in 1942 and 1943. Most of the men who filed past Beckwith and his paratroopers wore the medal ribbons of the North African campaign on their chests and their commanding officer was already the holder of a DSO. As far as the lieutenant was concerned, Thompson's plan for taking Bréville was a tried and tested formula they had used successfully in Africa. But he and his men were about to find out that the tight-knit countryside of the

Norman bocage was very different to the flat empty deserts of Egypt and Tunisia.

At 0425 hours the supporting artillery opened fire, while the men of the Black Watch lined the sunken lane and waited. Five minutes later Major John McGregor and his men climbed the steep banks and pushed through the trees into the open field with their bayonets fixed. A Company shook out into formation with 7 Platoon front left, 8 Platoon front right and 9 Platoon following up behind them. McGregor followed his forward platoons with his company headquarters, as they advanced over the slight rise of the field and followed it down towards the first line of hedges. The artillery continued to fire as they moved forward, but it was not a heavy concentration and most of it was falling wide of the crossroads.

McGregor's men would have been visible to the enemy as soon as they crested the small lip of high ground beyond the sunken lane. The men of 9 PARA also watched them go. Paddy Jenkins was aghast as the neat orderly lines of Scottish infantry moved through his position and formed up in the open ground in front of them. With their white metal mugs fixed in regulation order to the back of their large packs, the whole thing looked like an exercise. The Paras fired smoke rounds over their heads from their hand-held two-inch mortars in a desperate attempt to provide some cover while the Black Watch moved across the open ground. The Germans concealed along the second hedge and the ditches around the crossroads 700 metres to their front watched the ranks of the lead company as they moved down the gently sloping field towards them. But they held their fire, as the smoke from the paratroopers' two-inch bombs built slowly and did little to screen the exposed line of advancing Scottish infantry.

A single round cracked out as the lead company reached the first hedge. It struck the platoon commander of 9 Platoon in his forearm, and the rest of McGregor's men went to ground. Someone in the enemy lines ahead of them had jumped the gun. The rest of the Germans remained silent, but the single shot made McGregor cautious. Studying the ground ahead of him from the relative cover of the hedgerow, he ordered 7 Platoon to advance forward while the remaining platoons went firm in the hedge. He told them to be prepared to give covering fire as he followed 7 Platoon into the small depression of the next field. The second hedge was 200 metres in front of them.

The Germans concealed in the line of tangled hawthorn and wild roses beaded each man with the foresights of their weapons, but continued to hold their fire. They let the leading sections come to within thirty metres and then they unmasked themselves in a storm of withering small-arms and machine-gun fire. Strung out in the open on a forward slope with two hedge lines between them, the Jocks in the middle of the killing ground didn't stand a chance. MG 42s swept across the extended lines of the advancing sections. Men jackknifed and fell as the bullets and shrapnel from incoming mortar rounds tore into them. Some dropped and fired from the prone position, but there was no cover and the attempt to return fire from the open ground was futile and momentary.

McGregor was hit twice by machine-gun fire and wounded four times by mortar fragments. His company signaller already lay dead in the hay beside him. Realizing he was the only one left alive, McGregor crawled back to the platoons he had left in the hedge line behind him. His second-in-command and another signaller went out to help him but they were killed instantly in the blast of exploding mortar rounds, which were now plastering the whole area. McGregor's men still in the hedge were also taking heavy casualties, as German fire chopped backward and forward through the hawthorn. With two-thirds of the men dead or dying, A Company's attack was going nowhere and some of those who had survived the initial storm of fire were beginning to break back across the field to the safety of the sunken lane.

Watching the disaster befalling his lead formation, Thompson ordered B Company to work their way round further to the left of A Company's flank, where a line of ditches and hedges converged as they ran up from the lower ground towards the crossroads. The terrain on the left offered a more covered approach, but the Germans had anticipated the move. As soon as the company started to advance, a barrage of enemy mortar fire pinned them down. Thompson then ordered his final reserve company to make a wider sweep to hook round the stalled advance of B Company. But as C Company worked their way forward into an open orchard of small apple trees, the Germans adjusted their fire to bring a pattern of exploding mortar bombs down on top of them. Like B Company, C Company began to take casualties and were unable to make any headway.

Walking wounded and individual Jocks, for whom the withering German fire proved too much, streamed back across the fields towards the Bois du Mont in ones and twos. Stretcher-bearers doubled into the open from its leafy perimeter and struggled back under fire with the more seriously wounded. Once an injured man had been dropped off, the stretcher-bearers went back out into the fields where other men were still being hit. John Gwinnett went out with them and helped carry a wounded Jock back on a stretcher while mortar rounds rained in and showered the padre with dirt. The Black Watch's small infantry Bren-gun carriers waited in the bottom of the sunken lane and ferried the injured along to where paratroopers and medics met them. They pulled men out of the open-topped armoured multi-purpose vehicle and plugged gaping shrapnel and bullet wounds with cotton first field dressing, in an attempt to stop them bleeding out before they reached the RAP.

The carnage of broken and bloody bodies was appalling and once again Watts's small medical facility was overflowing. The dead, dying and wounded were hastily placed together, while Watts and the regimental medical officer from the Black Watch conducted triage and decided which ones to treat first. Some men screamed in agony and fright as their life-blood poured away; others were silent and too close to death to make much noise. Jeeps were sent forward from the ADS at Le Mesnil and screeched to a halt outside the villa, where the medics indicated whom they should take and whom they should leave behind.

Still under German fire, with A Company virtually wiped out and the other two companies pinned down and many of his officers killed or wounded, Thompson knew his command cohesion was beginning to break down. He decided to pull what remained of his battalion back to the start line in the sunken lane. The unit had been effectively decimated; in just over four hours the Black Watch had lost 19 of its officers, 85 NCOs and 200 men. Half of A Company lay out in the field where they had been cut down on the other side of the first hedge line. Most of the bodies were lying face down, still in their assault formations. The enamel army mugs, fixed in regulation pattern to the backs of their large packs, spotted the open ground with a macabre marker of bright white dots.

The bravery of the Black Watch was not in question, but the lack of detailed reconnaissance, the assumption that tactics used in the desert would succeed in close country, poorly coordinated artillery and a lack of armoured support doomed the attack to failure. When the odds are stacked against them any unit can suffer a lack of offensive spirit, but like much of the 51st Highland Division, the Black Watch were tired after three years of campaigning in Africa and the Mediterranean. Montgomery's initial preference for using tried and tested combat units of the 8th Army in the forefront of operations was a false premise. In truth, although they had been in the line for longer and Normandy was their first campaign, the paratroopers had trained specifically for it and were fresher.

In the wake of the failure to take Bréville, Otway feared a German counter-attack would not be long in coming and intelligence was already reporting the movement of armour in and around the village. There was a pervading sense across the position that they were waiting for something to happen, and there was an uneasy calm. Otway used the opportunity to get Thompson to agree to position his six-pounder anti-tank guns along the front of the Bois du Mont position where they could cover the north-east approaches from Bréville and the paddocks in front of the château. The rest of the Black Watch remained in the sunken lane where they seemed to be suffering from a form of collective shellshock.

The lull in the fighting provided an opportunity to bury the dead. Usually those killed the day before or during the night were buried quickly in the burial patch behind the villa just after stand to. But the attack by the Black Watch meant that there were many more to lay to rest beneath the Norman soil. In the immediate aftermath of the attack the emphasis had focused on tending to the wounded, but with the failed assault over there was now time to deal with those who had been killed.

As the RAP was slowly cleared of casualties by the Jeeps, the bodies of the dead were tied into rough Army blankets and stacked in rows, then carried to the makeshift cemetery. They were interned in shallow graves, just deep enough to satisfy Christian decency and field hygiene. Their numbers were too great and time was too short to warrant much else. The padres of both units said a few words and then spades turned the earth and rough wooden crosses were placed at the head of each grave; no one wanted to be caught out in the open when the next stonk came in.

It remained quiet for the rest of the day, but as the last light began to fade Otway still expected to be attacked in strength. Hill had agreed that the 5th Black Watch would consolidate on their D Company positions around the château. B Company and what was left of A Company were placed on either side of the drive, while C Company were ordered to take over half of Bomb Alley from 9 PARA. When Otway visited Thompson in the château to tie up the defences between their two battalions, he noted how they were still suffering from the shock of their experiences during the morning's attack and the Highlanders had not yet started to dig in. However, the location of the unit's six-pounder anti-tank guns in 9 PARA's area would significantly bolster the Paras' few PIAT guns.

The Black Watch's position was reinforced by the arrival of a Vickers machine gun platoon from the 1/7th Middlesex Regiment, which was attached to the 51st Highland Division as its infantry support weapons unit. The platoon brought four additional medium machine guns with them. Jenkins watched them swing into the drive in their Bren-gun carriers, and the sound of their motors provoked the Germans to send up flares to probe the darkness. Jenkins's body was tired but he willed his mind to stay awake. He desperately wanted to sleep, but his nerves were on edge. Even though there were now friendly troops in front of him, he was still worried about the thick foliage around him and the enemy's ability to use it as cover to creep up on his position.

The German flares cast eerie shadows that flickered across the ground, swaying in their parachutes then fizzling out to cast the area beneath them once more into pitch blackness. There was none of the usual ambient light and an impenetrable cloud blanketed out the waning moon. Visibility was reduced to a few metres and Jenkins strained his eyes into the night, searching the dense foliage for signs of movement. His ears were cocked for any sound, the snap of a twig or the rustle of leaves, that might indicate the approach of the enemy. The darkness and his fatigue combined to play tricks on his senses and imagination. Strange shapes seemed to loom out of the bushes around his trenches, until he realized that he was hallucinating. He fought off the urge to sleep; he needed to stay alert and he wanted to stay alive.

Otway was worried too. Although there had been no counter-attack, the noise of enemy armour from the direction of Bréville had continued to build throughout the day and he ordered out a patrol under the cover of darkness to crater the road from the village. At midnight, Captain Robinson stole out into the night with a party of engineers. They used large hollow shape charges, which were designed to direct their explosive force downwards into the ground, to gouge out two huge holes in the road. The detonations attracted the Germans' attention further ahead of them at the cross-roads. As they withdrew, Robinson and his men were rewarded by the sight of a half-track armoured personnel carrier toppling into one of the craters, having roared up the road to investigate the explosions.

The paratroopers and Jocks had spent an uneasy night watching and waiting. Few got more than a couple of hours' sleep and the steady drizzle of rain added to their misery. Paddy Jenkins looked at his watch: it was 0330 hours. The rain dripped from the trees above him in the sunken lane as he stretched and emerged stiffly from his hole to ready his men for stand to. The hour between darkness and first light was always long and cold, while men waited for the trees and bushes around them gradually to take shape in the slate-grey half-light of dawn. Ron Tucker had awoken to the smell of wet leaves and hay. For a moment he had forgotten where he was. But the damp, hunger in his belly and the sight of red rivulets of water stained by the blood of the Black Watch casualties were stark reminders that he was in a trench dug into the banks of the sunken lane.

The perilous conditions at the Bois du Mont and the state of those who held it were all too apparent to Captain Bill Mills. As the battalion's logistic officer he commanded 9 PARA's small seaborne element of four three-tonne trucks and a water trailer. Packed with the unit's second-line scales of ammunition, water and rations, the vehicles had landed across the beaches on D+1, but only drove forward from 6th Airborne Division's logistic dump in the early hours of the morning on 12 June. The little convoy of vehicles moved under the cover of darkness, but they could see the parachute canopies still hanging in the trees at the sides of the road and they passed large numbers of German corpses piled on the verges. Mills noted the absence of other British units once he passed through the trench lines at Ranville, which made him realize just how isolated 9 PARA's position was compared to the rest of the division.

It was getting light by the time his party drove through the entrance of the Bois du Mont and pulled up outside the villa. The tops of the trees had been smashed by shellfire and the ground was strewn with the detritus of empty ammunition cases and spent cartridges and rent with small blackened craters from incoming rounds and bombs. He noticed how the battalion lived below the surface and how few of them came out to greet him. Each infantry unit has its own particular heart and character based on the individual nature of its constituent companies. But what he saw scattered around the leafy bastion of damaged trees and churned earth was unrecognizable from the battalion that had trucked past him on their way to the airhead at Broadwell transit camp just six days before.

The original unit structure of companies as Mills had known it had ceased to exist. Each sub-unit was now little bigger than a platoon and they were mixed up in amalgamated ad hoc groups. He was also visibly shaken by their appearance. They were indescribably filthy, their uniforms torn and shabby and their hair matted with dirt and sweat. The ravages of privation, fear and fatigue were etched on to their haggard features, which were pinched taut by stress and sleep deprivation. But what struck Mills most was how many of the familiar faces he had expected to see simply weren't there.

They were out of almost everything and Mills set about emptying his vehicles. The numbers of the battalion were so few that he had more than enough cigarettes to give every man a pack of Lucky Strikes and thin plumes of smoke were soon wafting from the bottom of trenches, as men inhaled hard and sucked in the nicotine they craved. Their bodies also yearned for the energy of food. Like tobacco, rations provided an important distraction from the rigour of field conditions and near constant combat. As a result, men who had not eaten properly for days searched feverishly through the fourteen-man ration packs for favourite items, such as tins of steak and kidney puddings and treacle deserts.

While Mills spent most of the morning breaking down boxes and distributing their contents to the men manning the forward trenches, the weather improved and a blue sky broke through the thick blanket of cloud. The sun came out and the birds returned to the trees. Their song filled the woodland, as cattle grazed nonchalantly on the summer hay among cows that had been killed by the fighting. The presence of their stinking carcases betrayed the bucolic charm and made for an incongruous scene. At midday the tranquillity of the summer's day was shattered by the crash of enemy mortar and artillery fire.

The ear-splitting cacophony of shell and mortar fire was joined by the shriek of the detested Nebelwerfer rocket launcher. The multi-barrelled weapon ripple-fired every two seconds, its heavy shells warbling through the air to add to the downpour of death and destruction.

Mills scrambled for his freshly dug trench, which was only three feet deep when the first rounds came in. The air was alive with shrapnel and he could feel the blast brush against the exposed parts of his skin as he tried to push himself deeper into his shell scrape. The rest of 9 PARA were relatively safe, as long as they stayed underground and did not receive a direct hit. Their slit trenches were well excavated and were covered by several feet of earth, which gave them overhead protection. But the men of the Black Watch were suffering the same level of exposure as Mills. The first screams of the wounded from around the château were testimony to the fact that the Jocks had been slow to dig and their short tenure meant that their trenches lacked depth and overhead cover.

Stretcher-bearers braved the storm of steel to fetch the wounded and bring them in to the medics. As shells and bombs rained in, some of them blasted into the tops of the trees, which made them detonate prematurely and shower down shrapnel and lethal wood splinters before they could hit the ground where the earth would have absorbed some of their explosive effect. Consequently, the men who moved above ground, or lacked overhead protection, came to hate being in close proximity to a wooded area. But even with the protection of a properly constructed trench, men pressed themselves hard into the earth as the ground shook and the awful noise assaulted their eardrums. They prayed for it to be over and that the next projectile would not be a direct hit.

The initial intensity of the bombardment was the heaviest to date and although it slackened after the initial stonk, it continued for three unforgiving hours. For the men on the receiving end of it, there was a fine line between sticking it and breaking down. For some the continual shelling was too much and they became 'bomb happy'. Today the acute incapacitating neurosis of shellshock would be described as 'post-traumatic stress disorder'. Most men felt it gnawing at their mental faculties, motivation and ability to stay alert to some degree. In more severe cases, soldiers became completely ineffective and some were ready to do anything to get taken out of the line. A sergeant in Gordon Newton's position in the part of 'Bomb Alley' 9 PARA still occupied was evacuated with a self-inflicted wound to his calf when the Sten gun he was cleaning accidentally went off. But the men around him were convinced that it was done deliberately, as a means of escaping the relentless torrent of shot and shell.

At 1500 hours the Germans turned up the heat and fired everything they had from at least three regiments of artillery and numerous mortar batteries. While the men of 9 PARA and the Black Watch hunkered down the earth was scarred with black smouldering holes and the air was thick with the stench of burned explosive. Mills pressed harder into the sides of his shallow trench and made himself as small as possible, as the blizzard of blast and shrapnel cut across the top of his body. He knew that the increasing intensity heralded a large-scale attack.

Behind the barns and along the lanes of the stone houses of Bréville, the assault troops and the armoured vehicles of the rump of 346th Infantry Division listened to the bombardment as it crashed on the British positions across the fields in front of them. The Germans were gripped with nervous tension, as crews sat in their half-tracks and tanks, their engines idling. The supporting infantry fingered their weapons and waited. They had spent the day receiving their orders, planning and rehearsing their attack. They had been fast to learn the lessons of the bocage after a week of fighting the British and there had been no complacency in their preparations. Forty-five minutes later, the bombardment lifted. German commanders spoke into their microphones, their drivers engaged the tracks of the vehicles, the grenadiers picked up their weapons and the formation of men and metal started to move forward as one.

Ahead of them, the Paras and the Jocks could hear the rumble of the engines and the squeal of tracks. NCOs and officers readied their men as they cleared the dirt of the bombardment from their weapons. Field telephone line was tested and, if it was cut, signallers were sent out to fix it. Mortar men primed their bombs and waited poised for their 'number ones' to shout out bearings and elevations, while machine-gun and anti-tank crews adjusted their sights and confirmed that the breeches of their guns were locked and loaded. The clanking rattle of tracks and tenor pitch of the engines grew louder, and commanders shouted themselves hoarse over the growing din and told their men to hold their fire.

The first assault was led by the German infantry in half-tracks and on foot. Their infantry support mortars fired over their heads, as the shielded MG 42 gunners mounted at the front of the vehicles opened fire. Receiving target coordinates from the forward trenches, Sergeant Hennessey's three-inch mortars replied in kind, as bombs slid down barrels and spat back out again in a flash of flame and smoke. At 200 metres, the anti-tank guns, Vickers and small arms opened fire. Germans started to fall and some of the half-tracks were brought to an abrupt halt by solid steel shot from the six-pounders, but it was a full battalion attack and there were too many of them. The vehicles gave the enemy speed, some cover and their numbers began to tell.

The weight of the attack came against the Black Watch positions dug in around the château. The enemy overran the forward trenches in the paddocks and forced the defenders back to the main house and along the ditch running up the side of the drive. The Vickers machine guns from the Middlesex and 9 PARA poured a murderous fire into the front of the German ranks and their flanks, as the man-killer weapon of the First World War did its bloody business. Combined with the rapid firing of the mortars, it was enough to stop the first attack and the line held. But the Germans were already forming up for their second assault.

The second attack was led by a mix of armoured vehicles including Panzer Mark IVs and StuG IIIs. The tanks and self-propelled guns crashed through hedges on the northern side of the stable block. Infantry-on-infantry fighting broke out in the stables and initially the Black Watch held the Germans off. But the use of the armoured vehicles firing at point-blank range in support of their dismounts overwhelmed the Scottish infantry and they fell back to the château. The tanks and self-propelled guns also made a point of seeking out the Vickers and anti-tank guns. Having lost any advantage of surprise regarding their location, the crews of the six-pounders in the hedge line along the road were quickly fixed and outmatched by the larger calibre 75mm guns, against which their small cut-down crew shields offered pathetically little protection.

A small number of the Black Watch continued to hold out in the château, but most of their Vickers guns had been knocked out and the rest of their line looked as if it was about to crack. The unit had thrown every available man into the fight, but the loss of a high proportion of their officers in the forlorn attack on Bréville began to tell. From his position in the Bois du Mont, Lieutenant Smythe watched individuals break and run from the Black Watch platoon dug in along the driveway back towards 9 PARA's trenches. They were without an officer and he feared that the whole platoon was about to break. He grabbed some bandoliers of ammunition and dashed across the road to restore order to the faltering Jocks.

Mills saw other soldiers from the Black Watch running back to the Bois du Mont. He fitted his short 'pig-sticker' bayonet to his Sten gun because he expected that the Germans would be close on their heels. Otway intercepted the retreating Jocks and ordered them to face the enemy. As he pushed them into positions among 9 PARA's trenches, he fired a burst from his Sten into the ground at their feet to make his intent clear.

The Paras continued to pour fire at the advancing Germans as they washed round the château, where a few of the Black Watch still held out. Enemy armour began to advance on both 9 PARA's A and B companies' positions. German infantry crouched behind them, as the metal monsters stopped to fire and their 75mm guns chopped the trees and branches around the trenches into matchwood. Wehrmacht infantry had already begun to flank Bomb Alley and were advancing through the wood behind the ditch. Some of the enemy managed to cross the road and the small barn at the southern end of the Bois du Mont was soon under fire.

A steady stream of wounded were being brought into the RAP, but John Gwinnett sensed his spiritual services were needed by those who were still capable of fighting. Armed with nothing more than his dog collar and Bible, he strode to the entrance of the Bois du Mont and nailed the 9 PARA flag made by the women of Oxford to the trunk of a tree as a rallying signal to the 9th Battalion. Lieutenant Slade grabbed the German officer's sword he had looted from the château and ran up and down the A Company trenches along the road exhorting Paras and Jocks alike to keep firing.

In the centre of the position, Bill Mills was aware that every man was needed in the forward trenches. When Lieutenant Murray Christie of B Company called for someone to help man the Vickers at the top of the sunken lane, Mills ran up the track and found two dead machine gunners lying on either side of the weapon. A number of enemy dead were also piled up to its front. Mills cocked the gun and aimed it at German infantry dashing across the road; it fired twice then stopped. He re-cocked the gun and it spat out another two rounds before jamming again. Stripping out the breech he noticed that it had been damaged by shrapnel and was mis-feeding. He belted back down the track to the villa to get the reserve machine gun.

With an all-up weight of just over fifty pounds, the Vickers is a heavy gun, but it can be carried bodily by one man if the front two legs of the tripod are lifted across the shoulders. Mills managed to get the spare gun back up the lane, swung it off his back and jammed the spikes of its tripod into the earth of the bank, and snapped a canvas belt of rounds across the feed tray. He cocked the gun and pressed the trigger. To his relief it fired on full automatic. But he needed help to crew it properly. He shouted at two paratroopers in a nearby trench and handed the gun over to them. He adjusted the tripod and started to give them fire control orders as a Panzer Mark IV advanced up the road from Bréville towards them.

While the bullets rattled off the top of the tank's turret, its commander dropped back inside his hatch and barked his own fire control orders to his gunner. The turret traversed and stopped. As the 75mm HE round exploded into the machine gun's position, a piece of shrapnel struck Mills in the hand. When he looked back at the Vickers, another two paratroopers lay dead by the shattered machine gun. One of them was Terry Jepp's younger brother Ron.

Sergeant Knight's men had also spotted the tank, which was more vulnerable since Jepp's brave action of engaging it with the Vickers had forced it to close down. Two PIAT bombs hit the front of the vehicle. They failed to penetrate its armour, but the panzer backed off down the road, firing as it went. One of Knight's PIAT men stalked the tank along the ditch running beside the road as it withdrew. He fired an anti-tank bomb at its tracks, where he knew it was most likely to do damage. It hit, but failed to blow off the running gear. However, it alerted the battened-down crew to the presence of the anti-tank gunner in the ditch. The turret traversed once more as it depressed its gun barrel and fired. The round obliterated the PIAT man in a momentary flash of flame and smoke, leaving nothing more than a burned scar in the earth where a human had once been. But the vigorous defence at the top of the sunken lane was enough to convince the tank commander to quit the field.

Other tanks were still in action and were bearing down on A Company. With his anti-tank screen of six-pounder guns gone and defences of the Black Watch in front of him breached, Otway feared that his own position was about to be overrun. At 1600 hours he sent a radio message to 3rd Parachute Brigade appealing for help. The Le Mesnil crossroads was also under attack, but the Canadians were holding and Hill called on the forty men of their reserve company. Hill decided that he would lead them and used engineers from his own headquarters as additional reinforcements. With his pistol in hand and his scratch force following him, Hill set off at the double towards the Bois du Mont.

Corporal McGuinness knew that his own position was becoming rapidly untenable. He was manning one of the two medium machine guns still in action. The other was a Middlesex Vickers holding out in the Château St Côme but that was damaged. McGuinness was covering the junction where the drive met the road. Private Fenson had been hit and he needed to reposition his Vickers before the panzers flattened him. Then McGuinness saw a party of Paras led by Major Smith wrestling with an abandoned anti-tank gun. He knew that it would be a more effective weapon in any duel with armour, but only if they could get it into a decent fire position. Leaving the Vickers, he jumped into one of the Black Watch's Bren-gun carriers and drove it over to Smith.

McGuinness hitched up the gun and towed it at speed to a better firing location along the hedge line, where Smith and his men unhooked it and manhandled it into position. McGuinness pulled back the loading lever and rammed in the slim brass-cased anti-tank round then slammed the lever forward to snap the breech shut. He screwed his eye to the sight and set it on a panzer at the edge of the château. McGuinness fired. The six-pounder sight shot back into his face with the recoil of the gun, almost taking his eye out. But the round hit the tank. Without thinking, McGuinness opened the breech, ejected the spent case in a swirl of acrid smoke, reloaded and fired two more armour-piercing shots to make sure the tank was properly accounted for.

Regimental Sergeant Major Cunningham and Sergeant Major Beckwith had similar ideas to Smith and McGuinness, and also managed to get a carrier started. They cleared the dead bodies of its crew from the trails and picked up another gun. An enemy tank spotted them and engaged the carrier with its coaxial machine gun. The open-topped vehicle was lightly armoured and vulnerable to anything but small-arms fire and Cunningham and Beckwith ducked below the rim of its sides as the bullets bracketed them. They survived the short journey and managed to get the six-pounder into action in front of the château and added to the anti-tank fire that began to check the advance of the armour towards 9 PARA's trenches.

With two of the six-pounders back in action the German armour started to withdraw, but not before having knocked out nine Bren-gun carriers. Six were already smouldering blackened hulks and three more of the small armoured vehicles were burning fiercely in front of the château, their ammunition and fuel tanks alight. Although the majority of the Mark IVs and self-propelled guns pulled back behind the main house and the area of the stables, Otway's right flank was still in danger of being turned, as the Black Watch's line crumbled in the line of trees. By the time Hill got there, the woods had become a mêlée of confused fighting.

Some of the Black Watch had already fallen back across the road into the Bois du Mont. Hill ordered his men into extended line and began to clear systematically through the trees. Mortar bombs were exploding in the treetops showering men with fragments and splintering wood. A bullet hit a Canadian next to Hill and others fell. But the brigadier urged his men on. The German infantry had also lost their cohesion in the confusion of the fighting and the timely launch of Hill's counter-attack began to force them back out of the wood. When they reached the edge of the line of trees as it curved towards the château, Hill ordered his men to reoccupy the trenches. He could see the German armour around the main house and a Panzer Mark IV advancing towards them spraying the undergrowth with its machine gun.

The Canadians and engineers returned fire, forcing the German commander to duck back into his cupola and close down when bullets ricocheted off the steel of his tank. Anti-tank bombs from PIATs fired by the engineers hit the front of its armour. They caused no damage, but the tank was exposed and, lacking protection from its own infantry, it pulled back. Hill ordered some of his men to push across to the château where they reinforced Thompson's position and the small band of machine gunners from the Middlesex Regiment. With Hill's arrival and the fire of the six-pounders manned by the makeshift crews of 9 PARA, the position was stabilized and the German attack defeated. But the battle was not yet won.

Earlier in the day the 13/18th Hussars had moved across the Orne. In the late afternoon B Squadron was put on notice to help 3rd Parachute Brigade, while the rest of the regiment was warned off to support an attack 6th Airborne Division planned to make against Bréville later that night. Just before dusk, the troops in the Bois du Mont heard the rattle and clank of Shermans coming up the road from Le Mesnil. The men cheered from their dugouts when the first troop of three tanks lumbered into view. Finally, after six days of fighting, 9 PARA had their own friendly armour with them to help even up the odds.

The Shermans passed Fred Milward where he was dug in opposite the drive to the chateau; he was pleased to see them, but he was also bloody glad that he was not a tanker. The tanks had closed down and, cocooned within the cramped confines of three inches of armour, the crews had limited visibility of the outside world. Blue-grey smoke coughed from their rear engine decks as they slewed their tracks and lumbered cautiously down the château's drive. The lead tank stopped momentarily for its commander to ask a soldier in the ditch about the location of the enemy. The young tanker did not expose himself and it would have been impossible to have a satisfactory conversation over the deafening noise of the engine and the constant buzz of static in his headphones.

The tank lurched forward slowly, as the driver engaged the gears. The avenue of trees and the main house ahead of him bounced in the narrow-framed slit of his periscope, when the crack of an anti-tank round sounded from the stables. Travelling at around 2,000 metres per second and at a distance of less than 200 metres, the solid armour-piercing shot slammed into the side of the tank with shattering force less than half a second later. Even though not the dreaded 88mm of the larger German Tiger tank, the 75mm gun mounted on the Panzer Mark IV and StuG III self-propelled guns could do great damage to the under-armoured Sherman, especially with its propensity to burst into flames when hit.

Bill Mills heard the almighty metallic clang as the German round hit the Sherman and brought it to an abrupt halt. It sounded like a 'gigantic blacksmith's hammer hitting a giant anvil'. Inside the tank, the crew felt the kinetic shock of the projectile's energy as it punched through the metal of their vehicle. The smell of smoke and burned cordite confirmed that they needed to get out fast, before the flames reached the fuel tanks and the turret ammunition. They flung open their hatches, tore off their headsets and clawed their way out of the Sherman in a desperate attempt to escape the terror of being burned alive. They tumbled off the side of the tank, half falling and half roll-ing, their clothes torn and smouldering, and crawled into the ditch running alongside the drive. Behind them orange flame was already jetting through the hatches from which they had just escaped. The driver of the first tank dropped into Milward's trench. Visibly shocked by the experience, the young crewman didn't hang around and shot off back across the road towards the relative safety of the sunken lane.

The commander of the second tank had caught the flash of the muzzle in his periscope. He was already screaming fire control orders into his microphone, while his gunner frantically cranked the traverse handle of the turret to bring the sighting vane of his gun to bear on the enemy self-propelled gun in the stables. Inside the third tank, the crew were taking the same action; with the yells of his commander crackling through his headphones, the gunner's foot was already poised on the firing pedal, ready to get his first round away as soon as he acquired the target. But it was already too late. The German gun crew were quicker and two more sharp cracks rang out.

The remaining Shermans were hit in rapid succession and their crews also bailed out while thick dark smoke began to pour from their engine decks and turret rings. Miraculously all the tankers managed to escape from the stricken vehicles and the blackened shapes of men crawled into the relative safety of the ditch. Behind them their tanks had become roaring infernos, as the white-hot armour-piercing rounds set petrol from severed fuel lines alight and the ammunition began to cook off, sending up huge smoke rings from the turret hatches.

The other two troops of the Hussars pulled back off the ridgeline, much to the bitter disappointment of the paratroopers and Jocks. It had been an expensive lesson in the need for proper infantry-armour cooperation in close country. With their 75mm armament, machine guns and magnified gun sights, the remaining six tanks of B Squadron could still have provided much useful observation and fire support. But in those early days of the Normandy campaign, the idea of 'penny-packeting' tanks to work individually with infantry was considered a cardinal sin. Armoured doctrine insisted that tanks should be used en masse in manoeuvre operations and both combat arms still had much to learn about fighting together in the bocage.

With the withdrawal of the Shermans, the enemy attempted one more attack, but it was quickly broken up by naval fire from the combined six-inch guns of HMS *Arethusa* and the *Mauritius*. This restored the men's morale after the defeat of their own armour and they cheered once more as the heavy shells screamed in to wreak death and destruction among the Germans. It was the last attack the 346th Division would make. After bleeding its offensive capability in an attempt to retake the ridge over six days of fighting, the Wehrmacht Grenadiers were forced back permanently on to the defensive.

As the enemy crawled back through the burning fields, the men in the trenches around the Bois du Mont and in the ruins of the château could hear the cries of the German wounded calling out for their comrades and their mothers. The paratroopers and Jocks felt little pity for them. Most did not hate the enemy and respected them for their fighting prowess, and when they came across them as prisoners they recognized them as fellow human beings and victims of war. But regardless of what they thought, the day's fighting had anaesthetized them to the suffering of the enemy and they were just too tired to care.

There was a crimson sky in the west as the last vestiges of daylight faded and Otway completed his rounds of the position by visiting B Company in the sunken lane during stand to. The fighting around the Bois du Mont appeared to be over and the men sat back in their trenches and waited for the cover of night and the prospect of a few hours' rest. In the distance towards the beaches they could hear the rumble of gunfire from five regiments of British artillery and naval ships firing on Bréville, which heralded the start of the 6th Airborne Division's attack to force the Germans finally out of the village and plug the hole in the British line. The men drew comfort from the sound of the guns and the fact that the Germans were taking it instead of them.

Hugh Pond heard the whine of incoming enemy artillery and threw himself flat into a trench. There was a stupendous bang as a shell landed close by and filled his mouth and nose with dirt. He sneezed violently and felt an agonizing pain in his chest. When he tried to get up he found he could not move.

Others had been caught out in the open by the blast. Lieutenant Christie and Captain Greenway were accompanying Otway on his rounds as he moved along B Company's lines in the sunken lane and all three had been caught by a shell that punched through the canopy of leaves and landed smack between the high banks of the track. Greenway was blown bodily into the branches of a tree and Otway was knocked unconscious as he was blasted across the lane. The redoubtable McGeever was also felled and Christie slumped dying against one of the banks with half of his face ripped off. The sharp concentration of German rounds lasted for ten minutes. Then there was silence until the cry for medics went up and men rushed with stretchers to get Otway and the other wounded to the RAP.

There was no further activity against 9 PARA's position for the rest of the night, none of the normal flares or bursts of probing auto-matic fire to puncture the blackness. The sky was clear and the stars were out. Men not on sentry duty slept, while those on stag covered their arcs and listened to the bloody fighting raging around Bréville

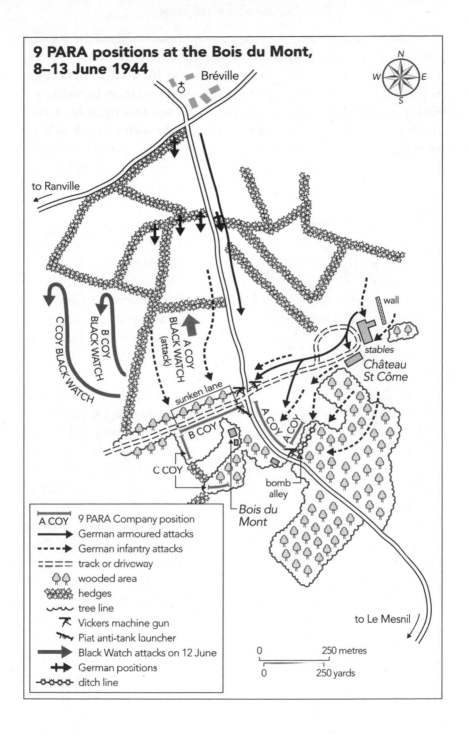

9 PARA positions at the Bois du Mont, 8–13 June 1944

Bréville

N
W E
S

to Ranville

wall

C COY BLACK WATCH

B COY BLACK WATCH

A COY BLACK WATCH (attack)

stables

Château St Côme

sunken lane

A COY

A COY

B COY

C COY

bomb alley

Bois du Mont

to Le Mesnil

A COY — 9 PARA Company position
→ German armoured attacks
╌╌➤ German infantry attacks
==== track or driveway
🌳🌳 wooded area
🌿🌿 hedges
〰〰 tree line
⚔ Vickers machine gun
🔫 Piat anti-tank launcher
➡ Black Watch attacks on 12 June
✚ German positions
✳✳✳ ditch line

0   250 metres
0   250 yards

less than a kilometre to their east, as it became an inferno of bursting artillery and blazing buildings. By midnight 12 PARA and a company of the Devons had captured the village at a cost of 162 men. In the wake of the attack, the small Norman church on the north-eastern side of the Bréville crossroads burned. As the fire took hold, one of the pipes in its organ stuck open and the draught from the flames sounded a single forlorn note in the darkness.

17

Aftermath

THE NEXT MORNING dawned warm and clear. Just after stand to, Bill Mills took the roll call: 126 members of the battalion answered it. Otway and Pond were still in the RAP and while the commanding officer's name was added to the daily strength return, the young subaltern's was not. Otway had awoken from his concussion to be informed that 9 PARA were being relieved in place by the 2nd Battalion the Ox and Bucks. He was declared fit enough to stay with the battalion, but Hugh Pond was informed that he was being evacuated for treatment in England. The force of the sneeze the dust from the shell had provoked had split three of Pond's ribs, which had been cracked when he crashed in his glider behind the Merville Battery on D-Day. Despite his protests, he was loaded on to a Jeep and driven to the beachhead while his comrades collected their kit and prepared to quit the position.

Two hours later the remnants of the battalion left the Bois du Mont in single file with their bayonets fixed. They were asleep on their feet and Ron Tucker swayed as he struggled to keep his eyes open and avoid jabbing the man in front of him with the spiked blade at the end of his rifle. Private Dennis Edwards of the Ox and Bucks watched the ragged line of men trudge past him with Otway at their head. The shock of battle was still etched on their haggard faces and their dark sunken eyes made men who were in the prime of their youth look a good deal older. They were filthy and their uniforms were bloodied, torn and soiled after six days of constant combat and living in the Norman dirt.

Pushing up towards the château revealed the true nature of the bitter fighting that had taken place. Edwards was no stranger to combat; he was part of the company from the Ox and Bucks that had seized the Orne Bridge in the daring glider *coup de main* operation that had taken place on 6 June, but he was horrified by the scene of utter carnage that stretched as far as the eye could see. The bodies of men, British, Canadian and German, were scattered across the open fields and lay on top of each other in the ditches and along the hedgerows. Twisted and blackened Bren-gun carriers dotted the landscape and the hulks of the three knocked-out Shermans smouldered on the drive.

Every square foot of ground seemed to be strewn with mangled body parts of men and animals, discarded weapons, clothing and equipment. Tank tracks and infantry boots had beaten down the fields and the ground was scorched black and pockmarked by hundreds of shell holes. Trees were shredded by direct hits, uprooted or reduced to shattered stumps. The air was pervaded with the awful smell of burned flesh, cordite and the corruption of corpses that had lain out too long in the sun. The stable block was a charnel house of dead thoroughbreds, some bloated with their entrails spilled out on to the cobblestones, others incinerated into dark shrunken shapes. And everywhere a plague of flies crawled on rotting meat, lifting into a vile buzzing swarm when they were disturbed by the arrival of the relief force.

What shocked Edwards the most was the scene he witnessed around the ruins of the château and in the wood where men had been killed by the effects of shell blasts. Seemingly undamaged, the dead were stuck in the attitudes of their last action in life. Edwards saw a dead NCO from the Black Watch lying prone by the remains of a tree, his Thompson sub-machine gun still tight in his shoulder, his finger closed round the trigger and one eye shut, while the other remained open and lined up the sights of the weapon. A dead German sat closed up around an ammunition tin with a belt of cartridges wrapped around his hand. Behind him another German lay propped up on one arm with the feed tray snapped open on an MG 42, his fixed expression seeming to urge his dead comrade to make haste with the bullets for his empty gun.

Some men were half buried with limbs sticking out of the ground, as if raised in a supplicating gesture to ward off the incoming rounds that had killed them. Nearby a Canadian paratrooper had been run through by a German with a bayonet that had pinned him to a large oak tree. One arm was curled around his assailant, his hand still clasping the dagger that he had plunged into the back of the man who had impaled him. All were like ghostly figures from a macabre waxworks museum, frozen in the agony of their last breath in a scene of sheer hell.

There wasn't a man among the defenders who wasn't glad to be moving out and leaving the carnage, detritus and stench of the battlefield behind them. Like most of the men who marched from the position, Fred Walker thought that 9 PARA were going to be pulled out of the line. But instead of heading back towards the safety of the rear areas towards the beaches, they moved further along the ridgeline to the shell-torn brick factory at Le Mesnil. Before occupying themselves with the routine of preparing another defensive position, they were deloused with a metal probe that sprayed white caustic powder up the sleeves of their battledress and down the fronts of their trousers. Then they set about filling sandbags, laying line and excavating dugouts.

The remnants of the Black Watch also pulled out from the château and relocated to the area of the brickworks. They took further casualties later that day when an RAF Typhoon mistakenly strafed them. One of its cannon shells also killed the pregnant wife of the farmer at Hill's headquarters.

With the plugging of the Bréville gap and the offensive capability of the German's 346th Division expended, the defence of the high ground became a static affair. The positions dug between the orchards and fields turned into a string of deep bunkers, with thick overhead timbered protection. There was little offensive action by either side save the odd patrol. But the ridge nonetheless remained a dangerous place and there was a steady trickle of casualties from enemy stonks and sniping. On 17 July Regimental Sergeant Major Cunningham was killed by shellfire and Sid Capon was wounded by shrapnel and evacuated.

In the valley below them the battle for Caen was in full swing, as the British 21st Army Group fought to break through the German defences into the open ground to the south. On 18 July 9 PARA had a ringside view as 1,000 Allied bombers droned overhead and pulverized the city with sixty tonnes of explosives. They felt the ground shake beneath their feet when three armoured divisions then advanced behind a bombardment of 400 guns until they were lost in the smoke and dust that hung over the whole Orne valley. It was the beginning of one of a series of Monty's offensives to take the city. The fighting raged for two days until the offensive petered out on 20 July.

On the same day 9 PARA were finally pulled back for a rest in the reserve area in a quarry on the banks of the Caen Canal just outside Ranville. It was the first chance they had to sleep undisturbed, out of range of enemy mortars and without their boots on. They had their first showers since leaving England and fresh bread to eat, which made for a welcome relief from a diet of hard tack compo biscuits. They listened to the radio and read newspapers and slowly reconnected to a world beyond the battlefield, away from death and destruction.

It was also a time to write letters to loved ones of both the living and the dead. By the time Dyer set pen to paper to write to the parents of Sergeant James Rose, his family had already received a copy of Army Form B.104-82B. As Rose's company commander, Dyer struggled to find words that would provide more comfort than the standard prose of the formatted War Office telegram that informed them of their son's death. 'It is my painful duty to inform you . . .' and 'I express the sympathy and regret of the Army Council . . .' had little meaning to devastated next of kin who had not the faintest idea who the Army Council were. But there were so many letters to write and the words did not come easily.

The respite in the rear area was not to last and after five days the battalion were sent back into the line at the brick factory. But as the defence of the east flank of the invasion consolidated, the Airborne Forces could also look to their men who were missing and had no known grave. The division's casualty levels had been appalling. During the Normandy campaign the formation suffered 4,457 dead, wounded and missing. The majority occurred during the first six days of the fighting to secure and hold the high ground of the Bréville Ridge. Most of the dead lay in makeshift graves like those from 9 PARA behind the villa at the Bois du Mont, but many lay interred or lost among the anonymous nature of the bomb- and shell-torn battlefield.

3rd Parachute Brigade had suffered 60 per cent casualties from its strength of 2,200 men. 9 PARA's strength when they went back into the line at Mesnil had increased to 11 officers and 218 other ranks. By the time they were eventually withdrawn from Normandy, 9 PARA alone had suffered 423 casualties, of whom 192 were estimated to have drowned in the floodwaters of the Dives. Hill knew that the men who had been dropped wide of the DZ would remain lost until the marshes decided to give them up, but with so many of his paratroopers unaccounted for, he wanted to discover what had happened to the men he had been forced to leave when they had been caught in the open and bombed by the American air force on 6 June.

John Gwinnett was given the task of finding them. The spot where they had been hit was easy to find. A stick of craters ran across the track from the DZ where Hill's party had been bracketed by 250-pound US bombs. Some of them had been filled in and were marked by a clutch of rough wooden crosses, which suggested a hasty field burial by the Germans. A partially buried radio set also poked out from the loose-filled soil of one. Excavating below it revealed the body of one of the naval signals party, who had jumped with 9 PARA to radio the success or failure of 9 PARA's attack on the Merville Battery. Underneath the rating's body lay that of a young man who was still holding the lead attached to a collar round the neck of an Alsatian dog: it was nineteen-year-old Jack Corteil.

Thirty-eight men were exhumed from the craters in a tangle of torn bodies and a gory pile of body parts, clothing and equipment. They had been fused together in a gruesome embrace of mutilated death in the wet earth for several weeks and the corpses were badly decomposed and impossible to recognize. Newton opened their smocks and probed for ID discs between their ribcages with a pencil.

The smell was horrific and sent Gwinnett rushing to the side of the track to spew up his guts. The stench stayed with those in the disinterment party for days and their comrades studiously avoided them when they returned from their grisly task to the defensive position at Le Mesnil.

Given their depleted number, the battalion reorganized into two weak companies. They remained in their static defensive positions until 17 August, when 6th Airborne Division received the general order to join the Allied advance across its entire front. After six weeks of fighting, the agony of Caen had finally ended. By the time the city had fallen, US forces had already broken free from the bocage in the west and swept rapidly inland. By 16 August they had linked up with British troops south of Caen to encircle the German Army, which had been bottled up in a constricting salient around the Falaise Gap. By 21 August the gap had been closed and the remaining enemy forces were in full retreat. While American and British armoured forces raced to the Seine in pursuit of the remnants of the withdrawing German Army, 9 PARA waded the River Dives and marched in the direction of Cabourg with 3rd Parachute Brigade and the rest of the Division.

On 27 August the British Airborne arrived at Honfleur, the day after Paris surrendered to the Allies. The paratroopers and glider troops had liberated 400 square miles of occupied territory and taken over 1,000 German prisoners. It was the end of the battle for Normandy, but Terence Otway was not there to see it, because 9 PARA had a new commanding officer. While still in the line on the Bréville Ridge, Otway had begun to suffer from splitting headaches, blackouts, temporary loss of vision and chronic back pain. His behaviour grew increasingly erratic and he was urged to report sick. A medical examination determined that Otway was still suffering from the impact of being blown up and he was declared medically unfit for continued frontline service. On 15 July he was replaced as CO of the battalion by Lieutenant Colonel Napier Crookenden and sent back to England.

By the time 9 PARA reached the banks of the Seine, Steiner and his guns had also left Normandy. Since the commandos' failed attack on 7 June, no further effort had been made to take the Merville Battery. The cost of launching another assault had been deemed too great at a time when the British were focused on taking Caen and the threat of massive naval counter-battery fire was considered enough to keep the guns quiet. On 16 August the young lieutenant received orders to withdraw his howitzers as the German Army began to collapse.

As the rain fell through the darkness on the night of their withdrawal, Steiner stayed with the last gun. He wanted to be with it as it fired its final fire mission in Normandy to cover the remainder of the guns as they pulled out. He ordered it to discharge six rounds before it was hitched up to a team of horses, which then caught up with the rest of the battery as they towed their guns across the beach to Cabourg. Steiner and his battery travelled alone through the French countryside until they re-joined their own forces on the Seine and managed to cross the river ahead of the advancing British units.

When men of the 2nd Ox and Bucks arrived at Merville on 17 August, the battery position against which the British had invested so much blood in their attempts to destroy Steiner's guns was deserted. It was a relief to the British soldiers. As they wandered round the abandoned position and empty gun emplacements they were struck by the enormity of its defences. The extent of its wire, machine-gun posts and the thick bastions of its casemates gave the battery the appearance of an impregnable fortress and none among them would have relished the prospect of having to take it by force.

On 6 September 9 PARA were withdrawn from France with the rest of 6th Airborne Division to refit in England. They sailed for home on the SS *Empire Gauntlet*, which was anchored off the invasion beachhead. They were taken out to the ship in a pitching sea by landing craft. As they climbed up the scramble nets, the rise and fall of the swell created a gap between the hulls of the two vessels, which each of the heavily laden men had to judge as they leapt for the roped netting draped on the transport ship's side. The risk of being crushed or drowned if they missed their footing made them spare a thought for the men who had landed from the sea across the invasion beaches on D-Day. Men for whom they and their comrades they were leaving behind in the shallow Norman earth had sacrificed so much to protect.

The nature of living in the field under the constant threat of their own death had not allowed much time for mourning those who would not be going home. But as they settled into bunks, looked for the galley and stared out to sea over the rail of the ship, they had time to reflect. Paddy Jenkins thought of the young men under his command that he had lost. He thought of their families, devastated parents and loved ones, whose sons, brothers and fathers would return home no more. He knew each man well. He had been like a father to them and he felt each loss keenly.

Those who survived had all been deeply affected by the loss of comrades and the experience of battle. Its privations, risks, horrific images and the mind-numbing terror, combined with the anticipatory dread of approaching combat or incoming shells, had all placed a huge physical and mental demand upon them. The responsibility of command had helped Jenkins to focus on something other than himself. The self-motivating fear of not letting others down, along with a ferocious pride in their platoon, company and regiment, had also played a collective part in sustaining them all. It was an ethos reinforced by being part of an elite and the comradeship between paratroopers, which helped mitigate the fatigue, hardships and fear that had formed part of the distressing world of systematic violence that they had lived through.

It was a culture which had kept them going when the odds were stacked against them and they fought in isolated positions only a few metres from the enemy. Teenagers and young adults who had not been soldiers for very long had become seasoned veterans in six days of bloody fighting. Although hardly older than the men he had commanded, Jenkins had watched boys become men and he was fiercely proud of them and what they had achieved. They had coped with the threat of being killed or maimed, becoming fatalistic in accepting death or injury as part of their conviction in the cause they fought for and the men with whom they fought.

Their D-Day mission was mired in the controversy of faulty intelligence, command intrigue, enormous cost and the disastrous drop, which nearly consigned it to failure. But whether at the Merville Battery or on the Bréville Ridge, they had triumphed in adversity. Although the guns at the battery were not the large 150mm calibre Allied planners had assessed them to be and although they were not destroyed, in taking the guns in the last crucial moments before the first waves of British troops hit the beaches, 9 PARA's costly assault on the Merville Battery had undoubtedly saved hundreds of lives.

Having taken their D-Day objective, they clung on to a small patch of vital terrain around the Bois du Mont and the Château St Côme in the first critical days of the invasion. 9 PARA bore the brunt of the fighting to hold 3rd Parachute Brigade's thin line on the Bréville Ridge. They did so as a lightly armed force, without close air support or armour, against an enemy three times their number and equipped with tanks. 9 PARA's contribution to holding the ridge played a crucial part in denying the German armour the most direct route to attack into the beaches when the Allies' foothold on the Normandy coast was tenuous. It resulted in the enemy having to make a long detour to the south-west of Caen and having to feed their panzers into the battle piecemeal, rather than being coordinated in a decisive blow that might have driven the Allies back into the sea as Rommel intended.

It was a feat of arms that had taken them to the edge of human endurance. Had they broken, the entire eastern flank of the invasion would have been put at risk and the very success of the Normandy landings would have been threatened. Whether landing by glider or parachute, what 9 PARA had achieved fully justified Montgomery's words about the 'manner of men' who served in the Parachute Regiment; they were indeed, in his words, 'every man an Emperor'.

The first shades of autumn were already in the leaves of the trees around Bulford when four canvas-covered three-tonne lorries came down the hill and turned right into Kiwi Barracks. Nearly four months had passed since twenty-two army trucks had taken nearly 700 men of 9 PARA to their transit camp at RAF Broadwell, when the leaves of spring had been a deep shade of vibrant green. Dusty Miller watched the trucks as they came through the gates and dropped off their loads on the barrack square. Having been evacuated back to England after being wounded at Le Plein, Miller had recovered and had been sent back to Bulford on promotion to await the return of the battalion. Miller stopped Gordon Newton as he hauled his equipment off the tailgate of one of the trucks and asked where the rest of the battalion were. Newton paused and looked at 9 PARA's new regimental sergeant major. 'This is all that is left of us,' he said, then shouldered his kitbag and headed to his barrack block and the long line of empty bed spaces that awaited him.

Epilogue

THE HEAVENS HAD opened by the time the new French President's car pulled up at the sombre stone archway located on the far side of the small tree-lined village green. The West Yorkshire Police band struck up 'La Marseillaise' when the presidential entourage alighted and made their way past the ranks of standard-bearers who lined the rain-soaked entrance to the cemetery. François Hollande had been in office only a matter of weeks, but in Normandy 6 June remains an important day of remembrance and celebration of the beginning of France's liberation and it was not something that he was going to miss.

Each June, commemorations are held all along the coast where the Allies landed almost seven decades ago, but for the British Airborne the focal event is the service at the Ranville cemetery. The first village to be liberated on D-Day, it is where most of their dead now lie in neat rows of graves, each marked by a simple elegant headstone fashioned in white Portland stone. Tended by the Commonwealth War Graves Commission, the cemetery is situated on the southern side of the village's distinctive Norman church with its separate bell tower. The medieval stone has been burnished a rich ochre by the wind, rain and sun, but the weather has not polished away the scars of battle. The frames of its doors and windows are still chiselled and pockmarked by the cut of bullets and shrapnel. But Ranville, like the other villages and hamlets scattered round the seaboard of the Calvados region, is not a community that wants to forget.

Each year thousands of local people and tourists gather to remember. Predominant among them are the veterans, proud in their faded berets, smart regimental blazers and rows of campaign medals on their chests. They come to reminisce about the events they took part in, to visit the objectives they fought over and ultimately to remember their comrades who did not make it home. Wearied by age, their ranks have grown thinner. Some are now wheelchair-bound, some walk with the aid of sticks and some cannot come any more, but the gratitude and affection they command from the local people have not been diminished by time.

The three 9 PARA veterans who sat in the front ranks of the open-air congregation felt it every time they returned to Normandy. Fred Glover, Gordon Newton and Geoff Pattinson felt it as they stood in the rain without umbrellas and watched the laying of the wreaths to the musical accompaniment of 'Nimrod'. Their blazers soaked, they stood rigidly to attention and saluted as the last strains of the last post sounded. In the silence that followed they thought of their comrades who lay to their left in the right forward sector of the cemetery. Men such as Private E.S. Corteil who lies in grave number 1AG. Buried with his dog Glenn, the inscription on the bottom of Jack's grave from his parents reads: 'Had you known our boy you would have loved him too.'

The sun broke briefly through the clouds and the standards fluttered in the wind when the bell in the church tolled at the end of the two minutes' silence. The congregation broke up and began to wander among the headstones. Fred Glover stopped in row 1AJ, his head cocked on one side, his beret dampened a darker maroon by the rain, as he read the names of Regimental Sergeant Major W.J. Cunningham, Lieutenant Christie, aged twenty-four and killed on 12 June 1944, as well as many others who died at the battery, Le Plein, the Bois du Mont and around the Château St Côme.

But Ranville is not the only place of pilgrimage and remembrance for the men of 9 PARA and their families. The Merville Battery is easy to find once in the village of Franceville-Plage, where Steiner had his OP, which still nestles sunken in the sand dunes across from where the Orne estuary flows into the sea. The signs for 'Les Batteries de Merville' are visible on the main trunk road and point to where the four guns were once based. Despite new road layouts, roundabouts and the increasing growth of urbanization on its fringes,

Merville itself is still a village of scattered houses and farmyards and the centre is little changed. The château and old school house that once accommodated Steiner's men are still there and the mairie that the RAF bombs destroyed has been rebuilt.

The orchard where 9 PARA formed up to make their attack is no longer there, but the four large casemates still squat menacingly in the centre of the three-hectare site. The barbed-wire entanglements are long gone, the anti-tank ditch filled in and the land once churned into a lunar landscape of deep bomb craters has been bulldozed flat again to how it was before the bombers came. In 1981 work started to preserve the battery: water was pumped out of its foundations, paths were laid between the casemates and the site was restored as a museum and a monument to the paratroopers and commandos who died there. Close to where the 20mm anti-aircraft gun was once located, a telegraph pole erected to carry German telephone lines has taken root, as if to prove that life springs eternal.

There are both changes and continuity at the other places where the 9th Battalion fought. The château at Le Plein is no longer there, but the Château St Côme and the villa at the Bois du Mont are once again family homes. The stable block has been rebuilt and horses graze once more in the paddocks either side of the château drive. The trees around the perimeter of the villa have long been repaired by nature, but if you look carefully you can still make out the shallow impressions of where the line of slit trenches were once dug along the hedgerows. Scratching away at the surface reveals old decayed ammunition tins, which were filled with earth to build up overhead cover and protect their occupants from the shot and shell that rained down on the position. In the wood shelter next to the villa, the names of the wounded who once waited for evacuation can still be made out chalked on the walls of what was the makeshift dressing station to the RAP.

The battery, Le Plein, the château, the Bois du Mont and the cemetery at Ranville are the places that the veterans come to visit, but Normandy was not 9 PARA's last battle. After three months spent rebuilding their strength in England, the battalion was rushed to the Ardennes to help stem the tide of Hitler's last-gasp offensive in the west. By the time they arrived, von Rundstedt's panzer divisions had been halted in the Belgian snow and the German Army retreated eastward towards Germany. The battalion jumped again during Operation Varsity in March 1945, when the Allies crossed the Rhine and broke into the Third Reich.

9 PARA was dropped accurately and the parachute and glider assault was the biggest and most successful airborne operation of the war, coming in the wake of the disaster that had befallen the 1st Airborne Division at Arnhem. The battalion advanced through Germany with the rest of 6th Airborne Division and took part in the race to the Baltic coast to get there ahead of the Soviets driving in from the east. They arrived in the German city of Weimar on 2 May, just ahead of the Red Army and six days before the German surrender in Europe, when the first shadows of the Cold War were already beginning to fall. Later that summer the battalion set sail for the Far East to take part in the final attack on Japan.

They were at sea on 9 August when the second atomic bomb was dropped on Nagasaki. With the Japanese surrender, the 6th Airborne Division was diverted to Palestine, where it conducted internal security operations against Jewish insurgents, until the division's withdrawal and subsequent disbandment on its return to England in 1948. But 9 PARA had already ceased to exist before 6th Airborne Division left the troubled mandate. The battalion amalgamated with 8 PARA in October 1947, when the wartime British Army reduced in size and the men who had survived the jump in Normandy and lived to see the end of the war had already started to go home and return to a civilian life that few had known as adults.

Despite the horror they had witnessed, the fear, privations and the death of friends, for most their wartime service and being part of 9 PARA, was the most significant experience in their lives. Their feelings on being demobbed from the Army were of overwhelming loss; many found it difficult to adjust to the world outside and they missed the sense of structured purpose, belonging, discipline and comradeship. For many there were also deeper, darker mental issues to overcome. Many suffered from what today would be called post-traumatic stress disorder, with its hypersensitivity to unfamiliar surrounds, loud noises and an erosion of inner psychological integrity, which brought with it an overwhelming sense of being unable to cope.

Whenever he went out, Gordon Newton was always looking for cover. Geoff Pattinson felt like a 'broken reed' and for several years he would wake up in the night screaming. But they were from a generation where few people had not been affected by wars, privations, loss and its horrors. The term 'shellshock' was reserved for only the most acute cases and the vast majority of hundreds of thousands of wartime service personnel suffered alone and in silence. Geoff Pattinson just 'knuckled down and got on with it'. He had a wife and a new baby daughter to feed, but the journey of adjustment was not easy.

Fred Glover returned to Bulford in September 1944, having escaped as a POW from a German hospital in Paris. He linked up with the Resistance and took part in the city's uprising before its final liberation by the Free French. He fought in the Ardennes, jumped at the Rhine and was finally demobbed after serving in Palestine in 1947. Fred took time to settle back into civilian life. He had a succession of jobs that led nowhere, until he enrolled in night school and that led to a meaningful career in engineering. Paddy Jenkins also felt the sense of loss keenly and missed the responsibility of leading others. He found it hard to stick at a job until he started working at a hospital in Braintree. One day in 1950 he heard the strains of Strauss's 'Roses of the South' being played on a piano by a young refugee from the Soviet-occupied East Germany. Their mutual love of music and love for each other resulted in sixty-two years of happy marriage, which continues today.

For some the loss was too great. Ron Tucker was demobbed in 1947 and re-enlisted in the Parachute Regiment as a private, later retiring in the rank of sergeant in 1954 and embarking on a civilian career in sales. But slowly, most of the men who had grown up in the Great Depression before embarking on what were the most formative experiences of their lives, adjusted to the drab reality of peace in post-war Britain. Geoff Pattinson spent thirty years working in the plans office of a shipping company. Although he hated every minute of it, the pay was good and his family enjoyed the benefits. Gordon Newton had a successful career in the police, eventually retiring as a chief superintendent.

Hal Hudson survived the wounds that shredded his guts during the assault on the battery and was eventually knighted as the chairman of Lloyds. Alan Jefferson left the Army in 1946 and followed a career in music and the theatre. Hugh Pond returned to the battalion while it was still in Normandy after recovering from the injury to his ribs. He stayed on in the Army after the war, until he retired to become the defence correspondent for the *Daily Express* and then pursued a successful business career in PR; he eventually retired as president of the plastics company Tupperware's divisions in Europe, Africa and the Middle East. The last surviving officer of the 9th Battalion, he now spends his time living between Spain and Surrey.

Sir Martin Lindsay never spoke of the episode that led to his removal from the command of 9 PARA and there is no mention of his service with 9 PARA in his entry in *Who's Who*. Although demoted to major, he went on to have a highly successful wartime career as the second-in-command of the 1st Battalion the Gordon Highlanders in Normandy, Belgium, France and Holland, where he was in the thick of the fighting experienced by the 51st Highland Division. On several occasions he commanded his unit in action and was awarded the DSO for personally leading one of his companies in an attack. He was also mentioned in dispatches and wounded in combat on two occasions.

Lindsay left the Army as a lieutenant colonel and was elected in 1945 as the Conservative Member of Parliament for Solihull, a position he held until retiring from politics in 1964. He was awarded a CBE in 1952 and created a baronet in 1962 for his services during nineteen years in politics. He was also a successful author, publishing his acclaimed account of his wartime service entitled *So Few Got Through*. Characteristically, he made no mention of 9 PARA or his strong suspicion that Terence Otway had connived in his removal from command. Although he maintained an affiliation with the 9 PARA reunion association after the war and retained the affections of the men he once commanded, he never attended an event when the man who had replaced him as CO was present. Sir Martin Lindsay of Downhill CBE DSO Bt died in 1981.

Terence Otway was awarded a DSO for his command of the battalion in Normandy, before being sent back to England six weeks after the jump into France. Disillusioned with the post-war army, he resigned his commission in 1948 and joined the Colonial Development Corporation working in Africa until ill health led to his return to the UK. He followed a mixed career in business and became active in promoting the welfare rights of Parachute Regiment soldiers. Otway died in 2006 and he remained prickly to the end. He never forgave the RAF for the disastrous drop on D-Day and on meeting Steiner at the Merville Battery after the war was reluctant to shake his former adversary's hand. However, although often criticized for his command style and the complexity of his plan to attack the Merville Battery, it was Otway who commanded 9 PARA successfully through all it endured in those first critical six days. His role as the CO was crucial to the unit's successful defence of the Bois du Mont and his impressive feat of leading his men when the odds were stacked against them cannot be taken away from him.

As most veterans came to terms with life out of the military and the challenges of making their way in the civilian world, the majority put their experiences behind them. Marra McGuinness rarely spoke of his wartime service and the Military Medal he had won for his daring exploits with the Vickers gun at the Bois du Mont remained hidden out of sight in a drawer. But as they advanced in years, many began to experience a yearning nostalgia for what they had experienced, the comradeship they had once had and what they had achieved. Like many, Geoff Pattinson did not return to Normandy until the fiftieth anniversary in 1994. Until then he had never really enjoyed the reunion dinners held at the Parachute Regiment's TA barracks at White City. As a young soldier the place names of Le Plein, the Château St Côme and the Bois du Mont had meant little to him. But when he returned five decades later, being in the places where he had fought and had been wounded rekindled his pride in his regiment, what they had achieved and what he had once been part of.

James Hill made regular visits back to Normandy and retained the respect of the men who had once been part of his brigade, which he commanded until the end of the war in Europe. Had he stayed in the Army, there is no doubt that he would have reached the highest ranks. He was offered the command of a division heading for the Far East, but the holder of an MC, DSO with two bars, had had enough of conflict and left the Army to pursue a highly successful career in business. Before he died in 2006 in a nursing home in Chichester, the town where he had made his home, he would spend hours reflecting on the men he knew, those he had led and those who had been lost. In war he had had to harden his heart, but it never conflicted with his compassion, which, with resolution and courage, he saw as an essential attribute of a commander. He once said that 'love is the greatest thing and if you love your soldiers, they would respond and follow you'.

Hill last visited Normandy in 2004 with failing eyesight and while suffering the effects of a stroke. Despite his ill health, his love for his men was undiminished. Under a cloudless blue sky, he and other veterans watched the men of 1 PARA, the unit of the Parachute Regiment he had first served with and commanded, jump over one of the drop zones used by the 6th Airborne Division. As he looked up and saw hundreds of green canopies blossom above the DZ in the slight breeze, coming in to land in the green fields, he and his companions thought of the young soldiers above them and what it meant to be a paratrooper. They remembered the fellowship forged in the days of war and how they had stood together and how human endurance had triumphed over adversity. They felt the swell of pride in their regiment and, above all, they remembered the manner of men they had once been.

Picture Acknowledgements

Alan Jefferson, *Assault on the Guns of Merville* (John Murray, 1987): 1, 4 above right. Airborne Assault Museum, Duxford: 2 above and below, 3 above and below, 4 above left, 6, 7, 8, 9, 11 above left, 12 below, 14 below, 15 above, 16 below. Courtesy of Neil Barber, *The Day the Devils Dropped In* (Pen & Sword, 2002): 4 below left and right, 5, 10, 12 above, 13, 15 below. Imperial War Museums © IWM-FLM-3021: 11 centre. Author's collection: 11 below, 14 above, 16 above.

Acknowledgements

I AM ENORMOUSLY grateful to a numerous variety of different people who helped me write this book. I am particularly grateful to the veterans of 9 PARA: Paddy Jenkins, Gordon Newton, Geoff Pattinson, Fred Glover, Hugh Pond, Fred Milward, Harry Grey, Mick Corboy, Fred Walker and Dom McArthur. It was a great privilege to interview them and walking the battleground with some of them was a humbling experience, which will stay with me for ever. This is their story and my only hope is that I have captured the spirit of their remarkable courage and fortitude appropriately. I must also thank those veterans I spoke to from the other units, arms and services who were connected to the battle, as pilots and ground crew from the RAF and the Glider Pilot Regiment, sailors, Army commandos, tankers, sappers, paratroopers from other units of 6th Airborne Division and the 5th Black Watch, who all played their part. Alistair MacKie DFC, Tony Pickering, Jimmy Taylor, Alan Hartley, Lenny Lambert DFC, Laurie Weeden, John Carlill, Bob Reeve, John Waddy (156 PARA), Tony Leake (8 PARA), Fred Walker, Stuart Watson, Tom Renouf, Alan Graham and Jim Heyward MM, whether in the air, at sea or fighting alongside 9 PARA, formed part of the story of the Merville Battery and Bréville Ridge. They also helped me capture the combined-arms nature of this one small, but critically important part of the Normandy campaign.

The wives and families of the veterans have also played a role in my research. My thanks go to David Delius, who served in the 13/18th Hussars and lost his father serving in the same regiment at D-Day, for linking me to Normandy veterans from the unit. Joan Hill, the wife of Brigadier James Hill DSO★★ MC, Audrey Pattinson and Ruth Grey, who were in relationships with Geoff Pattinson and Harry Grey at the time that they flew into Normandy, assisted me in better understanding the manner of the men they loved who did the fighting. I also owe enormous gratitude to Mark Giffard-Lindsay, who gained his family's consent to allow me to examine some of the private papers of Lieutenant Colonel Sir Martin Lindsay and I hope that I have done something to set the record straight regarding his remarkable grandfather and his essential contribution in preparing 9 PARA for Operation Overlord and their success in Normandy, during those first crucial days of the invasion.

As the deputy chairman of the Normandy Air Assault Trust, Lieutenant Colonel Alan Edwards deserves a special mention for repeatedly putting me up in his home near the Merville Battery during several research visits I made to France and for introducing me to local residents and historians connected to what happened there in June 1944. I must also thank Neil Barber who has done so much to capture the detailed experiences of scores of other 9 PARA veterans who are no longer alive. As a subject-matter expert, his support to my research and the many detailed discussions I had with him have been invaluable; as was the help and guidance of fellow Trust members Ron McCaffery and Mike Strong.

I am indebted to Jon Baker for allowing me unfettered access to the archives at the Parachute Regiment's Air Assault Museum at Duxford in Cambridgeshire and to Mark Worthington and Nigel Steel, who both provided invaluable assistance during my research trips to the Pegasus Museum at Bénouville in Normandy and research facilities at the Imperial War Museum in London. I am also very grateful to Graham Pitchfork for pointing me in the right direction at the National Archives in Kew and providing me with the flying logs from 512 Squadron RAF and connecting me with some of the airmen who flew 9 PARA into combat or made reconnaissance missions over occupied Europe.

Finally, it's a pleasure once again to be published by John Murray and I owe a vote of thanks to Roland Philipps and his excellent publishing team at John Murray, as well as my agent Annabel Merullo.

Sources

PUBLISHED SOURCES

Ambrose, S., *Pegasus Bridge* (Pocket Books, 2003)

Bailey, R., *The Forgotten Voices of D-Day* (Ebury, 2010)

Bishop, G., *The Battle – A Tank Officer Remembers* (privately published, n.d.)

Brady, S., *Normandy 1944 Allied Landings and Breakout* (Osprey, 1997)

Capon, Sid, *Sid's War*, ed. M. Strong (Michael Strong, 2012)

Crookenden, N., *Dropzone Normandy* (Ian Allan, 1976)

Crookenden, N., *The 9th Battalion The Parachute Regiment – The First Six Days in Normandy – 1944* (privately published, n.d.)

Edwards, D., *The Devil's Own Luck* (Pen & Sword, 2009)

Golly, J., *The Big Drop* (Jane's, 1982)

Harclerode, P., *The Fighting Brigadier* (Pen & Sword, 2010)

Hastings, M., *Overlord* (Guild, 1984)

Hennessey, P., *Young Man in a Tank* (privately published, n.d.)

Jefferson, A., *Assault on the Guns of Merville* (John Murray, 1984)

Kershaw, R., *D-Day: Piercing the Atlantic Wall* (Ian Allan, 2010)

Liddell-Hart, B.H., *The Rommel Papers* (Collins, 1953)

McGregor, M., *The Spirit of Angus* (Phillimore, 1988)

McNab, C., *Hitler's Armies* (Osprey, 2011)

Miller, C., *History of the 13/18th Royal Hussars 1922–1947* (Chisman & Bradshaw, 1949)

Neave, J., *The War Diary of Julius Neave* (privately published, 1994)

Nesbit, R., *The Eyes of the RAF* (Sutton, 1998)

Newnham, M., *Prelude to Glory* (Samson Low, Marston, n.d.)

Ruge, F., *Rommel* (Presidio, 1979)

Ryan, C., *The Longest Day* (Coronet, 1988)

Shannon, K. and Wright, S., *One Night in June* (Airlife, 1994)

Thompson, J., *Ready for Anything* (Weidenfeld & Nicolson, 1989)

Treloar, G., *The Memoirs of Trooper G. Treloar, B Squadron, 13/18th Hussars* (privately published, n.d.)

Tucker, R., *A Teenager's War* (Spellmount, 1994)

Wheldon, H., *Red Berets into Normandy* (Jarrold, 1982)

Wilmot, C., *The Struggle for Europe* (Clay, 1954)

OFFICIAL PUBLISHED SOURCES

By Air to Battle: The Official Account of the British Airborne Divisions (HMSO, 1954)

Otway, T., *Airborne Forces* (The War Office, 1951)

UNPUBLISHED SOURCES

5th Battalion, Black Watch War Diary, WO 171/1266, National Archives

6th Airborne Division – Operation Order: Operation Overlord (Neptune), 23 May 1944 (6 AB/119/G(Ops))

6th Airborne Division – Report on Operations in Normandy, 5 June–3 September 1944, Air Assault Museum, Duxford, 4E2 2/7/9

9 PARA Battalion Operations Order, Number 1, 30 May 1944, Air Assault Museum, Duxford, 4E2 2/7/9

9 PARA 'Immediate Action Report' – Capture of a Coastal Battery at 155775 by 9 Para on 6 June 1944, Air Assault Museum, Duxford, 3E6 3/9/1

9 PARA War Diary, WO 171/1242, National Archives

9th (Home Counties) Parachute Battalion Strength Returns (March–May 1944), WO171/1242, National Archives

21st Independent Parachute Company War Diary, WO 171/1248, National Archives

512 Squadron RAF – Operational Log, June 1944, Air 27/1972, National Archives

541 Squadron RAF – Operational Log, October 1942–May 1945, Air 27/2013, National Archives

716th Division Operational Report on the 'Invasion on 6 June 1944', for Commander Army Group, MS B-621 Ia Nr.3050/44, dated 23 June 1944, Imperial War Museum

Assault on a Strongly Defended Battery Position, an appreciation by Major
    T. Otway and Captain R. Gordon-Brown, dated 22 March 1944, Air
    Assault Museum, Duxford, 4E2 2/7/10

Battle of the 716th Infantry Division in Normandy, Generalleutnant
    Richter, Mansfield State College Library, Pennsylvania

Covering letter on Otway's appreciation of attacking a strongly defended
    battery, from Lieutenant Colonel M. Lindsay to HQ 3 Para Brigade, Ref:
    G/16, dated 29 March 1944, Air Assault Museum, Duxford, 4E2 2/7/10

Diary of 9th Battalion, The Parachute Regiment North-West Europe 1944
    (WO 223), Air Assault Museum, Duxford, 3E6 3/9/1

German Account of the Assault on the Merville Battery, by Paul Carell, Air
    Assault Museum, Duxford, 4E2 2/7/10

HMS Arethusa – Ship's Log (Officer of the Watch), dated 5 and 6 June 1944,
    Pegasus Museum, Normandy

Immediate Report on Operations of PARA Bn, 6–12 June 1944, account
    by Major George Smith, Air Assault Museum, Duxford, 3E6 3/9/7

Letters from Allen Parry to the family of Martin Lindsay

Notes by Major Allen Parry, Officer Commanding A Company, 9 PARA,
    made on 10 June 1944, Air Assault Museum, Duxford, 4E2 2/7/9

Notes by Major C. Stafford on discussions with French civilians who were
    involved in the construction of the Merville Battery, 1941–1944, Air
    Assault Museum, Duxford, 4E2 2/7/10

Notes on 512 Squadron RAF, by L.H. Cullingford (Navigator 512 Squadron
    1944), to curator of the Airborne Forces Museum, dated 9 December 1990

Notes on HMS Arethusa, by Captain Dalrymple-Smith RN, 1944, Air
    Assault Museum, Duxford, 4E2 2/7/9

Notes on the Merville Battery sent to the author by Louis Adelin, covering
    local French accounts of the fighting at Merville, dated 23 February 2012

Notes on the Middlesex Regiment fighting at the Château St Côme sent to
    the author by Jeff Haward, dated 5 April 2012

Operation Neptune – US Army Intelligence Report, 8 May 1944 (by R.A.
    Gooch, CWO, USA, Asst Adj. Gen.), Air Assault Museum, Duxford,
    4E2 2/7/10

Operation Overlord – Glider Pilot Administrative Instructions, Glider Pilot
    Regiment, Air Assault Museum, Duxford, 6 AB/198/G, dated 2 June
    1944

Research Notes on the Merville Battery by Major M.R. Strong, dated
    August 2004

IMPERIAL WAR MUSEUM: ARCHIVE
RECORDINGS

James Baty, 9 PARA: 21192
Herbert Beddows, 3 Commando: 20373/4
Sid Capon, 9 PARA: 21061/3
Lieutenant Colonel Napier Crookenden, 9 PARA: 16395/7
L.F. Edwards, 2nd Ox and Bucks: 92/37/1
Brigadier James Hill, 3 Para Brigade: 12347/4
Lieutenant Alan Jefferson, 9 PARA: 13723/3
Flying Officer Walter Jones, 100 Sqn RAF: 17646/4
John Rooke Matthews, 9 PARA: 21591/4
Captain William Mills, 9 PARA: 22685/10
Corporal Gordon Newton, 9 PARA: 17988
Lieutenant Colonel T. Otway, 9 PARA: 12133/4
Lance Corporal Martin Phelps, 9 PARA: 21292/4
Lieutenant Hubert Charles (Hugh) Pond, 9 PARA: 13143
Lieutenant Raimund Steiner, 1/716th Artillery Regiment (BBC Dangerous
    Films): 28408/6
Albert Watt, 9 PARA: 22672/5
Leslie Young, 9 PARA: 22246/2

Index

355

From Byron, Austen and Darwin

to some of the most acclaimed and original
contemporary writing, John Murray takes pride in
bringing you powerful, prizewinning, absorbing
and provocative books that will entertain you
today and become the classics of tomorrow.

We put a lot of time and passion into what we
publish and how we publish it, and we'd like to
hear what you think.

Be part of John Murray – share your views with us at:

www.johnmurray.co.uk

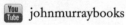 johnmurraybooks

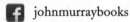 @johnmurrays

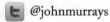 johnmurraybooks